OP Hero Commendations

"In a world where technology is transforming every aspect of our lives and children spend more time on video games, Yu-kai Chou's 10,000 Hours of Play offers an essential perspective. By blending deep insights into human behavior, he connects the dots in a way that will resonate for those spending their most valuable time gaming. By doing so, this book provides a guide to turning life into a game worth playing."

Jeff Booth, Best-Selling Author of The Price of Tomorrow: Why Deflation is the key to an Abundant Future.

"Yu-kai Chou's 10,000 Hours of Play is a revolutionary guide that transforms everyday challenges into opportunities of joy and fulfillment. At Zoom, my mission has always been to deliver happiness to my employees as well as our customers. Similarly, this book offers a playful yet powerful roadmap for anyone looking to bring happiness into their personal and professional lives. An essential read for leaders and individuals alike who strive to infuse more play and purpose into their work and beyond."

Eric S Yuan, Founder & CEO of Zoom

"As we step into the age of AI, it's important to remember our human essence and the playful spirit that propels our progress. 10,000 Hours of Play by Yu-kai Chou combines practical insights with the power of gaming to foster self-discovery and continual growth. This book is a practical guide for anyone eager to gamify their journey through life and unlock their full potential."

David Ku, Former CTO of AI & Research at Microsoft

"This book offers a great way to give your inner mammal everything it needs to be happy. It helps you spark dopamine by focusing on your next step in the game of life. It gives you a way to spark serotonin by making you the hero of your life. And it helps you spark oxytocin with a plan to build your team."

Loretta Breuning, PhD, Best-Selling Author of Habits of a Happy Brain and Founder of the Inner Mammal Institute

"A hugely optimistic book, packed with inspiring examples that use the metaphor of a role-playing game to illustrate the principles that will help you succeed in the greatest game of all: life."

Richard Bartle, Legendary Game Designer. Creator of MUD (the first virtual world) and Bartle's 4 Player Types

"Life is full of challenges, fun, epic wins and losses. 10,000 Hours of Play by Yu-kai Chou brilliantly captures the essence of turning life into an engaging journey of growth and discovery. This book guides readers to find rhythm and joy in their journey, transforming the path to success into a deeply rewarding experience."

Charles Huang, Creator of Guitar Hero (first billion dollar game in the world)

"In 10,000 Hours of Play, Yu-kai merges the science of gamification with the principles of exponential growth and Exponential Organizations. 10K HP offers a 6-Step program to turn your life into an ever-expanding game, and I recommend it for anyone who feels inspired to live an exponential life."

Salim Ismail, Founding Executive Director of Singularity University and Best-Selling Author of Exponential Organizations

"In a future defined by abundance, living with passion and purpose is essential. 10,000 Hours of Play serves as a powerful guide for those eager to transform their lives, accelerate their achievements, and contribute to a world of limitless possibilities. Chou's insights inspire you to think bigger, act faster, and reach new heights—all while enjoying every step through the transformative principles of play."

Peter Diamandis, Founder of XPRIZE Foundation, Singularity University, and Best-Selling Author of Abundance and Bold

"Yu-kai Chou's "10,000 Hours of Play" is a fascinating look into how the principles of gamification can be applied not just to products, but to our very lives. This book offers a compelling roadmap for anyone looking to harness the power of applying gameful mindsets to enhance personal and professional growth. Chou's engaging narrative and practical insights equip readers to turn everyday challenges into a game worth playing. 10,000 Hours of Play is an essential guide for transforming play into progress and aspirations into achievements."

Nir Eyal, Best-Selling Author of Hooked and Indistractable

"The best stories begin where a crisis disrupts a stable world, and a mentor propels the protagonist to embark on their journey to become a hero. Today's world is also filled with crises, and Yu-kai Chou, through his methodological 10K HP six-step process, acts as a mentor to guide readers on their own Hero's Journey. 10,000 Hours of Play seamlessly weaves storytelling with strategy, empowering readers to unlock their potential in a fun and fulfilling narrative. Read this book - you won't regret it!"

Gareb Shamus, Founder of Comic Con and Wizard Entertainment

10,000 Hours of Play

Unlock Your Real-Life Legendary Success

Yu-kai Chou

ISBN 979-8-9920065-0-6

Co-Authored by Mark Diaz.

Significant Contributions by Jun Loayza, Howie Ju and Anna Notovska.

Professional Editing by Highpoint Executive Publishing.

Publisher: Octalysis Media

30 N Gould Street STE 4000

Sheridan, WY, 82801

USA

Octalysis Media is the publishing branch of The Octalysis Group, specializes in content related to gamification, motivational psychology and behavioral design.

© 2025 Yu-kai Chou

This book is dedicated to those who seek more from their lives in this fast-changing world. It is for those who wish to become thriving players in the game of Life, rather than victims of circumstance. In any worthwhile game, playing is winning. The only way to lose is by not playing. We are grateful for the chance to live in these exciting times and to play our part in the great game of Life. We did not choose the game; the game chose us. However, we can choose how we play the game and the allies who will accompany us on our adventures. With the right mindset, tools, and strategies, we can become masters of our own destiny. And we can achieve it together.

Contents

CONTENTS

Foreword

We live in an era defined by exponential change, where the lines between work, learning, and personal fulfillment blur. As technology accelerates and opportunities multiply, the question we must ask ourselves is: How do we make the most of this unprecedented potential?

This is where Yu-kai Chou's 10,000 Hours of Play comes in. Rather than focusing on struggle and sacrifice, he presents a vision where the path to mastery is an engaging, purposeful experience. Much like the breakthroughs I champion in space exploration, artificial intelligence, and healthcare, Yu-kai's approach shifts our mindset toward possibilities rather than limits. He shows that the key to success lies in transforming our lives into a game, one where each milestone is a quest and each challenge a chance to level up.

In 10,000 Hours of Play, Yu-kai encourages us to reframe our lives as a series of opportunities for growth, play, and impact. By doing so, he unlocks a powerful truth: we perform at our best when we are deeply engaged in what we do, when work and play become indistinguishable.

If you're ready to take control of your own journey and elevate your life to a new level of meaning and achievement, this book is your roadmap. Yu-kai's insights will inspire you to approach your goals with renewed energy, creativity, and a sense of adventure. And in a world full of exponential possibilities, that mindset is more valuable than ever.

-Peter Diamandis, Founder of XPRIZE and Singularity University

Preface

I've spent a considerable amount of time contemplating what my second book should be. After my first book, *Actionable Gamification: Beyond Points, Badges, and Leaderboards*, became more established - selling over 100,000 copies worldwide and becoming a standard in some industries - I had to decide what to follow up with.

It's not that I lacked material - in fact, I have content for about five other books planned. However, with my limited time running a design company, a mentorship platform, and a Web3 platform to preserve memories onto the blockchain, plus three young kids, it's challenging to find time to work on a full book.

One option that is popular among my readers is to write a sequel to my first book, taking gamification and behavioral design to the next level. Roughly 500,000 people a year learn about my work and The Octalysis Framework, so there would surely be a strong market for this kind of book.

However, it occurred to me that my previous book focused on helping professionals create better motivating environments for their respective audiences, such as experience designers, product managers, HR professionals, educators, and policy makers. It doesn't necessarily help the common individual elevate their own life while enjoying every step of the way.

Instead of going deeper into technical design with the Octalysis Framework, I decided to go upstream to help a much wider audience by expanding on the revelation I had in 2003 that completely changed my life: how to turn one's own life into a game.

For years, I've been motivated by Malcolm Gladwell's book "Outliers," which claims that 10,000 hours of practice and experience help a person achieve industry-leading mastery. That may or may not be entirely true. Regardless, the premise of this book is this: if you gamify your life correctly, instead of suffering through 10,000 hours of blood, sweat, and tears, you could experience through 10,000 hours of enjoyment, fun, and purpose.

And at the end of all this gameplay, there's a good chance you will have become successful in your life and the endeavors you care about.

Since the concepts in this book completely changed the course of my life when I first started my journey, I hope this book can have the same impact on many others so that as 10K HP players we can all tackle the world's challenges.

Head to the next page, and let's begin this journey together.

Ready Player One: The Ultimate Level Up

Hack, hack, slash. Slash, slash, bash.

I checked the clock. It was 2 am. I had been grinding and killing monsters for the past four hours so that I could get the last piece of the Paladin set equipment: Griswold's Legacy in the game *Diablo II*. After obtaining this final piece, my Paladin would officially become overpowered (OP), and my friends would finally envy my achievement. "They're going to want me to be part of every single quest once I complete this!" I thought with anticipation, feeling the dopamine fire between my brain cells.

Hack, hack, slash. It was now 3 am. My homework lay on my desk, begging to be finished. But I was strong. I was motivated, and I was determined. I wouldn't sleep or touch my homework until I found that set item.

A few weeks later, I walked to my friend's house, beaming with pride: I had finally completed my Griswold's Legacy set. With the extra set item bonuses, I was going to be unstoppable. I didn't care that it took me hundreds of hours of dedicated gameplay to achieve this feat. Those late nights grinding and persevering were worth it in order to become the best. To accomplish great things, there must be great sacrifice.

My friends were already in the living room playing video games.

"Griswold's Legacy. It is completed. I am complete like Perfect Cell,"* I not-so-subtly bragged. "Who wants to check out how powerful my Paladin is now?"

---

*Cell is the name of one of the main villains in the iconic manga/anime series *Dragon Ball Z*, who was obsessed with achieving his perfect form by absorbing two other androids.

None of my friends seemed to hear me; they were all in a trance, staring at their screens. The rapid and thunderous mashing of controller buttons and joysticks seemed to just get louder and louder.

"Uh... guys?" I tried again, slightly confused. Maybe they forgot what Griswold's Legacy was. "I just completed the ultimate Paladin equipment set in *Diablo II*. You guys should come check out my awesome aura stats."

"Yu-kai, we don't play *Diablo II* anymore," my friends responded. "Yea, we're all playing *Warcraft III* now."

"I was speechless. Did over a thousand hours of grinding, killing monsters, and leveling up really all just amount to nothing?" My friends felt okay dedicating their lives to a new game every one to two years, but not me: I felt defeated, discouraged, and demoralized knowing that my years of investment were just wasted.

I thought, "There has got to be a game that everyone is playing and people can't just quit and move on to new things whenever they want to. How can I make sure I don't spend massive hours on a game again but end up having nothing to show for it?"

If I can figure this out, then that would be the best game in the world.

You Are Already a Gamer

Whether you know it or not, you're playing a game right now.

Just consider this: Popular games such as *Diablo II* are categorized as role-playing games (RPGs). In these, you take on the role of a protagonist (the hero) on an epic quest (usually to save the world). At the beginning of your journey, you are weak (low level), with few abilities, have limited access to locations on the map, and you are carrying few or no items. But as you slay monsters, level-up in your abilities, and discover items, your character gains the strength and experience to progress through more difficult levels in the game.

After my *Diablo II* debacle in 2003, I realized that the game I was searching for – the one worth dedicating thousands of hours to – was life itself.

I was still just in high school, but I started seeing myself as my own RPG character. Instead of seeing classes and extracurricular activities as chores I needed to do before I could play games, I treated all those activities as quests within the game I was playing.

Once I redirected my gaming mindset to productive activities, I suddenly thrived in everything I was doing in high school. I went from a B student to an A student (98%). I wrote a Chinese novel and three musical pieces for string quartets. I competed in the state competition for debate, forensics, swimming, and violin, and finished second in my state for chess.

After all, you don't just do the bare minimum possible in a game and move on. No, you become the best you possibly can!

All that gameplay enabled me to attend UCLA, which was supposed to be miles above my academic league. After all, I barely spoke English two years prior to applying for college.

While in college, I took this life game concept even further.

- Instead of slaying demons, I started my own business as a freshman at UCLA.
- Instead of searching for treasure chests, I networked with strong talents and investors.
- Instead of gaining and assigning ability points, I read books and found mentors to enhance my professional skills.

Because of all this play that I was doing in my life game, I now, in my later 30s, have obtained some of these (to put it in game terms) achievement badges:

- Founded over eight companies, most relating to gamification, with a variety of successes and failures.
- Created over thirty frameworks and models, including the Octalysis Framework for Gamification and Behavioral Design, which has impacted the experiences of over 1.5 billion users.
- Published a book about gamification that has sold over 100,000 copies and has been referenced in more than 3,300 Ph.D. theses and academic journals around the world (according to Google Scholar).
- Won the #1 Gamification Guru in the World award out of the top 100 gurus for three out of four years by the Gamification World Congress and Gamification Europe (I was #2 one year and, later, I became a judge).
- Traveled to over fifty countries delivering keynote speeches and workshops, including at places such as Harvard, Stanford, Yale, Oxford, Tesla, Google, and the governments of the UK, Singapore, Taiwan, and Kingdom of Bahrain.
- Built a multi-million-dollar consulting business that has helped organizations such as LEGO, Uber, Microsoft, McDonald's, Salesforce, and Shopify.
- Operated as the Head of Digital Commerce and Head of Creative Labs for HTC and VIVE, pioneering VR/AR/Metaverse technology.
- Functioned as a Chief Experience Officer of Decentral, working alongside Ethereum Co-founder Anthony Di Iorio to craft engaging blockchain experiences.
- Became a Fellow for the Royal Society of Arts in London, joining an esteemed lineage that includes luminaries such as Adam Smith, Stephen Hawking, and Benjamin Franklin.

- Invited as a Council Member of the Taipei Smart City Council and also knighted by His Imperial Highness King Yi Seok of the Joseon Imperial Family of Korea (yes, strange story).
- Launched Octalysis Prime (OP), the first ever gamified mentorship *guild* to learn gamification and behavioral design, with over 40,000 OP Players.

By most intents and purposes, the nerdy kid that was obsessed with video games from a young age has turned his hobby and passion into a powerful life-changing game.

If you're a gamer, then I have great news for you: You can immediately apply 10,000 Hours of Play to your own daily activities to start living a healthier, more productive, and more fulfilling life.

If you're not a gamer, don't fret. 10,000 Hours of Play (10K HP) is a strategy guide that will teach you the mindset and techniques to supercharge your life and build something meaningful. *And just like the rest of us, you're a gamer too. You just haven't realized it yet.*

So welcome, dear gamer. You are about to embark on an epic journey as the hero of your own game. Get ready for the life-transforming adventure that awaits you!

Are You a Non-Playable Character (NPC) or a Hero?

"Hey, Tiffany, it's been such a long time. How are you?" asked Billy.

"It's going fantastic!" Tiffany exclaimed. "I just hired two new agents for my real estate business and started a platinum-level membership for my referral program. I'm on track to break my sales record this year and become the top real estate agent in Los Angeles! How about you, Billy?"

"Oh, you know... same old, same old...the usual," Billy responded. At this moment, he could only think about the Netflix series he binge-watched until 3 am the night before.

Awkward pause. Tiffany quickly changed the subject. "So, how's your mom doing?"

I'm sure you've been in this position before: you get in touch with an acquaintance and ask, "How's it going?" only to get a "same old, same old" response. You've just met a person that lives the life of a non-playable character (NPC).

The NPC

Every role-playing game is riddled with NPCs. They are pro-grammed, predictable, and stagnant characters in an RPG that consistently serve a specific function: sell the hero items (such as weapons or potions), provide hints (when the plot demands it), exchange gossipy conversations, or just take up space in the game world so that it looks busy and vibrant for the Hero.

A lot of people in our society live like NPCs. They passively do the same activities every single day, complain about their school, work, and other people, spend many of their waking hours watching TV (and yes, even playing games!), and have no bigger vision for their lives.

A person who is stagnant, who hasn't done anything new in a few years, who doesn't have a clear vision about who they want to be and what they want to accomplish – that's someone living their life like an NPC.

The Hero

In contrast to NPCs, the Hero of an RPG is never stagnant. The Hero must travel to new places, slay more monsters, obtain new abilities, form new alliances, conquer new quests, and perhaps even save the world. As the protagonist of the game, the Hero is on a journey of discovering and accomplishing epic missions.

In real life, a Hero learns new skills, meets new people, gets into positions of opportunity, achieves new accomplishments, builds their family with nurturing love, strategically invests their money and resources, and continuously grows as an individual and a professional toward a greater goal – the objective of their game.

I believe life is so much better when you live as a Hero rather than an NPC.

Sure, life as an NPC is safe and secure: you stay in one place, you serve one function, and you're never in any danger (until some cataclysmic event happens to the world).

And sure, life as a Hero can be scary: it's risky, it's new, you may fail, you need to work harder than NPCs, and you must learn new skills.

If you truly enjoy the life of an NPC and would like to stay the same for the rest of your life, that's completely fine. We are not here to judge people's lifestyles, as long as you are happy with it, too.

But if you're excited about being the Hero of your own game and leveling up in real life, experiencing greatness and fulfillment you didn't think was possible for someone like you, then continue reading. It's time to start your first hour of play.

10,000 Hours of Play (10K HP): Turn Your Life Into a Game

This book's transformative life strategy is based on over twenty years of research and has been experienced by over 40,000 passionate 10K HP Players who have chosen to live their lives like an epic game within my Octalysis Prime (OP) community.

Here are examples of quests accomplished by 10K HP Players:

- **The Kickstarter Quest**: a 10K HP Player raised over $20,000 on Kickstarter to publish a children's book to inspire the next generation of kids, no matter how humble their beginnings.
- **The Mentor Quest**: a 10K HP Player found a mentor who helped her significantly improve user acquisition for her startup and raise funding.
- **The Dream Job Quest**: a 10K HP Player transitioned from an NPC job to a dream job that combines his three passions: music, games, and education.
- **The Podcast Quest**: a 10K HP Player started her own podcast and built an audience of passionate followers who are in love with her ideas.
- **The Blogger Quest**: a 10K HP Player started his own blog and established industry expertise for his consulting business.
- **The Parenting Quest**: a 10K HP Player upgraded his skills to become a better parent and designed a gamified learning journey for his children to grow up strong, emotionally stable, and with the right values.

In each of these quests, 10K HP Players gained experience, learned valuable skills, and met new teammates and mentors. All the quests you do in your life should come together and form your 10K HP journey. If you know what you want your 10K HP journey to be, then you can strategically plan out the quests in your life that will give you the right skills, resources, and support.

Why 10,000 Hours?

As mentioned in the Preface, the title of this book is inspired by Malcolm Gladwell's 10,000 hour principle, as described in his bestselling book *Outliers.*[1]

One of the more prominent studies behind Gladwell's 10,000 hour principle was done by psychologists K. Anders Ericsson, Ralf Th. Krampe, and Clemens Tesch-Römer at Berlin's Academy of Music, a prestigious music school.

Working with the academy's professors, the researchers divided the violinists into three groups. The first group included students who had the potential to become world-class soloists. The second group included pretty good violinists who could likely play professionally in established symphonies and orchestras. Finally, the third group included students who were unlikely to ever play professionally but intended to be music teachers in the public school system.

What they discovered was that the first group had an average of roughly 10,000 hours of deliberate practice *before they reached the age of twenty.* In contrast, the second group practiced 8,000 hours on average, while the third group only practiced 4,000 hours. They then saw the same patterns when comparing professional pianists to amateur pianists.[2]

The 10,000 hours principle was further validated by Daniel Levitin. Levitin is an OP cognitive psychologist, neuroscientist, writer, musician, and record producer who has written five books that have collectively sold over *three million copies* (in contrast, my first book, *Actionable Gamification,* only sold 100,000 copies). He is a Distinguished Faculty Fellow at the Haas School of Business within UC Berkeley and a member of the Board of Governors for the Grammys. The records and CDs that he has contributed to have sold more than thirty million copies, and he consults for the Rock & Roll Hall of Fame.

Note that Levitin is not just an accomplished scientist or musician; he has astonishing accomplishments in both fields, on top of being an esteemed academic. There is even a cognitive neuroscience term named after him: the Levitin Effect. Later, in Chapter 5, I will reveal how synthesizing skills from two or more unique fields could help 10K HP Players become their strongest roles within their Games.

In his book, *This is Your Brain on Music: The Science of a Human Obsession*, he writes, "The emerging picture from such studies is that 10,000 hours of practice is required to achieve the level of mastery associated with being a world-class expert – in anything. In study after study, composers, basketball players, fiction writers, ice skaters, concert pianists, chess players, master criminals, and what have you, this number comes up again and again."[3]

In *Outliers*, Gladwell continues to provide an impressive list of examples, citing Bill Gates, The Beatles, and chess legend Bobby Fischer, all of whom accumulated approximately 10,000 hours of experience before becoming world-class. He notes that even child prodigies like Mozart did not compose any of his great pieces until he was twenty-one years of age, ten years after he began composing concertos.

Of course, 10,000 hours is just a symbolic number[†]. It could very well be 8,000 or 30,000 hours, eight years, or twenty years, depending on your field and other variables[4]. "10,000 hours" is the symbolic representation of the *long journey* it takes to achieve mastery and success.

There are many other variables that define true mastery and success, including passion toward the subject, natural talents and attributes, picking the right roles, *deliberate practice* of such skills, support circles and mentors, and life encounters that lead to pivotal opportunities. These six variables come together to form the six steps within 10K HP that are covered in this book.

Regardless of exactly how many true hours or years "10,000 hours" represents, it is an incredibly long time to invest in the wrong skill or to work painfully hard without meaningful results. This is why I believe 10K HP is so important. It helps you identify which "game"

[†]There has been much debate, even by the researcher Ericsson himself, about whether the violinist study proves that 10,000 hours makes someone an expert. Regardless, it wouldn't change any of the ethos and takeaways of the 10K HP principles explained in this book. The proverbial 10,000 hours would simply represent the idea of putting significant time into a skill and taking up a strong role in your life game.

to play so that you know that your 10,000 hours of investment are going into something meaningful and fulfilling.

It helps you turn painful practice, which requires substantial discipline, into gameful fun that is effortlessly engaging.

Start Your Play

10,000 Hours of Play is a strategy guide that can help you turn your life into a game worth playing. By following the six steps outlined in this book, you can become the Hero of your own game and achieve your goals while having fun through a meaningful life.

It's important to remember that the journey is its own reward. Most people I talk to have never beaten the original Super Mario Bros game on the Nintendo NES. However, they still have fond memories of playing the game.

It could be the people you played with, the friends you made while trying to figure out how to beat certain levels, the frustration from not being able to overcome a challenge, or the elation of finally triumphing over a quest. All of these experiences add up to joyful memories, regardless of whether you have beaten the game or not.

This is the nature of games: **By playing you are winning. The only way to lose is by not playing.**

The same principle applies to your OP Hero's journey. You may choose several games that you may never beat, but that's okay. You will feel proud knowing in your heart that you tried and will be grateful for the allies you made, the skills you gained, and the quests you conquered along the way.

Ready Player One Highlights

- Whether you know it or not, you are playing a game.

- Many people live their lives as an NPC (non-playable character). They aren't passionately pursuing something greater.
- Unlike stagnant NPCs, living as a Hero means constant growth, new experiences, and achieving greater goals.
- Inspired by Malcolm Gladwell, the 10,000-hour rule emphasizes dedicated practice. However, in 10,000 Hours of Play (10K HP), it's about enjoying the game and finding fulfillment in the journey.
- Embrace your 10K HP, enjoy every quest, and turn your life into the most exciting game you've ever played.

Chapter 1: Your Hero's Journey Begins

Are you ready to embark on this fulfilling journey of living your life like an epic game?

Depending on where you currently are in your real-life adventures, you might say to yourself, "How am I supposed to turn my life into a game when the world is falling apart? I don't have the circumstances that allow me to become a great Hero anywhere. Life just isn't fair to me."

And it's true – the world seems to be headed toward more chaos and disarray with every passing day.

Various pandemics and sicknesses have had a profound impact on people's daily lives, causing the loss of countless loved ones, economic downturns, and imposing lockdowns that still have lasting effects to this day.

Wars and rumors of upcoming wars are causing families to fall apart, lives to be lost, supply chains to break, and countries to become hostile toward one another. The financial system seems to be crumbling as nations experience insurmountable debt, un-controllable inflation, and collapsing financial institutions.

What makes things worse is that people are becoming even more divided and hateful toward one another due to politicians who build tribalism through demonizing the other side and media that feeds on blood-boiling reactions to drive more views that please their advertisers.

It all just seems so hopeless.

But what if I told you that you are in the perfect position to become the Hero in your own life game, and that there's almost no better setup in which a Hero can rise?

Don't believe me? Think about the beginning of virtually every great saga; Chapter 1 of each great epic; Stage One of every story-driven game.

What do they have in common? They all had weak heroes living in worlds that are falling into crisis.

You probably wouldn't even call these individuals heroes if not for the fact that they decided to start their journeys in ways that made their stories worth telling to begin with.

What happens in most of these stories is that the world prior was peaceful and in harmony. The pre-hero lived a life of stability and comfort (maybe like you are right now, or you were a few years ago). But then, suddenly, something significant happens, and the world goes into crisis. People panic, and society descends into chaos.

This is the setup where the pre-hero decides to take on her journey to fully realize her potential as a True Hero.

Fictional characters like Luke Skywalker from *Star Wars* and Frodo Baggins from *The Lord of the Rings* lived relatively stable and comfortable lives until a crisis shattered their world – whether it's a distress signal from Princess Leia followed by the tyrannical empire killing Luke's family, or the discovery of the one ring that could bring utter evilness to Middle-earth.

In the real world, historical OP Heroes also lived through dramatic changes that were often scary and confusing at first, but later proved to be the prelude to their amazing stories.

Think about Nelson Mandela, who was born as a Black man in South Africa when people were segregated and humiliated regu-larly because of their skin color. He was a lawyer and believed in peaceful protests. This was before his call to adventure, and if there weren't any new shocks to the system, he would have had marginal impact in South Africa, and we probably wouldn't know his name today.

Then chaos struck in the form of the 1960 Sharpeville Massacre, where sixty-nine Black South Africans were brutally killed as they peacefully protested against unfair laws. This made Mandela realize that he had to do more. He helped start an armed group called the Spear of the Nation to fight for Black citizens' rights and force the government to take their pleas more seriously.

Later, he was caught and was then sent to prison for a whopping 27 years. During this time, his conviction toward his *game* never wavered while his allies outside of prison continued to rally for him.

Even though Nelson Mandela's 10K HP journey began through armed sabotages of government infrastructure, later, as a higher-level player he regretted those actions and claimed there were better ways to put pressure on the government. He continuously discouraged armed and violent methods toward the racist government, which earned him respect from both sides. After his release, 27 years later, he made history by becoming South Africa's first Black president, playing a pivotal role in fostering unity among the country's diverse races.

You see, just like in fictional stories, real-life OP Heroes often start with fairly uneventful or passive lives until something unexpected and paradigm-shattering happens.

So, what if the turmoil engulfing our world – pandemics, devastating wars, and the economic downturn – are collectively serving as our own call to adventure? Even though we like being comfortable and don't like things to change, it's important to remember that big shocks to the system can lead to legendary accomplishments in one's life.

This is where you embark on your own Hero's Journey.

The Hero's Journey

This big transformation from chaos into being an OP Hero doesn't happen easily. When you have a world in crisis, and you have aspirations of becoming the Hero to resolve that crisis, those legendary achievements won't just pop out of nowhere. If this were so, anyone could have easily accomplished them, and the achievements would not be considered legendary. It's first necessary to go through a Hero's Journey where you experience ups and downs, achievements and failures, and growth and let-downs to reach your final form.

This is where Joseph Campbell's Hero's Journey becomes critical. This is a narrative structure identified by Campbell in his book *The Hero With a Thousand Faces*.[1] Campbell outlines seventeen stages that many heroes undergo in myths and stories worldwide. Building on the concept of adversity and growth, this journey offers a framework for understanding transformative journeys through key stages, ultimately leading to personal growth.

Christopher Vogler, a Hollywood screenwriter, later adapted Campbell's seventeen-step framework into a simplified twelve-step version to suit the needs of modern storytelling, particularly in film.[2] (See Figure 1.)

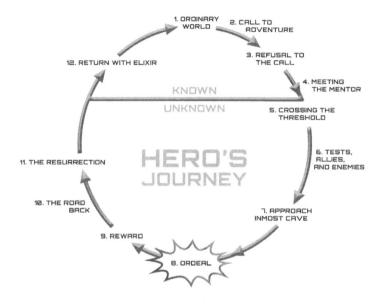

Figure 1. The Hero's Journey

Consider these stages through the fictional character Luke Sky-walker from the iconic *Star Wars* movie.

1. Ordinary World: Luke lives a mundane life on Tatooine, setting the stage for his adventure.
2. Call to Adventure: A distress message from Princess Leia draws him into the conflict between the Rebel Alliance and the Empire.
3. Refusal of the Call: Luke initially hesitates but ultimately resolves to join the fight after the Empire kills his family.
4. Meeting the Mentor: Obi-Wan Kenobi introduces Luke to the Force and the Jedi ways, guiding him throughout his journey.
5. Crossing the Threshold: Luke leaves Tatooine, embarking on a daring mission to rescue Princess Leia.
6. Tests, Allies, and Enemies: Facing challenges and encountering allies and adversaries, Luke's courage and commitment are tested.

7. Approach to the Inmost Cave: Infiltrating the Death Star, Luke and his companions confront their fears and the Empire's power.

8. The Ordeal: Luke faces a crisis when Obi-Wan sacrifices himself, forcing him to confront his vulnerability.

9. Reward: Rescuing Leia and escaping the Death Star, Luke is celebrated as a hero.

10. The Road Back: Luke joins the Rebels in assaulting the Death Star, using his growing mastery of the Force.

11. The Resurrection: Barely avoiding death, Luke destroys the Death Star, dealing a significant blow to the Empire.

12. Return With the Elixir: Luke emerges stronger, wiser, and embraces his destiny as a Jedi.

Luke Skywalker's transformation demonstrates the potential for personal growth through hardship, adventure, mentorship, loss, and triumph. It is a journey that many storied heroes go through, and it might surprise you how much these epic fables can be applied to our own lives too.

Of course, not every life game needs to be about saving the world. Sometimes it's about changing your immediate world or protecting the world of those around you. In the face of adversity, it is essential to recognize that heroism and extraordinary achievements can come in many forms.

Becoming a loving spouse, devoted parent, responsible student, landing that dream job, or becoming an exceptional friend can all be life-changing, as these smaller-scale achievements hold immense value and dramatically impact the lives of everyone around you.

So throw away your doubts. Now is the perfect time to start your Hero's Journey. This is your call to adventure. Maybe you need a mentor (such as me as you read this book, or it could be someone at a higher level). Maybe you need to go through some loss such as losing a job or a significant relationship. Whatever the reason, it's important to take the next step in life. You absolutely can turn your life from being comfortable and mundane to epic and world-changing.

The Six Steps to Master Your Game

Now that you acknowledge the importance of starting your Hero's Journey, you need the right tools and methodology to grow from a pre-hero to an actual Hero. This is where the 10K HP (10,000 Hours of Play) journey becomes the step-by-step model for your growth and adventure.

It guides you to turn your life into a game worth playing by dividing your journey into two sections: *knowing yourself* and *growing yourself*, with each section rewarding to explore in its own right.

Take a look at Figure 2 to see how this plays out.

Figure 2. 10K HP Six Steps Journey

Phase 1: Know Yourself

The first three steps within 10K HP are focused on knowing what you want, what you are good at, and who you should be. This is essential if you want to play your game at maximum potential, allowing you to surpass others in the same field.

Step 1: Choose Your Game (Mission)

The first step to becoming a hero in your own game is to identify your mission in life. In video games, the hero always has a clear objective to achieve. In real life, you need to define your mission, which should be something that excites you and gives your life purpose. It could be a career goal, a personal ambition, a cause you believe in, or anything that makes you feel alive.

Take some time to think about what you want to achieve in life. Don't be afraid to dream big and go beyond what you think is possible. Whether it's solving climate change or being a better parent, the game you choose must be meaningful enough to dedicate thousands of hours to play, master, and achieve.

Chapter 2 provides a variety of methods you can use to discover what game you should play in your life.

Step 2: Know Your Attributes (Talents)

In video games, characters have natural attributes such as strength, agility, or intelligence. In real life, your attributes are your talents and natural abilities. Knowing your attributes can help you identify your strengths and weaknesses in order to select your role as well as develop a plan to enhance your skills.

Talents and attributes (Step 2) are different than skills and abilities (Step 4). Talents are traits you are born with whereas attributes can only be acquired over years of life experiences. On the other hand, skills and abilities can simply be acquired by taking a class, reading a book, or going through some form of short-term training. More often than not, an attribute such as *perseverance* only comes with experiencing much hardship and cannot be obtained by simple learning sessions.

Chapter 3 examines the various ways to determine your attributes and form a *Talent Triangle* a model you can use to better decide what role you should play in your game.

Step 3: Select Your Role (Specialty)

In video games, players can choose to be a warrior, wizard, archer, or a myriad of other characters. In real life, your role is defined by your profession, identity, or your "side hustle." Ideally, your role should align with your mission and attributes.

Take some time to consider your role. What do you want to be known for? What profession or activity aligns with your mission and attributes? Knowing your role is key to making good career and personal decisions.

Chapter 4 explores a variety of layers that make up your *Role Sphere*, including your aspirations, identity, occupation, and specialization. You will also explore finding your unique *Hero name* that will empower you through your game.

Phase 2: Grow Yourself

The latter three steps within 10K HP is about taking actionable steps to play the game. Once you know your game, your attributes, and your role, you can begin your questing journey to level up your skills and connect with new allies.

Step 4: Enhance Your Skills (Craft)

In video games, players can earn skill points and spend them to learn new spells or abilities. In real life, you can enhance your abilities and craft by taking classes, reading books, doing jobs/internships/projects, and developing your personal and professional skills.

Once you identify the skills you have and the ones you need to acquire to achieve your goals and become the strongest player on your "Earth server," you can craft a strategic action plan to develop those skills.

Chapter 5 also explores a variety of real-life game skills such as *enchant* (gamification), *charge* (approaching strangers), *iron skin* (becoming immune to rejections), *thunderclap* (delivering great speeches), and more.

Step 5: Build Your Alliance (Network)

In video games, players at higher levels can help those at lower levels gain experience quickly. In real life, your network can help you gain knowledge, skills, and opportunities.

In your life game, you want to surround yourself with friends who are not only playing the same game but also bring complementary skills to the table. Additionally, having mentors can accelerate your progress by helping you gain knowledge quickly and unlocking opportunities that would otherwise be inaccessible to low-level players.

Chapter 6 explores the differences between factions, guilds, parties, and partnerships, so you can be strategic about building your alliances and never feel alone in your endeavors.

Step 6: Achieve Your Quests (Milestones)

In video games, quests help players progress through the game by recovering a lost sword, raising a "champion chocobo" (a fantasy species in *Final Fantasy*), or unlocking a new skill.

In real life, quests help you progress in life: start a company, get your Ph.D., find a mentor, buy a home, or start a family. These quests allow you to acquire the skills you need to tackle even harder quests, while also growing chemistry with your allies.

Chapter 8 dissects a variety of different quests, from main quests to side quests, major quests to minor quests, learning quests to health quests. It also will help you zoom out to see your life quests as a cohesive journey, divided into separate *sagas* and *arcs* (series of major quests)*.

Six Steps for Changing Your Life

These six steps within the 10K HP journey hold the key to unlocking immense success in your life. While the "Knowing Yourself" phase may only require revisiting once every few years, it is the continuous practice of the "Growing Yourself" steps that facilitates genuine progress and enriches the gameplay experience. If you embrace this mindset and see your life as a game, you can unlock your potential to achieve incredible feats while enjoying every moment of the adventure.

Playing the 10K HP Game: Cloud Strife

Later chapters of this book explore how historical OP Players have unintentionally applied the 10K HP principles to change the world we all live in. Legendary humans such as Mahatma Gandhi, Walt Disney, and Marie Curie all have exemplary growth journeys that can be seen through the lens of the six steps introduced in this book.

But before we dive into real-life examples, first consider how the 10K HP steps play out for a fictional game character - Cloud Strife from Final Fantasy VII, one of the most iconic RPGs of all time. Cloud's role began as a warrior within the powerful but evil megacorporation Shinra, but Cloud later left to join a protagonist group to take down Shinra and save the planet.

Here you can see how someone like Cloud needed to follow the six steps within 10K HP to achieve his goals and save the planet.

Phase 1: Know Yourself (Cloud Strife)

Following are the first three steps of 10K HP applying to Cloud Strife from the game *Final Fantasy VII*. Notice that the first three steps are set up quite early in this 10K HP journey and the key is that they must align with each other, as opposed to the Phase 2 three steps where it is about execution and achievements.

- **Step 1: Choose Your Game (Mission)**: In Cloud's case, his game is his life's mission. His mission is to stop the evil company Shinra from destroying the planet. This company is draining the planet's energy, and Cloud became disillusioned by his former employer to the point that he started dedicating his life to stopping their actions. That's his purpose, and his success within the game is only measured by how well he can accomplish this purpose.
- **Step 2: Know Your Attributes (Talents)**: In *Final Fantasy VII*, each character has their unique distribution of five major attributes: strength, dexterity, magic, spirit, and luck. Cloud immediately stands out with extremely high strength compared to all of his other stats. This indicates that he can likely deal a lot of damage with his attack moves. On the other hand, his magic is pathetically low, which means he is not very effective with magical spells.
- **Step 3: Select Your Role (Specialty)**: In most RPG games, you basically choose one of three main roles: Damage, Tank, and Support. The Damage role is used to take out enemies as quickly as possible; the Tank role is very resilient and can sustain a lot of damage from enemies, so a Tank's task is to get the enemies' attention while their teammates fulfill their separate duties. Finally, the Support role has the ability to heal, protect, or boost the party members.

Within this structure, in *Final Fantasy VII*, because Cloud's attributes are so weighted toward strength, it makes the most sense that he picks up a gigantic sword and becomes the main damage dealer.

Now that Cloud has figured out his role in his game, it's time for him to figure out how to level up and become the strongest Damage character in the game.

Phase 2: Grow Yourself (Cloud Strife)

While the first three steps were all about selecting and identifying, the next three steps focus on growth and action.

- **Step 4: Enhance Your Skills (Craft)**: In many RPG games, you level up your characters by fighting enemies. Every time they level up, they get stronger, unlock special abilities, and can sometimes upgrade their weapons with money. In Cloud's example, he starts with only two abilities, including *braver*, a strong physical attack that deals heavy damage to a single enemy. Later, he is able to unlock much more powerful moves to use against his enemies. He must determine for himself, in order to defeat his strong enemies more effectively, what skills he must acquire. This could be a variety of new skills and attacks, including ones that attack multiple enemies at the same time.
- **Step 5: Build Your Alliance (Network)**: Cloud understands that he cannot accomplish his goal of defeating Shinra by himself. He needs a whole group of allies to fulfill his mission. During the game, Cloud meets many characters with the same goal of stopping Shinra but have complementary attributes and skills. These are characters such as Barret (as a Tank), Tifa (another Damage), Aerith (Support), and many more. Cloud can unlock a total of eight companions in the game but can only adventure with two at a time. Therefore, he must be very strategic about who he chooses as his accompanying allies and make sure their abilities are complementary to each other.
- **Step 6: Achieve Your Quests (Milestones)**: Cloud isn't going to accomplish his major objective right at the start, no matter how much effort he puts into it. He's simply too weak and inexperienced — perhaps like many 10K HP readers may feel today in relation to their own goals and aspirations.

He would need to first do small tasks that can help him gain experience and grow in his relevant skill sets.

The great thing is that Cloud can take on his quests alongside his allies, growing stronger together while building chemistry as a team. In *Final Fantasy VII*, Cloud's first quest is called "Bombing Mission," where Cloud and his allies blow up one of Shinra's energy reactors, similar to Nelson Mandela's earlier quests against the South African apartheid government. Then, another quest is when Cloud needs to "Escape from Midgar," followed by "Journey to Kalm," until the very end where Cloud confronts his nemesis Sephiroth and fights the ultimate evil, Jenova.

After defeating Jenova, Cloud finally accomplishes his mission to stop Shinra from destroying the planet, hence beating his game. Of course, his life doesn't end at that point. After that, he could find a new game and a new mission in life, where he would need to learn new skills and grow even further. Maybe he has to learn to grow a loving family. Unfortunately, the real-world video game player says goodbye to Cloud at that point and does not get to experience his future adventures.

Speaking of real-world video game players, let's now look at how a historic OP Hero applies these same principles in the world we live in to achieve legendary success.

Even though Steven Paul Jobs didn't dismantle Shinra and save the entire planet from destruction, he accomplished some pretty good feats of his own in his life game. Mr. Jobs is the visionary behind Apple and the leading force behind the creation of the first personal computer, the iPhone, and many other innovative products we use today. He was also the Chairman of Pixar, which eventually sold to Disney, making him the largest shareholder of the conglomerate before he passed away.

Clearly, this guy knows how to play his game. Let's look at exactly how he did it and what we can learn from it.

Steve Jobs' 10K HP Journey

Below I break down Jobs' life game playthrough into the six steps of 10K HP.

Phase 1: Know Yourself (Steve Jobs)

Similar to Cloud Strife from *Final Fantasy VII*, the first three steps are about understanding your game and yourself, whereas steps four to six are about growth and action.

- **Step 1: Choose Your Game (Mission)**: Steve Jobs' goal was to "put a dent in the universe" by simplifying complex technology and making it accessible to everyone at a time when computers were primarily for engineers and tech-savvy people. This mission led him to revolutionize the personal computing industry with the Apple II, enhance graphical user interfaces with the Macintosh, transform music consumption with the iPod, introduce groundbreaking touch screen technology with the iPhone, and contribute to computer-animated storytelling through Pixar.
- **Step 2: Know Your Attributes (Talents)**: Jobs possessed an array of qualities that contributed to his success. These included *experience sensitivity*, which granted him the ability to envision how consumers would interact with and feel about his products; *innovative thinking*, which inspired him to conceive products that made users feel intelligent and fulfilled; and *persuasive communications*, which enabled him to effectively convey his visionary ideas. Additionally, his *confrontational proactivity*, which allowed him to challenge and push people beyond their limits, combined with his persuasive communications attribute both contributed to his famous *reality distortion field*- the ability to convince anyone

that something seemingly impossible was actually possible and needed to be executed.

- **Step 3: Select Your Role (Specialty)**: Throughout his professional life, Steve Jobs held various roles: as an entrepreneur, co-founding Apple and NeXT Computers; as an innovative technologist, overseeing groundbreaking products like the iMac and iPhone; as a captivating storyteller, mesmerizing audiences with his keynote presentations; and as a highly effective CEO of Apple and Chairman of Pixar. Under his leadership, Apple became a global powerhouse, while Pixar became the first 3D animation studio to achieve worldwide recognition with the massive success of its first film, *Toy Story*.

Phase 2: Grow Yourself (Steve Jobs)

Now that Steve Jobs knew his game, his attributes, and the role in his game, the rest was about leveling up and tackling activities that would help him beat his objectives.

- **Step 4: Enhance Your Skills (Craft)**: Over the years, Steve Jobs continued to level up his skills as an entrepreneur and innovator – including marketing, branding, product design, user experience, public speaking, negotiations, management, and synthesizing technologies. He continuously improved his attention to detail in user experiences, making product design and presentation the company's hallmark. This dedication to crafting products as experiences, from unboxing to first use, became integral to Jobs' skillset and success. All these skills came together to drive his culture-changing product launches across multiple companies, as well as his sale of Pixar to Disney for $7.4 billion.
- **Step 5: Build Your Alliance (Network)**: Even though Steve Jobs was known to be very demanding and difficult to work

with, he placed substantial value on working with others who had exceptional abilities. Even before his storied alliance with engineering genius Steve Wozniak, Steve Jobs found a mentor-friend at Reeds College named Robert Friedland. From Friedland, Jobs acquired an ultimate skill, his reality distortion field, similar to a *war cry* skill that boosts teammates into working overdrive and accomplishing feats that were previously thought to be impossible.[‡] And of course, Steve Jobs' collaboration with Steve Wozniak laid Apple's foundation and birthed the Apple I computer. Their early investor, Mike Markkula, taught Jobs presentation and design skills. Jonathan Ive, the mind behind iconic Apple designs, became a close ally. Tim Cook, a supporting teammate during his most difficult times, succeeded Jobs as Apple's CEO, ensuring ongoing success after Jobs' passing.

- **Step 6**: **Achieve Your Quests (Milestones)**: In the late 1970s, Jobs aimed to make computers user-friendly, resulting in the Apple II. In the early 2000s, he revolutionized the music industry with the iPod and iTunes through the slogan "1000 Songs in Your Pocket." In the late 2000s, his quest to change communication led to the iPhone, a groundbreaking touch screen device made with scratch-resistant gorilla glass. During these quests, Jobs faced many challenges and setbacks along the way such as competition, betrayal, near-bankruptcy, and health issues.

These were just some of the major quests Steve Jobs took under his belt. There were many other minor quests he completed that guided him to becoming the iconic figure he is today. You will learn more about various categorizations of quests later in this book in Chapter 8.

[‡]Steve Jobs was impressed by the leadership style and persuasive charisma that Friedland had and followed Friedland into an apple orchard commune, where Steve Jobs got the name Apple. Even though they had a falling out later, Friedland himself also became a billionaire, clearly indicating that his unique skills were substantially valuable in the life game he himself was playing.

Unlock OP Mode: 10K HP Alignment

Through the accomplishments of Steve Jobs, it's easy to see how all six steps within 10K HP came together to achieve what we call *10K HP alignment.* It is the state where Jobs was – playing the right game, relying on the right attributes, choosing the right role, honing the right skills, aligning with the right allies, and embarking on the right quests. With his 10K HP alignment, he eventually played his life game on OP (overpowered) mode, where his actions and contributions were able to impact the rest of his game world for ages to come. (See Figure 3.)

Figure 3. The 10K HP Player Pyramid

So, what is OP (overpowered) mode? Within the 10K HP termi-nologies, before a person starts their 10K HP journey, they are considered an NPC. They are in passive mode. Once you start your 10K HP journey by engaging in the activities in this book, you become a 10K HP Player. This is when you are in adventure mode, knowing and growing yourself through all six steps within 10K HP.

When you become successful in aligning all six steps, you cross a threshold and start operating at OP mode. OP Players are generally people who are powerful, successful in their fields, and able to change society.

Once these OP Players operate at a high enough level that they become legendary and remembered by history, they ascend to the ultimate position of OP Hero. In Chapter 9, you will read how a variety of OP Heroes in history achieved their 10K HP alignment and started to operate at a level unmatched by their peers.

It's Your Turn to Play: Begin Your Journey

In the next few chapters, you will learn about all of the 10K HP steps in detail and how you can apply them to live a more playful, purposeful life. Pay close attention to how these steps connect with one another in a cohesive way so that you can obtain your own 10K HP alignment.

Pick from One of the Three Game Modes

Easy: Imagine vividly in your mind what it would look like if following the steps in this book helped you achieve your most passionate dreams. What would your lifestyle be like? What would you be doing on a daily basis? How would others perceive you? When we can clearly envision success, it becomes much easier to stay motivated and accomplish our goals. Since you are the ultimate winner when 10K HP fulfills its objectives, adopting a playful and committed attitude from the start ensures your questing journey reaches its full potential - anything less would be leaving success on the table.

Medium: Reflect on the Six Steps and identify which ones you're already strong in and which ones you're currently lacking. Rank them from strongest to weakest, and consider how your weaker steps might be holding you back from achieving your ultimate goals. After finishing this book, revisit this exercise to see if your hierarchy has shifted and whether you've made progress in strengthening your weaker steps.

Hard: Write down a list of the obstacles and frictions in your life. Then, consider how they could make you a stronger player in your 10K HP journey. Think about other players who have overcome similar challenges. What can you learn from their stories? How might your struggles help you build unique attributes or resilience? If this exercise feels too challenging right now, don't worry. You can try the Easy or Medium Mode exercises instead and continue reading the following chapters. Over time, you'll gain the perspective and inspiration needed to tackle this challenge and reframe your obstacles as opportunities for growth.

If you would like a physical album to document your personalized 10K HP journey, you can access hands-on printouts and workbook materials at 10KHP.com/worksheets

Chapter 1 Highlights

- Global challenges and adversities such as failing economies and world conflicts are often prerequisites for your Hero's Journey.
- Great heroes, both fictional and real, such as Luke Skywalker, Frodo Baggins, and Nelson Mandela, emerged from crises that transformed them.
- Joseph Campbell's *The Hero's Journey* outlines personal transformation through stages such as the call to adventure, meeting mentors, facing ordeals, and achieving growth.

- Now is the perfect time to start your Hero's Journey. Embrace your call to adventure, seek mentors, and take the next step toward an epic life.
- The 10,000 Hours of Play (10K HP) journey is a six-step game worth playing, divided into *knowing yourself* and *growing yourself.*
- Step 1: Choose Your Game (Mission): Identify a life mission that excites you.
- Step 2: Know Your Attributes (Talents): Understand your natural talents, attributes, strengths, and weaknesses.
- Step 3: Select Your Role (Specialty): Define your role in life, aligning with your mission and attributes.
- Step 4: Enhance Your Skills (Craft): Continuously develop your skills through learning and practice.
- Step 5: Build Your Alliance (Network): Form alliances with mentors and peers for knowledge, skills, and opportunities.
- Step 6: Achieve Your Quests (Milestones): Pursue meaningful quests to progress and grow your abilities.
- Aligning all six steps allows you to operate in OP mode, becoming an *overpowered player* who can significantly impact your field and society.

Chapter 2: Choose Your Game (Mission)

STEP 1	STEP 2	STEP 3
WOW / LOL		
Choose Your Game MISSION	*Know Your Attributes* TALENTS	*Select Your Role* SPECIALTY

STEP 4	STEP 5	STEP 6
Enhance Your Skills CRAFT	*Build Your Alliance* NETWORK	*Achieve Your Quests* MILESTONES

"If you don't know where you want to go, then it doesn't matter which path you take."

—— Lewis Carroll, Alice in Wonderland*

As you begin your 10K HP journey, the first step in embracing a life of play is selecting the right game with which to engage. As Simon Sinek wrote in his book, *Start With Why*, [1] the purpose of *why* we live our lives dictate *how* we live our lives and *what* we choose to do. The life game you choose to play will end up determining your relevant attributes (Step 2), your appropriate roles (Step 3), the skills you need to learn (Step 4), the allies you need to connect with (Step 5), and the quests you need to take (Step 6).

In the gaming world, there is a wide variety of video game genres, such as RPGs, fighting games, puzzle games, first-person shooters, platformers, racing, party games, and many more. Personally, I really enjoy multiplayer online battle arena (MOBA) games such as *Heroes of the Storm* or *League of Legends*, strategy games such as chess and *Starcraft*, and virtual reality games where I can get some exercise in at the same time as playing. Others may be drawn to different genres, like fighting games (*Street Fighter*), casual puzzle games (*Candy Crush*), or action/adventure games (*Metal Gear Solid*).

In your 10K HP journey, the game you choose represents your life's mission: the purpose of your existence and the reason you are here. It could be to become the best parent to your children, make humanity an interplanetary species, create emotionally moving music, or solve the homeless crisis in San Francisco.

While many people focus on how to improve themselves and grow their abilities, it is extremely important to first identity what your game is so you don't grow aimlessly into someone incapable of tackling it at a high level. Otherwise, you might spend your life doing something you are not passionate about and feel miserable every step of the way. Without a clear vision of your game, you become a decorative NPC for other peoples' games.

Bronnie Ware, an Australian nurse who dedicated many years to palliative care, attended to patients during the final twelve weeks of their lives. She meticulously documented their regrets and found a common pattern among them. She later published a book, *The Top Five Regrets of the Dying*,[2] which includes:

1. I wish I'd had the courage to live a life true to myself, not the life others expected of me.
2. I wish I hadn't worked so hard.

3. I wish I'd had the courage to express my feelings.
4. I wish I had stayed in touch with my friends.
5. I wish that I had let myself be happier.

Analyzing these regrets, it's evident that they encapsulate the essence of living as an NPC in someone else's game, rather than the subjects being the heroes in their own games.

This serves as a potent reminder to break free from the chains of conformity and passive existence! Instead, take control of your own narratives to emerge as the hero in your own life story. My goal in these pages is to help you achieve this and avoid having those five regrets.

Dr. Stuart Brown, the founder of the National Institute for Play, famously wrote the following in his book *Play: How It Shapes the Brain, Opens the Imagination, and Invigorates the Soul*: "The opposite of play is not work — it is depression."[3] Unfortunately, when you are a non-playable character, a life of depression and unfulfillment often follows.

That's why you must play as if your life depends on it.

Your Game Is Not Your Job

Your game is not the same as your occupation or industry (that would be covered in Step 3: Select Your Role). It's not about becoming an accountant or a doctor, but rather the underlying motivation for pursuing that career (e.g., to save lives, to gain wealth, to achieve prestige).

At this point in the process, you should not pick a life game based on your natural talents or gifts, as that would come later in Step 2: Know Your Attributes. Instead, pick a life game based on your *passion and aspirations*. If you are doing something that resonates with those, you will much more likely enjoy spending more time playing the game, hence putting in those 10,000 hours to achieve mastery.

Even in the theoretical but more extreme case where you lack unique skills or talents, where you are only qualified to become a janitor and nothing else, passion still matters. If you were passionate about music, I believe you would be much happier being a janitor for a music company than a truck company. If you had a passion for trucks, it would be the other way around.

So, first you identify your passion and purpose, decide on the game you want to play, and then the rest of the 10K HP steps will help you determine what roles (Step 3) you should play to thrive.

Keep in mind that your game doesn't have to remain the same for the rest of your life. Still, it's ideal to commit to a game for at least three to eight years. The game shouldn't just be about "finishing law school and passing my bar exam" (that would be a major quest within Step 6 instead of your game). Rather, think about why you want to become a lawyer in the first place: Do you want to uphold social justice? Do you want to be respected by people? Or do you just want to make loads of cash?

Whatever your reason, it probably shouldn't change too frequently, unless you have a whole epiphany about what your life's purpose should be instead. Of course, if you realize you've chosen the wrong game, don't feel trapped. Pivot, apply the skills you've learned, rely on the allies you have met, and move on to your next game.

Also, your game doesn't have to be as grandiose as Elon Musk's. It doesn't need to be something as big as taking humanity to Mars; it could be as simple as living a quiet, stress-free life with your pet. It also doesn't have to be altruistic. Dell Computer Corporation's Founder Michael Dell, when pressed consistently why he started his business, finally responded with, "I wanted flags in front of my building."[4] He saw having a whole building named after himself, with its own dedicated driveway decorated with flagpoles, as the epic achievement for the game he wanted to play in his life.

Wear Your Game Like a Badge

Once you know the game you are playing, I recommend sharing it with everyone you meet. Wear it like a badge of honor. In essence, there should be no one close to you who doesn't know you are playing this game.

Wearing your game like a badge has many benefits:

1. Enhance visibility and validation: Regularly talking about your game makes it more tangible. It transforms a private aspiration into a public commitment, inviting both support and accountability.
2. Gain respect: When people hear that you have grand goals, they often hold a higher respect for you. People tend to judge you not on where you are right now, but what your goals are. I've seen it many times myself and will share a few examples later in this chapter.
3. Attract allies: When people know what you stand for, they're more likely to connect with you on a deeper level. You'll attract like-minded individuals who can offer their talents, resources, and network to help you accomplish your game objectives.
4. Inspire and influence: Sharing your game can inspire others to pursue theirs. You become a beacon for those who might share your aspirations but haven't yet found their strength or courage to go for it.

Consider the example of Monkey D. Luffy, the main protagonist from the iconic Japanese manga and anime series *One Piece*. Whenever Luffy meets new people, he would declare proudly, "I'm gonna be the King of the Pirates!" which in the world of *One Piece* means he would be the one individual above all. Especially in the early sagas, Luffy was not particularly strong, and he faced many individuals who were much stronger than him yet didn't dare to dream of becoming King of the Pirates.

As expected, Luffy's audacious declaration to become the King of the Pirates met initial disbelief and even mockery. However, Luffy's unwavering commitment and repeated affirmations very quickly transformed skepticism into respect. His boldness drew people to his cause, turning doubters into allies and companions (Step 5).

What can we learn from Luffy? First, there's clarity of purpose: Luffy's goal is clear and specific. There's no ambiguity about what he wants to achieve. Second, there's consistency in messaging: He repeats his mission at every opportunity, reinforcing his commitment to himself and others. Third but not least, there's conviction over skepticism: despite initial disbelief, Luffy's conviction remains unshaken, demonstrating the strength of his commitment to his game.

Invading England

In one of the greatest movies of all time, Braveheart, the main protagonist, William Wallace (portrayed by Mel Gibson), regularly shouted out his life game through his *war cry* skill. This is a *Real-Life Game Skill* that harnesses intense energy to inspire a team and drive them toward achieving results that would normally seem impossible. § I will cover extensively a variety of Real-Life Game Skills and how to use them to become successful yourself in Chapter 5: Enhance Your Skills.

William Wallace's war cry enabled him to inspire his men to achieve the impossible. After avenging his loved one and chasing the English army out of Scotland, William Wallace scolded the

---

§Chapter 1 noted that Steve Jobs was also skilled at his reality distortion field. Chapter 6 explores how Elon Musk uses war cry to drive his team into accomplishing seemingly impossible tasks.

Scottish nobles about how they just talk politics and nothing else. When they annoyingly asked, "Well, what would you do then?" Wallace replied, "I will invade England, and defeat the Englishman on their own grounds."

I remember the moment I first watched this scene. I was in total shock. "What is he talking about? How is that possible? Fending off one wave of attack is one thing, but some small Scottish rebels surely can't take on the dominating English Empire on their home turf?" Sure enough, the nobles regurgitated my uninspiring doubt: "Ahahaha - Invade? That's impossible!" But William Wallace snaps back with his soul-stunning war cry that I can still hear in my head today:

Why? Why is that impossible? You're so concerned with squabbling for the scraps from [the English King] Longshanks' table that you missed your God-given rights for something better!

Everyone was shocked by how much conviction he showed, and I, as the viewer, along with millions of other Braveheart fans, felt so inspired during that moment that we all started believing in taking on challenges that seemed impossible. We feared that we, too, might miss our God-given rights for something better!

Wallace's declaration is a demonstration of how a strong, clearly articulated life game can shift perspectives and galvanize action. It demonstrates the power of believing in something greater than the present circumstances, no matter how daunting they may seem.

As you discover your quests (Step 6) to master the game of life, consider what "invading England" means to you. It could be a career goal that seems out of reach, an innovative project that no one has attempted, or a personal transformation that others deem unachievable.

Remember, by sharing your audacious goals with conviction and clarity, you not only set yourself on a path of determined action but also inspire others to reconsider their boundaries. Like Wallace, dare to voice what others might not even dare to dream. Your bold vision could be the spark that ignites change, not just in your life but also in the lives of those around you.

Everyone Knows Bill's Game

In 1968, William Jefferson Clinton was just a young Rhodes Scholar at Oxford University, where he met another student, Jeffrey Stamps, at a party. Curiously, Bill Clinton started to ask Stamps questions about what he was doing in life, and then wrote all the replies down like a reporter. When Stamps asked, "Bill, why are you writing this down?" Clinton responded, "I'm going into politics and plan to run for Governor of Arkansas, and I'm keeping track of everyone I meet."[5]

Clinton's strategy underscores the same essential aspect of Step 1: Choose Your Game: vocalize your ambitions. By wearing his goals like a badge of honor, he made them an integral part of his identity (Step 3: Select Your Role). This approach not only keeps you focused but also magnetically attracts resources, people (Step 5: Build Your Alliance), and opportunities (Step 6: Achieve Your Quests) aligned with your game.

As we all know, Bill Clinton not only beat his initial game of becoming governor of the lesser-known state of Arkansas, but by utilizing his unique attributes (Step 2: Know Your Attributes) and interpersonal skills (Step 4: Enhance Your Skills), he eventually achieved the ultimate game objective of becoming the most powerful man in the world: President of the United States. His only downfall was that he ended up pursuing a "relationship side quest" that unfortunately canceled him from the presidency game.[¶]

[¶]Chapter 8: Achieve Your Quests, takes a look at side quests that can distract you from your main game and the importance of avoiding them.

I'm Going to Harvard One Day

During my own college years, I embarked on a cross-America bus tour with my family. Among our travel companions was another family with a daughter who was attending middle school. At first glance, she seemed like any other young girl, unassuming and perhaps shy. However, my perception changed dramatically upon engaging in a conversation with her. The moment we began to chat, she found a way to assert her ambition: "I'm going to Harvard one day." This didn't come out as a tentative dream or a casual mention – it was a declaration, a statement of certainty. Her words resonated with confidence and clarity, cutting through any usual pre-teen self-doubt.

Her statement immediately commanded my respect. In those few words, she transformed from a seemingly typical middle schooler into someone with a vision; someone who seemed to be destined for great things. Her certainty instilled a belief in me about her becoming a very accomplished individual in the future, regardless of whether she got into Harvard or not.

This brief six-word interaction underscored the same crucial lesson in the game of life: the power of wearing your game like a badge. Her example serves as a powerful illustration of how confidently articulating your goals can impact not only your own belief in them but also how others perceive and remember you.

It's been almost twenty years since that encounter, and though I don't know if she ever made it to Harvard, her ambition left a lasting impression. I remain convinced that today she must be a very successful woman, pursuing whatever is most meaningful for her own happiness.

If one day she found a way to get in touch and said, "Hey, remember me? On a trip twenty years ago, I told you I would go to Harvard. I was wondering if you could help me with something," I can say with confidence that I would immediately agree to assist her as much as I was able. This is because I already saw myself as her ally (Step 5) when she declared her game to me two decades ago.

As you navigate your own journey, consider openly and confidently sharing aspirations. Are you declaring your game with the same conviction as the young Harvard aspirant? Are you allowing your ambitions to shape your identity and interactions, just like Monkey D. Luffy, William Wallace, and Bill Clinton did? Once you have chosen your game, it's important to invite others to play.

How to Choose Your Life Game

I just touched on multiple examples illustrating how powerful it is to wear your game like a badge, but how do you pick a game to begin with? Choosing your life game is more challenging than picking a video game genre. It requires significant time, mental effort, and even trial and error to get it right. However, it is of utmost importance to choose the right game. After all, this is your life that we are talking about.

When asked what they want to do later in life, most young people shrug the question off: "It's too big of a question...I can't really think about it," is a typical response. The fact that it is a big and difficult question is the very reason to spend daily time and energy to figure it out, as opposed to hiding away from it until you discover yourself in a place in life where you seemingly have no more control over your trajectory. That's when people experience their mid-life or quarter-life crisis.

To make it all more manageable, here are four methods for finding your game. Utilize all four to increase your chances of finding the right game for you. These methods have some overlap. However, since Step 1: Choose Your Game is an important yet abstract endeavor for many, seeing the same concept from multiple lenses and perspectives will help produce that "aha!" moment when the path becomes clear.

Method 1: Identify Your Passions

It's common advice that you should find your passion and pursue it. For some, turning passions into their life game comes easily. For others, it is difficult to imagine how to build a life journey around their particular passion. I believe that through enough creativity and hard work, there are opportunities to convert all sorts of passions into a life mission.

Just look at me. I had a passion for playing games, and through dedicatedly achieving my quests (Step 6) over many years, I turned it into a career that is more rewarding to me than the careers of some of my friends who went through medical or law school.

As another example, take the story of J.K. Rowling, who turned her love for storytelling into a successful career as author of the best-selling Harry Potter fantasy series; or Steve Jobs, who merged his passion for design and technology to change the world with Apple. Have a passion for Smurfs? Become the ultimate expert on Smurfs and host yearly conferences that attract Smurf-lovers like you.[*]

In this method, create a list of your interests, hobbies, and things that genuinely excite you. It's essential to be honest with yourself and differentiate between fleeting interests and long-lasting passions. Reflect on how these passions have shaped your life thus far and consider how they can be translated into a life game.

If you spent every day for the next thirty years doing activities related to this passion, would you still love your life? Do you find yourself talking about this topic with great enthusiasm whenever it is brought up? When you are browsing YouTube, do you always stop to click on videos related to this topic?

---

[*] Yes, I must admit that this is a weird passion...but there are people like that out there. No one can tell you what your game ought to be. To each their own!

Some people love animals and can imagine spending their whole lives studying or taking care of them. What role they pick (Step 3), such as being a veterinarian or zookeeper, would depend on their Step 2 (knowing their attributes). Some people love doing experiments and want to invent new mechanical devices throughout their lives. Others love interacting with people and could see themselves teaching or counseling the next generation for as long as they can.

Again, it would be better if your life game was more than having a certain occupation, which would be covered as you move onto Step 3: Select Your Role. Ideally, your game should be closer to your aspirations, such as, "make children around the world smile," "become extremely famous," or "make creations that are seen by the world." Also, there is no shame in having a life game focused on trying to find a spouse who understands, loves and takes care of you, and is supportive of your dreams. When choosing your life game, it is often appropriate to ignore pressure from society, expectations from parents, and mockery from peers who are playing different games than you.

If in your heart you long for a stable, happy family with the cheerful joy of children in your home, then ignore the TV series that display a single kick-ass protagonist shaming those who are pregnant or having children as "awkward" or "repelling." If you have ambitions to change the course of humanity and want to be remembered as legendary on the *Earth Server Leaderboard*, then ignore the media that says somehow you are limited to certain roles simply because of your background or societal expectations.

The point is, it is your life, and your game. At the end of the playthrough, you are the only person responsible and taking the full consequences of the path you chose. Don't let the political agendas or ideology of someone else dictate or override what you are passionate about.

Method 2: Think About What Inspires You Whenever You Are Exposed to It

Are there certain types of movies, news stories, or encounters that especially touch or inspire you? Maybe it was the last time you saw someone taking care of an injured animal found in the wild? Or when you watch brave warriors charge into danger to protect something they believe in? Hearing stories of people overcoming their weaknesses and achieving greatness could also inspire you.

Whatever these moments are, take note of them. Try to determine if there is a life game that similarly touches and inspires you.

Of course, being inspired by something doesn't necessarily mean you will do the exact same thing. For example, witnessing brave warriors charging into danger doesn't mean your game is to pick up an axe and become a warrior, or to join the military as a weapons specialist. Instead, you might start with the essence of the pattern you observed – a simple direction for your life game: "I want to dedicate my life to something greater than myself, even if it involves danger and sacrifice."

As vague as it is, that in itself is a valid life game to pick, even if you're not yet certain about the significant cause you're willing to dedicate yourself to. By adopting this life game, you can already start to live your life with passion and direction. You can begin to assess your talents and attributes (Step 2), which will help you determine the most effective ways you can contribute to a greater cause. You can also start considering which roles (Step 3) best leverage your strengths and mitigate your weaknesses. If you really want to feel cool about being a passionate person who doesn't know what your mission is, you could even assume the role of a *ronin*, which is a samurai without a master to serve and die for yet.

You might focus on refining your general skills (Step 4), such as persuasion or leadership. You would also benefit greatly by associating with allies (Step 5) who share your aspiration to dedicate their lives to something larger than themselves. Essentially, they are engaged in the same game as you, and you will find it much more rewarding to undertake main quests (Step 6) together than to spend time with friends who are content playing video games all day.

Finally, you could embark on discovery quests that send you on a journey to explore the vast landscape of values worth defending – such as your country, free speech, democracy, and equality. After all, as a ronin in search of a master, it's crucial to ensure that person is worthy of your life and loyalty.

See how cool this sounds for someone who essentially doesn't yet know what they want to do in life? By defining even a vague game that inspires you, your life already transforms into a 10K HP journey, where every day brings enjoyment, direction, mission, and purpose.

Method 3: Determine What You Would Do If You Didn't Need to Worry About Money

People who aren't living the 10K HP life might assume that everyone is motivated purely by money. After all, money is the fuel that keeps our lives running. Without it, we could end up as struggling NPCs, waiting for other 10K HP Players to rescue us as part of their epic quests to make a difference. However, money is just that – fuel that propels us forward. We use fuel to travel toward destinations that hold meaning for us. It is nonsensical to treat fuel as the final destination we aspire to. If the only reason why you need fuel is to travel toward more fuel, you could see how that becomes a circular life path that doesn't lead to meaning and purpose.

In fact, many extremely wealthy individuals find their lives to be meaningless and miserable – I've personally worked with quite a few. They have all the fuel in the world but no meaningful destination to drive toward – isn't that depressing? What's worse is that they may have sacrificed their childhood, their youth, and the first twenty years of their careers amassing this fuel, yet they still don't know where they are going in life. To add insult to injury, they might even continue working eighty to a hundred hours a week just to add to their already vast reserve of fuel. This is when the non-10K HP Player experiences a mid-life crisis and decides to buy an expensive Lamborghini to feel a bit better about himself. Hey, if you can't love your own life, at least make others envious of it, right? Now, this privileged but lost soul can finally find some solace.

On the other hand, most top 10K HP Players don't treat money as their ultimate game destination. Because of that they transcended into legendary OP Heroes (do you even know who was the richest person in your country 40 years ago?). Figures such as Mother Teresa may not have a lot of feats in terms of wealth accumulation, but her selfless dedication to uplifting others has made her an enduring symbol of kindness. She is consistently the first name that comes to mind when people think of someone in human history with a compassionate heart for helping others. Even though she had little fuel, she made all her destinations count, and she *played* her game through her entire life.[**]

Similarly, we can look at modern-day China founding father Sun Yat-sen, who left his well-paying job as a doctor in order to build a *revolutionary faction (Step 5: Build Your Alliance)* aimed at overthrowing the corrupt Qing Dynasty government and bringing a democratic republic to the Chinese people. For decades he was under constant danger and assassination attempts, being exiled by almost every nation in Asia, and he lost friends and supporters, most of whom were put to death, whenever his uprisings failed.

[**] Mother Teresa has her own critics and controversies, with many suggesting that her organization was poorly run and the care she provided was insufficient. She was also regarded as a stern nurse and harsh manager to her staff. But the fact that she had dedicated her life to this cause and went through many hardships herself means she would still be considered a role model and respectable figure to many. Remember, if you look deep enough into any historical hero, you will find that they are mere human beings, just like you and me. No one is a true saint, but if you take actions similar to theirs and achieve your own 10K HP alignment, you could also ascend to their levels while forgoing whatever flaws they have that are distasteful to you.

However, he stuck to his game, eventually becoming a key component to ending two thousand years of imperial rule in China and becoming the first President of the Republic of China. What about money, you say? Even though Sun Yat-sen wielded large sums of it throughout his life, enough to fund governments and armies, when he died, he only left a humble house and many books to his family. Money was just his fuel to fund his game and his mission, instead of being the game itself.

The game we choose for ourselves should focus on the life we want to live, as opposed to how much money it could make for us. More often than not, we make money to increase the quality of our lives; but we spend so much time in our lives working, it in itself becomes the quality of our lives. It makes little sense for us to be miserable for the majority of our lives, just so we could buy some cool things on the side. Rather, it makes way more sense to focus on what we enjoy doing regardless, do it well enough to achieve success in it, and make sure there is enough fuel to keep the game going.

Just like many others, I never beat the original Super Mario on the Nintendo Entertainment System (NES), yet I have many fond memories playing that game. It would be absurd if my failure to complete the game left me disappointed, depressed, and traumatized. The fact that I tried made me meaningfully happy. Similarly, living your 10K HP journey is not necessarily about succeeding. By *playing* the game, you are automatically winning. The only way to lose is by not playing the game, especially if it is driven by the fear of failure.

Find the game you would love to play every day of your life if you didn't need to worry about money. Make sure that's a game worth playing even if you would never "beat it." Once you find it, you will be set for life.

Method 4: Identify Your Role Models

Another way to determine your life game – what truly matters to you – is to find people you admire, fictional or nonfictional, and decide that you want to leave a legacy like theirs. It doesn't have to be the exact same industry or role (don't feel pressured to defeat a world-conquering dictator with your sword skills), but find out what is the core of their endeavors that makes you respect them. Do they care about others? Do they apply smarts and hard work to solve some of the world's hardest problems? Do they climb out of an underprivileged upbringing and make the world respect them? Or do they sacrifice themselves so they can save the lives of many others?

One popular role model I greatly respect is Suzy Batiz, the founder of Poo~Pourri. Having endured a challenging upbringing, including being a homeless single mom while enduring two bankruptcies, Batiz ultimately bootstrapped her bathroom fragrance product, Poo~Pourri, into a $500 million company in her forties and into her fifties. Despite facing greater hardships than almost anyone I know (you will see more of her entire 10K HP journey in Chapter 9), she leads her life with inspiration, hope, and empathy. Those who see her as a role model might also be inspired to take on the challenge of inventing new products that transform whole industries, just as Suzy did.

Role models don't always need to have massive industry success. They could just be people in your life who inspire you with the way they live. One of my friends, Hyunchul Park, has a Ph.D. in mechanical engineering and is a material science researcher in South Korea. As Hyunchul was starting his new family and preparing to be a father, he told me that his role model is a professor he met in Switzerland named Jonathan B. Boreyko, a visiting scholar from the United States. Enjoying a one-year sabbatical, Professor Boreyko took his wife and *five* children, the youngest being two years old, to tour Europe together.

Seeing how Professor Boreyko was able to take such a big family to so many countries as an academic while always radiating positive energy, Hyunchul was inspired to feel hopeful that he could also live an adventurous life with many kids of his own. His life game is to help as many people as possible through his research, while serving as a role model for his growing family, mentally, emotionally, and spirituality. When I asked him how many kids he wanted to have, he just answered, "I'm not putting a limit on it. If more kids come, they come." I've known many richer and much more "ambitious" people in my life who don't dare to make a comment like that because they believe they simply won't be able to handle the challenges of having a big family.

Yu-kai's Role Model in Terminator 2

One of my own fictional role models is from the popular classic movie *Terminator 2*. If you haven't seen it, feel free to jump to the next section to avoid spoilers. (It's one of the all-time best action movies to watch despite its age.) But if you *have* seen it, my role model is likely not a character you would have guessed. Most of the time, a person's role model from a movie is the main character, his/her master, or the loyal supporting character (and on occasions, the villain). But my role model is a seemingly unimportant side character: the Director of Special Projects at Cyberdyne Systems Corporation: *Miles Bennett Dyson.*

You might be a bit surprised why I chose Miles Dyson as my role model. It's true, in a film that is action-packed with robots killing each other with epic weapons, Miles Dyson does play the role of the wimpy scientist that is powerless and humiliated. But if you look deeper into his character, you'll find that he is actually one of the most respectable people you could know if he was actually a real person.

To start off, Miles Dyson is one of the smartest people on the planet. He has ultimate science authority in Cyberdyne, a company that created the technology that would later become the humanity-eradicating Skynet and Terminators. He is extremely wealthy with a big pool at his mansion by the beach, and he is completely passionate about what he's working on, much like most entrepreneurs.

Besides the brains and wealth, he is a man with a heart. In one of the scenes, his wife and kids wanted him to take them to the theme park, Raging Waters. However, he was glued to his computer because he was "this close" to making the biggest technological breakthrough for mankind. After some patient nudging from his wife, he was willing to stop working on it and take them out to play.

You might be thinking, "What's so special about taking a break from work and hanging out with your family on a weekend?" However, some of you may know that when you are working on a project/problem/startup (basically your favorite game), you are completely obsessed about it to the point that it absorbs you into a totally different world and you think about it 24/7. In this frame of mind, it's difficult to keep your hands off the project. Miles Dyson was able to take a break from his state of flow because he truly loves his family. He is a package of brains and heart, plus wealth and respect. When he was first introduced in the movie, his life almost couldn't get any better.

Okay, he's a quality guy – so what? The real reason why Miles Dyson is my role model is because of the *choices* he makes during the movie. In the film, the heroine protagonist Sarah Connor tries to kill Dyson because she wants to prevent him from inventing Skynet in the future and destroying most of mankind. After being convinced that what she said was true (by seeing a real terminator), he immediately makes the determination that they must destroy his work together. He tells them that they can't just destroy his work at his house; they must go to the Cyberdyne headquarters and destroy everything there. He instantly makes a decision to drop his high status in society and become a criminal in order to save the future.

In one of the scenes, after being shot by Sarah Connor and being given an explanation as to why they wanted to kill him, Miles Dyson says, "I feel like I'm gonna throw up. You're judging me on things I haven't even done yet. Huh! How were we supposed to know?" As if in this life-threatening moment, the biggest concern of his is that his character has been personally insulted.[6]

And to back up that pride about his character, he immediately jumps to the conclusion: "There's no way I'm going to finish the new processor now. Forget it. I'm out of it. I'll quit Cyberdyne tomorrow...We'll have to destroy all the stuff at the lab, the files, the disk drives, and everything here. Everything. I don't care."

Being smart or attractive isn't necessarily a reflection of one's own merits, but doing what is right is. This capacity to set aside everything for the sake of what's morally right is truly admirable. Miles Dyson was on the brink of establishing himself as the foremost influential genius in the world, fervently dedicating his life to his passion day and night for over a decade. However, the moment he understood that his creation could potentially doom humanity, he made the instantaneous and resolute decision to forsake it all, along with his life. That's role-model character right there.

If I had been working on a truly world-changing technology for over ten years and was on the cusp of finally completing it, and then suddenly a desperate woman tried to shoot me, claiming it would destroy the future of mankind, I'm not sure I could just drop everything and destroy it as Miles Dyson did.

Yes, a gun would be pointed at me, but I might just give it lip service, or perhaps secretly keep a backup file to use after the confrontation blows over. If anything, I would likely reason with myself, "The future was destroyed not because I invented this, but because it was put to wrong use. We can just stop the government from making the stupid decision on putting Skynet in charge of all the computers! Since I am the lead on this, I would be able to directly influence how it is used."

Regardless, I don't know if I could be as decisive as Miles Bennett Dyson. While I might eventually decide to destroy everything, it would certainly take me longer to reach that resolution, especially when it means potentially forfeiting my life.

Because I have such a strong role model like Miles Bennett Dyson, I could consider my life game as, "Create world-changing inventions and companies while maintaining my heart and integrity to always do the right thing."

If you can identify what traits these role models have that inspire you the most, you can possibly align your life game with their trajectory before you break out and find your own unique path.

Now that you have these methods to help you determine which life game you want to play, take your time to choose your game. This process may take weeks, months, or even years, but it's crucial to find the right game to make your life a worthwhile journey. Enriching your life with meaning is worth the time and effort, no matter how great the scale.

Yu-kai's Own Life Game

To help make things more concrete, here's an example of the life game I set for myself. When I was in college, I had a life game that consisted of three game objectives:

1. Create a company that starts a whole new industry. For instance, before the computer was invented, there was no computer industry nor accessories; before the car was invented, there was no automotive industry nor associated services.
2. Make a global positive impact. At the time, I just defined global as being more than one country, and positive is something that generically makes the world better.

3. Make everyone around me successful. This of course is a game objective that can never be fully completed, but just like an *asymptote*, a line that continually approaches a given curve but never quite meets it, I could continue to get closer and closer to the goal without fully accomplishing it.

Ever since I was in college and for many years after, I made sure I spent every day of my life getting closer to these goals. Literally, I was playing my life game for ninety to one hundred hours a week. When I took a class, I asked how it would help my life game. I started my first few companies outside of academic hours (Step 6: Achieve Your Quests). I joined the business fraternity, Delta Sigma Pi, and met many amazing like-minded people (Step 5: Build Your Alliance).

When I watched a YouTube video for twenty minutes and realized it wouldn't help me toward my game objective, I would get mad at myself and refocus. For a time, I even set an alarm clock on my watch that would go off every fifteen minutes. When my watch rang, and I wasn't doing something to further myself toward my game objectives, I would course-correct before wasting more time.

And the thing is, that wasn't painful at all. It didn't require "discipline." It was fun, and I was excited to live life every single day. I was on my own Hero's Journey, and every day was a new opportunity to learn and play my game in a better way. At the time, I had a passionate spiel for people I met:

Building a startup company is like embarking on a Lord of the Rings journey. You don't do it because it's comfortable or because you get a nice house or TV. You do it because, first, you believe in the mission of destroying the Ring; and second, you like the people you are traveling with. You don't say, "Oh, I think I'm going to travel for forty hours a week and then just relax in the town I'm in." No, you say, "I'm so tired...maybe I can afford to sleep for four to five hours before continuing my travels." And during this journey, some people might join, some might leave, and some might die, but we press on because the mission is worth it.

That was not merely a feel-good speech I used to motivate or impress people. I genuinely believed in it and felt that every minute not pushing toward my goals was like a gamer trying to control an idle character in a game. If an in-game character was just being idle and, defying the gamer's control, not going out to defeat monsters, gain experience, and level up, the gamer would be shouting, "What are you doing? Go out there and level up!" It would be an incredibly frustrating experience because precious time would be lost.

Years later, after completing (and failing) many quests (Step 6) along the way, I finally looked back at my life and realized that I had accomplished quite a lot in those game objectives.

Even though I was not the sole creator of the gamification industry, I am credited as one of its founding pioneers due to my 10K HP journey into the industry since 2003 and having created the Octalysis Framework in 2012. As my designs have impacted over 1.5 billion users worldwide, and as I have conducted talks and projects in over fifty countries and contributed to lifesaving safety and healthcare projects, I believe it is fair to say that I have made a tangible global positive difference.

Regarding my goal of helping everyone around me become successful, I continue to strive toward this even today. I've helped hundreds of people find their dream career paths, improve their relationships, enhance their parenting, secure funding, and level-up their daily habits, but I'm still far from reaching *"everyone around me."*

Today, my online mentorship platform, Octalysis Prime, has helped over 40,000 members improve their lives through my knowledge of gamification and behavioral design. One of the core reasons to write this book is to advance toward this goal so that I can help hundreds of thousands more people improve their lives through the 10K HP process.

So what is my current life game? It can be summed up as making the largest positive impact I can in the world. I do this via a few game objectives:

1. Make Important activities more enjoyable, and make enjoyable activities more productive. This, in fact, is also the company motto for my gamification design consultancy, The Octalysis Group.
2. Help as many people as possible transform their lives into games they are passionate about and can thrive in. Both this book and my mentorship platform Octalysis Prime aim to accomplish this.
3. Optimize my spiritual, physical, emotional, and mental health. Ensure that I enjoy what I am doing and avoid spending over a year on quests that do not make me happy.
4. Be there for my family. I want to be a dependable and loving husband to my wife, and a good role model and mentor to my three children.

Note that these are not quests. They are high-level aspirations as opposed to specific activities that can be accomplished via a series of to-do lists. But specific activities such as writing this book, growing Octalysis Group, taking a class, or recruiting new members into Octalysis Prime would be considered quests, which I cover in Chapter 8.

Others, like my ally and business partner (Step 5) Jun Loayza, have different but complementary game objectives:

1. Raise his daughters to bring light, happiness, and joy to the world.
2. Create consumer products that positively impact millions of people.
3. Live healthily and happily beyond one hundred years with his wife.

You can see that, together, these game objectives represent family, work, and health, essential parts of our playthrough here on the Earth Server.

It's Your Turn to Play: Finding Your Life Game

Now that you have seen how I think about my life game, it's your turn to select your own.

Pick from One of the Three Game Modes

Easy: Reflect on your passions and the aspects of life that excite you the most. Write down two things you love doing or could see yourself dedicating years of your life to. Ask yourself: Which of these makes me feel the most alive? What excites me enough to wake up early or stay up late? This simple exercise will help you uncover the foundation for choosing your life game.

Medium: Use the four methods described in this chapter to narrow down your life game. What are you passionate about? What excites and inspires you? What would you do if you didn't have to worry about money? Whose life or work do you admire most, and why? Write down one or two potential life games that combine these elements.

Hard Declare your life game and wear it like a badge. Once you've chosen your game, practice articulating it clearly and confidently to others. Share your life game with at least three people, including one new acquaintance or ally you would like to bring into your network. This bold step will help you align your life game with your identity and attract others who can support your mission.

To maximize your probability of getting transformative results, you can also use our 10K HP Workbook materials, which can be found at 10KHP.com/worksheets   .

OP Hero Profile: From Courtroom Flop to the Nation's Top – the Strategy Sage

With each step of the 10K HP journey, I will examine the life of a historical OP Hero, demonstrating how their epic life game was significantly influenced by each specific step. As mentioned in Chapter 1, once you have achieved 10K HP alignment, you begin to live your life in OP mode and become an OP Player. OP Players are already the successful individuals we respect in society, but when you play your game at such a high level that you become *historically* important to the field you are involved in, you ascend to being an OP Hero.

For Step 1: Choose Your Game, let us cover the journey of a notable *Strategy Sage* who freed an entire nation.

Imagine a courtroom lawyer so burdened by shyness that he freezes when it's his turn to speak. His hands tremble, his throat is parched, and his forehead is damp with perspiration – yet he remains silent, not uttering a word. It's difficult to envision such a person becoming a proficient barrister, much less steering the course of history, isn't it?

Believe it or not, there was such a lawyer who ended up becoming one of the most famous figures in the world, noted for his speeches and influence over leaders and the masses. His life changed dramatically when he decided to shift his life game's mission – from making a good living to freeing a nation.

This lawyer was born in India and then moved to London to study law. His initial game was simple: earn a decent living and enjoy a good life in England. Everything he did, therefore, should have aligned with the objectives of this game. He decided that his role (Step 3) in this game would be a barrister, or trial lawyer (like Keanu Reeves' character in *The Devil's Advocate*, though I wouldn't say Keanu Reeves inspired this decision).

However, he may have skipped Step 2 of identifying his attributes before committing to his role (Step 3). It turned out that he was so shy that he even failed to speak up during his court appearances. After a few failed court quests (Step 6), his reputation took such a hit that no one in London wanted to hire him anymore. Because of that, he had to press the reset button and start over in a new country where nobody knew who he was. He chose South Africa, hoping for a fresh start.

On his way to South Africa, he faced severe racism, being forced out from his first-class seat. He protested, insisting he had paid for this expensive ticket. But despite his explanations, security ejected him and his luggage off the train at Pietermaritzburg, far from his destination in Pretoria. Instead of feeling demoralized, he took this shameful experience deep in his heart as he began his new saga in South Africa.

This resilient man is none other than the renowned pacifist and Strategy Sage Mahatma Gandhi.[7]

Finding His Mission

Gandhi's experience of being thrown off the train in such a humiliating manner inspired him to find a new mission (game) in life: creating a fair and equal India. This was quite a challenge, considering India was then under British rule and people of color were considered second-class citizens. To most people, pursuing this game would have seemed insurmountable for the failed British lawyer, Gandhi, now in South Africa, as he wouldn't seem to be the right person nor in the right place to accomplish this great mission.

However, Gandhi, now with his new game, knew that he could already undertake quests (Step 6) to advance toward his game objectives. He evolved his role (Step 3) from being a barrister to an activist. He founded the Natal Indian Congress, an organization to combat discrimination against Indian traders in Natal. Through this, he worked on unifying the Indian community in South Africa. During this time, he also built influence among Natal Indians and established network connections with important political figures (Step 5: Build Your Alliance).

Gandhi realized that his attributes (Step 2) were a better fit with civil law, helping people (rather than pursuing criminals), along with providing advice, guidance, and representation in civil matters such as contracts and property disputes. So this time around, utilizing his other attributes (resiliency, logic, and compassionate charisma) while enhancing his (Step 4) skills (diligent research, logical persuasion, and empathetic listening), Gandhi finally proved successful as both an activist and a civil lawyer in South Africa.

He was now a successful lawyer. Had he stuck with his old game of living a comfortable life, he would have already made it and might have stayed in South Africa. But no, he was now playing a much bigger game: liberate India from British oppression. He had to move onto his next big saga.

Once Gandhi had achieved success in the South Africa saga, in order to really achieve his game goals, he returned to India and transitioned his role to its final form: Strategy Sage.[††] He pioneered the wise and profound philosophy of *satyagraha*, which means "insistence of truth," or as I prefer to call it, *truth force*.[‡‡]

Gandhi knew that just being a Revered Wise Sage was not enough

---

[††]This is of course, a hero name we gave him in the 10K HP literature. Gandhi did not write any press releases announcing his role change from activist lawyer to a Strategy Sage when he set foot in India. But it would be extremely cool if he did, right?

[‡‡]I find *truth force* to be one of the most epic terminologies out there, so I'm going to use this term more than the commonly used *satyagraha* within the 10K HP context. You'll find that I like to use cool, fun names for existing phenomena or abilities because it makes learning and applying new knowledge more effective and enjoyable, which is the main goal of this book.

to accomplish his game objectives. He needed to move the politics of an entire nation and garner attention from the world. He strategically extended the philosophy of satyagraha into a peaceful revolution – a mass civil disobedience powered by the truth force. For this he needed to be a Strategy Sage.

In 1930, Gandhi led the Salt March, a transformative 390-kilometer journey that spanned twenty-four days across India, inspiring 50,000 protestors to join him. During this pivotal service quest (Step 6), Gandhi delivered public addresses, rousing the masses to defy British authority by creating their own salt at the edge of the Arabian Sea, a poignant act of civil disobedience against British salt laws.

Leveraging his key attributes (Step 2) and skills (Step 4), Gandhi's strategic application of the truth force successfully pressured British officials and led to several important concessions.

OP Hero Mahatma Gandhi: Takeaways

Ghandi's nonviolent resistance movement galvanized the Indian populace, shifted the tide of public opinion, and put pressure on the British government. His influence was so profound that international outcry eventually precipitated his release when he was imprisoned for challenging British policies during World War II.

Gandhi's truth force protests, and the resulting global pressure, eventually led to India's full independence on July 18, 1947.

Gandhi's wise and strategic maneuvering led to the decolonization of India, placing him on the Earth Server's legendary leaderboard as a Strategic Sage. His embodiment of the truth force (or satyagraha, if you prefer to avoid game-speak) also became a *faction* — a loosely connected yet powerful alliance bound by shared belief rather than formal hierarchy. The faction later included legendary OP Heroes like Martin Luther King Jr. and James Bevel in the U.S. civil rights movement, as well as Nelson Mandela in the fight against apartheid in South Africa.

True to his own Hero's Journey, Gandhi transformed from a shy lawyer to a global game-changer. By pivoting his life's game from the pursuit of personal comfort to liberating India from British dominion, he rose to greatness and made the world a better place to live. A game well played.

Chapter 2 Highlights

- Your life game represents your life's mission and guides your journey. Defining it prevents you from becoming a background character in others' stories.
- Wearing your game like a badge garners respect, attracts allies, and inspires others.
- Find your life game by doing these things:
- **Identify Your Passions**: Reflect on what excites you and imagine dedicating your life to it.
- **Consider What Inspires You**: Note moments of inspiration to find direction for your life game.
- **Imagine a Life Without Financial Worries**: Determine what you would love to do daily if money were not an issue.
- **Reflect on Role Models**: Identify individuals you admire and analyze their core endeavors.
- When OP Hero Gandhi changed his game from becoming a wealthy barrister to liberating India, he effectively changed his life, and it led him to become a legendary OP Hero.

Chapter 3: Know Your Attributes (Talents)

"The meaning of life is to find your gift. The purpose of life is to give it away."

—— Pablo Picasso

In the popular video game *Mega Man X*, the main character is endowed with amazing attributes:

- He has a blaster that shoots energy orbs.
- He can charge his blaster for more powerful shots.

- He can absorb powers from defeated enemy bosses.
- He can wall jump.

These attributes help Mega Man progress through the game on his mission to defeat the final boss, Sigma.

What would happen if you took Mega Man out of his video game and dropped him into the world of *Super Mario 64*? Try as *Mega Man* might, he wouldn't be able to beat the game of *Super Mario 64* because he doesn't have the necessary attributes such as long jumping, triple jumping, swimming, and flight (with a magical winged cap).

In the game of life, you are endowed with attributes encompassing an array of physical characteristics, intellectual capabilities, emotional temperment, personality nuances, and innate talents. You may find some people display phenomenal athletic prowess. Others possess a persuasive eloquence, or seem to naturally excel in fields such as mathematics or music.

Before we deep dive into the world of attributes, it's useful to distinguish attributes (Step 2) from acquired skills and abilities (Step 4). Just as Megaman's attributes are base-level kits that are inherited as opposed to learned, your attributes are not skills for which you can just take classes, such as search engine optimization (SEO), software development, jurisprudence, medicine, or gamification. These are *developed abilities*, not inherent attributes.

Attributes constitute an integral part of your identity. They are a composite of your genetic blueprint, the influence of your upbringing, and the molding power of your life experiences. While it is possible to *develop* your attributes, they improve slowly through an array of quests and encounters, such as environmental changes, experienced hardship and failures, or years of dedicated training.

In addition, it's important to understand that attributes alone are not enough to beat a game. You need to pick the right role (Step 3) that aligns with your attributes (Step 2). You need to learn skills

(Step 4) that are empowered by your attributes (for instance, having spatial reasoning attributes could empower learning architecture design skills), and you need to take on quests (Step 6) that help you level-up in all these fields.

We can all play Mega Man X, but very few of us put in enough time and effort to overcome the final nemesis, Sigma. Similarly, many people have musical talent, but it takes continuous practice and learning quests (Step 6) to play for the San Francisco Symphony.

It's important to know and be honest about your attributes because you don't want to be Mega Man playing in the Super Mario 64 world. Similarly, you don't want to be an orca stuck on land, or an eagle dwelling in a cave. The moment you find the right environment for your talents and strengths, you will discover the *flow* all around you and begin to soar.

Remember: don't get discouraged if you weren't born with the attributes of Lebron James or Beyoncé. With your unique attributes, you are able to do things that Lebron James and Beyoncé cannot do, and you should be proud of that. You just need to identify what those attributes are and pick the right role (Step 3) within your game that takes advantage of them.

Attributes: Your Unique Talents

Video games have stat sheets that detail the attributes of each character. Unfortunately, in real life we are not born with character sheets that list and explain our attributes. Therefore, it is an important quest (Step 6) for you to discover your attributes while helping your allies (Step 5) do the same.

Some natural attributes are easier to identify, as they not only are part of most school curricula but also are easy to compare with other students. For example, many physical or musical attributes become obvious because they manifest themselves in a public setting: you run or swim faster than everyone else; you learn to play the guitar incredibly easily; or, alongside your unique charisma, you start to entertain your followers on Instagram with comedy skits.

At times, natural attributes with numbers, writing, memorization, or speech can manifest themselves in school as well: you get As in classes without needing to work as hard as your classmates; you become a champion on your school's speech and debate team; or you can recite lines from movies that you have seen better than most of your classmates. Some people are luckier because they get exposed to their natural attributes early in life, often because of where they grew up or investment by their parents in various activities.

In *Outliers*, Malcolm Gladwell puts light on research that indicates the defining difference between two prominent parenting styles: Natural Growth vs Concerted Cultivation.[1] The Natural Growth parenting style is statistically more applied by working-class and poorer families. In this style, parents care for their children but allow them to grow and develop on their own. They do not interfere significantly in their children's development or leisure time with organized activities. They're less likely to reason with their children, using directives instead. These children may develop a sense of constraint and may be less likely to challenge authority or navigate institutional settings successfully.

Concerted Cultivation, on the other hand, is often observed in middle and upper-class families. Parents using this approach actively foster their children's talents, opinions, and skills. They're heavily involved in planning and organizing their children's leisure activities, making sure these are educational and developmental in nature. They are more likely to reason with their children, encouraging them to ask questions, challenge assumptions, and negotiate rules. These children are often exposed to a wider range of experiences, develop a sense of "positive entitlement," and are comfortable in interacting with adults and authority figures.

Gladwell argues that the Concerted Cultivation parenting style often gives children certain advantages, such as the ability to advocate for themselves and navigate social institutions, which can lead to occupational success later in life. As you can see, being born in certain families, or *starting zones*, can definitely give an advantage in defining and developing attributes - the playthrough of the last generation can accumulate and boost the current one, much like teammates in a relay race.

Of course, as you will see from the majority of the historical OP Heroes, starting zones only paint a small picture of one's 10K HP journey, and those with higher difficulty sometimes even help 10K HP Players develop unique attributes that wouldn't be obtained any other way (such as the *perseverance* attribute).

But even for those raised with Concerted Cultivation, most attributes aren't so glaringly obvious until later in life. Often, it is only slowly revealed when we have tackled enough quests (Step 6) through self-awareness and observing our advantages against other players. If you have been to college, you would have observed that most college students, many from really good starting zones, have no idea what they want to do in their lives and change their majors regularly.

This was the same situation for my business partner Jun Loayza, who took more than a decade to realize and thrive on his attributes. Jun Loayza was raised in Westminster, California, as a half-Peruvian, half-Japanese second-generation immigrant. Jun, alongside his brother, was raised by a hardworking single mother employed in the local school administration. During his high school years, Jun demonstrated a knack for sports, particularly distinguishing himself on the basketball court.

Due to financial constraints in his family, he first attended a community college before transferring to UCLA, where he and I crossed paths as we pledged at the business fraternity of Delta Sigma Pi – a perfect embodiment of Step 5 (Build Your Alliance), by joining a *guild.*

Jun had a magnetic personality; his social prowess made him the focal point at parties (whereas I was the trusted friend who looked after others when they started to throw up). However, a devastatingly disappointing hunt for his post-college job triggered a game-changing shift in Jun. Much like Gandhi relocating to South Africa, as I described in the previous chapter, Jun chose a new game — redirecting his energy into entrepreneurship and finally stepping into his own 10K HP life[§§].

Jun's quest achievements (Step 6) were many: He launched numerous companies, selling two of them to bigger entities. His professional journey took him to Bunny Inc, a voice actor platform. As the Chief Marketing Officer and Head of Product there, Jun drove the annual revenue from $1 million to $5 million within just two years. His product lead role at Gliffy culminated in a lucrative sale of over $100 million. In his next saga, he joined Google/YouTube, where his product management abilities helped him launch and scale several services that generated over $100 million in annual revenue. Jun's life game didn't just stop at making companies rich, as he cares intensely about raising the next generation and instilling family values. He also started a parenting podcast named *Dad Smarter, Not Harder* and authored a children's book, *How Many Stars Are in the Sky?*

Jun's life narrative is a testament to overcoming adversity. From humble beginnings as part of a minority, single-parent family, he ascended the ladder of success in his game of life. And because of that he can now provide his daughters with a better starting zone through Concerted Cultivation. I will use Jun as an example in various other points of this book, so don't forget him too quickly!

[§§]Although the consulting company he last interviewed with gave him an offer, I was fortunate that he quit after working there for three months to pursue his entrepreneurial dreams with me.

How to Identify Your Attributes

At 10K HP, we have developed a two-step process to identify your attributes. Step 1 is to gather information through various internal and external sources, while Step 2 is to develop your 10K HP Talent Triangle.

Even though it seems like a simple two-step process, it still requires a great deal of self-awareness and analysis. There are various methods to explore this, so here we explore the best ways to complete these two steps.

Step 1: Gather Information

Carve out an hour or two in your busy schedule to sit down alone with a pen and paper to reflect and analyze your experiences. You can also use our 10K HP Workbook at 10KHP.com/worksheets

Take Some Time for Self-Reflection

Here is how your mental process should work:

1. Think about some important moments in your life.
2. Analyze why they are important to you.
3. Identify attributes associated with those moments.

Here is Jun Loayza's mental process:

Important moment: Founding the student organization Bruin Consulting at UCLA

Why it's important: Bruin Consulting was Jun's first entrepreneurial project. After receiving many rejection letters from consulting companies during the student recruitment season, he realized that it was extremely difficult for UCLA students to get a career in consulting due to a lack of specific business programs for undergraduates. He thus started the first undergraduate consulting organization at UCLA with a group of three other founders, including me, and successfully launched the first undergraduate case competition.

Identified Attributes: Jun is able to quickly turn ideas into action (thought-to-action cycle, execution agility); he's able to build a team of motivated individuals and harness their skills toward a common goal (decisive leadership); he's able to win over people easily (charismatic persuasiveness).

Important moment: Co-founding the startup company RewardMe

Why it's important: RewardMe was a loyalty platform for restaurants and retailers, and it was one of the earliest startups where Jun Loayza and I raised over $1 million. We operated it for over two years and managed to build a product, sell it to customers, get it into stores, generate revenue, and achieve major user engagement goals well before our competitors at the time. Even though it didn't ultimately succeed, this major entrepreneurial quest (Step 6) shed a lot of light on Jun's strengths and weaknesses and helped him acquire a great deal of new skills (Step 4).

Identified Attributes: Jun feels comfortable taking risks; he is able to sell products through diligent hustle; he prefers to learn through action rather than through reading or mentorship; he is impatient and desires to achieve success as quickly as possible.

Ask Other People to Identify Your Attributes

Unsurprisingly, your friends, family, and co-workers can offer great insights into your attributes. It's often very difficult for us to identify our attributes because they come so naturally to us. We simply think, "Oh, everyone is able to do this easily, too."

To help your friends uncover your attributes, send them a message with the following questions:

1. You are the CEO of a company. What would you hire me to do at your company?
2. I'm giving a TED talk next month. What do you think would be the title of my TED presentation?
3. Your friend has an open position at his company. You refer me and I get the job. One year later, you meet up with your friend and he tells you how I'm doing at his company. How does your friend tell you about me?
4. I was just fired from a company. What do you think was the reason for me getting fired?

Although these questions won't give you an exact answer, they will help you to identify your attributes (yes, even question #4, which reveals your weaknesses).

Be aware that many people are not accustomed to requesting and getting feedback from their peers. It can often be jarring to know how others view you. When you do receive some answers, don't worry if they aren't the "right" ones – simply jot them down. Understanding and utilizing your attributes can be a lifelong exploration process, starting with small steps.

Also, start examining if you can break these attributes down into more detailed ones. If a peer identifies that you are good at math, then you can explore what is behind that. Is it doing arithmetic calculations in your head, because of the tenacity at which you practice it, or perhaps because of concentration during stressful moments that require patience. Perhaps it's all these? By looking at these dimensions of your strengths you can more accurately understand your innate attributes and understand where else to apply these talents.

If a peer identifies that you have a good memory, then you can explore deeper into it. Are you good at remembering events, people, numbers, images, or all of them? Exploring the specifics about your memory will help you identify your unique strengths.

If a peer identifies that you are likable, then you can explore what characteristics enable that attribute. Are you a lot of fun to be with because of your humor, positivity, or charisma? Or are you likable because you can quickly convey that you are a sincere empathetic person and can earn the trust of others?

Take Standardized Strength Tests

There are a myriad of self-assessment tests on the market, many of them claiming to help you find out what you are good at. With my 10K HP model I aim to make very clear whether specific assessments help you determine your attributes (Step 2), skills (Step 4), your mission (Step 1), or just how you make friends and build alliances (Step 5).

Another one of my close allies, PH Chen, didn't know what attributes he had as he was growing up, other than having some talents in athletic sports and persuasion. But in high school, his teacher gave the class a standardized test on spatial reasoning – the ability to process 3D objects and environments in your brain. The test was 90 minutes long, and many students struggled to finish it before the time was up. But PH finished it in just 30 minutes with a near-perfect score. This was the moment at which he understood he actually had great talent in this area, which motivated him to develop his role (Step 3) into becoming a prominent architectural designer later on.

I had a similar experience. When I applied to college, I actually thought I was going to become a chemistry major because I had exhibited some talent in that subject in 11th grade. However, in the last semester of high school, I took the economics AP (advanced placement) exam, which is a college-level test that gives you a score between 1 and 5. If you score a 3, then you will receive college credit with a C grade, while scoring a 5 will give you college credit with an A grade.

Similar to PH Chen's experience, the test was 130 minutes long, but somehow I finished it in 35 minutes. When I put down my pencil, I looked around and wondered why the other smarter students had not yet turned in their tests. Then I rechecked my work, which I normally never do. After that, I decided to go up and turn it in at the 45-minute mark and was the first to walk out of the exam. When I exited the room, I felt a little confused and thought, "Either I got a perfect score of 5, or I am just crazy and I got a 1." When the results came out, I received a 5, which allowed me to recognize that I had a natural talent in the subject of economics. Later in this chapter, where I analyze my own attributes, I'll discuss how the same attribute allowed me to be naturally talented in chemistry, economics, and chess.

My business partner Jun Loayza also raves about the Clifton-Strengths test by Gallup (formerly known as StrengthsFinder 2.0). This is a psychological assessment tool designed to identify an individual's top five strengths from a list of thirty-four themes. Its purpose is to help people understand and leverage their unique talents for personal and professional development. Jun took the test, and these are his top five themes:

1. **Significance**: People who are especially talented in the significance theme want to be very important in the eyes of others. They are independent and want to be recognized.
2. **Competition**: People who are especially talented in the competition theme measure their progress against the performance of others. They strive to win first place and revel in contests.
3. **Futuristic**: People who are especially talented in the futuristic theme are inspired by the future and what could be. They inspire others with their visions of the future.
4. **Achiever**: People who are especially talented in the achiever theme have a great deal of stamina and work hard. They take

great satisfaction from being busy and productive.

5. **Activator**: People who are especially talented in the activator theme can make things happen by turning thoughts into action. They are often impatient.

From his top five themes and from personal experience, Jun concluded the following:

I have the ability to get a project started incredibly fast. If an idea fascinates me, then I'll take action and get the idea started faster than anyone else I've ever met. I have the ability to recruit and inspire others to join my team. Whether it be at RewardMe, Chou Force, or Humble Bee, I've continually shown the ability to build a strong team. I have the ability to make a strong and positive first impression. This strength has proven incredibly valuable in interview and sales settings when time is scarce and a deal needs to be closed. If the pressure is on or I'm in the spotlight, then I have the ability to take ownership, work even harder, and do what it takes to succeed.

Recognize Your Weaknesses

In addition to uncovering your strengths, CliftonStrengths can indirectly help you identify your weaknesses. These are weaknesses that Jun Loayza identified from his results:

While I'm quick to start a project, it's too easy for me to get bored, drop my current project, and move on to the next one. For this reason, I've made a decision to say "no" to any new opportunities and focus solely on my current, ongoing projects. Although I make a strong first impression, I am terrible at keeping up strong friendships with many people. I have many acquaintances, but very few close friends. If I'm not getting recognized for the work that I'm doing, then I usually ignore the work and move on to something else that will bring me greater recognition.

With these insights, Jun can move onto Step 2, which is creating his 10K HP Talent Triangles.

Step 2: Establish an 10K HP Talent Triangle

Once you identify some potential attributes, it's time to make them concrete and arrange them into a useful order. I call this the 10K HP Talent Triangle. The 10K HP Talent Triangle is a simple visual representation of your attributes aligned in a triangle shape to display their hierarchy based on the intensity of your strengths. It's broken down into a few different groupings, such as the *Edge*, *Ring*, and *Base*.

I believe that each individual has at least one unique strength that is better than that of the majority of others around the world. When we can define what that unique superpower is, we call that the *Edge*. (See Figure 4.)

Figure 4. The 10K HP Talent Triangle Edge

Then, there are two to five other skills that may not be as strong as your Edge attribute but are stronger when compared to most of your peers. Our top five attributes, including our Edge attribute, become the *Ring*.

From personal experience, knowing exactly which attribute is your Edge attribute is not as important as knowing the collective Ring attributes, because it is how you harness your unique combination of attributes that establishes your life game character.

After that, there is a whole batch of other attributes (often five to fifteen) called the *Base* attributes where an individual is generally more talented than the average person, but a single one cannot be harnessed as a competitive advantage on its own.

As individuals begin to understand their strengths, they can start to chart this onto the triangle shape and form a 10K HP Talent

Triangle.

Creating Your First 10K HP Talent Triangle

As mentioned earlier, deriving a proper 10K HP Talent Triangle is not easy and could require a long time in self-discovery. However, you can start with a basic one and eventually develop it over time as you better understand yourself and develop unique attributes through your life experiences.

In Figure 5, I illustrate how I derived some of my attributes in the early days. This will hopefully help you *observe* the process of self-discovery, as opposed to my describing what other people do. Here's how I began putting together my strength triangle. The first thing I did was to first randomly jot down all of what I felt could be my strengths.

Figure 5. Yu-kai's Strengths

Strengths = Attributes

These are just attributes thrown around in no particular order besides what comes top of mind. Below is a list of explanations of what each of them mean. I define them here in case you wish to get some ideas and references on what could be considered an attribute.

1. Emotional Intelligence: I tend to be able to control my emotions well and interact with others in constructive ways.

2. Creativity: I tend to come up with more creative solutions than those of my peers. Later on, I realize that my creativity is really due to the next attribute: associative thinking.

3. Associative Thinking: My brain is able to make connections between things that others see as very random.

4. Empowerment: I'm quite good at empowering others, helping them believe in themselves and, therefore, perform at a higher level than they otherwise would.

5. Empathy: I almost involuntarily care about how others feel to the point that I sometimes cannot operate if I feel that they might be uncomfortable. This became something I needed to work on, since being afraid of upsetting others could also become a handicap.

6. Networking: I felt I was good at networking with others, because when I went to events, people really liked connecting with me. Later on, I realized this is a skill (Step 4) that is empowered by my empathetic attribute as opposed to being an attribute on its own.

7. Learn-Use Conversion: I discovered that, somehow, I would subconsciously find a way to apply anything I learned within two weeks.

8. Optimism: I saw that in situations of setback or uncertainty, I would always have a positive outlook, seeing the best-case scenario while emotionally prepared for the worst-case scenario.

9. Strategy: Since I was quite good at chess in high-school, I felt I was good at this thing called "strategy." However, it turns out that, more specifically, my "strategic thinking" was due to my attributes in logical analysis, pattern recognition, and associative thinking.

10. Systems Creation: I felt I was good at creating "systems," which allowed me to understand the best way to operate in new situations.

11. Adaptation: Since I moved around a lot growing up, I felt I was better at adapting to new environments and circumstances.

12. Quirky Humor: Growing up, I've always had this awkward humor that likely came from my mix of various cultures. It made it harder for me to fit in with my school groups, but it helped me stand out when I became more of a public figure.

13. Analytical Skills: I was good at analyzing situations and coming up with the right components to derive a mode of operation. Since I had to change environments a lot, I couldn't rely on how I always did things, but had to always analyze what was more beneficial in the new situation.

14. Interpersonal Speaking: Despite having a bit of that Quirky humor, when I talk to a new stranger, somehow they immediately felt I was very trustworthy. Many people I just met would tell me some of their more personal secrets, and I was surprised that they entrusted that information to me with such short engagement times.

15. Events Memory: I don't particularly have a good memory in numbers or names. However, I end up having a good memory of specific past events. Friends throughout my childhood were surprised how often I could recall how we met and what we talked about.

16. Leadership: I felt I was a good leader, as I led a high school chess club to become the state champion of Kansas, and also because as an entrepreneur, people who were twice my age liked my leadership. Later in this chapter I will explore the three attributes that actually make a good leader.

17. Gem Spotting: I felt I was good at spotting talented people who haven't yet found an opportunity to shine. This is a win-win, as I can find people who didn't demand an extremely high salary while providing an opportunity for them to showcase their strengths to the world. Later on, I would realize this, too, is more of a skill that is powered by the attributes empathetic intelligence, optimism, and empowerment.

Later in this chapter, after I show how I finalized my ring attributes, I will take a deeper analysis on how I discovered these attributes from various life experiences.

At this point, the next step I took was to start moving the stronger attributes to the top of the triangle while moving moderate ones to the middle or bottom. Then I charted the order to create, in 2010, my first 10K HP Talent Triangle (See Figure 6).

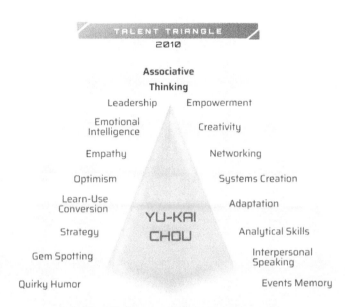

Figure 6. Yu-kai's 10K HP Talent Triangle 2010

I wasn't completely confident in the arranged order, but that did not present a problem. We all must start somewhere, and as long as it reflected some indication of how I perceived my strengths, it was already useful to help make some decisions in life.

Many years later, after a significant boost in additional life experiences, self-understanding, and feedback from others, I eventually modified my 10K HP Talent Triangle to that shown in Figure 7.

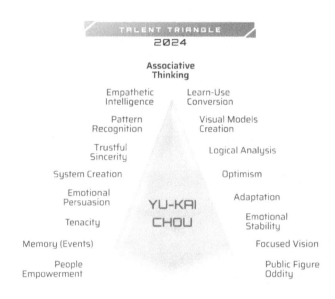

Figure 7. Yu-kai's 10K HP Talent Triangle 2024

I decided that associative thinking is my Edge, while empathetic intelligence, learn-use conversion, pattern recognition (events), and visual models creation together formed my Ring attributes. Below I go into detail to explain what these five attributes mean and their implications for my life. Pay close attention not just to what these attributes mean but to how I figured out that I have these attributes based on early observations and experiences during my student years.

The Associative Thinking Attribute

Associative thinking is the ability to connect two or more seemingly unrelated things. Perhaps because I grew up in multiple cultures, I was particularly adept at this. Initially, I thought one of my strengths was creativity, but I later realized it was due to this associative thinking attribute that I was able to produce creative thoughts and ideas.

However, depending on the environment, the same attribute could become a weakness instead of a strength. When I was in college, I took a course that required reading specific books and writing essays to demonstrate a good understanding and analysis of their content. Since I was already an entrepreneur at that point, I did just the bare minimum for most of the classes to obtain a B+ grade. However, for one of the essays, I found the topic fascinating, so I applied maximum effort to the paper. I read the book in detail twice, conducted outside research, applied what I considered great analysis, and turned in a paper I was extremely proud of.

Unfortunately, when the paper came back, I received a very low grade. The professor's note was, "What you wrote had nothing to do with the course material, clearly showing a lack of understanding of it." I was baffled. *If I didn't understand the course material, how could I have come up with this amazing piece of work?*

Now, of course, there was a chance I was just being arrogantly delusional and truly didn't understand what the book was talking about. But later, for the same course, when I didn't even read the books, conduct outside research, or put in any effort at all, I would simply write down what I remembered my professor saying and then achieve a very high grade.

This left me feeling disappointed because it seemed like my efforts were not being rewarded. It encouraged me to only put minimal effort into school while focusing on my startup and entrepreneurial endeavors.

On the other hand, when in the right environment, associative thinking can be very useful. It enabled me to conceive concepts like gamification – the merging of productive activities and gaming – before many others saw the connection. It also allows me to come up with interesting analogies to help people understand my concepts better. Additionally, it turns out that I am good at creating names that factor in multiple components.

My online mentorship platform, Octalysis Prime, was given that name not just because it is based on my Octalysis Framework and is a premium program. When people hear Octalysis Prime, they also think of Optimus Prime, the iconic Transformer robot, which they associate with fun, cool, and prestigious qualities. It also abbreviates nicely to OP, which, as I have noted, is often gaming jargon for "overpowered" – the ethos of what the OP community strives to achieve.

Similarly, the title of this book, 10,000 Hours of Play, not only connects well with Malcolm Gladwell's 10,000 hour rule but also abbreviates nicely to 10K HP, which in the gaming world could mean 10,000 hit points or 10,000 health points, indicating how much damage you could sustain before dying.

One of the most creative YouTubers with twenty-one million sub-scribers before he retired, Ryan Higa, is also big on pun jokes using his associative thinking attribute. Once he created an elaborate video that made a copy of a candy mint and put it into a refrigerator, just so he could use the pun joke of "copied-right in-fridge mint" (copyright infringement).

It's important to remember that the right attributes have to be in the right environment to output as a strength. If I was in an environment that required me to do things exactly as they are prescribed, such as many school or corporate environments, I would likely suffer because I always end up coming up with new ways to do things. Only when I am in a free creative space does this attribute shine.

The Empathetic Intelligence Attribute

Empathetic Intelligence is about applying empathy to practical situations. I grew up with an involuntary amount of empathy, which made me very sensitive to how others felt. Sometimes, it was just in my own head. For example, when watching movies at home with friends, if they needed to go to the bathroom, I would always pause the video. They would say, "No, just keep it playing. Don't worry about me!" But for some reason, I was incapable of continuing because I was concerned that they would miss important plot information and lose out on a potential "wow" moment later.

Similarly, when I'm traveling on an airplane, I initially thought it would be best to sit in window seats because I could lean against the windowed wall and didn't need to stand up when others needed to use the bathroom. However, I realized this approach didn't really work due to my empathy attribute. Since I felt uncomfortable bothering other people, I would just hold my urge to visit the restroom for the entire flight. It turned out I would rather be repeatedly disturbed by other passengers on the plane than to bother them. As a result, sitting in an aisle seat was the only option that suited my personality.

Eventually, I learned how to harness my empathy attribute to develop empathetic intelligence, leading to the development of the field of human-focused design. This approach helps people feel motivated and cared for. Sensitivity to how people feel in gaming environments enabled me to create my Octalysis gamification framework, which underpins much of my career success.

Having high empathy also allows an individual to become a coach-like leader within groups, helping people grow over time, but it doesn't necessarily make one a good commander-like leader who thrives in the crisis of wartime. I discuss attributes that empower different leadership styles later in this chapter.

The Learn-Use Conversion Attribute

The learn-use conversion attribute is the ability to quickly apply something that you have just learned. It's like when you learn a new math formula in class and then immediately use it to solve a problem. This attribute is about making immediate use of new knowledge, turning learning into action.

Initially, I wasn't consciously aware of this attribute in myself. In school, learning often felt like a chore that needed to be completed to avoid failing a test. However, over time, I noticed a pattern: whenever I learned something new, whether from a book, a lecture, or even by observing the world around me, I would find a way to use that information within two weeks. It could be as simple as mentioning it in a conversation or as complex as solving a real-world problem.

This process of applying new knowledge was not something I intentionally set out to do; it was almost like a reflex. It seemed as if my brain was eager to use this new information so as to integrate it into my understanding of the world.

Eventually, I began to enjoy learning, especially when I focused on subjects that genuinely interested me, such as business, psychology, and game design. This enjoyment stemmed from seeing how the things I learned could be applied in real life, often in creative and unexpected ways.

Generally, there aren't many scenarios where one could be penalized for this attribute, as applying what you have learned is typically beneficial. However, there are some scenarios where people are expected to merely regurgitate what they have learned and are actively discouraged from applying it in new ways. Nevertheless, even repeating what was learned in the right scenarios is an active demonstration of the learn-use conversion attribute.

The Pattern Recognition Attribute (Events)

Pattern recognition (events) involves observing past events and using that knowledge to predict future outcomes. From this definition alone, we can see that pattern recognition synergizes heavily with learn-use conversion. Initially, I thought pattern recognition was a basic skill for everyone, as essentially this is what our brains do to help us function in the world.

However, I've noticed that people often repeat the same mistakes, without realizing that they are falling into the same negative patterns repeatedly. Interestingly, most pattern recognition tests focus not on events but on shapes and figures. I think I am mediocre at identifying patterns within abstract shapes, but I excel at recognizing patterns that have narrative elements within them.

When I played chess as a student, I was quite good at remembering all the moves made within a game because I remembered the "events" that occurred – *my opponent's knight* moved to the center and challenged my rook; my rook then moved to attack his king; he blocked my rook with his other knight. I can recall these events so clearly that I could reenact the entire game, from the first move to checkmate. However, if I had to remember just the board positions where all the pieces lay, I would struggle a lot more.

With my pattern recognition attribute, I was able to identify various motivational or design patterns within a game, allowing me to derive over 180 game design techniques that could be applied to contexts outside of gaming. These included "easter eggs," "mystery boxes," "group quests," and more advanced ones like "bandwagon streak" – a complex combination of multiple lower-tier game design techniques. I could also recognize patterns in how the stock market behaves based on external triggers and make profitable decisions to buy low and sell high, yielding solid returns on my investments.

In my relationships, I applied my pattern recognition skills to avoid repeating the same types of conflict. Whenever things became heated with my wife, I would recognize the pattern and realize that if I said what I would naturally say, it would escalate into a heated argument. So instead, I chose to break the pattern and say something else, which often prevented the conflict before it even started.

The Visual Models Creation Attribute

Visual models creation is the ability to transform abstract concepts into concrete visual tools to solve problems. This attribute played a crucial role in my academic and professional journey, beginning in my high school days.

Remember I said I was good at chess and chemistry in high school and, later on, economics? While these disciplines seem distinct, their acquisition relied on a common skill set – my innate capability to visualize abstract ideas on a 2D interface.

In chess, this attribute manifested as a mental chessboard in my head where I could strategically see my future moves and my opponent's countermoves, visualizing the game several steps ahead. Chemistry, often perceived as a complex interplay of elements and reactions, often outputs itself as visual symbols of molecules and electrons connected as predictable patterns on a sheet of paper. Economics, with its supply and demand curves, transforms consumer and supplier behaviors into dynamic charts that I could see and manipulate in my head.

In introductory economic classes, I excelled at this compared with my peers. But once my economics classes started focusing on "proving each theory through calculus," I lost my edge and struggled like most other students. It turns out that I didn't have the patience or interest to do algorithmic calculations and, therefore, started to dislike my studies.

Of course, my attribute of visual models creation became the cornerstone of many of my later achievements. It enabled me to develop over thirty innovative models and frameworks in various fields, including the Nationcraft Framework, REMOTE Work Framework, Digital Convergence Model, Economy Design Framework, and, of course, the Octalysis Framework. I have a fun goal in life to create one hundred models and frameworks (on top of various products, services, and companies), just so I could harness my talent to create useful things in this world.

As you can see from my example, by digging diligently into your past experiences, you can begin to derive various components of your natural talents and attributes.

Applications of the 10K HP Talent Triangle

Once you have created your own 10K HP Talent Triangle, you can align your activities and quests (Step 6) with your top strengths. The main idea is to maximize your time spent on the activities and quests that harness your top five ring strengths, while avoiding quests that severely punish your weaknesses. If that is done well, then you could potentially become best-in-the-world at those skills (Step 4) and activities.

Because I knew my ring attributes, I could strategically plan my role in my game, the skills I needed to develop, and the quests I needed to take on to be the most successful in my 10K HP journey. So, I started to take on the following quests:

- Create useful models such as the Octalysis Framework.
- Study how games affect feelings and motivations.
- Read books on behavioral science.
- Write/speak about empathetic and emotionally persuasive content.
- Apply knowledge learned to brand-new cases for others (as a consultant). Motivate others to become their best (as a coach or mentor).
- Lead in tough environments where team morale is often low.

After tackling many of these quests, I eventually became an author, speaker, entrepreneur, and consultant in behavioral design and gamification (Step 3). I also started my own *guild*, Octalysis Prime, in order to inspire others and guide people toward their own 10K HP journey (Step 5).

Even though our Base attributes are not as strong as our Ring attributes, the more you find yourself in environments that can harness a combination of those talents, the better. For instance, because I have strengths in adaptation, if I always stay in the same environment, then this strength attribute is wasted. For this reason, when I planned to relocate my earliest startup from Los Angeles to Silicon Valley, I chose to first move there myself for six months in order to set up for my team's eventual move. This is because I believed I was better at adapting to new environments than my team, so I wanted to utilize my strengths to uniquely contribute to them.

Similarly, if someone has strong attributes in tenacity, that means it would not be utilized in scenarios where everything is going smoothly. As painful as that is, individuals with tenacity attributes would thrive more in scenarios that are difficult, where many others would quit, such as in startup or sales environments.

You don't need to constantly run toward painful places that utilize your attributes the most, but it is good to recognize that your full potential would be better realized in those environments – just in case you feel trapped in your current one. Just like any game, being trapped in the same area for long periods of time is significantly worse than facing difficult yet evolving challenges.

The 10K HP Weakness Triangles

Now that I had a better understanding of my strengths, I could move on and use the same process to determine my weakness attributes, with my greatest weakness on the bottom of the (inverted) triangle. (See Figure 8.)

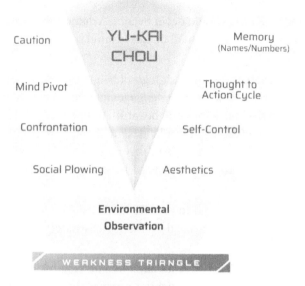

Figure 8. Yu-kai's Weakness Triangle

This list is smaller not because I have fewer weaknesses, but because I didn't spend as much time on it compared to determining my strength attributes. That is because I believe that knowing my weaknesses is not as useful as knowing my strengths, because building on strengths generally trumps improving on weaknesses.

Still, it is beneficial to have an understanding of your perceived weaknesses so that you can avoid scenarios where you would be punished by them. For your reference and later practice, following is an analysis of my own weaknesses and how I make conscious plans to make up for them.

- **Environmental Observation**: Since I'm always thinking about something in my head (such as making associations between concepts), I have a severe weakness in observing the physical environment around me as I go through my daily life. (My wife is not a fan of this particular weakness.)

Actionable Plan: I should never become a detective, spy, or any role that is expected to see small details around me.

- **Aesthetics**: While I am a good behavioral designer who understands how to create engagement and motivation, I don't have the knack to create beautiful designs, nor do I appreciate trendy fashion. I could design a mall that optimizes for people to shop, enjoy, eat, play, and repeat, but not a visually stunning palace for everyone to admire.

Actionable Plan: I need to acquire many allies (Step 5) in my 10K HP journey who have visual aesthetics as strength attributes.

- **Self-Control**: I have an addictive personality and lack discipline. If I end up touching a game that I was just curious about, I could immediately pour over ninety hours within a week just playing that game. Many people are surprised when they hear I have no self-control because I have started so many companies, published two books (including this one), and made over 1,400 videos (as of 2024) on Octalysis Prime.

Actionable Plan: I developed a way to *gamify* my life so that I don't need self-control to achieve what others consider very successful. When my work is transformed into my favorite game, I don't need discipline or self-control to devote ninety hours a week to it. In fact, just like any hardcore gamer, I need discipline or self-control to take a break from my favorite 10K HP game. This is why I am so passionate about teaching my methodologies to those who lack discipline, so that they too can live their lives with 10,000 Hours of Play.

- **Mind Pivot**: All my relatives who grew up with me know that I am a very stubborn person. When I make up my mind, it is very difficult for me to "give up" and change directions. As a flip side of the tenacity attribute, I tend to push toward my goals even if there aren't notable results after years of trying. This works when my focused vision attribute is effectively at play and there truly is a promised land ahead of us. For instance, when I started developing concepts of gamification in 2003, it was seen as an excuse to play games. But I kept at it until things really took off in 2010. However, if I had the wrong vision, then I might have gone down the wrong path without ever letting go of it.

Actionable Plan: To combat this weakness attribute, I also surround myself with allies who have mind pivot as one of their attribute strengths, so that I can get important feedback to adjust and pivot when things aren't looking too promising.

- **Thought-to-Action Cycle**: When I consider doing something, I like to ponder in my head all the ways that it could go wrong and how to resolve these obstacles before I take action. It's important to note that I am not intimidated by these dangers but see them as engaging problem-solving before jumping into the trenches. This means that while my execution is still better than those who only think about ideas but never end up doing anything, I am slow with my thought-to-action cycle. If I plan on doing something new, it might take three to six months for me to actually take steps to do it, which is slow compared to some driven entrepreneurs.

Actionable Plan: To mitigate this, I surround myself with allies who exhibit quick thought-to-action cycles and who can execute plans swiftly. Additionally, breaking down actions into smaller, manageable steps will enhance cognitive ease, making the start of each new venture feel less daunting.

- **Memories (Names/Numbers)**: While remembering events is one of my strength attributes, names and numbers often slip my mind, which can be awkward in both social and professional circles. Somehow, personalities and circumstances are just way more interesting to my brain than names and numbers.

Actionable Plan: To overcome this I've developed some unique strategies and tools to help jog my memory. For example, I connect new acquaintances with common names, say "Tony" to another "archetype Tony" I already know. By visualizing the archetype Tony next to the new Tony, I create a mental link that aids recall. Odd as it may sound, this technique is quite effective and adds a touch of quirky fun to meeting new people. I just hope that I will become your "archetype Yu-kai" rather than a less charming Yu-kai you meet before me.

Having Complementary Allies: Jun Loayza

Based on the actionable plans of my own Weakness Triangle, one of the important ways to counter *your* weaknesses is to work with allies (Step 5) that make up for these shortcomings. This is where Jun Loayza comes in. Remember Jun Loayza's attributes analysis from earlier in this chapter? In Figures 9 and 10, I showcase his talent and weakness triangles.

Figure 9. Jun Loayza's Talent Triangle

Figure 10. Jun Loayza's Weakness Triangle

Without going into each attribute in detail, notice that many of his strength attributes are actually my weakness attributes, and many of my strength attributes are related to his weakness attributes. This means that, as long as we can work well together in good chemistry, we actually greatly complement each other.

This symbiotic relationship with Jun Loayza is a perfect example of the power of complementary strengths. Jun's keen eye for aesthetics fills the gap left by my lack of attention to design and visual detail. His ability to swiftly pivot mentally compliments my stubborn tenacity, allowing us to navigate challenges with a balance of persistence and adaptability.

Jun's fast thought-to-action cycle is especially valuable. While I take time to meticulously plan and anticipate every possible outcome, Jun's prompt decision making propels us forward, ensuring that we don't get stuck in the planning phase. This contrast in our approaches creates a harmonious balance, ensuring thorough preparation on top of maintaining momentum. While Jun is not as strong at remembering events from the distant past, I often serve as a historian and remind him of important happenings to help him make the best decisions in the present.

As a result, Jun and I have done many projects and co-founded many companies together as allies. Our collaboration is a testament to the philosophy of 10K HP. By aligning with allies whose strengths balance our weaknesses, we create a powerful synergy. This synergy is about not only compensating for each other's shortcomings but also integrating our combined strengths to accomplish quests that neither of us could achieve alone.

I will expand more on the intricacies of Step 5: Build Your Alliance, in Chapters 6 and 7.

It's Your Turn to Play: Talent Triangles

It's time to get to know your attributes. Use the above methods to identify your attributes and develop your talent triangle. Feel free to use just a piece of paper, a digital canvas such as PowerPoint, or our worksheet and workbook materials, available at 10KHP.com/worksheets

Pick from One of the Three Game Modes

Easy: Start identifying your natural talents and attributes by asking yourself: What are the things I do well without much effort? What compliments have I received from others about my strengths? What activities make me lose track of time because I enjoy them so much? Write down your answers, aiming for at least five attributes. These might include things like creativity, problem-solving, or empathy. Remember attributes are different than skills. Attributes are something you innately have or slowly develop through life experiences. Skills are more technical, something you were professionally trained to be equipped.

Medium: Reach out to 3–5 friends, family members, or co-workers and ask them to help you identify your attributes. Use questions like: What would you hire me to do at your company? What do you think my TED Talk would be about? What qualities make me stand out from others? Jot down their responses and look for patterns or surprising insights to refine your understanding of your unique talents.

Hard: Create your 10K HP Talent Triangle by organizing your attributes into three levels: Edge (Your single most unique and powerful attribute that sets you apart), Ring (The next 2–5 attributes that are strong and complement your Edge), and Base (5–15 attributes where you have above-average abilities but not enough for a competitive edge on their own). Visualize this as a triangle with your Edge at the top, Ring in the middle, and Base forming the foundation. This exercise will help you understand your strengths and how to align them with your life game.

OP Leadership Attributes of 10K HP

While attributes can be extremely varied, I will cover a set of key attributes that are likely to become important in your 10K HP journey. In Chapter 6, you will learn about the six core attributes for becoming a successful alliance builder: integrity, sincerity, optimism, confidence, initiative, and persistence.

But first, take a look at another key set of important attributes I call the Three OP Leadership Attributes.

As you'll notice in the stories of the OP Heroes featured in this book, achieving top scores in your life game often involves stepping up as a leader, no matter what field you are in. To excel as an OP Leader, there are three key attributes you should focus on developing: vision, empathy, and execution.

The First Attribute for Being an OP Leader Is Vision

The leader must understand where the group should be heading – not just today or tomorrow, but also over the next year, five years, and even ten years. *Vision* involves (1) seeing the big picture, (2) envisioning a path to a brighter future, (3) realistically assessing the feasibility of that path, and (4) sharing that conviction with the team.

Without vision, the team might simply drift in a pool of busyness, while never reaching an outcome of substance.

The Second Attribute for Being an OP Leader Is Empathy

Merely knowing where your team should go is insufficient. A truly outstanding leader, or OP Leader, must grasp the emotions and motivations of their team members to foster high morale and effective collaboration.

Without *empathy*, team members become disgruntled, the workplace culture deteriorates, and the turnover rate skyrockets.

Finally, the Third Attribute for Being an OP Leader Is Execution

Once you have defined your team's destination (vision) and grasped the motivations of your members (empathy), the final OP Leader attribute centers on mobilizing your team toward that vision.

Without *execution*, aspirations remain merely pleasant dreams. Eventually, the team must wake up to the reality that, despite good intentions, nothing has been achieved.

With Their Powers Combined: OP Leadership

When you put all three attributes together, that's when you have what we call *OP Leadership*. When studying other leaders, you'll notice that most of them will have two out of the three, but very few people have all three of these pillar attributes.

This applies to me as well. You already know from earlier in this chapter that my strength attributes are more related to empathy and vision. I'm very sensitive to people's feelings, which allowed me to create one of the most referenced human motivation frameworks. I tend to also spot trends five to ten years before they become publicly recognized, hence my experience in gamification and virtual worlds in the early 2000s, as well as blockchain and augmented reality in the early 2010s.

However, my primary weakness lies in execution. My strong empathy attributes mean I often feel significant emotional pain when a teammate is upset or disappointed. Consequently, I find it challenging to push people to enhance their performance or speed. This style of leadership is often effective with self-driven, creative individuals, but it falters with tasks that require high amounts of discipline, leading to an overly relaxed culture. Over the past decade, I've been working to strengthen my execution attribute by prioritizing progress toward my vision rather than becoming preoccupied with other people's feelings.

At key moments, I've had to remind myself that some of the most successful leaders, such as Steve Jobs and Elon Musk, are noted for their relentless focus on their product vision and their intolerance for anything that compromises their standards for high quality.

Eiichiro Oda, the author of *One Piece*, the iconic manga and anime series that sold over 510 million copies (more than Harry Potter and Batman comic books throughout history), is extremely harsh on himself and his team when it comes to execution. Once, a new editor joined his staff, and Oda literally asked the editor to "die for *One Piece*," adding that, "If you destroy your health due to overwork, I'll take care of your family financially."¶¶

Even though this request is harsh and perhaps only seen as possible in Japanese culture, it sometimes is what it takes to achieve world-dominating visions. Of course, good execution leaders don't just order people around – they lead by example. Eiichiro Oda is known to work until 2 am, just to wake up at 5 am to draw again.

He only sees his wife and daughter four times a month, and on one occasion where he passed out from fatigue and health issues, his visiting friend Masashi Kishimoto (who happens to be the author of another famous manga/anime series, *Naruto*) saw Oda on his hospital bed still drawing *One Piece*. Most people at that point would have urged Oda to stop, but knowing Oda's dedication, Kishimoto decided to sit down and help him with his drawings

---

¶¶Due to *One Piece*, Eiichiro Oda has amassed a wealth of over $200 million.

instead. What a crazy, intense yet warm moment![***]

Elon Musk is also very demanding of his employees, but he himself often spends over 90 hours a week working and also sleeps on the factory floors, more hardcore than any of his hard-working employees. When people see their centi-millionaire and centi-billionaire leaders working harder than them, and that this execution results in being the number one team in the world, many people can't see themselves being anywhere else.[†††]

Keep in mind that I need to focus more on the merits of execution because that is the attribute I lack. Many leaders naturally excel in execution but may act too harshly toward their employees. In such cases, they needn't validate the effectiveness of leaders like Steve Jobs and Elon Musk; instead, they should remember that gentle and empathetic leaders, such as legendary NCAA basketball coach John Wooden, also achieved extraordinary results. The key is to recognize your strengths and weaknesses, and then use that knowledge to enhance your role as a leader.

When I consider the right balance between my innate empathy and developing execution, I realize that winning is actually one of the biggest morale boosters. When some of the smartest people in the world – who could earn a handsome paycheck anywhere – see that their efforts and struggles result in world-changing products that everyone loves, the emotional boost surpasses what any empathetic manager could provide.

[***]I am not advocating that everyone should work themselves to death as a way to live a fulfilling life. Many workaholic leaders who are extremely successful look back and regret that they sacrificed their health and families just for their career, as mentioned in the previous chapter with *The Top Five Regrets of the Dying. The whole point of 10K HP is that everyone should live a life that is consistent with their passionate game, pick roles that are appropriate for their talents, and do quests that are aligned with their beliefs and values. I am simply noting here that the leaders who do end up sacrificing everything else just to maximize their team's execution tend to get more done than other teams who don't make that sacrifice, for obvious and fair reasons.

[†††]In fact, according to Walter Isaacson's biography of Elon Musk, a Tesla employee named Phil Duan quit after two years of being completely burnt out by Musk's leadership style, but then "begged" (in his own words) his manager if he could return to Tesla nine months later because other companies were too slow-paced. "I decided I'd rather be burned out than bored," he said.

If you are on a team that is constantly losing simply because nothing is being accomplished, even if your leader makes you feel loved and appreciated (which is still essential, especially for losing teams), it ultimately feels demoralizing in the long run.

Finally, one thing I realized is that if someone isn't pulling their weight on the team and I don't hold them accountable, it actually demoralizes the people who are working hard and achieving great results. I would fail miserably as a leader if I frustrated those who are giving their all just because I was afraid to discomfort those who are underperforming. As a result, I understood that in order to be an empathetic leader, it was imperative to keep the lower performers accountable so that the morale of high performers can be maintained.

After acknowledging this, I was finally able to improve my execution attributes and acquire skills (Step 4), such as respectful confrontation and candid communication.

Notice how both my personal insights on "winning boosts morale" and "high-performer feelings" emphasize *emotions* as the main justification for good execution? This is because my inherent attribute is empathy, which makes it very difficult and slow for me to develop new attributes such as execution capabilities. I couldn't just "be myself" or take a class to become strong in execution. Instead, I had to creatively leverage my empathy to gradually enhance my execution leadership.

This is a crucial insight about our 10K HP growth. I could only make this progress by recognizing that as a leader, I am strong in empathy and weak in execution. Rather than struggling against my natural inclinations, I utilized the strengths I already possess to find a more indirect but more feasible path to my growth goals.

This approach is similar to how I dealt with another one of my weaknesses: self-control (or the lack thereof). Because I lacked discipline, I employed my strengths in systems creation and empathetic intelligence to develop my own motivation methodology

- later known as gamification. This allowed me to accomplish an impressive amount of productive activities without relying on self-control. Instead of brute-forcing my weaknesses and pushing myself to be disciplined, I simply relied on my strengths to overcome my weaknesses. I no longer needed ten thousand hours of discipline. Instead, I needed ten thousand hours of play.

True to gamification fashion, once we have a foundation of the three Leadership Personas, they can develop into a variety of "7 Leadership Personas." Let's explore them here. (See Figure 11.)

Chou's 7 Leadership Personas

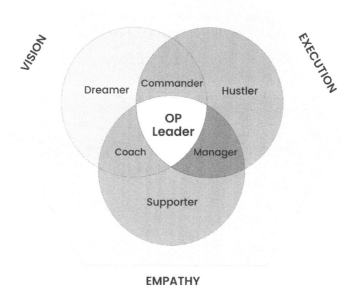

Figure 11. Chou's 7 Leadership Personas

Based on the three attributes of OP Leaders, we can derive seven different Leadership Personas. These 7 Leadership Personas explain the team dynamics between each person and how they can work together effectively.

The 7 Leadership Personas are as follows:

- The Dreamer
- The Supporter
- The Hustler
- The Coach
- The Commander

- The Manager
- The OP Leader

The Dreamer (Only Vision)

If a person possesses only vision without the other two leadership attributes, we classify them as a *Dreamer* in the context within a team and leadership roles.

A Dreamer is someone who envisions a better future and has great ideas about what needs to be done. However, they lack the motivation or initiative to take tangible steps toward realizing that vision or engaging with a team to make it happen. Ultimately, whether or not the vision is fulfilled depends on someone else.

You may have encountered individuals who passionately discuss their ideas but never take action. They continue to talk about their brilliant vision for years, only to see someone else bring a similar product to the market. This person usually finds emotional closure by repeatedly saying, "They stole my idea!" However, the truth is that their ideas remained dreams while others transformed them into reality. Without developing other leadership attributes, Dreamer ideas could often just be seen as science fiction, akin to saying, "I have an idea for building a time machine!"

Of course, if you are a Dreamer and don't find yourself inclined to pick up the other leadership attributes, you still have paths to success. You could become a thought leader in a chosen field (Step 3: Role) and educate the world about your vision. You could also become an ethicist or a scholar to help steer the world toward higher enlightenment or a better future.

You could also become an advisor or a strategist for a leader who values your thoughts. You just shouldn't be the leader yourself because your current attributes do not favor it. If one or more of these *roles* become your path, then it would be important to enhance your skills (Step 4) such as presenting, writing, public speaking, and personal branding, while developing and growing your supportive attributes (Step 2) such as intellectual curiosity and pattern recognition. That way, you can still inspire the world with your vision based on what you have learned and how effectively you communicate.

Again, by applying the 10K HP principles, we demonstrate that with any set of attributes, you can select a path and environment in which you can uniquely succeed. You just need to recognize this and align your role (Step 3), skills (Step 4), and quests (Step 6) with your game (Step 1).

The Supporter (Only Empathy)

If a person possesses only empathy without the other two leadership attributes, they are considered a *Supporter* in the 7 Leadership Personas.

A Supporter excels at being a friend and displaying care for everyone in the group. They have a remarkable ability to make others feel good and provide emotional support when needed. Having great Supporters in a team is advantageous as they boost team morale and foster a collaborative culture. They create an environment where people genuinely want to be present.

However, if the group leader is solely a Supporter, there may be a significant lack of an action plan (vision) and, consequently, a lack of action (execution). The group becomes a gathering of individuals spending time together and feeling good but without clear direction or progress.

If you primarily identify as a Supporter and haven't recognized other significant attributes (Step 2) beyond your 10K HP leadership attributes, there are still many commendable roles (Step 3) that focus on these traits. Examples include nursing, counseling, caregiving, teaching, and customer service. The role you choose, along with the associated prestige, income, and fulfillment, will depend on your life goals/mission (Step 1), the quests (Step 6) you undertake, and the skills (Step 4) you acquire through your quests.

However, if empathy is your main identified attribute and you are not inclined to develop others, pursuing quests and acquiring skills that are more suited for a software engineer could likely lead to a life of misery and dissatisfaction.‡‡‡

Supporter personas would benefit from learning skills (Step 4) such as rapport building, empathetic communication, and proactive listening. Supporters thrive when they connect with others and receive appreciation, so developing these skills can lead to greater happiness and fulfillment in their lives. It's worth noting that as you excel in your chosen field, you may also need to gradually develop leadership skills through the other two leadership attributes: vision and execution. This is because you would eventually need to lead and mentor another generation of junior Supporters and keep the torch of human connections going. The takeaway: never dismiss the other leadership attributes as irrelevant.

The Hustler (Only Execution)

A *Hustler* is an individual predominantly possessing execution who is able to complete tasks with effective efficiency, yet lacks empathy and has a limited vision of the path going forward.

Hustlers exemplify the essence of "getting things done." They are dynamic and relentless in action, often preferring to spring into motion rather than contemplate or consider others' viewpoints or

---

‡‡‡While there have been strong societal pushes for all sorts of people to become software engineers regardless of their attributes, it's important to recognize that the software development lifestyle is filled with bugs, error messages, and "hard-cold-code" that returns errors again and again until it provides the pure joy of a clean run. All of this comes with stressed people telling you that you need to fix something in five minutes or their own lives would be ruined. As a person who cared about connecting with people and receiving regular positive reinforcements, I didn't have it in me to do software engineering, despite working heavily in the industry and respecting my engineering allies. It's important to remember this: Any role you pick (Step 3) would not be fulfilling at all if doesn't align with your game (Step 1) and attributes (Step 2).

long-term outcomes. These individuals may regard speculation about the distant future as unproductive, preferring instead to concentrate on immediate responsibilities, delivering results with speed and efficiency.

Having a Hustler on your team can prove highly advantageous due to their work ethic. However, their leadership style often leaves much to be desired, generally adopting a "do as I do" approach rather than guiding and developing their team members. While they are the most industrious among the three Leadership Personas discussed so far, their insensitivity for the feeling of others and lack of strategic foresight can lead to friction within their teams.

Despite these challenges, Hustlers have the potential to achieve significant success in their life game. They are the grinding machines of the game, always striving to level up, especially when provided with a clear roadmap. If a well-defined strategy exists for their chosen game (such as rigorous study for medical school, attending a code bootcamp for an engineering role, or door-to-door selling of a product), Hustlers can obtain great success and earn respect in their fields.

Hustlers are often the driving force behind a big part of the economy, turning the wheels of progress with their ceaseless action. However, they can grow resentful when their tireless efforts are not recognized with leadership opportunities. Rather than fostering bitterness, it would be beneficial for Hustlers to focus on nurturing their other leadership attributes to become effective leaders. Remember: It is unproductive to complain about the landscape of the game. Rather, the way to play the game of life is to constantly grow in the right direction so that you are able to overcome your landscape challenges.

From Player to Leader: Combining Two or More Attributes

So far, I have reviewed the three *single-trait* Leadership Personas. It's crucial to remember that only having a single leadership attribute doesn't diminish your potential to be a powerful player in this world. However, to evolve into an effective *leader*, you will need to embrace and develop one or two additional leadership attributes along your journey.

Now it's time to explore that next level with Leadership Personas that embody two leadership attributes.

The Coach (Empathy + Vision)

If a 10K HP Player possesses both vision and empathy attributes but lacks execution, we classify them as a *Coach* in our 7 Leadership Personas. Recall how I mentioned that vision and empathy are my strengths? That's why, throughout most of my entrepreneurial career, I have identified myself as a Coach-style leader.

Coaches typically maintain a clear vision of the direction the team needs to take to achieve success. They also prioritize the emotional well-being of their team members, thereby sustaining a certain level of team morale. Working with a competent Coach fosters respect and sometimes willingness to even work at below-market rates. In fact, some individuals may choose to work for an inspiring Coach-style leader pro bono, finding meaning and appreciation in their tasks that is often absent in their regular jobs.

The Coach leadership style excels when paired with a team of Hustlers. The Coach sets a firm direction, ensuring that the Hustlers are driven toward a common vision. However, when paired with Dreamers and Supporters, this pairing may lead to pleasant yet noncompetitive teams. Even in competitive sports, a

Coach-style leader working with Dreamers and Supporters often results in teams that play for enjoyment rather than competing at a higher level.

Coach leaders excel in inspiring and nurturing environments rather than cutthroat competition. Places like co-working spaces, wellness centers, educational institutions, think tanks, and design agencies provide fertile ground for Coach leaders to thrive. We know from behavioral science that when people are relaxed, they can focus on their intrinsic motivation and become more creative. They end up solving problems faster and in more innovative manners, which as a result makes the group become more competitive in the right industries.[2]

Furthermore, Coach leaders are well-suited for monarchs or leaders of established countries, where the goal is to guide and maintain a sense of well-being rather than constantly striving for an edge. A Coach is an appropriate leader when things are already on a positive trajectory, and the focus is on sustaining momentum and team morale.

The Commander (Execution + Vision)

If you are a leader who possesses strong vision and robust execution attributes but potentially lacks empathy, we refer to that as a *Commander* within our 7 Leadership Personas.

It's important to clarify that being a Commander does not inherently imply a negative persona. However, due to their decisive vision and relentless drive for progress – often at the expense of others' feelings – Commanders can inadvertently upset their team.

Their lack of empathy can make it challenging for them to inspire people positively. They operate primarily on rules and objectives, emphasizing, "This is our target by January, so get to work!" When a team member struggles under pressure, a Commander, devoid of empathy, might respond dismissively with, "What's your problem?

I don't care how hard it is. Either you can do it, or you're off the team." At times, their approach may even adopt a more abrasive tone, resorting to public shaming or impassioned outbursts.

Importantly, it is a practical reality that even though team morale can be extremely low with high chances of burnout, Commanders can still lead a company to remarkable success. Numerous iconic CEOs exemplify this, including Steve Jobs of Apple, Elon Musk of SpaceX, Travis Kalanick of Uber, and Jack Welch of General Electric. Known for their autocratic leadership styles and fiery tempers, these leaders often adopted a "my way or the highway" approach. Any disagreement or excuse might result in termination from a project or even employment.

However, when a Commander possesses true vision (as not everyone who acts like a Commander necessarily has vision) and the tenacity to relentlessly push their team toward achieving this vision, their leadership can inspire employees to accomplish more than they ever could have imagined on their own.

The side effect is that this leadership style often results in unhappy employees and high turnover rates, with the accompanying stress significantly impacting the team's quality of life.

On the other hand, if the team members themselves are "type A" Hustlers and Commanders,§§§ they might value being on a winning team under a strong, visionary leader over a gentle, empathetic leader who merely nudges everyone at a comfortable pace. Many people have spoken about the harsh conditions of working under Steve Jobs, but at the same time, they declared that it was the best work they had ever done in their lives. As a result, the work they accomplished there truly changed the course of human history, enabling powerful computing devices to be accessible in every household.

Finally, company shareholders typically welcome Commander

---

§§§Type A refers to aggressive and competitive personalities, according to work done by cardiologists Meyer Friedman and Ray Rosenman.

leaders in their corporations, as Commanders relentlessly drive results and increase stock prices. Therefore, in the worlds of business and politics, Commanders often are the ones who change the world, pushing the status quo to new, but sometimes uncomfortable, heights.

The Manager (Execution + Empathy)

A *Manager* is the team leader persona who is proficient in execution and has an abundance of empathy but lacks strong vision.

A Manager leader's role is straightforward yet critical. These individuals are adept at understanding and responding to the emotional states of their teammates. They possess keen insight into what motivates their team members and are skilled at fostering a supportive and harmonious work environment.

Their strength lies in their ability to implement strategies, ensure tasks are completed efficiently, and meet deadlines consistently. They are the backbone of day-to-day operations, especially in large organizations that already have a visionary leader, ensuring that the team's immediate goals are met with precision and reliability.

However, their Achilles' heel lies in their difficulty in formulating an overarching vision for the long-term direction their team should pursue. Managers may prioritize immediate tasks and short-term goals over long-term strategic planning. This lack of foresight can hinder meaningful or effective progress. The team may feel comfortable and busy but often ends up doing work that becomes obsolete in the foreseeable future.

Managers can reach their full potential when they collaborate with visionary leaders who provide direction and strategic insight. When paired with a strong vision from a Dreamer advisor, a Coach supervisor, or a Commander executive, Managers can transform their teams into highly effective units.

While Managers may lack the innate ability to formulate a long-term vision, their proficiency in execution and empathy makes them invaluable to any team. By complementing their strengths with the visionary input of other leadership personas, Managers can ensure their teams not only meet immediate objectives but also contribute to the long-term success of the organization.

As you can see from these Leadership Personas, the key to success is not about having all of the necessary successful traits yourself. It's about finding your own 10K HP alignment with the right role (Step 3) to play, the right allies that make up for your weaknesses (Step 5), and developing new attributes and skills to tackle the right quests (Steps 2, 4, and 6).

So here we arrive, finally, at the center of the 7 Leadership Personas Venn diagram.

The OP Leader (Vision + Empathy + Execution)

Becoming an OP Leader represents the pinnacle of leadership within 10K HP. This role requires a balanced combination of the three 10K HP leadership attributes, as shown in Figure 11.

- **Vision**: An OP Leader possesses a clear understanding of their goals and the path to achieve them. They set objectives, chart a course toward the future, and inspire others to share and believe in this vision. Their ability to turn ideas into actionable plans sets them apart from others.
- **Empathy**: An OP Leader is grounded in a genuine understanding and care for their teammates. This empathy fosters deep connections, building trust and loyalty within the team.
- **Execution**: An OP Leader knows when to be firm and when to be flexible, understanding that tough decisions are sometimes necessary for the team's success. They balance compassion with the discipline needed to meet deadlines and achieve objectives.

An OP Leader creates an environment that attracts people to join them. Their care for the team, combined with effective execution, ensures that goals are met in a respectful and uplifting manner. Their vision serves as a guiding star, leading everyone toward achievement and fulfillment.

An OP Leader understands that challenges are inevitable but sees them as opportunities for growth. Their balanced approach keeps the team motivated, focused, and aligned with the vision, even in tough times. Their empathetic leadership makes these challenges more bearable for everyone involved.

By embracing OP Leadership, they enhance their ability to navigate life's challenges with resilience and foresight. Mentors and peers find joy and fulfillment in supporting and collaborating with them. Their leadership becomes a beacon, attracting success, support, and shared achievements.

Historically, few have achieved the status of an OP Leader. Most people master two of the three attributes and spend their lives developing the third. Unlike skills (Step 4), which can be acquired quickly, attributes develop slowly over time, making it difficult for anyone to achieve real OP Leader status. Some historical individuals whom I consider to be OP Leaders include Winston Churchill, Eleanor Roosevelt, Indra Nooyi from PepsiCo, and the Chinese revolutionary Sun Yat-sen.

It's Your Turn to Play: Your Leadership Attributes

Now that we have explored what the OP Leader Attributes and various 7 Leadership Personas, it's your turn to explore where you fit into the model and how to upgrade yourself as a leader.

Pick from One of the Three Game Modes

Easy: Reflect on your Leadership Personas. Which Leadership Attributes do you excel in naturally? Which ones feel like weaknesses? Which circle do you most want to strengthen? Write down your thoughts and consider how your strengths have helped you contribute to teams in the past.

Medium: Share the 7 Leadership Personas = framework with three trusted friends or family members. Ask them: Which OP Leadership Attributes are your strongest? Which Leadership Personas do they think you are, and why? Which Attributes do they think you should improve, and how? Reflect on their feedback and look for patterns in their observations. This external perspective can help you better understand your strengths and weaknesses.

Hard: Create an action plan to strengthen your weakest Leadership Personas and grow as a leader. Identify one or two Attributes you'd like to improve, and define clear, actionable steps to strengthen them. Develop a strategy to put yourself in the right place and surround yourself with the right allies who can help you grow. Set a timeline for these actions, track your progress, and share your plan with an accountability partner.

To bring structure and focus to your journey, visit 10KHP.com/worksheets to unlock practice worksheets and discover the 10K HP Workbook.

OP Hero Profile: From Child Worker to Weaving Worlds – the Industrious Storyteller

For this chapter's OP Hero story, consider the journey of a young boy from Kansas City who impacted millions simply by bringing smiles to their faces. This boy was born into poverty, laboring as a paperboy at the tender age of nine to help his family make ends meet.

Growing up was not easy for our young OP Hero. He faced harsh conditions at home, often bearing beatings from his angry father, and was forced to work from an early age. This boy, however, found solace in his vivid imagination. During his most stressful moments, when his father's yelling was at its peak, he would disconnect from the harsh reality and lose himself in a world of enchantment where animals could talk.

Raised on a farm in Missouri, this boy had plenty of animal companions. He would spend hours sketching these creatures, weaving imaginative tales around each one of them in his mind. Eventually, he also discovered a profound sense of joy when he could make other kids laugh and allow them to temporarily forget the painful hardships in their lives.

His challenging childhood experiences led him to select a very specific life game (Step 1): to make children smile. He wanted as many children as possible to feel happiness and joy so they didn't need to go through life as painfully as he did.

He became a devoted admirer to the crafts of comedy, acting, and drawing. He obsessed over his idol Charlie Chaplin, whom he felt was a master at making people smile. He regularly impersonated Chaplin, performing skits with his best friend Walter Pfeiffer.

To begin his journey of making other children smile, he mimicked the role (Step 3) portrayed by his role model Charlie Chaplin and started off as a *comedic entertainer*. His remarkable talent even won him several local theater talent contests.

This little, unassuming child grew up to become the undeniable titan of the entertainment industry, engraving his name in history as the legendary Walt Disney. (See Figure 12.)

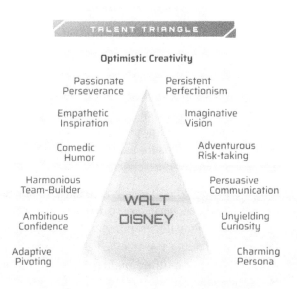

Figure 12. Disney's Talent Triangle

Even though Disney was a very promising comedic entertainer, among all his attributes (Step 2), his most outstanding strength, as recognized by himself and his peers, was his optimistic creativity. He was constantly creating – always confident that his work would bring smiles to people's faces.

Upon discovering animation at the age of nineteen, Disney decided to transform his role into an *enchantment storyteller.* He figured that if he could create magical animations with breathtaking storytelling, he could stimulate fantastical imaginations in children's minds all over the world, no matter how harsh their realities were.

Shortly after, he found an ally (Step 5) in a new talented artist called Ub Iwerks. Together they ventured in their first major quest (Step 6) of opening their own studio: Iwerks-Disney Commercial Artists.

Disney honed his abilities (Step 4) by attending art classes, delving into numerous books about animation, and practicing incessantly to gain more skill points in this art form. He worked tirelessly, saving up to buy books about animation as he was eager to perfect the craft.

Disney's obsessive nature stems from another powerful attribute: *persistent perfectionism*. This led him to pursue perfection in his artwork. This tenacity toward perfection led him to achieve great breakthroughs when he transitioned their studio into Laugh-O-Grams at the age of twenty-one.

It was during that time when Disney realized that dreams without money don't make it very far, so the new venture focused on creating advertisement illustrations and occasional animated commercials. His meticulous eye assessed each frame of animation with rigorous scrutiny, outputting higher quality work than their competitors in the industry.

During this time, Disney and Iwerks also created original and immersive animations such as *Alice Comedies* (based on *Alice in Wonderland* by Lewis Carrol), a series where a real little girl enters a world of cartoon characters.

Of course, along with his strength attributes, Disney also had several weakness attributes, as shown in Figure 13. He was impulsive and disorganized, which led him to become overly emotional at times. He also lacked competency in the skill of managing finances (Step 4) due to him being so disorganized. In order to play his game well, he needed an ally (Step 5) with complementary skills to handle the business and financial aspects of the studio.

Unfortunately, Walt Disney did not do his 10K HP exercises at the time and didn't realize he needed to find such an ally. Because of this, *Alice Comedies* struggled to find distribution partners and eventually led Laugh-O-Grams to financial bankruptcy.

After two consecutive failures, many people would have given up and "found a real job," as family members of many 10K HP Players would often suggest. It's a common yet painful experience to put yourself out there, believing you can do better than the status quo, only to fail repeatedly. Admitting to others that they were right and that you were in over your head the whole time can be deeply humiliating.

Often this leads to a great deal of self-doubt. "Maybe I am not as special as I thought I was. Maybe I'm just mediocre like everyone else. Maybe I should just go back and live out my mediocre life like everyone else." This is where many 10K HP Players give up on their game and become NPCs.

But not Disney. During these challenging times, his attributes of optimistic creativity, passionate perseverance, and ambitious confidence played an important part in how his life played out.

Disney was perseverant, but not in an unwavering manner. As mentioned, he was very emotional and would go through extreme grief when he failed. However, he would immediately transition that sorrow into anger and make a new determination to do much better the next time around.

Figure 13. Disney's Weakness Triangle

This tendency of having a lot of emotional ups-and-downs while never truly giving up is why we termed his attribute *passionate perseverance*. Following the 10K HP literature, if one has talent in any type of perseverance, they should strongly consider putting themselves in environments that are difficult and risky. If they always stayed in a safe and comfortable environment, then this amazingly powerful attribute would have no opportunity to be utilized.

As Walt Disney once said, "You may not realize it when it happens, but a kick in the teeth may be the best thing in the world for you."[3] Of course, it wouldn't work if people gave up easily, so you want to make sure, like Disney, that you have strong teeth and can tank through a few roundhouse kicks.

After Laugh-O-Grams failed, Walt Disney took the little money he had and sought opportunities in Hollywood, trying to sell the few animations of *Alice Comedies* they produced before closing shop.

This was when Walt Disney finally realized that he needed a strong ally (Step 5) to help with the business aspects of the company, which led him to recruiting his brother, Roy Disney. Together they formed their next major quest (Step 6) adventure and formed Disney Brothers Studio (renamed Walt Disney Studios two years later).

Thanks to Roy, Walt Disney finally had someone to help manage his finances and operations. This allowed Walt Disney to focus on developing and fully realizing his enchantment storyteller role.

In addition, Roy helped with the sales and business development of the company. He negotiated a pivotal contract with the distributor agent Margaret Winkler, who purchased the rights for *Alice Comedies*. This allowed Walt Disney to continue working on his cherished creation, though he now had to answer to Winkler's company. Little did he know, this would become the roundhouse kick to his teeth.

Not long after, Margaret Winkler's husband, an aggressive businessman named Charles Mintz, took over as executive producer of *Alice Comedies*. Mintz immediately began pressuring the Disney brothers to produce animations at a faster pace.

At that time, Walt Disney had not invested many skill points into his communication and negotiation abilities (Step 4). Consequently, he suffered another significant heartbreak when he lost the rights to his highly successful creation, *Oswald the Lucky Rabbit*, to Charles Mintz. As a higher-level commander-type leader, the assertive Mintz employed many aggressive tactics to pressure Disney into relinquishing not only the rights to the character but also the related animations of Oswald the Lucky Rabbit.

This was an extremely demoralizing event, and it made the passionately perseverant Disney realize that the true way to play his game of making children smile was not to personally create the most enchanting pieces of work, but to own the intellectual and distribution rights for the best content in the world.

It was at this time that Disney transformed into his final role – from enchantment storyteller to *Industrious Storyteller*. Instead of doing most of the work himself, he would start a *guild* (Step 5) that would attract other enchantment storytellers to join and create the best content in the world to make children smile. He would delegate most of the creative details to other animators, scriptwriters, graphic designers, voice actors, and special effect artists, all while owning the intellectual property and distribution rights himself.

It is important to note that not all storytellers are industrious. Many remain craftsmen who personally create engaging content no matter how high-level or successful they become. For instance, Hayao Miyazaki, the famed Japanese animator behind masterpieces like *My Neighbor Totoro*, *Spirited Away*, and *Princess Mononoke*, achieved OP Hero status early on in life but continued his journey as a top-level enchantment storyteller. Walt Disney uniquely built an international media conglomerate because of his negative experiences with Charles Mintz, which pushed him to become industrious toward his game of making the most children smile.

Leveraging his role as an Industrious Storyteller and guided by his potent attributes of optimistic creativity and persistent perfectionism (Step 2), Disney forged a new team that brought to life an even more successful character in 1928. This character's name was Mortimer Mouse.

Does the name sound familiar? Perhaps you're more acquainted with the name they subsequently adopted for this character – the iconic Mickey Mouse. It really goes without saying that Mickey Mouse has become a household name, appreciated and recognized in virtually every corner of the globe.

Fueled by the attributes mentioned in this chapter – optimistic creativity, persistent perfectionism, and passionate perseverance – Disney embarked on a series of pivotal quests (Step 6), such as successfully selling his groundbreaking animated short film, *Steamboat Willie*, to Universal executives. This endeavor proved to be a monumental success and significantly propelled his 10K HP journey forward.

That eventually led to even more legendary quest achievements (Step 6), such as introducing the world's first fully animated feature film, *Snow White*, in 1937, launching the fantasy theme parks Disneyland and Walt Disney World, and winning twenty-two Academy Awards from fifty-nine nominations. Today, Disney's Mickey Mouse is over 100 years old and remains one of the most recognizable fictional characters in the world.

For these amazing achievements, Walt Disney sits on our 10K HP Earth Server's storyteller leaderboard as a top Industrious Storyteller.

It's important to note that Disney's unique attributes may not have been as effective in other contexts. For instance, they would likely have been less impactful for a task like liberating India from British rule – Gandhi's game.

Case in point: During the challenging period of World War I, Walt Disney served as an ambulance driver. Using his distinct attributes, he brought joy and laughter to fellow soldiers with his sketches and amusing skits during tough times. His ambulance didn't wear the usual camouflage; instead, it was adorned with humorous cartoons.

Starting a social movement for political change would not have been Disney's best play style because his attributes didn't naturally align with that mission. However, boosting soldiers' morale and bringing smiles to their faces was a play style that was perfectly suited for him, playing to his strengths.

OP Hero Walt Disney: Takeaways

In summary, the synergetic combination of Disney's attributes was optimal for creating an organization that creates and distributes joyful content to children, just as Gandhi's attributes made him more suitable for liberating India through his compassionate charisma and empathetic love. In both cases, the attributes of these iconic figures impeccably aligned with the roles they played in their respective spheres. That is the focus of the following chapter.

Chapter 3 Highlights

- Attributes are inherent traits; skills are learned abilities. Knowing your attributes helps align your role and enhance skills.
- You can identify your attributes by analyzing important life moments, getting feedback from others, and using strength assessments such as CliftonStrengths.
- The 10K HP Talent Triangle is a hierarchy of attributes arranged by their edge, ring, and base strengths.
- The three leadership attributes are vision, empathy, and execution.
- Based on the combination of these attributes, individuals can be divided into 7 Leadership Personas such as dreamers, supporters, hustlers, coaches, commanders, managers, and OP Leaders.
- OP Hero Walt Disney wanted to be a comedic actor but saw that he had attributes in being an animator or enchantment storyteller. However, after many failures and losing his intellectual property, his attributes of optimistic creativity and persistent perfectionism led him to create one of the largest conglomerates in entertainment history.

Chapter 4: Select Your Role (Specialty)

STEP 1	STEP 2	STEP 3
Choose Your Game MISSION	*Know Your Attributes* TALENTS	**Select Your Role** **SPECIALTY**

STEP 4	STEP 5	STEP 6
Enhance Your Skills CRAFT	*Build Your Alliance* NETWORK	*Achieve Your Quests* MILESTONES

"Choose a job you love, and you will never have to work a day in your life."

—— Confucius

In the iconic game *World of Warcraft*, players start off with some very important decisions that will affect the entirety of their gameplay. They must select their faction (Alliance or Horde), a race (human, dwarf, undead, etc.), and a skill class (Priest, Warrior, Rogue, Warlock, etc.)

Besides the faction, which determines the side you play on in the game, a player's class is their most impactful choice. As of the software expansion *The War Within*, released in 2024, there are thirteen different classes, and the gameplay generally boils down to three roles:

- **Tanks**: Players who become tanks play aggressively, charging into battle to lead the team, attract damage from all the enemies, and provide cover for their allies.
- **Healers**: Players who become healers like to play outside the thick of battle, supporting their teammates and making sure everyone is empowered to play their best.
- **Damagers**: Players who select damagers like to play fast, aggressively, and strive to get the most damage and kills on enemies.

As you can see, each role is best suited for a specific type of player: patient, methodical players tend to choose Tanks; strategic players who like to support their team choose Healers; impatient, adrenaline-filled players who love the spotlight choose Damagers. In the game of life, you too must select a role for your game.

Roles Are Powered by Attributes

In my discussion earlier about Step 1: Choose Your Game, I wrote about how your game should not be determined by your attributes (Step 2). That's because it's essential to first discover a meaningful pursuit you can dedicate your life to before figuring out how you fit into it. I know plenty of people who choose their life path not because they resonated with it, but because their parents wanted them to take that course, it made the most money, or they seemed to be talented at that activity. Regardless of how successful they became, they felt empty and hollow. That's because they were not *playing* their 10K HP life game.

But once you have identified the game that is worth playing, the role you pick in that game should align with your talents as much as possible. For instance, if your game is to protect the earth and improve on ecological sustainability, the role you pick should be determined by your talents. If you are talented in quantitative and arithmetic attributes, then you could become an engineer and invent eco-friendly machines that reduce emission into the atmosphere.

If you don't have quantitative talents but have more attributes in the communications and humanities space, you could become a diplomat to negotiate international treaties that help protect the environment. Or you could become an activist or lobbyist to help push for positive policy changes. The point is, only when you know your game will your role be purpose-driven.[111]

Defining Your Role Sphere

Most of the time, people think of their roles as their occupation: accountant, software engineer, professor, researcher, writer, artist, or full-time-parent, etc. That is because our occupation is the value we contribute to society and those around us and is, therefore, easily observed and recognizable. But there are more layers to our roles that interplay with our occupation. I call the layers our *Role Sphere*, as they are like layers of an onion that surround a more fundamental core, much like how the planets orbit the sun. Figure 14 shows the four Role Sphere layers that together form our 10K HP roles.

---

[111] I understand there is much more involved to tackle these challenges. This is just a simplified way of understanding how different Roles could empower the same life goals or game in different meaningful ways.

Figure 14. Role Spheres

1. The Aspiration Layer: Who You Want to Become

The Aspiration Layer is the foundational layer and your most inner core, encompassing your dreams, ambitions, and the ideal version of what you strive to become. In the context of your 10K HP journey, who you want to become is mostly determined by the life game (Step 1) you choose to play.

In the Aspiration Layer, it doesn't matter who you are and where you are at. Where you want to be and who you want to become defines your existence more than anything else because it presents your trajectory and *journey*. This is why, in Chapter 3, the middle-schooler who said "I am going to Harvard" defined her existence to me with those words, which told me more than anything else about her. This is also why Monkey D. Luffy in *One Piece* is defined by his goals of becoming the "King of the Pirates."[17]

In essence, the Aspiration Layer is at the innermost core because your mission defines your role more than anything else. The OP Hero Mahatma Gandhi was a lawyer for many years, but when he changed his Aspiration Layer from someone who just wanted to live a comfortable life to someone who strived to create equality in India, the most fundamental shift in his role occurred, more than any occupational change could.

2. The Identity Layer: Who You Believe You Are

The Identity Layer is about self-perception and self-awareness. It's how you see yourself and your place in the world. Your identity is shaped by your experiences, beliefs, values, and how you interpret your place within these contexts. Identity is also something more fundamental than your occupation, involving beliefs such as, "I am a person who takes care of my family," "I am a person who would never give up on my tasks," or "I am a person who would not stand aside when seeing injustice."

The Identity Layer is continuously shaped and reshaped by your experiences and interactions. It is not static but evolves as you grow, learn, and change throughout your life. The Identity Layer works hand-in-hand with the Aspiration Layer, as we often think about our aspirations based on who we believe we are, but we also think about our identity based on the aspirations we are inspired to pursue. For instance, a role model might inspire you to pursue a goal you never previously imagined, and because of that, your identity transforms to fit that aspiration.

---

[17] In fact, in the "Ocean's Dream" filler arc within the *One Piece* anime, Luffy and his crew woke up one day to find that they had lost all their recent memories, starting from the beginning of their adventures together. Understandably, everyone else started to panic because they didn't recognize each other and had lost a big piece of their identities. But not Luffy. After the initial confusion, he didn't care that he had no idea how he got there or why he was surrounded by strangers. All he cared about was that he still intended to become the King of the Pirates. This thought alone allowed him to stay happy and positive. Because his aspiration role was so entrenched in his system, the other Role Sphere layers were lower priorities that could be aligned later.

Of course, this doesn't mean you can be whatever you want to be. Everyone is born with certain talents and limitations, which are encompassed in Step 2: Know Your Attributes. Your identity should be based on your natural-born attributes. For instance, as a Mage, I would have a very hard time playing the game as a Tank, just as a Priest would have a very hard time playing the game as a Damager. You could still try to play these roles that aren't supported by your attributes in small niche communities or among your friend circles, but once you get onto a bigger stage with greater competition, you will often get obliterated by the Warriors playing Tanks and the Mages playing Damagers.

Once you have determined your Identity Layer, that will then help you determine a large part of the next layer – the Occupation Layer.

3. The Occupation Layer: Your Value to Those Around You

The Occupation Layer is where your inner layers – those for your aspirations and identity – become visible and influential in the real world. In this layer, your internal perceptions and aspirations translate into external contributions. This layer is about the expression of your roles in your communities and workplaces, the value you provide to others, and how you are perceived in these roles. It's a tangible representation of the work you do and its impact.

Occupation goes beyond mere job titles or career paths. It encompasses your broader contribution to the world around you, whether as a professional, volunteer, family member, or community leader. For instance, in your game you might aspire to help uplift other human beings (your Aspiration Layer) and see your own attributes as naturally empathetic and nurturing (your Identity Layer). Your occupation might then be that of a teacher, counselor, therapist, or full-time parent, where you can uplift others with empathy and nurturing ways.

Sometimes, your occupation does not align well with your Aspiration and Identity Layers. This misalignment can result from choosing a major or a job based on other people's expectations, the need for immediate money (this is called a "resource side quest" within Step 6 (quests), or simply not spending enough time planning our 10K HP journey so you have no idea what you want to do. The good news is that as long as you hold true to your Aspiration and Identity Layers, your occupation can be changed with good planning, counseling, or strong determination.

How smoothly or painfully your Occupation Layer can be enhanced or changed is highly influenced by how well you develop your Specialization Layer.

4. The Specialization Layer: What You Become Good At

The Specialization Layer is where your Step 2 (attributes) and Step 4 (skills) come together, leading to mastery and expertise in specific areas. Unlike the Aspiration and Identity Layers, which are shaped by your dreams and self-beliefs, the Specialization Layer is more grounded in your innate talents, as well as the skills you choose to develop.

Your specialization role is not necessarily related to your occupation role, but rather, it's what you are perceived as being very good at, either by yourself or with those around you. For example, a medical student (occupation role) might also be extremely good at playing the guitar, competitive card games, and creative writing. These specialties, while not directly related to her field of study, represent a unique combination of talents and skills that distinguish her. Even though it's best that your specialization role aligns with your occupation role, sometimes you discover new paths opening up because of the hobbies or interests you become good at. For example, the medical student might develop a way to combine these skill sets and create a narrative-driven game to help other medical students prepare for their exams. She now would have a unique specialization that very few people in the world would have.

Your specialization is the tangible proof of your development and growth. It is what we bring to the table in a unique combination of skills, knowledge, and experience that we alone possess. It is our personal brand, our signature in the world.

In this layer, your focus shifts to mastery and excellence in particular areas. For instance, the person with an aspiration to make meaningful societal contributions (Aspiration Layer) and who identifies as an empathetic, caring leader (Identity Layer) might find themselves in an occupation role such as a community organizer or social worker. Their Specialization Layer, then, would be the specific skills and expertise they develop in these roles, such as effective communication, conflict resolution, fundraising abilities, or deep knowledge in social policy.

Unless it is to overcome a critical weakness, the skills (Step 4) you learn should be empowered by your attributes (Step 2). Quantitative attributes, for example, suggest specialties in financial or engineering skills, as long as they can support the 10K HP mission (Step 1). Aesthetic attributes, on the other hand, are more likely to translate to graphic design or fashion-viable specialties. Only when your skills are empowered by your attributes do you achieve a strong Specialization Layer within your roles.

The Occupation Layer then acts as a bridge, connecting your Specialization Layer to the practical world. As you commit to your occupation, whether it be a professional role or a personal commitment, it serves to reinforce and refine your Specialization Layer.

When you have fully understood and aligned your entire Role Sphere, you then gain a profound understanding of your true self. This clarity guides you in developing yourself to excel in your chosen role on the Earth Server, allowing you to contribute in the most meaningful and impactful ways.

Roleplaying and the Power of Identity

Chapter 2: Choose Your Game (Mission) dedicates considerable attention to finding your game, which is intricately tied to your aspiration role. The right game in life provides clarity to your position in your journey and helps you understand the current role you should adopt based on that aspiration.

Now, explore your Identity Layer by understanding the power and science behind identity and how techniques like roleplaying can significantly impact how you play your game.

Roleplaying to Become a Public Speaker

Your Identity role is a set of beliefs about yourself that significantly influence your behavior across various environments. This concept holds true even in the realm of imaginary roleplay. In professional settings, individuals who imagine themselves as leaders or innovators are likely to take initiative, embrace challenges, and think more creatively. Similarly, in personal relationships, individuals who view themselves as supportive partners or nurturing parents are more likely to engage in behaviors that reinforce those identities.[18]

The transformative effects of roleplaying have had a huge impact on my own 10K HP journey. Many people who know me as an international keynote speaker are extremely surprised to learn that before college I was terrified of public speaking.

In eighth grade, having just moved to the United States and attending Prairie Star Middle School in Kansas, I remember walking

---

[18]The research and science on identity and its powers can be found in my first book, *Actionable Gamification: Beyond Points, Badges, and Leaderboards*, specifically Chapter 8: The Fourth Core Drive - Ownership & Possession.

by a drama class where a fellow student was rehearsing on stage. He passionately and excitedly yelled something to his small group of classmates, and I was in total shock, thinking, "Wow! I could *never* do something like that. It's just not me and not in me." At the time, just watching him struck fear into my heart, and I wondered if all Americans were that impressive.

I had a set of self-beliefs that convinced me I would never be able to do what my schoolmates could. My fear of public speaking was so intense that I would break into a sweat and feel like I was choking on my own breath, even when my friends were the ones on stage – a feeling that's connected to the double-edged sword of my empathy attribute, which I explored in the last chapter.

So, how did I go from being terrified of public speaking to a keynote speaker comfortable in front of thousands? I roleplayed. No, seriously. Whenever I had to step onto a stage, I employed a technique where I pretended to myself that I was a charismatic speaker with over twenty years of experience. Adopting this mindset, I *obviously* wouldn't feel nervous about addressing the crowd. If I misspoke, I could just laugh it off confidently, making light of the situation along with the audience, and smoothly move on.

Of course, this internal technique is very different from lying to the public about having many years of experience when you do not. I believe in radical honesty and have never suggested that friends or clients misrepresent themselves with false information. However, if you portray yourself confidently while telling your audience that it's your first time on stage or even charismatically saying you feel rather nervous, you are exerting the energy of an experienced speaker without being dishonest. This attitude instantly changes how you feel and how the audience views you.

By consistently roleplaying (to myself) as someone experienced in public speaking, I was able to use that new identity role to gradually grow into the occupation and special roles I was portraying. While

I still don't consider myself particularly charismatic, my "public figure oddity" attribute ended up charming a crowd of people who became fans after hearing my speeches. This transformation highlights the profound impact of roleplaying, specifically the identity roles that can tangibly impact personal development and confidence, especially in challenging situations.

Roleplaying Eating Habits

The power of roleplaying and your identity roles isn't limited to just achieving career goals; it even extends to seemingly trivial matters like eating spicy food. Before I turned twenty-five, my tolerance for spicy food was virtually nonexistent. I avoided it at all costs as it was unbearable for me, often leaving a negative impact that lingered long after the meal. One aspect of eating spicy food I particularly disliked was how, after eating something spicy, *everything else* seemed spicy, too, due to the continuous burn on my tongue.

However, that changed when I read an article highlighting the health benefits of spicy food, such as its potential to boost metabolism and aid in losing body fat. At that point I already had experience applying the skill of roleplaying a desired persona, to improve various aspects of my life, such as public speaking. So I did the same thing and started *pretending to myself* that I was someone who loved eating spicy food.

Almost overnight, I transformed from a person who couldn't handle the slightest hint of spice to someone who indulged in it regularly. My friends, who prided themselves on their spice tolerance, were astonished to see me out-eating them in spiciness levels. I simply convinced my own brain that the burning sensation on my tongue was preferable and enjoyable. Some people apply the same technique to manage certain levels of pain or hunger. Since these sensations are just messages sent to our brain, we have a certain amount of control over how we interpret these neurological signals. Roleplaying allows us to circumvent some of our previous attitudes and beliefs towards these neurochemical sensations.

After about six months of regularly eating spicy food, I recognized that using roleplaying still required some energy, and it was still more natural for me to prefer savory foods. Consequently, I gradually stopped favoring spicy food over other options. However, I retained the ability to easily switch back to enjoying spicy foods whenever needed, especially when dining with friends. The point here obviously is not to encourage 10K HP Players to eat spicy food, but to understand the power of assuming certain identities and self-beliefs.

You become what you eat, but you eat based on your self-beliefs.

Your Identity Layer Drives Behavior

In his book, *Atomic Habits*, James Clear states that there are three layers of behavioral change: outcomes, processes, and identity. He brings up the difference between two people who are resisting a cigarette. When offered to smoke, one says, "No thanks. I'm trying to quit," while the other says, "No thanks. I'm not a smoker."

When a person says, "No thanks, I'm trying to quit," they are still identifying as a smoker who is in the process of changing. This mindset often leads to a constant battle with oneself, where each cigarette avoided is a temporary victory against their ingrained identity as a smoker. This approach can be mentally exhausting and less effective in the long run, as the core identity of being a smoker remains unchanged.

On the other hand, the individual who responds with, "No thanks, I'm not a smoker," has embraced a new *identity*. This person sees themselves fundamentally as a nonsmoker. This shift in identity is profound. Each time they refuse a cigarette, they reinforce this new self-perception.

This is where the power of identity change becomes evident. By adopting a new identity, your actions naturally align with it. The effort required to resist temptation is lessened because the behavior (avoiding smoking, in this case) is an expression of who you are. Over time, as this new identity is reinforced through consistent actions, it becomes more ingrained, and the behavior becomes more automatic.

This principle of identity-based behavioral change applies to various aspects of life, from professional development to personal hobbies. When you start to see yourself as the person you want to become (Aspiration Layer), your actions naturally start to align with it (Identity Layer). Whether it's becoming a public speaker, a writer, or a healthier individual, the key lies in reshaping your identity to reflect your goals and aspirations.

Voters Are Better Than Those Who Vote

A 2011 study by Stanford social psychologist Christopher Bryan and his colleagues divided subjects into two groups, where one would answer on a survey, "How important is it to you to be a voter in the upcoming election?" while the other answers, "How important is it to you to vote in the upcoming election?" They then measured actual voting behavior based on the different survey prompts. The results were striking: those who were asked about "being a voter" showed a higher voting turn out rate compared to those who were asked about "voting."[1] This suggests that when people see voting as an intrinsic part of their identity, they are more likely to engage in it.

This finding is another testament to the power of identity in driving behavior. When actions are perceived as extensions of our identity, you are more compelled to act in accordance with that perception. In the case of voting, being a "voter" is not just about the act of voting, but about embodying the role of a responsible, engaged citizen. This identity alignment transforms an activity from a mere action into a reflection of who you are.

Identity Pacts Create Sustainable Commitments

Nir Eyal, in his influential book *Indistractable*, highlights the power of what he calls an *Identity Pact*.[2] This concept revolves around the idea of defining yourself not by what you can't do, but by what you *choose* not to do. For instance, Eyal himself was a vegetarian for five years. Instead of saying "I can't eat meat," he framed it as "I don't eat meat." This subtle shift in language reflects a significant change in perspective; it's not about having the willpower to resist temptation, but rather about making a choice that aligns with one's identity.

The essence of an *identity pact* is in alignment with one's actions based on their chosen identity. For Eyal's readers, this could be the identity of being "indistractable." Similarly, you could choose to be a "lifelong learner," a "health-conscious gamer," or a "resilient optimist." The key lies in the internal commitment to this identity. Once you firmly establish who you are, your actions and decisions naturally flow from this Identity. This strategy effectively removes the constant battle of decision-making, as your actions become a natural extension of your self-identity.

In your 10K HP journey, when you align your aspiration role and your identity role with your occupation role, you will start to perform in certain ways that elevate you to higher levels in everything you do.

Exploring Your Occupation and Specialization Roles With Career Circles

Now that you have a deeper understanding of your Aspiration and Identity Layers, it's time to explore what many people often contemplate intently regarding their roles: their Occupation Layer.

As a reminder, your occupation represents how you contribute value through your Specialization Layer to those around you. It doesn't necessarily have to be a paid job; it can be a role as a charity volunteer, a hobby craftsman, or a loving parent.

So, how do you practically select your occupation role in life? Let's start with this example:

If your aspiration role is to fill the world with beautiful music at an affordable price but you lack musical talent, you could still fulfill this aspiration by leveraging your skills differently. Perhaps you could work as an accountant for a music organization or start a music education nonprofit. In this way, the value you bring is not just in crunching numbers but in enabling more people to experience music.

This is where career circles become integral in guiding you to explore your occupation role effectively.

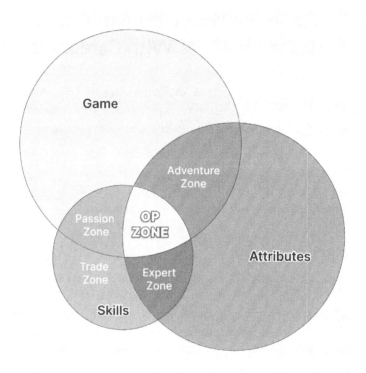

Figure 15. Career Circles

Figure 15 depicts a Venn diagram of three career circles. It includes two circles from the steps we've already journeyed through within 10K HP – your game derived from Step 1 (linked to your Aspiration Layer), and your attributes based on Step 2 (Powered by your Identity and Specialization Layer). Finally, the Skills Circle corresponds to your Specialization Layer and Step 4: Enhance Your Skills, which I cover in detail in the next chapter.

I'm introducing the Skills Circle at this juncture because, as mentioned earlier, your current skill sets are another key factor in determining the role you choose to play. However, these are considerably less critical compared to your game and attributes simply because the latter are likely already stable and developed, whereas skills can be quickly enhanced or acquired through practical means such as engaging in courses, immersive reading, or participating in platforms like Udemy, Khan Academy, or Octalysis Prime.

Based on this diagram, there are five possible zones in which your occupational role could reside, reflecting five different attitudes that aptly correspond to your identity roles.[19]

Your career circles encompass five zones from which you choose your occupation role.

1. The Trade Zone: I Just Want to Make a Living

If you choose an occupation role in the Trade Zone, then you're really just choosing your role because you already have skills in a certain area, and you just need a job that makes you money. Because this is not part of your game, you won't feel fulfilled. Because this is not where your top talents are, you won't be world-class at it no matter how much time you put into it to improve your skills.

- Pros: It's easier to find a job that matches your skills.
- Cons: You'll live an unfulfilled life because you won't be pursuing a greater mission. At the same time, it is unlikely to will ever achieve true mastery.

---

[19]Career circles might remind some people of the Japanese concept of *Ikigai*, which essentially translates to "a reason to live." There is a variety of literature out there that has a similar concept, such as The Hedgehog Concept from Jim Collins (*Good to Great*), Keith Ferrazzi's Blue Flame (*Never Eat Alone*), and more. While not directly inspiring career circles here, I'm happy to give them credit and appreciation for sharing these meaningful concepts to the world a lot earlier.

2. The Expert Zone: I Want to Be Highly Successful at What I Do

If you choose an occupation role in the Expert Zone, then you could become world-class as you align your skills (Step 4) and attributes (Step 2). But ultimately these may not fulfill you if they don't work together toward your actual game. You may make a lot of money, gain a lot of recognition, or achieve great professional success, but you might still lack personal meaning and fulfillment.

- Pros: Because this role is aligned with your attributes and talents, you have great opportunities to achieve mastery, leading to money, accolades, and recognition.
- Cons: This role is not aligned with your life mission, leading to a lack of fulfillment.

3. The Passion Zone: I Want to Do Things That Are Meaningful

If you choose an occupation role in the Passion Zone, then you're on your way to fulfillment because you're playing your game, but it will be more difficult to beat it if you don't have the attributes to be world-class in this profession. However, it may be something where just by doing it, you obtain a fulfilled life. Mastery and completion are not necessary for having meaning, purpose, and enjoyment. You'll be playing your game your whole life, and that's all that matters.

- Pros: You'll feel fulfilled because you're striving to beat the game that matters to you.
- Cons: You may never beat your game if you lack the attributes to become world-class at your role.

4. The OP Zone: I Want to Accomplish Great Results Toward Things That Are Meaningful

If you are able to find an occupation role in the OP Zone, you are in a great place. Not only are you playing your game, but you've also selected a role that utilizes your natural talents (Step 2) and leverages your current skills (Step 4). This choice allows you to build upon your strengths, enjoy the journey of playing the game, and excel at what you do. With the right allies (Step 5) and the right quests (Step 6), you would be well on your way to achieving 10K HP alignment and living life in OP Mode.

- Pros: There's a complete alignment between your mission and talent. The harder you work, the more your skills level up; the more time you invest, the closer you get to mastery and conquering your game.
- Cons: Finding this role can be quite difficult. It requires time, patience, and a willingness to try many things that could feel embarrassing. However, if you persistently seek this outcome, perhaps with guidance from resources like this book, mentors, and role models, you'll eventually find it.

5. The Adventure Zone: I'm Willing to Risk It All for a Brand-New Path

If you choose an occupation role in the Adventure Zone, I applaud you for having the courage to embark on a brand-new life journey. Similar to the OP Zone, you could become world-class in your role and feel fulfilled because you are playing your game. However, unlike the OP Zone, you may not have much experience or many skills in the roles within the Adventure Zone – you'll be starting from scratch. This means that at the beginning you won't be good at it, and you'll have to put in much more effort than your peers. However, if you stick with it, work hard, and develop the appropriate skills, you have a high chance of beating your game (effectively moving to the OP Zone).

- Pros: Similar to the OP Zone, there is alignment between your mission (game) and your talents (attributes). You'll likely find joy and fulfillment in this role, and you have the potential to become world-class.
- Cons: Unlike the OP Zone, you may not already have the skills needed to succeed in this role. It's risky to start a new career or endeavor from scratch, but because there is alignment between your game and attributes, you have a strong chance of becoming great at it and beating your game.

As you might guess, I recommend you find an occupation role within the OP Zone if possible. However, since that is difficult to achieve quickly, it is a plausible strategy to begin in the Adventure Zone and start doing quests that help you gain experience and skill points that can help move you into the OP Zone.

If you are very young, then there is barely any risk to starting off in the Adventure Zone, as you won't be giving up anything. If you have already been living your life in the Trade Zone or Expert Zone for decades, switching to Adventure Zone could seem scary, but it will be ultimately fulfilling and likely worthwhile. For the first time in your life, you would be *playing*, not just living.

If you are in the Expert Zone and can apply your already-mastered skills to a newfound passion or game, then you would immediately be in the OP Zone. That would be even more optimal than spending years in the Adventure Zone picking up brand new sets of skills, but you might be losing a lot of fun because there's not as much "adventure" to it.

How to Determine Your 10K HP Role

You may have noticed, the more you have developed Step 1 and Step 2 in your 10K HP journey, the more zones within your career circle open up. If you haven't identified your game yet, zones such as Passion, Adventure, and OP remain out of reach. Similarly, without clarity on your attributes, Expert, Adventure, and OP Zones are not yet viable options. Most people would be more aware of their skills circle and thus have access to their Trade Zone, since they spent significant time honing these skills. However, some still don't fully acknowledge or appreciate their greatest skills yet. This means that, as you gain more insights about your other 10K HP steps, more choices for your role open up. That is exciting and makes our 10K HP exercises even more rewarding.

Scenario 1: I Know My Game but I Don't Know My Attributes

Since not everyone can quickly figure out their game and attributes before they commit to certain roles, what should you do if you haven't figured out yours from the first reading of the previous two chapters? This section is intended to help you determine what you can immediately do to find your next role in life as you slowly work your way toward the OP Zone and 10K HP alignment.

When you have a clear idea of your game but don't have full clarity of your attributes yet, a practical method to find your role is to join organizations that are already engaged in your game. These organizations could offer opportunities that align with your existing skills, broadening your scope for growth within your chosen game. This approach encompasses various types of entities, including companies, nonprofit organizations, hobby clubs, or school associations. By questing within these organizations, you will have a better chance of discovering your unique attributes.

Consider the hypothetical case of Melissa, a thirty-year-old, college-educated, married woman living in London with one child. Melissa's chosen game is to help the next generation of underprivileged children overcome their disadvantages and grow up to lead happy, successful, and financially secure lives.

In pursuit of her game, Melissa did some online research and discovered TOMS, a footwear company that provides shoes, sight, water, safe birth, and bullying prevention services to those in need. Other organizations like Kiva.org and Khan Academy, which align with Melissa's mission to support underprivileged individuals, also caught her attention.

Joining these organizations would allow Melissa time to further explore and develop her attributes, engaging in more 10K HP discovery activities such as assessments, joining community guilds such as Octalysis Prime, or progressing through the 10K HP Workbook. This way, she actively pursues her passion while discovering more about herself.

Of course, if Melissa wanted to optimize even more, it would help if she spent a little bit more time thinking about her attributes before applying to TOMS, so that her first job there is set up for success. Although she hasn't fully grasped her edge, ring, and base talents as outlined in the Talent Triangle from Chapter 3: Know Your Attributes, she generally understands that she is creative, artistic, and has good taste in style (her friends usually ask her for fashion advice). Although she doesn't think of new, innovative ideas on her own, she works well in teams and can improve the efforts of other team members. She knows she is patient and understanding. While patience is a strength, it often leads to her not being as proactive as she can be.

With these insights, Melissa understood that she could explore roles at TOMS that align with her attributes, such as a *buyer, designer, brand ambassador,* or *partnership builder.* That way she is already set up to develop her full set of attributes and prepared to work on

Step 4: Enhancing Your Skills.

Scenario 2: I Have Ideas About My Attributes But Don't Know What My Game Is

If you're in the process of discovering your game and what you want to do, but you've already identified many of your attributes and talents, your goal is to find roles that harness these attributes, make you stronger, and expose you to more life experiences to see what you become passionate about.

For instance, say you have identified strong communication skills, creativity, and a penchant for storytelling. While you may not have a specific game in mind yet, these attributes can guide you toward roles where such talents are invaluable. You might gravitate toward fields like journalism, content creation, or education, where your ability to communicate effectively and engage an audience can be a significant asset. As a journalist or content creator, you might stumble upon social issues or recognize achievements in life that inspire you. That's when you can realign your newly developed expertise to contribute to the new game you found.

Suppose your attributes point toward bringing entertaining yet educational content to the world. In that case, roles such as a documentary filmmaker, educational game developer, or children's book author become relevant. These roles leverage your creative storytelling and communication skills to educate and entertain simultaneously.

Remember, your game doesn't always have to be a grand, lifelong mission; it can start as a small project with a role that aligns with your current talents and grows with you. As you explore your roles, your interests might solidify into a more defined game. The beauty of the Role Sphere model within 10K HP is its flexibility to accommodate and grow with your evolving understanding of your

Aspiration Layer on one end and your Specialization Layer on the other.

Scenario 3: I Don't Know What My Game or My Attributes Are

When you find yourself uncertain about both your game and your attributes, a practical approach is to seek out and emulate role models. This strategy can provide clarity and direction as you navigate your 10K HP journey. Role models serve as living examples of the game, attributes, roles, and even skills you might aspire to, offering a tangible representation of potential paths you could explore.

Take the case of SpaceX President Gwynne Shotwell, who during high school didn't have any career aspirations but focused on getting good grades, being a cheerleader, and playing basketball. Then her artist mother pushed her to begrudgingly attend a Society of Women Engineers conference. At one point Shotwell attended a panel discussion during which she was attracted to the mechanical engineer panelist because she had "a beautiful suit, fabulous shoes." This immediately made Shotwell decide that she wanted to be like that fashionable mechanical engineer.

Because of this role model, Shotwell applied to Northwestern University, which offered a strong mechanical engineering program, and started building up her specialization role. This eventually led to her occupation role of working at automotive and eventually aerospace companies. Note that this decision was made before she knew her life game and before she understood her attributes. She did it simply because it was the occupation role of a woman who inspired her.

This decision ultimately positioned her as a top industry leader in one of the most impactful engineering firms in the world, approaching $1 billion in net worth[3] and listed as one of the 100

Most Influential People in *Time* magazine, making her an OP Hero too.

As you can see, having role models and mentors are extremely impactful in anyone's 10K HP journey. I will return to this theme as we explore other steps, especially Step 5: Build Your Alliance and Step 6: Achieve Your Quests.

It's Your Turn to Play: Creating Your Role Sphere

Now that we have covered the variety of roles within our Role Sphere, it's time for you to explore what your roles are and how they connect to your game and attributes.

Pick from One of the Three Game Modes

Easy: Define your Role Sphere by breaking it into its four layers: Aspirations, Identity, Occupation, and Specialization. Write three sentences for each layer to map out your current and future roles. This exercise will help clarify the path ahead.

Medium: Reflect on your current roles and how well they align with your attributes and aspirations. Ask yourself: Do your current roles tap into your natural strengths, or do they unintentionally suppress them? If they do not maximize your unique attributes and skills, what roles should you be playing instead - ones that would bring you closer to your life game's finish line?

Hard: Share the Role Sphere framework with 3 trusted family members or friends and have a deep, meaningful conversation. Explain the concept and share your Role Sphere with them. Ask for their perspective: What do they think about the roles you're currently playing? Which roles do they see as a natural fit for you?

Turn the conversation around and ask about their Role Sphere. Who do they aspire to become, and what roles do they currently play? Use this feedback to refine your Role Sphere and identify the allies who can help you transition into future roles.

To make this exercise even more structured, visit 10KHP.com/worksheets for practice worksheets and tools to guide you through this process.

Role Advancements and Transfers

As you master your roles in your 10K HP journey, your ambitions will grow, and you naturally will expand into new ones. Initially, being proficient in just one role is sufficient for success. Don't be daunted by some of the OP Player examples showcased; those role models have simply been engaged in their games for longer. Their trajectory, too, is within your reach as you evolve into a high-level endgame player.

In the old classic Taiwanese term-based strategy game, *Flame Dragon II*, characters start off with basic classes like "Swordsman," "Warrior," or "Archer." With significant leveling up, these characters can advance to become "Swordmaster," "Holy Warrior," or "Magic Archer." Life mirrors this progression; we continually advance our roles, evolving from students to interns, to analysts, and beyond. The previous chapters illustrated this – how OP Hero Gandhi advanced from a barrister to an activist lawyer, and finally to a Strategy Sage. Walt Disney evolved from a comedic entertainer to an enchantment storyteller, and ultimately to an Industrious Storyteller. Our lives, too, should be marked by many such *role advancements*.

When it comes to games, the most adept players often meticulously plan their character's role advancements from the outset, often studying guides and optimizing strategies on spreadsheets. Similarly, astute 10K HP Players like you should thoughtfully plan how you will advance and evolve your roles through a defined trajectory based on your attributes, skills, and quests.

In certain games, advancing to higher-level classes involves mastering more than one lower-level class. For example, in *Dragon Warrior VII* characters start with basic classes such as cleric, fighter, thief, or mariner. Upon mastering the skills of two such classes, they can upgrade to an intermediate class. For instance, a character who masters both cleric and fighter skills can become a *Paladin*, whereas a character who masters both thief and mariner skills can become a *Pirate*.

This concept applies to life as well. Often, mastering two or more disciplines can lead to the creation of a unique role. For instance, combining proficiency in game design, business operations, psychology, and systems thinking led to my role as a gamification designer.

Another great example is Daniel Levitin, whom I first mentioned in this book's Introduction. Levitin mastered both music and neuroscience, becoming a leading authority on how music affects the brain. When you merge multiple disciplines to form your unique specialty, you carve out a powerful field of play for yourself.

Then, there are individuals who decide to change their career trajectory completely – what we call a *role transfer*. This involves switching career circle zones (see Figure 15) and embarking on a completely different path. This can be tangibly risky but also immensely rewarding. These role transfers are often about moving to the Adventure Zone, where people don't yet have skills for the new role. Such transformations often make you feel truly alive, especially when done for the right reasons.

Imagine a professional who has spent years in the technology sector, excelling as a software developer (their initial role). However, they discover a passion for environmental activism. This realization leads them to a role transformation, from technology expert to environmental advocate. This change can be risky, involving stepping away from a familiar domain into a new field. But the rewards can be substantial – personal fulfillment, a sense of purpose, and potential impact in a whole new arena. As mentioned earlier, it would still be optimal and, therefore, recommended if this environmental advocate utilized their previous specialization to advance their new role. In this case, the individual could transform into an *environmental technologist*, advancing environmental activism through better technological methodologies.

Of course, sometimes a role transfer is done for opposite reasons, such as someone putting their dreams aside for more financial stability in the Expert Zone due to added responsibilities in their own lives. This is fine, too, but as a 10K HP Player, one should always have an action plan to achieve 10K HP alignment by synergizing their game, attributes, role, skills, alliances, and quests. As long as you continue to make plans and tangible progress toward 10K HP alignment, you could one day reach it and start to live life in OP Mode. But if you give up and start to operate in passive mode, then you will likely live the rest of your life as an NPC.

Role Transformation Journey of OP Player: Joris Beerda

In the 1990s, Joris Beerda was a graduate student of international relations and economics at the University of Amsterdam. Recognizing the extensive wars and destructive forces in the world, he decided that his game was to help improve the lives of those affected by conflict and devastation. To understand both sides of the conflict in the Middle East, he studied both in programs within the West Bank, administered by the Palestinian Ministry of Education and Higher Education, and in Israel. While those who were simply on one side of the conflict saw this as a treacherous outrage, this gave him unique knowledge and skills (Step 4) to develop his specialization role and play his game properly. Upon obtaining his master's degree, he joined the Ministry of Foreign Affairs of The Netherlands to continue fulfilling his mission as a diplomat.

At this point in his journey, Joris already had a good understanding of his Role Sphere. His aspiration role was to help create stability and restoration within war-torn areas. His identity role was that of a Dutch man who continuously learns, is not afraid to take risks, acts on what he believes is right in the world, strives to make the biggest positive impact, and speaks his mind even if it is confrontational. His occupational role was that of a Dutch diplomat, and his specialization role was in economic and political relations, given his degree from a top 15 school in Europe.

While most diplomats seek stability and predictability, his unique aspirational and identity roles motivated him to venture into areas with the most conflicts so he could create a bigger impact. As a result, he enlisted himself in many dangerous zones. Based on United Nations mandates, he tackled the quest (Step 6) of building the first rebel-government soldier reintegration camp in the Africa Great Lakes region, notably in the Republic of Burundi. He also created innovative training and virtual engagement approaches with rebel groups, government soldiers, public-private partnerships, and refugees in Asia. In one of his engagements in Bangladesh, he was literally surrounded by mountain rebels pointing guns, bombs, and spears at him. His "assignment" was to convince these rebels to drop their weapons and join the opposing military, which had been mutually killing their colleagues and brothers just a few days prior, as a conclusion to the civil war.[4]

During the Afghanistan War that started in 2001, true to his game, Joris rushed into Afghanistan to help with the rebuilding efforts. He developed many new skills in persuasion, training, virtual work, and behavioral-driven strategies. He also authored and coached the virtual training missions for the NATO mission in Afghanistan (the ISAF - International Security Assistance Force). By completing all these quests (Step 6), he was given the rank of Lt. Colonel at a young age and appointed to create the first civil-military simulation for NATO/ISAF general staff at the Ramstein Air Base, headquarters for the U.S. Air Forces in Europe.

At the pinnacle of Joris' game, the Ministry of Foreign Affairs of The Netherlands received a personal letter from Ashraf Ghani, then Afghanistan's finance minister and, later, its president, requesting that Joris not be assigned to other posts but stay in Afghanistan to continue leading foreign donor efforts in raising $2 billion to rebuild the country.

At this point, Joris had accomplished multiple role advancements and earned the occupation role of Deputy Representative (second in charge of representing The Netherlands in Afghanistan) as well as Head of Development Cooperation. His specialization role had evolved to include post-conflict reconstruction, civil-military co-operation, virtual work and training, HR innovation, bureaucracy streamlining, and human behavioral design. If anyone in all of NATO needed to fill a role with those specialties, Joris would be the guy.

However, in 2004, even with his specialization in streamlining bureaucracy and the enormous success he had as a young diplomat, he felt things were moving too slowly in the government sector. He was no longer learning as much and felt that most of his efforts were spent on writing reports instead of doing fieldwork.

Consistent with his identity role, he still wanted to continuously learn and take risks in his life. As a result, he evolved his aspiration role to tackle a new game: to create a significant impact in the private sector as a business leader. With this new aspiration role, his first major quest was to leave his job as a diplomat and join the "Big 4" accounting firm PwC, as a Senior Manager of Advisory Services. Consequently, he made the brave move of doing a role transfer from his previous OP Zone to the Adventure Zone, where it aligned with his new game and attributes, but he didn't necessarily have experience or skills in that particular line of work.

At PwC, Joris continued to harness his specialties in creative persuasion, relationship building, and high-stakes negotiations, achieving remarkable success. He single-handedly closed two major deals totaling $14 million within two years, utilizing his contacts and personally negotiating the contracts to the finish line. Expecting this to greatly elevate his position in the company, now that he had proven himself in this new role, PwC only extended him a low five-digit bonus. Feeling a bit disappointed, Joris' candid identity role enabled him to directly ask the firm's partners, "I understand that I am still relatively new here, so my reward is proportionally small. What should I accomplish to prove myself and one day become a partner like you?" The response was that he needed to work there for at least twelve years to achieve such a role advancement.

Feeling that the company undervalued his contributions and specialty, and further driven by his identity role, Joris decided to seek out work environments built on meritocracy — where significant contributions to a company's success would be rewarded proportionally, regardless of tenure. He realized that the game he truly wanted to play was to "become successful in the business world in a fair and equitable manner."

Consequently, despite his early success at PwC, Joris opted for another role transfer, leaving PwC to become a professional recruiter. He was attracted to the recruitment industry because it operated on a system that he thought was fair: as long as he could effectively assist companies in finding exceptional talent and help individuals secure their dream jobs, he would be rewarded in proportion to the results he delivered. This system mirrored the mechanics of video games, where performance and results are valued more than a person's background or seniority.

Venturing into this entirely new industry again placed Joris back into the Adventure Zone within his career circles. However, his identity role of constant learning, combined with his specialization role in creative persuasion, relationship building, negotiation, behavioral design, and even HR innovation, enabled him to excel in this new environment. Within just a few years, he was able to make seven figures and had actually beat his game of becoming successful in business through a fair and equitable manner.

However, Joris again realized that he wasn't truly happy. Despite his considerable success in this third major occupational role within his 10K HP journey, he found that he wasn't intrinsically enjoying the nature of his work. His day-to-day tasks, though involving brokering win-win scenarios between companies and individuals, lacked the purposeful excitement and intellectual stimulation he craved.

Consequently, Joris decided to modify his game once more, aspiring to create positive impact in the world through activities that were intrinsically interesting to him. This game change meant that Joris' new aspiration role no longer aligned with his occupational role, and that he shifted from the OP Zone in his career circles to the Expert Zone, where he had alignment with talents and skills but not his game.

Driven by his Identity role of continuous learning and risk-taking (pay attention to how strongly his identity role continuously affected his life journey and choices), Joris decided that he preferred to be in the Adventure Zone again, rather than staying in his comfortable Expert Zone. He pressed the pause button on his recruiter quests and semi-retired to Bali, Indonesia, where he surfed every day for many months and took the time to explore his next significant role transformation.

During his time in Bali, Joris' aspiration, identity, and specialization roles were clear and consistent, yet he needed to find an occupational role that aligned with all of them. To understand what he was intrinsically motivated by, he listed all the nonfiction books he had enjoyed throughout his life and looked for common themes. He discovered that they all pertained to applying human psychology and behavioral science to solve problems. Reflecting on his past experiences, he knew he didn't want to pursue academia. So, he wondered, what was the best occupation that would utilize those specific specialties while creating significant business value?

Then it hit him, "Aha! If I could make business activities engaging, even fun, for employees and customers, that would be everything I was looking for!" Through his own 10K HP exploration, Joris had discovered the field of *gamification.* He then conducted some research and saw that I was consistently recognized as one of the top two or three gamification experts in the world (as my aspiration, identity, occupation, and specialization roles were all aligned).

Furthermore, he was extremely impressed by the Octalysis Framework that I conceptualized due to my unique attributes, as it tied together every piece of behavioral knowledge he had acquired over the years into an elegant and actionable tool. So, in 2014, Joris decided to reach out to me via my website, yukaichou.com.

A Legendary Alliance

When Joris initially contacted me, I was in my late 20s and he was in his early 40s. Besides the age difference, Joris had way more life experiences and wins under his belt than I did, as he had actually made big differences in conflict zones and survived multiple life-threatening scenarios. But because his identity role was a "Dutch man who continuously learns, who is not afraid to take risks, who acts on what he believes is right in the world," he came to me in a very modest position. He offered to *work for me full-time, without pay, for an entire year*, just so he could learn from me.

He wrote, "I will help you with whatever needs to be done (your website; preparing your programs abroad; input on your presentations; helping with business development). I am happy to do this for free for a while. If I prove myself in delivering top-notch work, I would like us to talk on how I could represent you at engagements where you cannot be due to time constraints." In other words, when he decided to undergo a role transfer to gamification consultant, Joris didn't simply attend a few workshops and then present himself to the world as an established gamification expert. He instead assumed the role of apprentice, virtually a full-time unpaid intern, with the hope of achieving *role advancements* to more impactful positions in the future. To this day, I find this decision astounding, and it greatly explains why Joris has achieved such great success, regardless of the game he plays.

During that period, there were also many others who reached out to me on a regular basis, hoping to work with or for me in some capacity. But, understandably, no one offered anything close to what Joris did. So I decided to try out this ally (Step 5) to see how it would go. During the initial phases, I just dumped a lot of work onto Joris and told him to join me in my virtual client meetings, which often occurred at 3 am to 4 am for his Bali time zone. Joris took my abuse like a champ and applied his specialization role (an accumulation of Step 2: Know Your Attributes and Step 4: Enhance Your Skills) to excel at everything he was tasked to do.

After a year of this apprenticeship, I felt very good working with Joris, so I decided to turn this ally into a *partner.* We created a new company together, called The Octalysis Group. Through this partnership, Joris accomplished a role advancement in his gamification game and became Managing Director, where he took the lead on creating significant business value for companies like Lego, Microsoft, Salesforce, and Porsche as well as funded startups in all sorts of industries and regions. Eventually, he unlocked the highest role advancement by becoming the CEO of The Octalysis Group. In this role, he oversees all of the company's business activities, while I focus on designing for clients and other creative projects, such as writing this book.

Joris now has full alignment within his Role Sphere. His occupational role is the top executive for one of the most prestigious gamification design consultancies in the world. He is obtaining more financial success than his days as a recruiter. Most importantly, he is enjoying the work he is doing and loving his life. Effectively, he is living his 10,000 Hours of Play.

As you can see in Joris Beerda's 10K HP journey, he maintained a consistent identity role since his graduate school days. He evolved his aspiration role as he gained a deeper understanding of what the world could offer him, and he continuously refined his specialization role, applying his attributes and skills across the various industries he played in. He underwent several significant occupational role transfers to ensure that his work aligned with his game (aspiration role), his values (identity role), and his abilities (specialization role). Finally, in his 40s, he achieved 10K HP alignment by playing the right game, harnessing the right attributes, assuming the right roles, acquiring the right skills, connecting with the right allies (including me), and undertaking the right quests. As a result, he continues to live life in OP Mode, making a meaningful impact, enjoying remarkable success, and relishing every step of the journey. To this day, Joris stands as one of my closest allies and best friends in our game of life.

I hope Joris' story encourages you to realize that no matter how deeply entrenched you are in an industry or how substantial the sunk costs you've accumulated, it's rarely too late to achieve success and fulfillment through role transfers. You can improve your game by strategically transferring to an occupation that aligns more closely with your true self, representing your entire Role Sphere. This holds true even if it means undergoing multiple transfers before discovering your true role, with each transition being an improvement over the last.

These transitions should be well-considered and strategic, not based on mere wishful thinking or whims. It's crucial to carefully apply your attributes and skills when determining your new role. Notice how in each new role Joris undertook, he effectively applied the attributes and skills that he'd previously acquired to adapt to his new environment. We will explore how to effectively do this in the next chapter on Step 4: Enhance Your Skills.

Choosing a Hero Name

In 10,000 Hours of Play, if you aspire to elevate your journey to even more "gameful" and fantastical realms, you can explore beyond the roles you assume in your professional and societal contexts. You can do this by adopting your very own *hero name* based on your Aspiration Layer – a transformative identity that propels you beyond the everyday boundaries of life.

Steve Kamb, in his book *Level Up Your Life*, discusses the concept of adopting an alter ego to break away from routine and embark on adventures. His alter ego, "Rebel One," reflects his aspiration to be a pioneering leader, guiding his gamified health guild, the Nerd Fitness Rebellion, toward a lifestyle of health and wellness. This hero name imbues him with a sense of being a pioneer, inspiring action as a trailblazer among his guildmates.

In a similar vein, Dr. Jane McGonigal introduces the concept of a "secret identity" in her book *Reality Is Broken*. This idea hinges on the belief that embodying a character with desirable traits can bolster personal resilience, confront challenges, and encourage growth. For instance, faced with a debilitating concussion leading to depressive thoughts, McGonigal assumed the secret identity of "Jane the Concussion Slayer." This persona instilled in her additional strength, hope, and enthusiasm, aiding her in overcoming her challenges and progressing toward a full recovery.

In the context of 10,000 Hours of Play, I believe the terms "alter ego" and "secret identity" are akin to Peter Parker's transformation into Spider-Man, where he works as a reporter most of the day but becomes a crime-fighting neighborhood protector when his true identity is needed. These terms indicate that our day-to-day identities are merely facets of ourselves, handling the mundane, while our alter egos or secret identities tackle life's grand, adventurous aspects.

At the same time, I believe that your hero role shouldn't be an external guise or a concealed persona, but rather the truest expression of your inner self. This is epitomized by the iconic superhero Superman. Unlike Peter Parker's Spider-Man or Bruce Wayne's Batman, Superman's real identity is his superhero form, Kal-El from Krypton. For Superman, his day-to-day identity as the glasses-wearing reporter Clark Kent is, in fact, his costume to conceal his true identity and powers.

In your 10K HP journey, discovering and embracing your hero role means acknowledging and embodying the extraordinary elements of your identity. It empowers 10K HP Players to cast off the metaphorical "costume" of societal norms and routine, unveiling their authentic, powerful self. As long as you identify your true role in life based on your game (Step 1), attributes (Step 2), skills (Step 4), and quests (Step 6), your jobs and daily activities aren't mundane tasks to escape from. They transform into the epic adventures that comprise your Hero's Journey. Your hero role isn't an escape from reality; it's the purest manifestation of your identity.

Crafting Your Hero Name

When you decide on your hero name, it should resonate with your values, fuel your motivation to overcome challenges, and serve as a constant reminder of your extraordinary path.

Your hero name should be a source of excitement and empowerment, symbolizing your ultimate potential and dreams. To find it, reflect on uplifting words, admirable characters, or qualities you strive for. Creatively merge these to form a name that feels authentically yours, embodying your commitment and purpose on this journey.

Start by considering the traits, values, or goals that define your hero role. Are you a *pathfinder* venturing into unknown realms; a *visionary* shaping a brighter future; or perhaps a *guardian*, protecting and nurturing your community? Select an archetype that aligns with your aspirations and strengths.

Next, draw inspiration from historical icons, leaders, or trailblazers. For those inspired by innovation, consider someone like Nikola Tesla, a symbol of ingenuity in electricity and engineering. If transformation and growth resonate more, perhaps Helen Keller, a figure of overcoming adversity and inspiring change, is more fitting. For missions of nurture or healing, look to individuals like Florence Nightingale, who redefined modern nursing with compassion and care.

Reflect on the qualities of these figures – their resilience, creativity, and dedication. Merge aspects of your journey with the attributes of these inspiring individuals to create your unique hero name. If your path involves innovation and leading change, a hero name such as Innovator Pathfinder or Visionary Guardian might emerge. This fusion forms a multidimensional identity, echoing your journey on different levels.

For instance, in my consulting company, The Octalysis Group, hero names of my guildmates include: Wisdom Harmonizer, Psychology Guardian, Dynamic Visualizer, Innovation Dragonlord, Cyberspace Craftsman, and more. As you can see, they often reflect one or more of the four layers of the guildmate's Role Sphere: aspiration, identity, occupation, and specialization.

For myself, because my Step 2 attributes suggest that I am good at creating visual models, pattern recognition, associative thinking, and empathetic intelligence, I realized I am skilled at constructing systems relating to human beings. As a result, I adopted the hero name Human-Systems Architect. This means my role in the game I play is to constantly create new systems that empower humans to mobilize toward a greater objective. This is not only a role that inspires me but also one in which I have found much success.

However, I also aspire to incorporate my spirituality and faith into everything I do. So, as an aspiration role, I want to evolve my hero name into The Spiritual Architect. This means that I receive inspiration from the spiritual realm above me and channel that inspiration with my hands to create systems that benefit society. Depending on your beliefs, you might not resonate with the spiritual angle as I do, but as you can see, when you decide on your own hero name, it's whatever name floats your ark.

Know Your Hero Code

Once you have determined your hero name, it's time to establish your *hero code*. After all, you don't just adopt these names to sound cool and feel good about yourself. Everything you do in your 10K HP journey should lead to actionable improvements toward beating your game.

Your hero code is a set of guiding principles and values that define how you approach your life and your role. It acts as a moral compass, ensuring that your actions are aligned with your true self and your ultimate goals. Here's how to create your hero code:

1. Reflect on Core Values (Identity Role): Start by identifying the core values that resonate most with you. These might include integrity, courage, compassion, innovation, or perseverance. Think about the principles that have guided you in the past and those you aspire to embody in the future.

2. Define Your Mission (Game): Your hero code should clearly articulate your mission. What are you striving to achieve in your hero role? This could be a commitment to helping others, advancing a particular field, or making a positive impact on the world. Be specific about your objectives and the change you wish to see.

3. Establish Non-Negotiables: Determine the non-negotiable standards that you will uphold, no matter what. These are the lines you will not cross and the compromises you will not make. Non-negotiables might include honesty in all dealings, never giving up on a challenge, or always putting family first.

4. Identify Daily Practices: Outline the daily practices that will keep you aligned with your hero code. These could be habits, routines, or rituals that reinforce your values and mission. Examples might include setting aside time for reflection, continuous learning, or volunteering regularly.

5. Create Accountability Measures: To ensure you stay true to your hero code, establish ways to hold yourself accountable. This could involve setting measurable goals, seeking feedback from trusted allies, or keeping a journal to track your progress. Accountability may sometimes feel less fun, but without accountable progress, you risk abandoning your hero role due to a lack of true results.

Example Hero Code: The Human-Systems Architect

As usual, it's easier to learn through examples. Since you are now familiar with my game, attributes, and role, here is an example of my own hero code as a Human-Systems Architect.

1. Core Values

- Integrity: Always do what I believe is right for the benefit of society.

- Compassion: Approach people and situations with empathy and kindness.
- Innovation: Continuously seek creative solutions and improvements instead of being content with the status quo.
- Perseverance: Do not easily give up, even in the face of adversity. Only quit when the mission is no longer worth pursuing or a greater mission takes priority.

2. Mission

- To create systems that empower individuals and communities, fostering growth and positive change in society.

3. Non-Negotiables

- Never compromise on ethical standards.
- Avoid actions that make me like or respect myself less.
- Prioritize the well-being of people in system designs.
- Commit to lifelong learning and self-improvement.

4. Daily Practices

- Practice gratitude and prayer every morning.
- Spend an hour each day reading or learning about new developments in human behavior and systems thinking.
- Exercise daily to improve physical and mental output.
- Dedicate time each day to creating or inventing something new.
- Do something fun each day and learn from the experience.

5. Accountability Measures

- Design SMART quests: Specific, Measurable, Achievable, Relevant, Time-bound.

- Set monthly goals and review progress toward minor and major quests.
- Publish these minor and major quests within my Octalysis Prime community for OP members to provide emotional support, encouragement, and accountability.
- Seek feedback and accountability from my wife and other allies to stay aligned with my hero code.

By establishing your hero code, you create a clear framework for how you will live out your hero name and achieve your aspirations. It ensures that every step of your 10K HP journey is purposeful, consistent, and aligned with your deepest values.

Once you know your Role Sphere, hero roles, and hero code, you will be ready to explore the skills (Step 4) needed to become the strongest player within that role on the Earth Server.

It's Your Turn to Play: Your Hero Name and Hero Code

It's time to explore what your own Hero Name is. Once you find a Hero Name you resonate well with, you can then define your new Hero Code.

Pick from One of the Three Game Modes

Easy: Brainstorm and decide on your Hero Name — a name that embodies your values, aspirations, and strengths. Ask yourself: What traits or archetypes inspire me? Draw inspiration from uplifting words, historical icons, fictional heroes, or role models you admire. Write down your Hero Name and reflect on why it resonates with your journey.

Medium: Create the foundations of your Hero Code by identifying your guiding principles. Write down three to five Core Values that represent your moral compass (e.g., Integrity, Courage, or Compassion). Define your Mission: What is the ultimate purpose of your game? How do you want to make an impact? Establish three to five Non-Negotiable. What are the lines you will never cross, no matter what. This exercise will help you clarify the principles that guide your actions as you pursue your life game.

Hard: Develop a full Hero Code and actionable strategy to embody it daily: Identify daily practices — habits or routines that align with your Hero Code. Design Accountability Measures to ensure you stay aligned: Set measurable goals. Share your Hero Code with trusted allies who can hold you accountable. Keep a journal to track your progress and reflect on how well you're living up to your code. When you share your Hero Name and Hero Code with two to three friends or mentors, ask them for feedback and discuss how they see you living up to your hero ideals.

To make this exercise even more structured, visit 10KHP.com/worksheets for practice worksheets and tools to guide you through this process.

OP Hero Profile: From Underprivileged Minority to Global Media Queen – the Inspirational Mogul

For an OP Hero representing Step 3: Select Your Role, journey back to 1954, to a modest home in Mississippi, where a young black girl with big dreams was born into poverty. From her earliest days, she thrived in the spotlight, dreaming of becoming a remarkable performer like her idol, the legendary Diana Ross. She admired Ross deeply, captivated by her melodious voice, commanding stage presence, and unyielding spirit.

The allure of Diana Ross extended beyond her exceptional talent; it was also found in her successful ascendance as a black woman in a society predominantly established by white men. Witnessing Ross' triumph against the odds inspired this girl to envision similar victories for herself. Through a role model, our young hero's aspiration role and identity role were developed.

Her childhood, however, was marred by severe hardships. Grappling with poverty, racial prejudice, and the trauma of sexual abuse, she found solace and empowerment in the realm of acting. She had a natural flair for it, and before long, her talents began to draw attention. This is when her attributes (Step 2) and skills (Step 4) helped her develop her specialization role as a performer in front of an audience.

During a visit to Hollywood's Walk of Fame, she found herself awestruck by the illustrious names etched into the ground. Each one represented a star in the firmament of celebrity, and right then she set a personal life game for herself (Step 1). She made a resolution: "I am going to place my own star among these stars." She yearned to join the pantheon of renowned celebrities and media personalities, thereby selecting her initial occupation role (Step 3) as an actress. Her chosen life game (Step 1) was to become a star – a media personality who would have a huge impact on the world.

Her distinctive attributes (Step 2) – inspirational charisma and empathetic intelligence – set her apart from the crowd. These qualities, critical for any successful actor, helped her achieve numerous quests and achievements (Step 6), notably securing first place at the Tennessee State Forensic Tournament and competing in the 1971 nationals at Stanford University in Palo Alto, California, where she ranked in the top five.

Throughout her school years, she skillfully harnessed her attributes to break barriers. At the tender age of sixteen she became the first black student to run for Vice President at East Nashville High School and prevailed against all odds. Her charisma was unmistakable, and the local community began to acknowledge her potential.

In addition to Diana Ross, she found another powerful female role model in Barbara Walters. A TV News Reporter for NBC's *The Today Show*, Walters was the first woman to successfully break into the male stronghold of news broadcasting and was recognized as a national and international figure in broadcast journalism. Walters' unique interviewing style, which gently nudged subjects to disclose more than intended, deeply influenced our hero.

Following in Walters' footsteps, our hero decided to transition her occupation role from actress to news reporter. She aspired to emulate the impact of trailblazers like Barbara Walters, aiming to make her mark as a young black woman in an industry lacking diverse representation.

To turn her aspirations into reality, she embarked on a series of ambitious quests (Step 6). Her journey began by hosting a radio show targeted toward black audiences. She then secured a high-paying role as a news reporter at WLAC-TV, making her television debut in Nashville at the young age of twenty. Her career continued to flourish with roles in Atlanta and Baltimore.

There, she achieved her goal of becoming an accomplished news reporter, earning a salary far beyond what her "starting zone" upbringing had prepared her for. She had finally made it. Just like Barbara Walters, she also succeeded in the TV industry.

Despite her rapid ascent, she hit a stumbling block when she encountered a *plot twist* event and was demoted from her role as a respected news reporter to the host of a morning chat show, *People Are Talking*. The demotion happened because the station managers saw her as unable to detach her emotions from her stories. This harsh reality brought her to tears as she pleaded with her boss to keep her position, but to no avail. As a young woman without the advantage of a prestigious university education, it felt as if all her sacrifices, the obstacles she had surmounted, and her relentless pursuit of recognition as a news reporter had been in vain.

As fate would have it, what initially appeared as one of the most heartbreaking setbacks became a launching pad for our OP Hero to achieve her 10K HP alignment. Her inherent attributes (Step 2), specifically her empathetic intelligence, energetic charisma, and investigative curiosity, resonated with the audience through the television screen. This magnetic pull resulted in an undeniable rapport with the viewers, leading to a significant upswing in her new show's popularity.

This plot twist event marked a significant shift in her role (Step 3). As she transitioned into the position of empathetic interviewer on *People Are Talking*, she experienced profound satisfaction. In stark contrast to the high-pressure environment of her previous reporting job, these interviews became a rewarding and liberating experience.

This once modest girl, who had begun her journey in an industry often lacking diverse representation, emerged as one of the world's most influential women. With her empathetic communication and insightful dialogues, she touched the lives of millions through her television presence. Today, she is universally recognized as the *Inspirational Mogul*, Oprah Winfrey.

Once Oprah had set her game (Step 1) to become a media star and began to excel in her role (Step 3) as an empathetic interviewer, it was time to cultivate her abilities (Step 4), build relationships with allies (Step 5), and embark on more quests (Step 6) to fully realize her dreams.

In her early years as a burgeoning talk-show star, Oprah frequently sought aid from one of her mentors (Step 5), Maya Angelou. Angelou was an influential figure in Oprah's life, consistently offering guidance, advice, and wisdom. She helped Oprah develop her empathetic interviewing and inspirational storytelling skills (Step 4). Among her teachings, Angelou would insist, "When people show you who they are, believe them."

Oprah took Angelou's counsel to heart, persistently refining her skills. As a result, her show's popularity skyrocketed, eventually paving the way for the launch of her very own program, *The Oprah Winfrey Show*, which premiered in September 1986.

Her difficult beginnings sharpened her skills in empathetic interviewing, charismatic presentation, inspirational storytelling, and more. Utilizing those skills strategically turned her into a beacon of inspiration who deeply connected with audiences from all walks of life.

After beating her initial game (Step 1) of becoming a star, Oprah, like most accomplished gamers, set her sights on her next game: leading, educating, uplifting, inspiring, and empowering women and children globally. With this new game, she transformed into her OP Hero role (Step 3): the Inspirational Mogul.

As an Inspirational Mogul, Oprah's quests (Step 6) extended beyond entertaining an audience as she did as an empathetic interviewer. Like the Industrious Storyteller Disney, she created her own guild named Harpo – a reverse spelling of Oprah – and began directing multiple organizations toward her goals of inspiration and philanthropy.

Harpo gave rise to numerous successful TV shows. Besides the household name *The Oprah Winfrey Show*, it produced other hits such as *Dr. Phil*, *Rachael Ray*, and *The Dr. Oz Show*, along with many Broadway productions. In partnership with Discovery, Inc., in 2011, Oprah launched the Oprah Winfrey Network (OWN), a channel filled with programs that inspired and entertained viewers, with Oprah taking the helm as CEO and Chief Creative Officer.

In the new millennium, Oprah teamed up with Hearst Communications to unveil *O, The Oprah Magazine*. This publication provided millions with advice on a wide range of topics, including health, relationships, fashion, and personal growth.

Her impact on literature also has been noteworthy. Oprah's Book Club has the power to catapult a book into best-seller status due to the extensive exposure she provides. There is even a term called the "Oprah effect," which means books or products become successful simply because Oprah featured them on her shows.

Initially inspired by Hollywood, Oprah has also acted in and produced several successful films, including *The Color Purple, Beloved*, and *Selma*. Her roles have received critical acclaim, earning her nominations for acting awards. Through the strong utilization of her attributes (Step 2), growth of her skills (Step 4), finding great mentors and allies (Step 5), and taking on impactful quests (Step 6), Oprah not only reached her goal of becoming an international star but in 2003 also became the first African American woman to become a self-made billionaire.

Alongside amassing great wealth, Oprah's philanthropic endeavors have made a substantial impact on the world. Through three key foundations – The Angel Network, The Oprah Winfrey Foundation, and The Oprah Winfrey Operating Foundation – she has funneled more than $400 million toward diverse causes. The Angel Network, which she actively promoted on her talk show, funded notable projects like the Oprah Winfrey Leadership Academy for Girls in South Africa and the rebuilding of the Gulf Coast after Hurricane Katrina, with Oprah assuring donors that every donated penny goes directly into these ventures. She operates The Oprah Winfrey Foundation independently, supporting it via an endowment, while The Oprah Winfrey Operating Foundation was created in 2007 specifically to finance the Leadership Academy for Girls in South Africa.

Oprah has made philanthropy integral to her persona and brand. In testament to her commitment, Oprah's will includes a generous bequest of $1 billion to various charities, establishing her as one of the twenty-first century's most notable philanthropists.[20]

OP Hero Oprah Winfrey: Takeaways

Oprah's journey illustrates a profound truth: great attributes in the wrong role or environment can actually become weaknesses. Her early career highlights that while her game and attributes remained consistent, it was her transformative and accidental change in role – the focus of this chapter – that set her on the path to becoming an OP Hero.

Her early-career role as a reporter did not resonate with her strongest attributes. Her energetic charisma was underutilized in the detached, fact-oriented world of news reporting. Just as an orca would flounder on dry land or an eagle would be confined in a cave, your unique abilities can be hindered if they are not aligned with your role. In the wrong environment, Oprah's empathetic intelligence sabotaged her own success.

Oprah was fortunate enough to accidentally discover her ideal role when she was involuntarily demoted. Of course, we don't want to wait around for other people to put us into our perfect roles.

Unlike Oprah, as a 10K HP Player you can purposefully and strategically *seek out* your ideal roles so that you do not need to leave anything to luck. You can achieve this by aligning your game (Step 1) and innate attributes (Step 2) with the role (Step 3) you aspire to play, eventually achieving 10K HP alignment. Like Oprah, you possess the potential to excel in a chosen role, charting your own path, enriching your life, and making a significant impact on the world around you.

---

[20]While Oprah's philanthropic endeavors are significant, it's important to note that in terms of sheer monetary contributions, many other *business moguls* have donated tens of billions of dollars, often without the spotlight or the goal of brand building. However, Oprah stands out not necessarily as the most philanthropic but as one of the most inspirational. Unlike many moguls, who are often perceived as stodgy businessmen or nerdy tech entrepreneurs, Oprah radiates a unique warmth and charisma that resonates with people. That's why on the 10K HP Earth Server leaderboard, we assign Oprah the OP Hero role of Inspirational Mogul rather than "Philanthropic Mogul."

You just have to find what that role is.

Chapter 4 Highlights

- Roles are powered by attributes. Select a role that aligns with your talents for fulfillment and effectiveness.
- Your Role Sphere consists of aspiration (who you want to become), identity (self-perception), occupation (your external role), and specialization (your expertise).
- Role-playing new identities aligned with your goals transforms your abilities and confidence, leading to greater success.
- Create identity pacts to create sustainable behavior changes. "I can't eat meat" should become "I don't eat meat."
- Explore your occupation and specialization roles with career circles.
- **The Trade Zone:** Skill-based roles lacking fulfillment.
- **The Expert Zone:** High success and mastery but may lack personal fulfillment.
- **The Passion Zone:** Fulfillment from playing your game, but hard to achieve mastery.
- **The OP Zone:** Full alignment with game and talents, leading to mastery and fulfillment.
- **The Adventure Zone:** Aligns with game and talents but requires skill development.
- Determine your 10K HP role by exploring careers in organizations aligned with your interests or by finding role models.
- Role advancements are natural promotions from your current role to the next one. Role transformations are complete shifts to another zone within the career circles.
- Establish your hero code to ensure your journey is purposeful and aligned with your true self.

- OP Hero Oprah Winfrey was demoted from a news reporter to a morning talk show host; this ended up being the perfect role for her attributes. She then thrived and became the billionaire Inspirational Mogul.

Chapter 5: Enhance Your Skills (Craft)

STEP 1 — Choose Your Game — MISSION
STEP 2 — Know Your Attributes — TALENTS
STEP 3 — Select Your Role — SPECIALTY
STEP 4 — Enhance Your Skills — CRAFT
STEP 5 — Build Your Alliance — NETWORK
STEP 6 — Achieve Your Quests — MILESTONES

"The secret of joy in work is contained in one word: excellence. To know how to do something well is to enjoy it."

—— Pearl S. Buck

When I played *Diablo II* many years ago, I took on the role of a barbarian. Each time I leveled-up, I gained a skill point to invest in my abilities. As my barbarian progressed, I had the option to allocate skill points to various "weapon masteries," such as blade mastery, mace mastery, and polearm mastery, among others. These investments made the corresponding weapons more powerful. As a novice, I distributed my skill points evenly across these masteries, sometimes favoring one category if I found a decent weapon for it.

However, I soon realized that my barbarian was handicapped because he could only wield one weapon at a time during combat. This meant he was only utilizing the skill points invested in that particular weapon mastery, leaving the points allocated to other masteries effectively wasted. As a result, my barbarian's combat effectiveness suffered, and he struggled to compete at higher levels.

With more experience, I learned that seasoned barbarian players often start a new character from level 1 and focus their skill points on mastering a single weapon type, such as *spear mastery*. They can then invest in synergistic skills like *iron skin* for physical damage mitigation, *natural resistance* for magical damage endurance, increased speed for mobility, and *leap* to jump to a new location with better tactical advantages. This strategic allocation of skill points ensured that all abilities supported each other, creating the most formidable *spear barbarian*. After that, the barbarian would do quests to find a powerful legendary spear, unlocking his full potential.

In the game of life, you too must enhance your skills and master your craft. And just like a *Diablo II* barbarian, this involves focusing on multiple synergistic skills to conquer your life game.

What Are Skills in 10K HP?

In 10K HP, skills are the abilities you acquire and refine throughout your life game, driving you forward in your quests. Take public speaking as an example. This craft, initially fraught with stumbles and nervousness, can be transformed into a powerful tool of influence and inspiration through practice, feedback, and perseverance.

Skills, unlike attributes (Step 2), are not innate. They require active learning and development through education, training, and diligent effort. For example, an online marketer is not innately equipped with knowledge in search engine optimization (SEO); this skill must be learned.

However, the effort required to master a skill does depend on your attributes. Enhancing your skill in conversion optimization, for instance, is greatly aided by possessing attributes like empathy and analytical thinking, which enable a deeper understanding of your audience through data analysis and emotional resonance.

In your 10K HP journey, developing skills is similar to how a character in a role-playing game acquires new abilities. Your skills may start basic but can reach higher levels of proficiency as you progress. This growth is rewarding and crucial for tackling increasingly complex quests.

Consider the journey of a musician mastering an instrument. Beyond learning notes and scales, she must grasp the subtleties of performance, develop a distinct style, and forge an emotional connection with her audience. Likewise, in your 10K HP journey, skill development is not solely about technical expertise but involves integrating a set of skills that enhances your specialty role.

As per 10K HP literature, the skills you cultivate should align with your game and augment your role. If your aspiration role is to become an innovative entrepreneur, your skills might include business acumen, digital marketing, and product development. Alongside that, if your identity role is deeply rooted in artistic expression, skills like digital design, storytelling, or creative writing might also be effective.

Prioritizing which skills to develop is crucial. Not all skills are of equal importance in your 10K HP journey. Some are fundamental to your mission, while others play a supporting role. Concentrating on skills that have a significant impact on your quests is vital for a triumphant 10K HP journey.

How Jacked Do You Want to Be?

When it comes to leveling up your abilities, should you aim to achieve world-class expertise in a single skill, or should you strive to develop as many skills as possible to become a jack of all trades? The ideal approach, of course, lies not in fixating on one extreme over the other, but rather in focusing on a few synergistic skills.

The Skill Spectrum

Figure 16. The Skill Spectrum

On the skill spectrum illustrated in Figure 16, you will see that veering too far to the left turns you into a specialist, an individual excelling within a very narrow scope. Consider chess as an example: you might be an absolute master of the King's Gambit opening. However, if your opponent avoids this opening, or you transition into middle game or endgame scenarios where your skills are weaker, you'll find yourself out of your depth and likely to lose.

Conversely, leaning too far to the right transforms you into a *dabbler*, someone who develops skills in various areas but never truly excels in any. Staying with the chess analogy, you might cultivate skills in openings, endgame, writing (to author a chess book), design (to create your chess logo), speaking (for book tours), negotiation (to secure better rates for chess tournaments), fashion (to present yourself well during games), among others. While these skills are undoubtedly synergistic if your role (Step 3) is to become a chess author or journalist, most are unrelated and distracting if your life game (Step 1) is to become the top chess master.

To conquer the game of chess, mastering a variety of synergistic skills is crucial. Magnus Carlsen, currently the world's leading chess player, has achieved his status by mastering skills in chess openings, positioning, pawn structures, endgames, exchange sacrifices, dark/light color plays, and others, far surpassing his peers.

Of course, Carlsen's formidable attributes (Step 2) such as concentration, memorization, pattern recognition, and mental endurance contribute significantly to his global supremacy in chess. He also routinely practices skills such as meditation to further enhance these attributes.

On the other hand, Emanuel Lasker, the second chess world champion in history and a professional psychologist, believed that an understanding of human psychology complemented his traditional chess skills. He was renowned for frequently opting for the second-best move instead of the best one – *if* he believed that his grandmaster opponents would find the resulting positions uncomfortable, leading them to play in a psychologically compromised state.

Equipped with his synergistic skills, Lasker maintained his status as world champion for an impressive twenty-eight years, from 1894 to 1921. Remarkably, he was still considered one of the top players in the world when he was sixty-seven years of age.

As you can see, there are many ways to "build" your character and learn various skills to become successful at what you do, depending on your creativity, interests, and other attributes.

Synergistic Skills

In the classic RPG *Final Fantasy VII*, players discover and earn *materia* (the main source of magic) to enhance the skills of their characters. For example, Fire materia allows players to cast fire spells on enemies to deal damage.

In addition, materia combos allow players to link two materia together to create a synergistic skill: link "Cure" with "All" ' and you heal all of your characters on the screen.

It was incredibly fun to collect materia and experiment with them to discover the best combination of synergistic skills. For example:

- Mug + Steal = deal damage while stealing items
- Magic Counter + Cure = heal when attacked
- Final Attack + Phoenix = revive everyone to maximum health upon death

In your life game, you too must discover and develop synergistic skills to beat your game objectives.

In many games, you can invest a limited amount of "skill points" into learning or enhancing various skills. Investing your skill points in one skill means you have fewer skill points to invest in other skills. In real life, be conscious of the opportunity cost of developing one skill over another. Every hour you are improving one skill means you are not improving another.

It's important to plan ahead so that your skills aren't wasted. It's not optimal to invest five years of dedicated learning to acquire a new language, when your life game only gets exposed to one language (this skill would then just be a costly "major side quest," which I expand upon in Chapter 8: Achieve Your Quests).[21]

By planning ahead, you can map what skills you'll most likely need to beat your game, improving your chances of obtaining and enhancing relevant and synergistic skills.

---

[21]Of course, if learning a new language is a fun hobby and you do it for quality-of-life purposes, you could definitely spend a lot of time on it. However, from the 10K HP angle, it would definitely slow down your progress toward actually beating your life game compared to others who didn't take on this major side quest. Those who focused on defeating world-ending villains would naturally stay ahead of those who spend a lot of time on side quests such as fishing or chasing after chickens.

How to Enhance Your Skills

In the realm of gaming, skill enhancement is often the difference between an average player and a champion. Similarly, in life, the continuous improvement of your skills can elevate you from being a participant to a leader in your chosen field. But how do you approach this complex process? How do you identify which skills to develop and the most effective methods to enhance them?

From mapping your current abilities to strategically planning their advancement, you'll explore proven techniques and innovative approaches to skill enhancement. You'll learn to recognize your unique capabilities, rank them effectively, and engage in targeted development that aligns with your life's mission and goals.

Remember, every skill you possess is a result of your dedication and experiences. Whether it's playing a musical instrument, coding software, leading a team, or communicating effectively, each skill you have today has its own story of how you obtained it, whether you remember it or not.

Following are four steps that will help you identify and hone in on the skills you must master to become the strongest role on the Earth Server.

Step 1: Map Your Current Skills

The first step is to create a map of your current skills. This exercise is about respecting and acknowledging the process and dedication it took to obtain them. To make the map, write down your chronological experiences through different phases in your life:

- Games you have mastered
- Networks you have built

- Clubs or organization to which you have contributed
- Books or blogs you have consumed
- Training and learnings that have enriched your knowledge
- Experience through work

Write or print out your meaningful experiences and start making notes about the skills you gained. Don't worry about being too broad or too specific; it's important to just write down your skills and only later rank and refine them.

Some examples of skills include debate, strategic planning, sprinting, brainstorming, programming, social media marketing, photoshop, plumbing, laughing wholeheartedly, meditation, interviewing, financial engineering, planning schedules, comforting others, carrying heavy objects, playing the piano, Spanish, gamification design, the Octalysis Framework, public speaking...you get the idea. Figure 17 depicts an example of my own journey map through my years at UCLA. The notable experiences and quests (Step 6) I had through my college years derived from a variety of attribute growth, skills acquisition, and ally formations. Eventually, you can add your skill growth throughout all your life sagas.

YU-KAI CHOU - UCLA SAGA (18-21)

Quest 1	Quest 2	Quest 3	Quest 4	Quest 5
Started eBay Business	History of Social Thought	Started FD Network	Joined DSP Business Fraternity	Started yukaichou.com Blog
+ Business Operations	+ Language	+ Networking	+ Professionalism	+ Writing
+ Confidence	+ Logic Tracing	+ Leadership	+ Guild	+ Language
	+ Critical Thinking	+ Startup Operations	+ Presentation	+ Branding
		+ Technology	+ Leadership	
			+ Visual Models	
		+ Ally (Jason)	+ Tenacity	
			+ Ally (Jun)	

Quest 6	Quest 7	Quest 8	Quest 9	Quest 10
Conceived FD World	Created FD Career	Co-Founded Bruin Consulting	Started Business Consulting Team	Attended Networking Framework Event
+ Startup Operations	+ Startup Operations	+ Professionalism	+ Business Operations	+ Confidence
+ Marketing	+ Game Thinking	+ Confidence	+ Visual Models	+ Visual Models
+ Branding	+ Marketing	+ Leadership	+ Leadership	
+ Leadership	+ Branding	+ Visual Models		
+ Creativity	+ Leadership	+ Guild		
+ Networking	+ Creativity			
	+ Networking			
+ Ally (Stephen)	+ Fundraising			
	+ Technology			

Figure 17. Yu-kai's Journey Map Through University

Figure 18 extends my journey map out further. You can see that over the years, I have had seventeen counts of improving my gamification design skills, fourteen for my leadership skills, and another fourteen for my presentation skills. By noting all the skills that are developed through a variety of sagas, arcs, major quests, and minor quests, you can get a great view of your top skills.

By the end of this chapter, if you happen to make some progress on your own journey map with the skills you have accumulated, keep this map close as you will develop it further in Step 6: Achieve Your Quests.

YU-KAI CHOU - SKILLS / ALLIANCE OBTAINED

Saga 1

South Africa

+ Emotional Strength
+ Empathy
+ Imagination
+ Perseverance
+ Pattern Recognition
+ Storytelling
+ Strategy

Saga 2

Taiwan

+ Strategy x3
+ Confidence x2
+ Emotional Strength
+ Game Design
+ Social Charisma
+ Social Dignity

+ **Ally (PH Chen)**
+ **Ally (Yi Chou)**

Saga 3

High School

+ Confidence x6
+ Abstract Visualization x3
+ Presentation x3
+ Craftsmanship x2
+ Language x2
+ Leadership x2
+ Stage Courage x2
+ Strategy x2
+ Tenacity x2
+ Adaptation
+ Creativity
+ Critical Thinking
+ Conviction
+ Drive
+ Empathy
+ Economic Thinking
+ Game Thinking
+ Imagination
+ Logic Tracing
+ Optimism
+ Persuasiveness
+ Responsibility
+ Storytelling
+ Vision

+ **Faction (Christians)**
+ **Ally (Todor Gogov)**
+ **Ally (Jason Kuo)**

Saga 4

UCLA

+ Leadership x4
+ Branding x3
+ Startup Operations x3
+ Marketing x2
+ Networking x3
+ Creativity x2
+ Technology x2
+ Business Operations
+ Confidence
+ Critical Thinking
+ Fundraising
+ Game Thinking
+ Language
+ Logic Tracing
+ Presentation
+ Professionalism
+ Tenacity
+ Writing
+ Visual Models

+ **Guild (Delta Sigma Pi)**
+ **Guild (Bruin Consulting)**
+ **Ally (Jun Loayza)**

Saga 5

Young Entrepreneur

+ Presentation x6
+ Fundraising x4
+ Leadership x3
+ Startup Operations x3
+ Persuasiveness x2
+ Technology x2
+ Tenacity x2
+ Behavioral Design x2
+ Branding
+ eCommerce
+ Empathetic Intelligence
+ Faith
+ Financial Projections
+ Game Thinking
+ Marketing
+ Networking
+ SEO
+ Social Media
+ Storytelling
+ Humor

+ **Ally (Stephen Johnson)**
+ **Ally (Angel)**

Saga 6

Gamification Expert

+ Pattern Recognition x4
+ Branding x3
+ Critical Thinking x2
+ Empathetic Intelligence x3
+ Creativity x3
+ Behavioral Design x2
+ Emotional Persuasiveness x2
+ Gamification Design x2
+ Visual Models x2
+ Business Operations
+ Economics Thinking
+ Game Design
+ Game Thinking
+ Leadership
+ Marketing
+ SEO
+ Storytelling

+ **Ally (Howie Ju)**

Saga 7

Octaysis Rising

+ Leadership x3
+ Gamification Design x3
+ Creativity x2
+ Faith x2
+ Empathetic Intelligence x2
+ Presentation x2
+ Behavioral Design
+ Business Operations
+ Corporation Operations
+ Critical Thinking
+ Emotional Persuasiveness
+ Imagination
+ Logic Tracing
+ Startup Operations
+ Storytelling
+ Technology
+ Tenacity

+ **Faction (Octalysis Kingdom)**
+ **Guild (Octalysis Prime)**
+ **Guild (The Octalysis Group)**
+ **Ally (Joris Beerda)**

Saga 8

10K HP

+ Leadership x2
+ Book Publishing x2
+ Emotional Persuasiveness
+ AI Usage
+ SEO
+ Social Media
+ Book Promotion

+ **Guild (10K HP Readers)**
+ **Ally (Mark Diaz)**

Figure 18. Yu-kai's Extended Journey Map

Step 2: Rank Your Skills

Now that you've listed your skills, it's time to rank them from strongest to weakest. You don't need to be completely precise, but it would be helpful to get close to reality, as you will use this information to make some growth decisions later on.

There are two main ways to rank your skills:

1. Compare them with one another.
2. Compare them to the similar skills of other people.

Compare Them With One Another

Comparing one skill to another can be a straightforward way to evaluate your abilities. For instance, before attending UCLA, my Chinese language skills were significantly stronger than those for my English. However, post-graduation from UCLA and after starting businesses in the United States, my proficiency in English eventually outpaced my Chinese. Similarly, I have devoted more time to learning and refining my chess skills than practicing the violin, making it relatively simple for me to discern that my chess abilities surpass my violin skills.

There are, however, instances where comparing skills becomes more complex, such as contrasting leadership skills with communication skills. These abilities are often developed passively through various activities; it's not as if one could say, "I spent three hours leading and then two hours communicating; therefore, I improved my leadership skills more."

To evaluate such skills, consider the following question: If I were to hire myself for a full-time position in an organization, for which skills would I employ myself? Would I hire myself as a violinist? Would I appoint myself to lead the organization? Would I engage myself to handle public communication?

It might be challenging to immediately pinpoint the answer, but it's often much easier to rule out certain skills. For example, I definitely wouldn't hire myself as a violinist or chess player, but I might consider myself for a teaching role due to the instructional skills I've cultivated over time.

Once you have an idea of the skills for which you'd hire yourself, or those you definitely wouldn't, you begin to understand which of your current skills are stronger than others.

Compare Them to Similar Skills of Other People

The best (and most rewarding) way to rank your skills is to compare them to those possessed by other people. Similar to evaluating your talents (Step 2), this is where you explore previous accomplishments, recognitions, and victories. Were you in a varsity sport in high school? Did you score well in a design competition? Were you making all of your friends look bad in karaoke? What skills do these achievements demonstrate? They might indicate you have talent in some attributes and, therefore, surpass others in the derivative skills. Make a note of that in your ranking process.

Remember, don't get stressed over the minute details of placing one skill greater than another. As long as these skills are in the right ballpark, your ranking will help you understand the skills you have obtained for later analysis on synergy and how it connects to your game. These orders change all the time anyway as we grow and learn more about ourselves.

Step 3: Create Your Skill Triangle

In Step 2: Know Your Attributes, you worked on your Talent Triangle by stack-ranking your top attributes to your generally strong ones. Once you have determined your skills and a rough hierarchy of which ones you excel at, it's time to create your own *Current Skill Triangle*, as shown in Figure 19. Similar to your Talent

Triangle, the Skill Triangle lists a few top skills at the top, strong ones in the middle, and comparably weaker but still competent skills at the bottom. Just like the Attributes Triangle, the top skill you have is called your *edge skill*, while your top five skills are your *ring skills*, and the rest are your *base skills*.

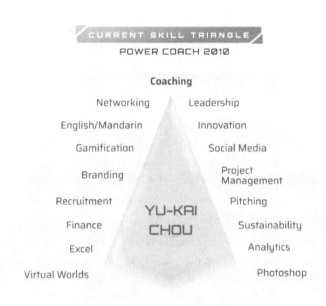

Figure 19. Yu-kai's Current Skill Triangle

The example shown in Figure 19 is my Skill Triangle from 2010. At the time, besides being an entrepreneur, I was heavily interested in becoming a "power coach," a role focused on helping others achieve success and become powerful in life. (Remember, one of my top three life goals in college was to make everyone around me successful?) During that period, I observed that my top three skills were coaching, networking, and leadership.

What do these skills have in common? They all deal with people and utilize my high empathetic intelligence, trustful sincerity, and optimism attributes. Often, our top skills are a build-up and utilization of our attributes, just like attributes such as running fast and jumping high can lead to high skills in various sports like basketball or volleyball.

At the time, I also felt that I had strong innovation abilities, based on my years of startup experience powered by my associative thinking attribute. Additionally, growing up in South Africa, Taiwan, and the United States gave me high proficiency in being bilingual in Chinese and English.

My years in startups also helped me understand gamification, social media, and branding better than most people I interacted with. Finally, there were some technical abilities that I picked up along the way, such as recruiting talent, sustainability knowledge (I was elected a "Top 50 Young Leaders of California" to attend Arnold Schwarzenegger's Governor Global Climate Summit), and other skills such as data analysis and Photoshop.

My life experiences have shaped these skills, but they don't necessarily align with my game or role. This particular Skill Triangle would be great if I wanted to be a one-on-one coach who gets business through networking and social media branding and uses gamification to make coaching more fun.

However, my game and role evolved into transforming people's lives at scale through an accessible and gamified platform (Octalysis Prime) and creating systems that would make the world a better place. Therefore, my skills from 2010 would not suffice for my game and role as a spiritual architect in 2024. I will discuss this further when I introduce the *Target Skill Triangle.*

Applying Synergizing Skills Together

Skills are not utilized in a vacuum. Combining *synergistic skills* and attributes can make you stand out and help you succeed in your game. For example, in 2012, I noticed there were many "gamification experts" with various levels of gamification design skills, just like I had. However, due to my startup experiences, I also had skills in branding and social media.

I therefore synergized my skills by having them support each other. I built a brand name under my unique methodology of gamification, called Octalysis, promoted it on social media, and drove millions of people to recognize my frameworks as high quality and actionable. From that, I secured many prominent public speaking engagements and clients like Microsoft, Uber, Lego, and Walgreens.

Many other gamification experts who didn't have these synergistic skills unfortunately couldn't grow in the same occupational role because they didn't attract as many inbound opportunities to support their livelihoods. As a result, many had to find other full-time employment that either underappreciated their expertise or disregarded it entirely. They were forced to be stuck in constant resource side quests until they acquired other synergistic skills, or until the game landscape changed in their favor.

Don't feel discouraged if someone at your work or in your class-room seemingly has stronger skills than you. If you train syner-gistic skills that complement your attributes, your capabilities will compound, and you'll become the strongest player in your unique role in this world.

Fast forward to 2024. My Current Skill Triangle as a gamification designer role now looks more like Figure 20.

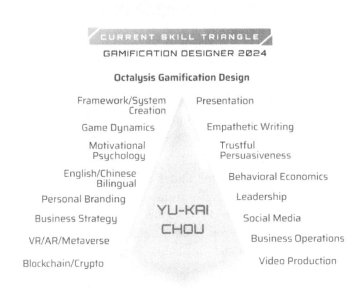

Figure 20. Yu-kai's Current Skill Triangle as a Gamification Designer in 2024

You can see that as a gamification designer my top skills now focus on being the strongest at Octalysis Gamification (which makes sense since I am the creator of that design methodology). Additionally, empathetic writing and presentation skills (both video and speech) also have become part of my ring skills. I need to present my ideas in compelling ways to truly transform the masses.

My Skill Triangle also includes some skills that are important for running my business, such as motivation psychology, business strategy, video production, personal branding, and finance. Additionally, I need to understand the latest technology trends, such as virtual reality and blockchain solutions, as many of my projects require the use of such technologies. So, those skills are listed as well.

Understanding your current Skill Triangle is key to seeing which quests (Step 6) you have the highest competency to tackle, what role transfers (Step 3) are possible paths forward, and which allies (Step 5) you need to complement your role while taking on those quests.

Step 4: Create Your Target Skill Triangle to Beat Your Game

In the previous chapters, you chose your game and selected your role. You also determined your current skills through the Skill Triangle. You'll now use these to identify the skills you need to develop. This is where the Target Skill Triangle comes in.

The Target Skill Triangle is a visual representation of what your top skills should be in order to become the strongest role in your game. To figure out your Target Skill Triangle, you must imagine a top master who has your role and determine what skills they are good at.

Occasionally, that person already exists, and you just have to closely study what skills they have mastered. If your role is to become a visionary product leader, you can look at Steve Jobs or Elon Musk and see that they have the key skills of persuasion, innovation, design, user experience, branding, marketing, leadership, and execution. Therefore, you can create a Target Skill Triangle that mimics that of Jobs and/or Musk.

In 2010, since I wanted to become a power coach, I studied unique skills from established coaches such as Bill Campbell and Tony Robbins. Based on their skills, I created my 2010 Target Skill Triangle, as shown in Figure 21.

In the chart, you can see that my goal was to have top skills in coaching, problem-solving, effective communication, and active listening. I also needed some business skills such as branding, networking, and negotiations. Once I had this Target Skill Triangle,

I could match it with my 2010 Current Skill Triangle for being a power coach and identify which skills I needed to hone. Based on that, I could design my next learning quest, whether it be reading a specialized book, taking a class, or volunteering for related projects.

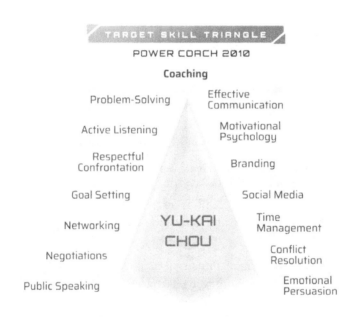

Figure 21. Yu-kai's Target Skill Triangle as a Power Coach in 2010

Of course, in 2024, my Target Skill Triangle would be different from fourteen years ago. Remember I mentioned that I aspire to become a spiritual architect? My Target Skill Triangle for that is depicted on Figure 22.

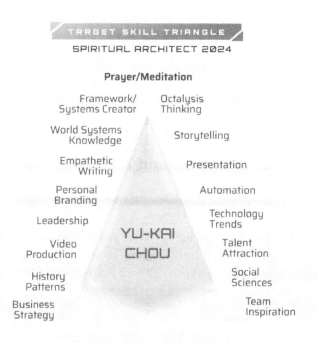

TARGET SKILL TRIANGLE

SPIRITUAL ARCHITECT 2024

Prayer/Meditation

Framework/ Systems Creator — Octalysis Thinking

World Systems Knowledge — Storytelling

Empathetic Writing — Presentation

Personal Branding — Automation

Leadership — Technology Trends

Video Production — Talent Attraction

History Patterns — Social Sciences

Business Strategy — Team Inspiration

YU-KAI CHOU

Figure 22. Yu-kai's Target Skill Triangle as a Spiritual Architect in 2024

In this new aspiration role, I aim to become top-notch at prayer and meditation (areas in which I am currently far from proficient), as well as in framework/systems creation. I have condensed many of my previous skills into something I call *Octalysis Thinking*, which is an aggregate of Octalysis Gamification, motivational psychology, behavioral economics, neurobiology, game design, applied psychology, and persuasive technology. While I would not be the top expert in most of these fields alone, I combine them in a unique way that forms my own system.

Beyond that, I still need to excel in abilities to improve thought-leadership, such as empathetic writing, presentation, and personal branding. Additionally, I want to understand world systems knowledge, technology trends, historical patterns, social sciences, and business strategy to integrate these into my framework/systems creation skill.

By harnessing these skills together, I will be able to create a variety of better human systems, alongside my *Nationcraft Framework*, *Silo-Busting Framework*, and the *Self-Pity Pyramid*.[22]

Comparing Current and Target Skill Triangles

Once you have identified your Target Skill Triangle, you can compare it to the Current Skill Triangle and start to plan the skills you need to acquire to improve your game. This is where quests (Step 6) come in. Quests tie everything in 10K HP together, focusing on the actions we take in life that will make the biggest impact on beating the game. More on that in Chapter 9.

For instance, if you decide that your Target Skill Triangle should be similar to mine as a gamification designer (perhaps you want to play a similar role in a similar game), you would first need to master Octalysis Gamification. This means reading up, practicing, and applying as much Octalysis Gamification knowledge as possible (Octalysis Prime then becomes an optimal major main quest to tackle).

You would also need to improve your empathetic writing and presentation skills. You could join your local Toastmasters to enhance your public speaking skills, study great video bloggers to learn their techniques, and find someone skilled in empathetic writing to help optimize your emails. Fortunately, the rise of AI and platforms like ChatGPT has made acquiring these skills much faster and easier.

The best craftsmen know how to use the best tools skillfully to get optimal results in any situation. Instead of complaining or being

---

[22] To find out more about these frameworks, go to my website: yukaichou.com/frameworks.

intimidated by AI, the most actionable step for any 10K HP Player is to quickly learn how to use AI effectively, as you would if you found a *legendary weapon* in a game.

Skills: I Still Have No Idea Where to Start

For some people, identifying their Target Skill Triangle is quite difficult, and the path to mastery is far beyond what they can currently imagine. Don't be intimidated. A simple way to get on the right path is to find job postings of similar roles to identify the skills they value. In this way, you can start small, and as you begin to master the game, you can eventually grow and upgrade both your Current and Target Skill Triangles.

Look Up Job Postings for Your Role

Let's say you want to play the role of a user experience (UX) designer. A simple online search might show that the following companies value the following skills for their UX designers:

Role: UX Designer

Airbnb:

- Excellent communication skills
- Lo-fi and hi-fi prototyping skills
- Strong collaborator with product managers and engineers
- Experience with shipping product
- Cross-platform design experiences (web, Android, iOS, e-mails)

Apple:

- Experience in delivering wireframes, UX flows, mockups, interactive prototypes, personas, and use-case development
- Ability and passion to understand distinct user groups quickly and distill complex needs into clean, understandable solutions
- Understanding of information architecture, design patterns, and interaction design
- Work as part of a cross-functional team with users, product owners, business analysts, and development teams to deliver business value
- Ability to work independently, managing schedules in a dynamic, multi-project environment
- Familiarity and ability to promote appropriate usability testing and user research endeavors
- Programs knowledge: Familiarity with design and prototyping software, such as Sketch, Adobe XD, Omnigraffle or equivalent
- Languages/Syntax: HTML, CSS, Javascript, React/Redux knowledge is desirable, but not required

From the above information, you can get a good idea of the skills required by multiple (ideally more than two) reputable companies. It is important to note that some of the requirements listed above are attributes ("work independently") instead of skills, and they cannot be acquired quickly through a class. Some are experiences, such as "have shipped product," which are not real skills but past endeavors/quests that have been accomplished.

Once you've identified at least two job postings, group the skills together to make them more actionable. I grouped the skills for a UX designer as follows:

- Prototyping (low fidelity and high fidelity), wireframes, mockups
- Cross-platform design skills

- Multi-department communications
- Consumer needs analysis, usability testing, and user research
- Information architecture
- Design patterns
- Interaction design
- Best-practice promotional skills
- Software: Sketch, Adobe XD, Omnigraffle
- Languages/Syntax: HTML, CSS, Javascript, React/Redux

But what is the right order of these skills if you want to create your Target Skill Triangle? Besides intuition and common sense for UX designers, the next step is to look up several more companies hiring such roles. After looking through a dozen, you will notice commonalities. The skills most frequently required are the ones you should target to develop first (and move to the top of your Target Skill Triangle).

Alternatively, let's say you have chosen the role of a "marketer." The following companies value the following skills for marketers:

Role: Marketer

Pete's Coffee:

- Project management experience working within a new product development process for food or beverages, including a familiarity navigating stage gate models
- Proven ability to drive results with a high degree of personal initiative and integrity in a fast paced, dynamic environment
- Strong ability to build and maintain highest-quality cross-functional partnerships
- Proven ability to successfully plan and manage projects with a close attention to detail and high level of organization
- Excellent problem-solving, communication, presentation, analytical, and process building skills

- Ability to self-motivate and motivate others to accomplish goals
- Bachelor's degree in marketing, philosophy, art history, biology, ethnomusicology, or related field of study; Master's degree is a plus

Gap:

- Interest in retail IT with strong analytical and critical thinking focus
- Understanding of the modern commerce technology stack: testing, personalization
- Strong written and verbal communication with understanding of the dynamics of large organizational politics; technical writing skills are a plus
- Ability to manage scope
- Segmentation and campaign management experience

Some commonalities:

- Strong communication
- Ability to manage multiple projects
- Ability to manage the people within an organization
- Analytical abilities to see what works and what doesn't

You can see that the technical skill requirement for being a marketer is actually lower than that of a UX designer, which often means the barrier to entry is lower and often correlates to lesser pay. (Of course, almost every career offers high pay if you become a top player on your "server.")

And lo and behold, one company above actually prefers philosophy and art history majors! When your family makes fun of you for choosing these passion-driven majors with limited career prospects, you can now righteously show them this job description and say, "What are you talking about? I am proactively preparing to be a marketer for Pete's Coffee."

Keep an eye out for skills that are repeatedly mentioned in job postings. These are the skills you need to target first. However, these descriptions above are minimum requirements to get into the industry and do not explain the skills required to become a high-level player.

For that, either follow the prior advice and look at great marketers to identify what skills they excel at or start reading books and taking classes from top experts in marketing. You will start to identify unique skills that the average marketer is not aware of, giving you an edge within your role.

The Skills Journey of an Architectural Designer

Remember PH Chen from Chapter 3: Know Your Attributes? He was the high school student who took a standardized assessment on spatial reasoning and realized that he had especially strong talents in it. This assessment guided him to select his role (Step 3) as an architectural designer. He then defined his life game (Step 1) as "creating productive living environments that inspire people."

Following is his 10K HP journey of becoming an OP Player. Pay special attention to the deliberate efforts and risks he took to acquire the skills he needed, and how he utilized those very skills to take on his subsequent quests.

So, how did PH acquire the right skills as an architectural designer? Being extremely fortunate to start his 10K HP journey early in his high school years, his first quest was to determine which college would maximize his skill enhancement.

Unlike most students who applied to schools based solely on their reputations, PH traveled through Taiwan to attend lectures at various universities and colleges, listening in on their architecture lectures.

However, he was somewhat disappointed after attending lectures at the top universities in Taiwan. He felt that all the skills they were teaching could be learned just by reading textbooks on his own. His last stop was Shih Chien University in Taipei, where he discovered something exciting. "Wow," he told me in an interview, "the skills taught here couldn't be learned any other way."

Shih Chien University wasn't particularly top-rated in Taiwan, but he saw that their curriculum was immersive and encouraged free thinking. You had to be there and be fully present to grasp the material, as opposed to being able to acquire everything at home. Impatient about waiting for high school graduation, PH became close friends with a student from Shih Chien and started attending classes there for six months while still in high school. These classes uniquely taught him to think outside the box using different paradigms.

One notable exercise required each student to lock themselves in a room and draw for 100 hours. They could only leave to eat or use the restroom. Initially, it seemed simple enough. However, after twenty to thirty hours, although PH felt his drawing was complete, he had to continue working on the same piece for another seventy hours! He believed it was already perfect, but with so much time remaining, he had to justify each change, recognizing how it seemingly detracted from the work's perfection, then figure out how to adjust it to make it perfect again. This cycle of breaking and rediscovering perfection stretched PH's brain and imagination beyond anything he had experienced in the past.

Another notable exercise was when the professor took all the students to a classroom's higher-floor balcony and asked them to make paper airplanes to see how far they could throw them to the floor below. Proud of their learnings from previous structure integrity and origami courses, the students were eager to demonstrate who could launch their airplanes the farthest.

However, after the throwing competition, the professor said, "OK. Now figure out how to retrieve your paper airplanes without leaving this floor." This baffled all the students. "What? How are we supposed to do that?" The professor responded, "It's up to you, but perhaps you can find some scrap materials in our classroom to build something that has enough structural integrity to reach and fetch your paper airplane."

Shih Chien University didn't just teach PH free-thinking skills; it also taught him survival soft skills, like going onto the streets and surviving without money for forty-eight hours. This forced the students to approach strangers and bargain for food, and to design their own outdoor shelters. All these skills allowed PH to grow into a stronger architectural designer.

PH dedicated four years to his studies at Shih Chien University, with just one remaining to graduate. During this period, he meticulously planned each day, hour by hour, from 6 am to midnight. His schedule included an hour for reading books, another for hand-tracing the work of master artists and designers to grasp their nuanced use of curves, and additional time for studying how biological structures could be integrated into building designs. He also devoted time to attending operas, enriching his understanding of how rich cultural elements can be woven into living spaces. His expansive studies spanned electrical and mechanical engineering, as well as explored the impact of light and sound on architectural environments. In other words, he designed a polymath curriculum for himself.

Seeking further inspiration, PH studied a list of designers who had won the prestigious Pritzker Prize and discovered the legendary Zaha Hadid, who became his role model. He embarked on tours to observe various buildings and projects by renowned architects, which prompted him to challenge traditional architectural norms. He soon realized that the future of architectural design would heavily depend on computer technology, making him the first student in his school to extensively use computers in his coursework. In 2007, he began learning a critical skill called *parametric design* using Rhino Script, positioning him as one of the earliest adopters and masters of this discipline.

This critical and innovative approach distinguished his work and made PH one of the most unique architectural designers in his industry for decades to come.

However, it was during this time when he realized that much of Shih Chien University's architecture curriculum was comparable to what the globally respected Architecture Association (AA) in London was covering five years prior. Aware that his course credits wouldn't transfer to AA, most people would have completed their undergraduate degree before making any drastic changes. But not PH. He thought, "If AA is teaching knowledge and skills that are five years ahead of Shih Chien, why should I waste a precious year here?" So, he decided to apply to AA. However, due to Taiwan's one-year mandatory military service, he had to withdraw from Shih Chien before AA accepted him. With only a 10 percent acceptance rate at AA, this was a significant risk. If AA did not accept PH, he would have spent four years in college but would only have a high school diploma. Naturally, this decision completely shocked PH's parents, who questioned why he couldn't just finish his university degree first.

Fortunately, after reviewing his unique portfolio, AA accepted PH. However, he had to immediately request to defer his attendance for a year due to his military obligations. Although AA agreed to the deferment, upon completing his military service, PH was surprised to find that AA had raised its English proficiency requirements from the previous year, and his English test scores no longer met the new standards. Unwilling to remain idle while pursuing his dream of attending AA, he moved to London to have the right immersive environment to improve his lacking English skills.

In London, PH was a young individual in his early 20s, armed only with a high school diploma. However, his education at Shih Chien University had fostered free-thinking and the belief that any man-made rule could be broken with the right approach. Consequently, he wrote numerous letters to the heads of Architecture Master's Programs in the UK and the US, explaining his eagerness to learn from them as part of their program.

Despite many schools rejecting him because he lacked a college degree, the head of the program at the University of Westminster – a top twenty school in the UK – interviewed him and was impressed by his work. Upon discovering that he only held a high school diploma, they apologetically explained that their policy required a college degree for admission to their master's program. Undeterred, PH argued that while their typical architecture undergraduate programs lasted only three years, he had already completed four years of undergraduate study in Taiwan. Although this was against their policies, the logic was appropriate, and the professor found PH's portfolio and skills very impressive. Consequently, they made an exception and enrolled him in their Master's Program of Architecture and Digital Media.

PH used this opportunity to enhance his skills in intelligent systems, mechanical engineering, the internet of things (IoT), and robotics, while further specializing in parametric design. Once PH obtained his master's degree from the University of Westminster, he became fully qualified to secure a high-paying job.

However, PH was intent on further developing his architectural design skills. With his improved English skills, he returned to enroll in the undergraduate program at the AA. Moreover, instead of choosing specialties where he already excelled, he deliberately selected professors who focused on areas where he was weak. Despite his subpar English and communication skills, PH managed to barely pass most of his classes. Impressively, after his graduation from the AA, he was promptly invited back to become a course instructor there for his specialized skills in IoT with architecture, digital fabrication, computational design, robotics, and parametric design. He also founded his own guild, Dezact.org, to help a new generation of architectural designers enhance their skills through his specialties.

During this time, PH made a couple attempts to join Zaha Hadid Architects, the firm of his earlier role model, but they didn't have a role for him in London. He then decided that he could learn more at a smaller design studio and joined Mamou-Mani Ltd Architects, which was founded by a visionary French architect specializing in digital fabrication-led architecture. According to PH, "The CEO had the vision to see what was possible in an industry where most people thought it couldn't be done. He also possessed the charisma and eloquence to convince people to give him a chance to prove it. On the other hand, I had unique skills to help the CEO execute and pull off his visions. Together, we pioneered many new method-ologies in the field that were previously considered impossible." During this period, PH contributed to the design of the Burning Man Temple of 2018, *Galaxia*, and invented the *Polibot*, a cable-driven parallel robot capable of building towers autonomously, which was later patented by Mamou-Mani Architects.[23]

With sufficient experiences from a smaller studio, PH then wanted to learn first-hand how large-scale architecture firms managed building projects from start to finish. Still with no available position at his dream company, Zaha Hadid Architects, he joined Kohn Pedersen Fox (KPF), a top-ten architecture firm known for designing many of the world's most iconic buildings. He acquired new skills and emerged as a leader in cutting-edge technology, de-veloping proprietary software that boosted the firm's productivity and fostered creativity in designing complex geometric structures. However, he did not forget his childhood dream, continuing to

---

[23]Unfortunately, since PH had not yet upgraded his business dealings skills, he later discovered that his name was not credited on the patent, despite being the primary innovator behind it.

apply to Zaha Hadid Architects.

After three failed attempts to join Zaha Hadid Architects, an opportunity finally presented itself. In 2021, Zaha Hadid Architects faced a challenging project, uncertain of its feasibility. Through an internal employee who admired PH's work, PH managed to arrange a conversation with the manager. Thanks to years of skill accumulation, PH demonstrated on the spot his knowledge and computational design expertise on tackling complex geometry projects from concept to construction. Impressed by his demonstration, they hired him immediately, fulfilling his dream of becoming a Zaha Hadid architectural designer. Later, PH became one of the main architects that helped create the breathtaking Shenzhen Futian Financial Technology Building, fulfilling his game of "creating productive living environments that inspire people."

It's important to recognize that PH's achievement of his dream job was not merely due to good luck or chance. While luck inevitably influences life's outcomes, he proactively embraced Quests in his upbringing that were neither safe nor comfortable. Not everyone drops out of college in their final year just to apply for a better learning environment. Not everyone moves to a new country to improve their language skills. Even after completing four years of undergraduate studies and several more in a master's program, PH re-enrolled at AA as an undergraduate because he believed it offered the highest leveling-up potential. After being rejected three times by his dream company, he still attempted that fourth time. The more you prepare and persist without giving up in your game, the more you allow luck to play a role in your success.

Respecting PH as a top master after so many years of crafting his skills, and also wanting him as a lifelong ally (Step 5), I asked him to help design the interior of one of my properties in Taiwan during his spare time. The end result was so satisfactory that I named the property The Octalysis House, a demonstration of how years of dedicated skill upgrades can turn something plain into a space that is inspiring and magical. Figure 23 shows The Octalysis House after the project was successfully implemented.

Figure 23. The Octalysis House After PH's Interior Design Project

It's Your Turn to Play: Skill Triangles

Now that we have explored a variety of examples regarding skills, it's time for you to define the skills you have and the skills you need to acquire.

Pick from One of the Three Game Modes

Easy: Identify and map out your Current Skill Triangle — the skills you already possess. Write down your top five skills that you feel are your strongest (these form your Ring Skills). Then, include other above-average but less critical skills as your Base Skills. This will give you a clear understanding of your existing strengths and how they currently shape your life game.

Medium Build your Target Skill Triangle by identifying the skills you need to master for your game. Think about a "Top Master" who has already succeeded in your desired role. What skills have they mastered? List the top three skills that will give you an edge in your role, along with supporting and base skills you'll need to develop. Compare your Current Skill Triangle to this Target Skill Triangle. Which skills do you need to improve or acquire?

Hard Create an Action Plan to level up your skills and close the gap between your Current and Target Skill Triangles. Choose one key skill to prioritize for the next three to six months. Design a strategy to grow that skill: Find a course, mentor, or project that will challenge you to improve. Commit to deliberate practice daily or weekly. Combine strategy with synergy: Think about how this skill enhances your other abilities and aligns with your attributes. Track your progress: Set specific milestones and measure improvement over time.

For structure and support, visit 10KHP.com/worksheets to access worksheets that will help you map and track your Skill Triangles effectively.

Going Gameful: Real-Life Game Skills

As you can see from the examples in this chapter, there are countless skills to learn in this world. Every subject, course, and training program can be developed into a skill with various sub-skills, each having its own learning curve – from physics to business to yo-yo tricks. I refer to these as *traditional world skills*. But just as in Step 3: Select Your Role, where you have a traditional Role Sphere (aspiration, identity, occupation, and specialty roles) alongside more playful hero names, I have also begun to collect a series of powerful *real-life game skills*. These are special abilities in the real world but are named using game terminologies.

Some of these skills can be categorized into *classes*, much like those in role-playing games. These skill classes include *Warrior, Ranger, Mage, Rogue, Druid, Paladin*, and *Warlock*. I describe these skill classes in detail later in this chapter, but first here's an overview of the skills themselves.

If mastered, these real-life game skills could fundamentally change the course of your future success. Readers who master any of the skills described in this section will likely experience a drastic transformation in their lives.

For example, one of my most notable traditional game skills is the craft of gamification design. In the realm of real-life game skills, this would be termed *enchant*. Enchant is a skill typically utilized by druids within games to make a target attracted to performing certain desired behaviors – a skill that captures the same gamification essence of motivating people to engage in activities by making the activities enjoyable. (My personal "ultimate technique" within the enchant skill is the Octalysis Framework, which I use almost on a regular basis.) As long as you are interacting with (and motivating) people, it's useful to have them enjoy their interactions with you as well as the tasks that need to be done.

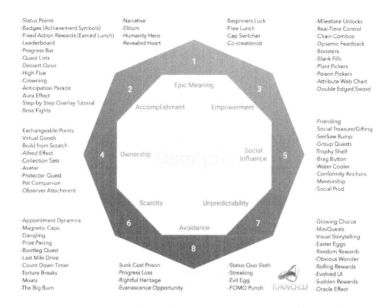

Figure 24. Octalysis Gamification Framework

The Intimidate Skill

Enchant stands in stark contrast to another real-life game skill, *intimidate*, a Warrior skill that compels people to perform desired behaviors through the imposition of a strong presence and enforced submission. In the television series *Breaking Bad*, there is an iconic scene where the main character, Walter White, confronts a thug who seems twice his size. During this standoff, Walter merely stares at the man and says, "Say my name." This intimidates the other person, who correctly guesses his alias as the drug kingpin: Heisenberg, before backing away.

This Warrior skill of confronting someone with such a powerful emotional frame that they yield and submit can be observed in various contexts, from boardroom negotiations where executives assert dominance, to historical battles where leaders inspired fear through sheer force of personality. For instance, Napoleon Bonaparte, one of history's most formidable military strategists, often wielded the intimidate skill with masterful precision, leveraging it to demoralize his enemies and secure victories with minimal conflict.

Heroic Strike vs Divine Shield

Another Warrior skill is called *heroic strike*, which is the ability to say or do something so audacious that it shocks the targeted individual and garners respect and compliance. An incredible example of a heroic strike was described by Oren Klaff, the author of *Pitch Anything*.[1]

Once, Klaff was having a pitch meeting in the office of a powerful hedge fund manager, Bill Garr. Flanked by his two Ivy-league MBA associates, Garr displayed such arrogance and disinterest in what Klaff was saying that he nonchalantly took out an apple, bit into it, chewed with crunchy loudness, and then set it down on the table. This act could be seen as rude and tactless, likely flustering most people into thinking they had lost the deal. However, in reality, this was a heroic strike by Garr, designed to be audaciously unsettling, causing his opponent to negotiate poorly and ultimately working in his favor.

Observing this, Klaff realized he needed to execute an even stronger heroic strike to counter this offense. He excused himself to get a glass of water and went to the kitchenette he had noticed earlier when walking in. He picked up a glass of water, a paper towel, and a plastic knife – the perfect tools for his heroic strike against this "raid boss."

Upon returning to the meeting, but before sitting down, he addressed Garr, "Listen, Bill, I hope that isn't how you do deals. In a real deal, everyone needs a piece. I'll show you what my deal looks like." Approaching Garr's desk, he playfully asked, "May I?" but did not wait for an answer. He picked up the apple with multiple bite marks, used the plastic knife to cut it in half, kept the clean side for himself, and handed the bitten side back to Garr. He then took a bite off his half, chewed it quickly, complimented its flavor, and reiterated the importance of splitting deals fairly with investors.

Understandably, the MBA associates were dumbfoundedly shocked by this heroic strike, nervously awaiting their boss' reaction. The boss, equally stunned, remained frozen with mean, squinty eyes for a long time but eventually burst into laughter, exclaiming, "Hahaha, I can definitely see why Dan said I should meet with you. Listen, tell me again who else you have in this deal." Oren Klaff's heroic strike had pierced the psychological defenses of his opponents, and later followed up with another Warrior skill: *execute* to close the deal by the end of the meeting.

So, how do you counter the Warrior skill heroic strike? With the Paladin skill *divine shield*. Divine shield represents the power and ability to say "no," regardless of how persuasive others are, including their use of social pressure or psychological tactics. On a small scale, divine shield is a useful skill to employ against a charismatic friend trying to convince you to attend a party you aren't interested in. On a slightly larger scale, divine shield can help someone respectfully reject their parents' wishes for them to choose a certain life path.

In 1982, when Steve Jobs tried to persuade John Sculley to leave his position as president of PepsiCo and join the much smaller Apple Computer as their CEO, Sculley was initially reluctant. But then Steve Jobs employed the heroic strike skill, asking, "Do you want to sell sugared water for the rest of your life? Or do you want to come with me and change the world?" According to John Sculley, the heroic strike landed like "a punch to the gut."[2] Sculley was so shocked by this proposition that he feared he would regret passing up the opportunity, leading him to say yes. Clearly, John Sculley didn't possess a divine shield that was as high-level as Steve Jobs' heroic strike.

Unfortunately, John Sculley's legacy ended up being the guy who fired Steve Jobs, brought Apple down, only for Steve Jobs to return years later to save the company with the comment, "What can I say? I hired the wrong guy."[3]

Rogue Skill: Masquerade

In the previous chapter on Step 3: Select Your Role, I discussed how my ability to roleplay other characters enabled me to adopt certain characteristics of my role models, even if those were fictional. This is the Rogue skill *masquerade*, which is the skill of pretending to be another person and performing soft skills at a comparable level.

I believe that while it is important to always tell the truth (e.g., "This is my first speech to such a large crowd"), speaking in the style of an experienced speaker can elevate your 10K HP journey to greater heights. Barack Obama, during his presidential campaigns and presidency, effectively used masquerade by adopting certain characteristics and speaking styles of past leaders he admired. For example, he studied and emulated the rhetorical techniques of Abraham Lincoln to enhance his own public speaking and connect more deeply with his audience. This approach helped him communicate more effectively and build a strong, inspirational public image.

If you can think of a person whom you admire and start behaving like them in all scenarios, effectively applying masquerade, you would eventually become more like them as part of your growth journey.

Ranger Skill: Track Treasure

Oprah Winfrey, the OP Hero from the previous chapter on roles, was extremely proficient in the real-life game skill *track treasure*, a strategy typically used by Rangers to identify hidden treasures and opportunities not obvious to others. Whether it was finding gems in each conversation with her interviewees or discovering great business opportunities that would expand her business empire, Oprah was adept at seeing the best approach to unearth the most optimal outcomes. This skill transcended her role from just a talk show host to a business tycoon, with billions of dollars within her stash.

If you have an eye for nonobvious opportunities leading to certain gains and a track record to show you aren't delusional, then you too have the track treasure skill. Make sure you use it on a regular basis and don't let those treasures pass you by!

Druid Skill: Hex

In Chapter 3 I discussed how OP Hero Walt Disney endured a very difficult childhood due to his father's harsh treatment. Whenever he faced abusive insults, he employed the real-life game skill *hex* (a Druid skill), to completely tune out anyone who was delivering unreasonable punishment. In games like *World of Warcraft*, hex can temporarily transform an enemy into a small critter. While in their critter form, they can neither deal damage nor be damaged. It's usually a reliable way to bypass difficult enemies but not necessarily for defeating them and gaining experience points for leveling up.

Similarly, Elon Musk also had an abusive father who would spend extended periods demoralizing his son's spirit during his youth. Musk used the hex skill in a similar way to tune out his father and instead focus on other topics. I will cover Musk's journey in more detail soon.

In his book, *Awaken the Giant Within*,[4] OP author and life coach Anthony Robbins shared a technique he calls the "scramble pattern," where when someone is traumatized by past memories of another person giving them harsh emotional abuse, they start to imagine that sequence with clown or gag comedic music playing in the background while the abusive person is growing long ears like Mickey Mouse. Effectively, when you "scramble the sensation" of that traumatizing memory, thinking about it no longer causes the same emotional trauma as before. The hex skill is very similar to that, but instead of using it on a past memory, you can use it in real time while the opponent is dishing out emotional damage to nullify its effectiveness on the spot.

However, just as in games where you do not gain experience when you hex a target and bypass them, in real life, when you hex someone who is giving you critical feedback, you also don't learn as much from the critiques and interaction.

Mage Skill: Arcane Wisdom

Another OP Hero, Warren Buffett, exemplifies the real-life game skill *arcane wisdom*, a Mage skill that involves the capacity to absorb a wide range of data, statistics, and information and synthesize them into clear, actionable outputs. Buffett's legendary investment strategy hinges on his profound ability to distill complex financial details into comprehensible investment decisions.

Knowing that he possesses the arcane wisdom skill, Buffett spends a significant portion of his day reading financial reports, industry publications, and other sources of information to stay ahead of market trends and make informed decisions. After all, if a 10K HP Player doesn't apply their skills, it's the equivalent of not having them at all.

By applying arcane wisdom regularly, Buffett was able to identify undervalued companies and predict market trends with uncanny accuracy, employing strategies that have consistently outperformed market averages. As a result, he maintained his status as one of the wealthiest investors on the Earth Server for extended periods.

Paladin Skill: Thunderclap

Moving on to civil rights movements, the OP Hero Martin Luther King Jr. masterfully wielded the real-life game skill *thunderclap*, a Paladin skill that involves delivering powerful public speeches that charge up and inspire people. This skill was evident in his iconic *I Have a Dream* speech, which resonated not only with hundreds of thousands on the steps of the Lincoln Memorial but also with millions around the world.

King's oratory prowess and his ability to connect with the hearts and minds of his listeners exemplified the thunderclap skill, as his words could electrify an audience, galvanizing them toward the cause of civil rights and social justice. His speeches often served as a rallying cry for change, imbuing his audience with a sense of urgency and a call to action that transcended racial and geographic boundaries. As a result, King's thunderclaps left an indelible mark on history, proving that whoever masters these same skills can indeed lead significant social transformation.

Warrior Skill: War Cry

The OP Hero Steve Jobs was also a quintessential practitioner of the real-life game skill: *war cry*, a Warrior skill used for motivating a team with intense energy and pushing for results that others might consider unreasonable. Like the barbarian in the *Diablo* franchise who uses war cry to buff his teammates, Jobs used his formidable presence and demanding expectations to elevate the performance of his team at Apple. Jobs was notorious for his reality distortion field, a unique blend of charisma, persuasion, intensity, and insistence that made the impossible seem achievable.

Under Jobs' leadership, teams developed groundbreaking products like the iPhone and MacBook, often under tight deadlines and immense pressure, achieving technological feats that set new industry standards. This approach led to a series of revolutionary products that transformed entire industries, demonstrating that the forceful motivation and relentless push of war cry can lead to extraordinary outcomes. Similarly, when Eiichiro Oda, the creator of the manga series, *One Piece*, asked his new editor to "die for *One Piece*," it was also a war cry that set the tone for an intense and hardcore journey in the fast lane.[24]

Warlock Skill: Terraform

Another example of a real-life game skill drastically changing the game for an individual or an entire industry is demonstrated by OP Player Keith Rabois, who employed the real-life game skill *terraform* (Warlock skill class) during his tenure as Executive Vice President at PayPal from 2000 to 2002. Terraform is typically a powerful spell in games that completely transforms the landscape to something more favorable. It tends to drain a lot of time and resources but has paradigm-shifting results when successfully performed.

At the time, PayPal was pioneering a new way of handling money online, essentially functioning like a bank but without adhering to the corresponding regulatory compliance typically required for such financial activities. This innovative approach placed PayPal squarely in the regulatory spotlight, as it did not neatly fit into existing financial regulations. Recognizing the potential regulatory challenges, Rabois led efforts to engage and lobby financial regulators and lawmakers, securing a favorable environment that allowed PayPal to operate legally without the stringent banking regulations that could stifle its growth and innovation.

A similar scenario unfolded at Square in 2010, where Rabois, then

---

[24]The editor later shared that his initial reaction was "What, really?" but then he felt impressed with the thought, "This person really works with that kind of resolution!" From the article by Evan Valentine. "One Piece Creator Told Editor to 'Die For One Piece' ". January 6, 2024, ComicBook.com. https://comicbook.com/anime/news/one-piece-creator-editor-die-for-one-piece/

the Chief Operating Officer, again had to navigate significant regulatory hurdles. As Square introduced a new way of processing credit card transactions through mobile devices, it disrupted the traditional payment processing industry. The company faced potential classification issues similar to those of traditional financial institutions that could have subjected Square to undue regulatory compliance. Rabois' terraform skill became invaluable as he guided Square through these challenges, fostering a regulatory environment that accommodated this innovative payment solution, thereby securing Square's position in the market.

In both instances, Rabois' adept use of terraform not only mitigated potential legal hurdles but also transformed the regulatory landscape to better suit the evolving nature of fintech. These examples prove that strategic influence over regulators and rule makers is crucial for disruptive companies that need to transform the status quo.

Warrior Skill: Power Leap

Sergey Brin, a co-founder of Google, effectively utilized another dynamic Warrior skill known as *power leap* to expand Google's advertising business. This skill involves taking the bold initiative to travel directly to someone's location for a face-to-face meeting without a prior invitation, a higher-tier upgrade to the Warrior skill *charge*, which entails boldly approaching someone directly when they are in front of you.

A notable instance occurred immediately after Google's IPO in 2004. While on their private jet to Spain, the Google founders Brin and Larry Page learned the bad news that Yahoo had beaten Google in securing an exclusive deal to provide ads for AOL's European internet service. Eager to secure the deal, Brin messaged Philip Rowley, then head of AOL Europe, and announced that they were diverting their flight to London to meet with him that very day.

Unfortunately, Rowley firmly rejected their request, stating that AOL had already concluded the deal with Yahoo. Rowley remarked with resolve, "That is the way it is going to go. The process is done." Taking fortune into his own hands, Brin refused to accept no for an answer. As his flight continued to soar toward London, he persisted, asking Rowley for a meeting location and time later that day. This power leap left Rowley uncertain of what to do, prompting him to contact Jon Miller, the CEO of AOL in Virginia. Although Miller was intrigued, he reminded Rowley that they had already committed to Yahoo and it would not be good to go back on their word. Nonetheless, he advised Rowley to meet with the forceful Google founders to see what they had to say.

In a private meeting at the Milestone Hotel in London, Brin and Page presented a much more attractive offer to Rowley. Subsequently, Miller advised his team, "The right thing is to let Yahoo get in the game." They informed Yahoo that Google had made a much better offer and asked if Yahoo wanted to increase their bid. Yahoo, understandably upset and lacking the power leap skill themselves, declined to enter a bidding war. As a result, Google transformed what seemed like a lost battle against Yahoo into a victory over AOL Europe, all thanks to the power leap. Rowley later commented, "Their physical presence made a big difference. You want to be able to trust the people you are going to work with. We were just getting to know Google from the European side of AOL, and for them to come over was really, really helpful," despite his initial firm rejection of the visit. His divine shield was not strong enough against Brin's power leap.[5]

Although power leaps can be extremely powerful, as you will see in more examples later in this book, they also represent a high-risk, high-reward skill. Much like in games, if you power leap to the wrong place at the wrong time, you might not achieve the desired results and may be caught out of position, losing precious time and resources. Thus, a master of any skill is not simply someone who uses it all the time, but also someone who knows when not to use it.

Mage Skill: Elemental Ensemble

The real-life game skill *elemental ensemble* (Mage skill class) represents the ability to mentally visualize and conceptualize complex compositions and then perform or execute them with precision and creativity. This skill is valuable among chemists, chefs, and musicians, allowing them to understand in their minds how various components can come together to form a pleasing outcome.

In 1998, the popular Taiwanese TV show, *Super New Talent King*, was underway. One evening, after a particularly lackluster performance by a singer, the audience was unimpressed. However, after the show, influential entertainer Jacky Wu happened to glance at the music sheet left behind. To his surprise, the music was extremely intricate and beautiful. Curiosity piqued, Wu asked, "Who wrote this music?"

It turned out that the composer was a waiter named Jay, who unfortunately (or fortunately) had not managed to secure good enough grades to get into college. Jay came from a single-parent family but had a lifelong love for music. His role models were musical OP Heroes like Chopin and Stevie Wonder. Jay started playing the piano at the age of four after his mother noticed his musical talents. By third grade, he had also taken up the cello. Despite his musical talents, Jay was too shy to enter the talent show himself, so his classmate booked him as an accompanying pianist instead.

Wu, impressed by the music, decided to hire Jay as an assistant music producer. This marked a dramatic turning point in Jay's life, as he immersed himself in music production, sound mixing, recording, and songwriting at Wu's studio. Determined to release his own album while also performing various errands for Wu, Jay regularly wrote songs to showcase for him.

After much persistence, Wu finally agreed to see if other singers would perform Jay's songs. However, they found his style too unconventional and turned the songs down. In a last-ditch effort, Wu challenged Jay: if he could write fifty songs in ten days, Wu would select the best ten and produce an album for him. Seizing this final opportunity, Jay combined his real-life game skills *undying rage* (Warrior skill: activating survival instincts to focus on defeating an overwhelming challenge) with *elemental ensemble* (Mage skill) and shockingly finished the fifty songs within the allotted time! True to his word, Wu produced an album for Jay, albeit with only half the budget of similar projects.

Jay Chou's debut album, *Jay* (2000), was named "Best Album" at the Golden Melody Awards in 2001. The following year, his album *Fantasy* won five awards, including Best Album, Best Composer, and Best Producer. Notably, he was named Best-Selling Chinese Artist by the World Music Awards in 2004, 2006, 2007, and 2008.

In 2022, Jay's album *Greatest Works of Art* was announced as the best-selling album of the year globally by the International Federation of the Phonographic Industry (IFPI), surpassing musical stars like Taylor Swift, BTS, Black Pink, and Seventeen. His unique elemental ensemble skill as a "Music Mage" propelled him to become the most famous artist in Asia and a true OP Hero, inspiring future generations.[6]

In fact, Jay's own team even used "mage-like" language to describe his talents and skills when I talked to them: "Jay's innate musical talent acts like magic, capable of healing hearts, inspiring creativity, and connecting people from diverse backgrounds. His songs and musical works are his way of casting spells, with each song carrying a unique ability to touch listeners' souls, bringing them joy, comfort, and resonance."

If you're wondering why you might not have heard of this huge musician, it's because his music is primarily in Mandarin Chinese, appealing to Chinese-speaking audiences worldwide. However, you might recognize him as Kato from the movie *The Green Hornet* alongside Seth Rogen, or as Li from *Now You See Me 2*. And no, Jay Chou is not related to Yu-kai Chou.

Gameful Skill Classes

As noted earlier, I have organized the key real-life game skills under various *gameful skill classes* – *Warrior, Ranger, Mage, Rogue, Druid, Paladin,* and *Warlock* – to illustrate the tendencies of each one, each unique in its own style. The most common gameful skill classes, each with its own distinct characteristics, are as follows.

Warrior: Confront and Persuade

10K HP Players who have mastered Warrior skills excel in selling, persuading, and closing deals. They are often conversion-oriented, preferring to directly sell or convince others of their agenda. Warriors often can win in life through their sheer audacity and aggression.

Some Warrior archetypes include: Jordan Belford (the "Wolf of Wall Street"), Muhammad Ali (boxing legend), Gary Vaynerchuk (media and tech entrepreneur), Jack Welch (Ex-CEO of General Electric), Tony Robbins (life coach), and Oren Klaff (sales coach and dealmaker).

Ranger: Observe and Innovate

10K HP Players who have learned many Ranger skills specialize in visionary management and planning. They are opportunity-oriented and win through strategy and leadership. Rangers excel at observing, planning, and careful innovation.

Some Ranger archetypes include: Sherlock Holmes (famous fictional detective), Ed Catmull (former President of Pixar), Steve Jobs, Walt Disney, Oprah (although often positioned as a Druid), and Richard Branson (Co-founder of the Virgin Group). As you can see, the current Earth Server meta[25] favors Ranger skills if one's game is to accumulate wealth, due to how technology and innovation can scale the 10K HP Players' means of income generation exponentially.

Mage: Analyze and Calculate

10K HP Players who have mastered Mage skills are problem-solving-oriented people who prefer to win through their sheer intellects. They rely on their quantitative, deep thinking, and analytical skills and often exhibit a "factual and frank" communication style. Mages often lead with the philosophy of "solutions over people."

Some Mage archetypes include: Sheldon Cooper (fictional physics genius from the show *Big Bang Theory*), Marie Curie (Nobel Prize Laureate for both chemistry and physics), Albert Einstein, Ada Lovelace (mathematician credited for writing the first computer algorithm in the 1850s), Bobby Fischer (legendary chess player), Warren Buffett, Alan Turing, Carl Sagan, Stephen Hawking, and Will Hunting (Matt Damon's character from the movie *Good Will Hunting*).

Rogue: Experiment and Optimize

10K HP Players who specialize in Rogue skills are often results-oriented and like to win through cleverness, productivity, and influencing others. They value creativity and efficiency, keen to adapt and overcome new environments, and often lead by example.

---

[25] Separate from the word "metaverse" or the company Meta, in gaming terminology, a *meta* (acronym for "most effective tactics available") is a strategy that is considered by the community to be the most optimal way to win.

These are often life hackers or people who continue to optimize on their lives to achieve breakout results.

Some Rogue archetypes include: Tim Ferris (author of *The 4-Hour Workweek*), Leonardo da Vinci, Frank Abagnale (author of *Catch Me If You Can*), Charles Ponzi (the originator of the Ponzi scheme), Masayoshi Son (the founder of Softbank who has one of the coolest rags-to-billionaire stories), Victor Lustig (con artist who fraudulently sold the Eiffel Tower, twice), Ramit Sethi (personal finance guru), and Loki from the Marvel Cinematic Universe.

It's important to recognize that being a Rogue archetype does not necessarily imply dishonesty, as clever optimization defines this class, not ethical values. However, many of history's clever scammers would also be considered Rogues, true to its theme of individuals who try to break traditional rules to achieve something greater. Rogues are often impatient and look for shortcuts, which you will soon see from the crazy and inspiring journey of Masayoshi Son later in this chapter.

Druid: Nurture and Empathize

10K HP Players who resonate with Druid skills excel in nurturing and empathizing, naturally gravitating toward roles that emphasize care, connection, and harmony. They create environments where people feel valued, supported, and empowered.

Druids are deeply people-oriented, thriving in community-building and mediation. Their strength lies in uniting others, fostering cooperation, and diffusing conflict through empathy and understanding. They succeed not through force, but by cultivating trust and guiding individuals toward collective growth.

Some Druid archetypes include: Mother Teresa, Fred Rogers (host of the pre-school television series *Mister Rogers' Neighborhood*), Patch Adams (founder of the free hospital nonprofit, the Gesundheit! Institute), Florence Nightingale (pioneer of modern nursing), Clara Barton (founder of the American Red Cross), Albert Schweitzer (humanitarian polymath), and Anne Sullivan (instructor and lifelong companion to Helen Keller).

Paladin: Inspire and Attract

10K HP Players who commit themselves to Paladin skills are often ideals-oriented and possess a strong capacity for emotional strength and perseverance. They inspire others through their conviction and ability to attract followers to a cause. Paladins lead by exemplifying hope, resilience, and the power of a shared vision, making them natural charismatic leaders who can rally people during times of hardship.

Some Paladin archetypes include: Mahatma Gandhi, Sun Yat-sen (founder of the Republic of China), Malala Yousafzai (youngest Nobel Laureate, receiving the Peace Prize at age 17), Winston Churchill (British Prime Minister who led his nation to oppose Hitler), Helen Keller (inspiring author and disability activist who grew up both deaf and blind), Martin Luther King Jr. (civil rights movement leader), Nelson Mandela (first President of South Africa), and Margaret Thatcher (first woman and longest-serving British Prime Minister).

Warlock: Compete and Crush

10K HP Players who dabble in Warlock skills are generally competitive and aim to crush their opponents. They use their skills to overpower competitors and establish supremacy in their endeavors. Warlocks are intensely dominance-oriented, employing competitive tactics to overpower their adversaries to get ahead. They thrive on creating and exploiting advantages, often leveraging others' weaknesses to achieve victory. Warlocks win through their ruthlessness and unfair use of the strongest tools and tactics to gain an advantage over competitors.

Some Warlock archetypes include: Larry Ellison (founder of Oracle), Donald Trump (US President), Rupert Murdoch (founder of News Corp), Leona Helmsley (New York businesswoman nicknamed "the Queen of Mean"), Vladimir Putin, and Niccolò Machiavelli (who wrote the Warlock playbook in politics: *The Prince*).

Collecting Real-Life Game Skills

Table 5-1 shows some of the real-life game skills typical of each gameful skills class (many more skills exist). To see all the up-to-date real-life game skills, you can visit the 10K HP website (10KHP.com/gameskills) and start using them in your real life too.

Class/Tier	Skill	Description
Warrior I	Execute	Finalizing deals and agreements through confident persuasion.
Warrior II	Taunt	Attracting others to approach the player as an inbound lead.
Warrior III	War Cry	Motivating a team with intense energy and pushing for results normally seen as unreasonable.
Ranger I	True Sight	Observing keen details missed by others.
Ranger II	Track Treasure	Identify hidden treasures and opportunities that aren't obvious to others.
Ranger III	Instinctual Pathfinding	Trusting your gut or intuition and finding the right thing to do.

Class/Tier	Skill	Description
Mage I	Temporal Freeze	Completing a calculation very quickly in one's head.
Mage II	Ley Line Infusion	Quickly absorbing a large amount of knowledge within a certain subject matter.
Mage III	Astral Projection	Ability to see all possible outcomes.
Rogue I	Ninja Focus	Sustained discipline and focus on tasks.
Rogue II	Decoy	Misleading others so one can execute on a covert plan.
Rogue III	Fulcrum Strike	Execute high leverage activities that could obtain transformative results that turn the tide.
Druid I	Mind Soothe	Calming others down through gentle communication.
Druid II	Shapeshift	Adapting to new environments and people to build relatedness.
Druid III	Enchant	Gamification skills to make activities more enjoyable or preferable.
Paladin I	Holy Barrier	Setting boundaries to protect mental and emotional well-being.
Paladin II	Thunder Clap	Public speaking that charges up and inspires people.

Class/Tier	Skill	Description
Paladin III	Phoenix Rebirth	Recovering from devastating failure such as failing a company or losing a loved one and coming back stronger.
Warlock I	Bind Fate	Leverage someone else's brand or resources to become powerful.
Warlock II	Siphoning	Extracting skills or knowledge rapidly from others.
Warlock III	Animate	Automate processes traditionally reliant on human labor by leveraging computing and robotics.

Evaluating People Based on Their Gameful Skill Class

While it might be tempting to use gameful skill classes as a type of personality assessment, it's crucial to remember that they merely categorize real-life game skills – things you learn to excel at, rather than defining who you are.

Unlike the archetype examples listed earlier, most people possess real-life game skills across multiple gameful skill classes, which is depicted in the attribute web charts in Figures 24 and 25. Since these skills are acquired to help you become more successful in life, it's wise to learn as many as possible that aid in playing your game within your role.

Figure 25. **Skill Web Chart of Walt Disney**

Figure 26. **Skill Web Chart of Oprah Winfrey**

If you are keen on categorizing 10K HP Players based on gameful skill class, you might use the two predominant skill classes as labels for each individual. For example, I could be labeled a Druid-Ranger because I possess numerous skills that are characteristic of a Druid, linked to my empathetic identity role, while my occupational role as an entrepreneur involves applying innovative leadership skills that are characteristic of a Ranger. The second term represents the main professional class, while the first acts as a modifier. However, some individuals may demonstrate equal dedication to real-life game skills from three or more different classes, so this labeling should be viewed as casual vernacular rather than a strict terminological system in 10K HP.

On the other hand, Gandhi could be described as a Druid-Paladin, as his main work focuses on inspiring and attracting a generation of people toward his ideals, like that of a Paladin, while he employs a methodology akin to the gentle Druid rather than the more combative style of a Warrior-Paladin, such as Martin Luther King Jr.

The Warrior-Rogue Billionaire: Masayoshi Son and His Fulcrum Strikes

Masayoshi Son, the founder of SoftBank, is one of the OP Heroes who has mastered the Tier III Rogue skill *fulcrum strike* (see Table 5-1). This real-life game skill involves executing high-leverage activities that can lead to transformative results and significantly alter the course of events.

From a young age, Son demonstrated an extraordinary ability to seize pivotal opportunities that few others dared to attempt. Growing up in an immigrant Korean family in Japan that struggled to put enough food on the table, Masayoshi Son admired Den Fujita, the man who introduced McDonald's to Japan. Son spent hours calling Fujita's office, attempting to start a conversation (Step 5: Build Your Alliance). Understandably, Fujita's assistants did not allow this random kid to speak with their boss.

Seeing his long-distance telephone bills mounting, Son realized it was a waste of money and decided to take a risky power leap (Warrior skill). He mustered enough funds to buy an domestic plane ticket, flew directly to Tokyo, and showed up at Fujita's office. Impressed by the young Masayoshi's conviction, Fujita agreed to a fifteen-minute meeting. During their conversation, Son asked Fujita which industry he should select for a business. Fujita advised him to pursue a career in computers, ideally in America.

At the age of sixteen, Masayoshi Son saved enough money to fly to California. He quickly learned English and enrolled in an American high school. However, just a few weeks into his tenure as an American high school student – a thrilling but unsettling dream come true for many foreign youngsters – Son felt that progress was too slow. He then executed a powerful fulcrum strike (Rogue skill): he requested the school administration allow him to take the college entrance exam early. Despite his limited English, Son barely passed the exam and graduated from high school just a month after enrolling.

With relentless drive, he attended the University of California, Berkeley, studying economics and computer science. Still lacking funds, and instead of finding a student job on campus like others would, he asked his friends if there were any jobs that could make $10,000 per month by working only five minutes a day. His classmates, of course, thought he was delusional to imagine such a thing. So, Masayoshi decided that the most efficient use of his time was inventing. Every day, he set his alarm for five minutes to brainstorm new inventions, aiming to patent the good ones and sell them for a good price.

By the end of the year, Masayoshi had a notebook of over 250 invention ideas. While not all were viable, he determined that the best idea was a pocket-sized device that could translate text into different languages. He then approached a physics professor using his *charge* skill (Warrior skill class) and convinced the professor to help him build a prototype by using another Warrior skill: execute. Once the prototype was created, Son started applying the Rogue skill *ninja focus* and relentlessly pitched his invention to companies, day in and day out. He even used another Rogue skill, *decoy*, by paying another Asian student to attend the lectures he was missing so his attendance record could still be high.

After much persistence, Son was able to sell his device patent to Sharp Corporation for $1.7 million. So, at the age of 19, Masayoshi Son had already transformed from a poor international student into a millionaire with his five-minutes-a-day ideas – all through his committed utilization of the fulcrum strike alongside other real-life game skills!

Still in his ninja focus mode with incredible discipline and hustle, Masayoshi Son began importing Space Invaders arcade machines from Japan to the US, installing them in bars and restaurants. Most entrepreneurs would approach such a venture cautiously due to its logistical complexities, compliance with customs, capital intensity, and uncertainty in market demand at each location.

However, the Warrior-Rogue Masayoshi Son would have none of that and continued to execute his fulcrum strikes. Within six months, he had imported over 350 arcade machines to the US. Instead of shipping these large and heavy machines by sea, he purchased them via credit and flew them over by plane. Although this method was significantly more expensive, it allowed him to start generating revenue much faster, enabling him to make enough before he needed to pay off the creditors. Through this strategy, Masayoshi Son made another $1.5 million in profits.

During this time, he also started a video game company called Unison World, which he later sold for $2 million. Following a promise to his mother, Son returned to Japan after completing his degree at Berkeley. Still focused on his entrepreneurial game, he conceived forty business ideas and ranked them based on their potential. Following advice from his previous mentor Den Fujita, he chose the idea that became a software distribution company called SoftBank.

SoftBank initially struggled for a few years, but Masayoshi Son continued to invest all his savings into the business. Eventually, SoftBank began to thrive. After being diagnosed with and recovering from a life-threatening case of chronic hepatitis, Son realized his time on earth was limited and decided he needed to level-up his fulcrum strikes even further. Before Son reached the age of forty, SoftBank had over 800 employees and more than $1 billion USD in revenue. He took the company public to scale even faster. Recognizing that the quickest way to achieve transformative growth was to invest in high-growth companies, in his early forties, he invested over $3 billion USD in 800 different startups, including companies like Yahoo! and E*TRADE.

One of Masayoshi Son's most famously successful investments was in a company called Alibaba. Masayoshi describes his initial meeting with Jack Ma, Alibaba's Founder, by noting, "He had no business plan, no revenue... but his eyes were very strong." Son's $20 million investment into Alibaba later soared to $70 billion. For a brief period of three days in 2001, Masayoshi Son even surpassed Bill Gates as the richest man in the world. However, during the infamous dot-com bubble burst, he experienced the largest recorded loss of wealth at the time, losing $70 billion in net worth in a single day.

Unfazed, Masayoshi Son continued to make big bets and execute strategic fulcrum strikes over the next decade. He believed the next major fulcrum strike would come from having the internet at your fingertips. Thus, he arranged a call with another one of his heroes, Steve Jobs, to inquire if Jobs would partner with him to create a mobile phone that functioned more like a computer and could access a wide range of internet-related features. Steve Jobs disclosed that they were already working on a top-secret project called the iPhone. Son then asked if he could secure exclusive rights to sell the iPhone in Japan. Steve Jobs laughed, thinking Masayoshi was out of his mind, especially since he didn't know what the iPhone would entail and he didn't even own a mobile phone carrier in Japan.

So what did Masayoshi Son do next? True to his style, he purchased a mobile phone carrier, Vodafone Japan, for around $20 billion, impressing Steve Jobs and becoming the exclusive seller of iPhones in Japan for many years.

But buying or investing in thousands of companies wasn't enough for Masayoshi. He felt compelled to execute more fulcrum strikes with even greater leverage. Masayoshi had an opportunity to invest in Jeff Bezos' Amazon in its early days but couldn't free up enough capital to make it happen. To ensure this never happened again, he started *The Vision Fund* in 2017, raising $100 billion – the largest fund in history and four times larger than the second largest.

To raise the fund, he flew to meet the Saudi Arabian prince, Mohammad Bin Salman, who was looking to transition Middle East oil money into future transformative technologies. On the plane trip there, Masayoshi flipped through the presentation his team had prepared, which asked for $30 billion from Mohammad Bin Salman. He changed the number to $100 billion instead, asserting that they needed to think big. This audacious move resulted in raising $45 billion during a forty-five-minute meeting with the Saudi prince – $1 billion per minute! This achievement made his previous fulcrum strike of making $1.7 million with his five-minutes per day inventions seem like child's play. To round up the fund, he also raised money from Apple, Foxconn, Abu Dhabi, and his own company, SoftBank.

With $100 billion in his war chest, he could now diversify his investments into a variety of trends and innovations, right? Not for Son. Just like his previous commitments to the computing and mobile revolutions, he declared he would invest the majority of his funds into artificial intelligence, believing it to be the next major trend for humanity. Of course, after the launch of ChatGPT five years later, the world again realized that the Warrior-Rogue, Masayoshi Son, was right on the money once more. They eagerly await his next fulcrum strike to disrupt the playing field.[26]

It's Your Turn to Play: Real Life Game Skills

As you can imagine, mastering even one of these real-life game skills could be transformative for many readers on their life journeys. If you have the courage to perform the Warrior skill, charge, on any stranger on the street, you could vastly increase your opportunities in your career, experiences, and even relationships. Imagine mastering the execute Warrior skill like Oren Klaff, who regularly closes centimillion-dollar deals, or the Druid skill *mind soothe* like Chris Voss, who expertly calms high-adrenaline criminals holding hostages. With just one of these skills, you could become a leading star in your organization.

Pick from One of the Three Game Modes

Easy: Review the table of Real-Life Game Skills in this chapter. Identify the skills you already have and write them down. Determine your class (e.g., Warrior, Mage, Rogue) based on your strongest skills. Write down an example of a time you used each skill to overcome an obstacle or complete a Quest.

Medium: Discover one Real-Life Game Skill you need to level up for your game and create an action plan to acquire them. Research

---

[26]While Masayoshi Son's story is extremely inspiring, it is important to note that playing a Rogue involves extremely high risks alongside the high rewards. In games, Rogues generally have high damage output but low defense, which means they either win swiftly through stealthy assassination of their enemies, or they make a miscalculation and quickly die from enemy fire. It is generally not for the faint of heart. While this section focused mostly on the successful fulcrum strikes, Masayoshi Son has also made many mistakes that led to devastating failures, such as when he lost the $70 billion in a single day. He famously invested $4.4 billion after Adam Neumann gave him a twelve-minute tour of a WeWork coworking space in 2016, which unfortunately led to an accumulated loss of $11.5 billion many years later. "WeWork Saga Cost Masayoshi Son $11.5 Billion and His Credibility." Bloomber.com [article behind paywall]. https://www.bloomberg.com/news/articles/2023-11-07/wework-saga-cost-masayoshi-son-11-5-billion-and-his-credibility]

or identify one Top Master who excels at your desired role. Break down their Real Life Game Skills and determine which ones are most important for your growth.

Hard: Go on a Skill Quest to actively practice and refine one key Real-Life Game Skill in the next four weeks. Choose one skill you want to master. Commit to a measurable practice routine. At the end of the month, share your results with a mentor, ally, or trusted group to get feedback and track your progress.

So, how do we learn these 10K HP real-life game skills? I've compiled a library of valuable resources on the best ways to acquire these skills, including books, courses, experts, and videos at the 10K HP website, 10KHP.com/GameSkills, for anyone serious about elevating their life to the next level. Just make sure your new OP Player skills are aligned with your game, attributes, and role.

OP Hero Profile: From Bullied and Broke to Top of the World – the Existential Innovator

This chapter's OP Hero, an embodiment of Step 4: Enhance Your Skills, is a widely recognized and often respected figure whose impact spans across society. He began his life game with a mission (Step 1) that extended naturally from his insatiable curiosity: uncovering the truth of the universe. Exceeding any other human being in this regard, he utilized his unique attributes (Step 2) and acquired a vast variety of synergetic abilities (Step 4) to become what we consider the highest-level player alive on the Earth Server today.

Let us begin with the captivating story of a young boy from Pretoria, South Africa – a tale often misconstrued by popular media. From the tender years of his childhood, this OP Hero was quite introverted and preferred to spend time alone reading books. His realm was one of science fiction novels and comic books, where a future among the galactic stars was an inevitability.

His very first quest (Step 6) was to read as many books from his local libraries as possible. Remarkably, by the age of nine, his insatiable thirst for knowledge outpaced both his school's and his community's library resources, leading him to petition the school to add new books.

It was during this period that our OP Hero read the entire *Encyclopedia Britannica*, a compendium brimming with over forty million words spread across 32,000 pages. This quest powered him up through his distinct set of synergistic attributes (Step 2): intellectual curiosity, learning agility, logical intelligence, learn-use conversion, and comprehensive recall.

These qualities facilitated not only rapid learning but also the amalgamation and practical application of the acquired knowledge. They became the underpinning forces of his intellectual prowess, enabling him to absorb, synthesize, and harness information in a manner that is rarely matched by others.

Unfortunately, akin to Saitama, the fictional character from the manga and anime series *One-Punch Man* who could defeat every opponent with ease and boredom, our young OP Hero found that, despite having overwhelming powers, navigating his social environment and climbing the social hierarchy were extremely challenging.

During his school years, he frequently found himself on the harsh receiving end of playground bullies. On one notable occasion, he boldly stood up against classmates who were propagating racial slurs, which caused him to endure another brutal beating.[7]

Sometimes the beatdowns would be so bad that he would be in the hospital for an entire week. In one of the worst beatings, the fracture in his nose was so severe that, thirty years after he left

South Africa, he still had to go through corrective surgery to fix the broken tissues within.[8]

Unfortunately, the physical torment was but a fraction of the profound loneliness and isolation that consumed him. The bullies didn't limit their actions to him. They also targeted his best friend and forced the friend to stop hanging out with him. Moreover, they coerced this friend to betray our OP Hero, luring him out of hiding into another harsh beatdown. This emotional wound cut deeply into his psychological state as he lived his school days rotating between evading bullies, enduring beatings, and suffering betrayals from people he considered close friends.

During this time, he was simply the right player in the wrong game, like Mega Man struggling in a *Mario 64* world. As you will see later on, our OP Hero *proactively* tried to solve this problem by changing his environment multiple times.

At home, things weren't much better. When he was just eight years old, his parents went through a divorce. For the first two years, our OP Hero and two younger siblings lived with his mother. This mother of three struggled so much financially that she had to balance an exhausting array of five jobs to ensure that the family's basic needs were met. On one particularly heartbreaking day, one of the children accidentally spilled their milk, and she reportedly broke down in tears as she couldn't afford to replace the milk until her next paycheck arrived.[9]

After living with his mother for two years, our OP Hero made the decision to reside with his father, an austere engineer with whom he maintained a tumultuous relationship. While this new environment was financially stable, his home morphed into a turbulent battleground plagued with daily tension and psychological abuses.

Despite the trials and tribulations, his engineering father's home gave him a much better environment to enhance his skills. In this new environment, our OP Hero procured his first computer at the ripe age of eleven – a Commodore VIC-20.[27] Bereft of playmates to share in outdoor adventures, he dedicated countless hours to his new digital companion. His powerful learning-centric attributes (Step 2) mentioned earlier served as a springboard, enabling him to acquire and cultivate new skills (Step 4). He diligently taught himself programming in BASIC (software engineering skills), honed in on his scientific problem-solving skills, and enhanced his knowledge application skill.

In a span of just two years, our thirteen-year-old OP Hero completed his inaugural business quest (Step 6). He crafted a video game christened *Blastar* – a space-themed adventure where players navigate a spaceship to defeat an alien freighter. He then sold *Blastar* for $500 in 1984 ($1,500 in 2025 dollars) to *PC and Office Technology* magazine – an impressive achievement for a child his age. Our OP Hero sold two more games to the same buyer shortly after.

Furthermore, it was clear that his father wanted to pass down many skills to his children. Both our OP Hero and his brother were required to go to their father's engineering work sites to learn how to lay bricks, install plumbing, fit windows, and put in electrical wiring. This equipped our OP Hero with foundational physics and engineering abilities that became quite crucial later on.

However, our OP Hero felt the emotional relationship with his father was causing too much trauma, and he wanted to leave. He noticed that in the novels and comic books he read, all the important events for humanity happened in the US, so he was determined to move there if possible.

When he was seventeen, he once again changed his environment through a zone shift quest. Since his mother was also Canadian, he obtained Canadian citizenship and moved to Saskatchewan,

---

[27] One of the most respected biographers, Walter Isaacson, reports that our OP Hero worked odd jobs to save up to buy this computer, as his father was vehemently against wasting money on one. However, the OP Hero did persuade his father to negotiate a discounted price for a $400 computer course at a university, where his son could stand in the back and learn.

Canada, to live with a second cousin he had never met. Besides working on a farm, he took on other unconventional jobs to survive, such as cleaning out a boiler room at a lumber mill in Vancouver.

This job was fraught with peril. Donning a hazmat suit, our OP Hero had to contort his body to squeeze through a minuscule tunnel and shovel out a mixture of sand and hot goop. Staying inside beyond thirty minutes would result in death due to the excruciating heat. Because of this, all but three of the thirty workers who started with our OP Hero quit their jobs within three days. Of course, our young protagonist was one of the three who persevered to the end. Despite his tender age, his emotional resilience attribute (Step 2) held steadfast, enabling him to endure until the gig's completion.

In the process of this demanding task, he once again leveled-up his skills (Step 4), among them mechanical engineering, with his underlying knowledge of physics at play along with some preliminary understanding of manufacturing optimization.

These skills eventually would make this young OP Hero the iconic expert on a variety of subjects, including spacecraft design and manufacturing, clean energy deployment, automated production systems, and a plethora more.

Yes, you might have guessed it. Our OP Hero who attained mastery over his life game by developing an unparalleled array of synergistic skills is none other than the unstoppable visionary Elon Musk, known for his groundbreaking enterprises such as Tesla, SpaceX, PayPal, and more.[10]

By applying his unique talents to acquire exceptional skills, the poor boy who was bullied and worked dangerous jobs to survive eventually ascended to become the wealthiest player on the Earth Server. He accomplished this through completing a variety of epic quests that were formerly laughed at by his critics as "humanly impossible."

While Musk has become a controversial figure in recent years owing to his political angle, his straightforwardness from having

Asperger's syndrome, and the demons his abusive father installed into him, it should still be indisputable that he is extraordinarily successful in the game he is playing. The goal of this book is to reveal how individuals conquer their respective games in a systematic way, allowing us to learn from them and apply their techniques to our own lives. In Musk's case, we examine his adept use of attributes to acquire a diverse set of skills and apply them harmoniously toward his quests.

But how did our young Musk, who had just left the dangerous lumber mill and had only acquired a variety of engineering skills along with knowledge from his books, go from poor, smart kid to become the world's most preeminent tycoon mogul?

Soon after his lumber mill adventures, he enrolled in Queen's University in Ontario, Canada, to get one of the most prominent skill boosts – a college education.

It is important to note that one's skills and abilities only are relevant to the game (Step 1) they are playing and their roles (Step 3) within the game. At this stage, Musk's main game, as interpreted by this book, is "strive for greater human enlightenment," which in essence means uncovering the truth of the universe for humanity. Through his mission of trying to extend human consciousness and his constant effort to build technology for businesses, we interpret his role in this game as an *entrepreneurial engineer.*

We already saw his performance as an entrepreneurial engineer when he built and sold the game *Blastar* at the age of thirteen. But to further level up his skills (Step 4) as an entrepreneurial engineer, he made sure he learned both business skills as well as engineering fundamentals. At Queen's University, he double majored in business and physics.

These skills were invaluable as they equipped Musk with a comprehensive understanding of "how things work." Physics unveiled the mechanisms of the natural world, while business and economics provided insights into finance and market dynamics.

With this combined knowledge, Musk was empowered to engineer both groundbreaking technologies and enterprises, challenging conventional norms by harnessing the concept of *first principles* – breaking down the problem to its fundamental principles to arrive at innovative solutions – toward these world dynamics.[28]

While attending Queen's University, Musk augmented his skill set as an entrepreneurial engineer by selling computer parts and fully assembled computers in his dormitory for additional income. Furthermore, acknowledging his own shortcomings in public speaking, he took the initiative to participate in schoolwide public speaking contests. This wasn't merely a pursuit of his innate interests or a straightforward progression on his academic path, but rather a deliberate and strategic move to enhance his skills (Step 4) by leveling-up in the game he had chosen to play.

It was during this time that one of his most important allies (Step 5) – his brother Kimbal Musk – joined him at Queen's University. In order to further expand their alliance via mentors and acquire more business skills, they flipped through newspapers to find prominent business people, taking on the quest (Step 6) of cold-calling these potential mentors to get lunch together.

Through this quest, they got in touch with Peter Nicholson, an executive from the Bank of Nova Scotia. Even though Nicholson was not in the same region and required hours of travel by train to meet, the Musk brothers were so determined to build alliances that they invited him for lunch. It took six months to get on Nicholson's calendar, but he agreed to meet these college kids because they had the boldness and gumption to cold-call him and arrange a meeting.[29]

---

[28] The first principles approach is a problem-solving method that involves breaking down complex problems into their most basic, fundamental elements. By questioning every assumption and starting from these core principles, innovative solutions can be developed without being constrained by traditional methods or analogies. This technique allows for original thinking and can lead to breakthroughs that are not achievable when relying on conventional wisdom.

[29] As indicated here, if you are impressed with Elon Musk's success and want to replicate it, a good starting point would be taking on the quest of cold-calling successful people found online and asking for mentorship.

Following their encounter, Nicholson was impressed enough by their unyielding determination that he offered a summer internship quest at his bank to Musk, cementing himself as a trusted advisor for years to follow.

The internship quest (Step 6) at Bank of Nova Scotia allowed Musk to acquire important skills (Step 4) and allies (Step 5) that would subsequently have a profound influence for his PayPal quests many years later.

Throughout this time, Musk seriously contemplated embarking on a career as a video game entrepreneur, driven by his passion for gaming. However, he felt such a path would not yield significant enough contributions to humanity. Consequently, he explored five engineering fields that he believed could wield the most substantial impact on humanity's future:

1. The Internet
2. Sustainable Energy
3. Space Exploration
4. Artificial Intelligence
5. Human Genetic Reprogramming or DNA Engineering

From this list, Musk unequivocally ruled out meddling with human genetics due to its ethical implications. However, he developed a profound fascination with sustainable energy and space exploration.[30] Such interest was fueled in part by influential literary works like *The Hitchhiker's Guide to the Galaxy* and his admiration for the iconic astronaut, Neil Armstrong.

If you recall from Step 1: Choose Your Game, one of the best ways to determine your game is to explore which books and people inspire you the most. This was literally the path that guided Musk toward his epic world-saving game.

---

[30]In fact, when he met Nicholson's daughter Christie, the second sentence he said after meeting her was: "I think a lot about electric cars. Do you think about electric cars?"

Of course, Canada was always the stepping stone for Musk to move to the US, so he later transferred to the University of Pennsylvania on a scholarship, where he obtained a double degree in physics and economics from the Wharton School of Business. UPenn is among the prestigious Ivy League universities, with Wharton being one of the top-tier business schools in the world that specializes in corporate finance. Here, Musk continued to level-up his skills in understanding how both the natural world and human systems work.

It was during his time at UPenn that he wrote many papers, such as "The Importance of Being Solar" and "Ultracapacitors," which received near-perfect marks. While some critics claim Musk doesn't deserve his success, his initiative of cold-calling notable individuals found in newspapers and earning a double degree from an Ivy League institution on a scholarship stand as commendable achievements above most people in society.

During the summer breaks, Musk moved to California to undertake two additional internship quests (Step 6) in the heart of Silicon Valley to further sharpen his skills (Step 4). By day, he worked at Pinnacle Research Institute, an intellectual hub teeming with some of the world's most astute engineers researching ultracapacitors. This engagement significantly bolstered Musk's knowledge and abilities regarding cutting-edge battery technologies.

At night, Musk transitioned into his internship quest at Rocket Science Games, enhancing his expertise in gameful design and software engineering. Interestingly, the industry-transforming Visionary Innovator, Steve Jobs, also initiated his illustrious journey within the gaming sphere at Atari. Jobs was deeply inspired by gameful design principles, notably the concept of intuitive simplicity – "insert coin and avoid Klingons" – with no manual necessary.

Along with Musk's first business quest of creating *Blastar*, there seems to be true gamification secrets of success hidden within games, just waiting to be discovered by those who are intellectually curious enough to dig into them.

After completing his internship quests and fulfilling his coursework at UPenn (though the official conferral of his degree was delayed two years due to graduation technicalities), Musk relocated to California, where he embarked on a Ph.D. program in applied physics and materials science at Stanford University. This quest seemed to be the best route for Musk to augment his knowledge and proficiency in ultracapacitors – a vanguard technology within the realm of battery innovations.

However, the vibrant innovation and abundant promise of Silicon Valley proved irresistible. Specifically, he found himself captivated by the burgeoning phenomenon known as the internet. To Musk, the internet was akin to humanity's nervous system.

This vision of the internet was so important to Musk's idea of human consciousness that in 1995, Musk dropped out of Stanford University after only two days of attendance.[31]

This decision officially transitioned Musk's game from "strive for greater human enlightenment" to "realize the transformative potential of the internet to change the world," as he hard commits from seeking scholarly knowledge to becoming a full-fledged entrepreneur pushing to pioneer the forefronts of internet innovation.

As a result of this game change, his role (Step 3) also evolved from an entrepreneurial engineer to an *internet entrepreneur.*

Of course, the following series of new quests (Step 6) meant that both Musk and his brother Kimbal Musk needed to develop new skills (Step 4). Together they co-founded Zip2, a web software company, with little more than their savings, some family help, and a daring vision. The task was tough: to offer business directories

---

[31]In fact, Stanford University could only find records of his acceptance to their school but no records of attendance, which was provided to Ashley Vance as proof for his 2015 biography of Musk.

and maps for newspaper company websites during the dawn of the online revolution.

Some of the default skills Musk needed to level-up on were software engineering and strategic thinking.

Thanks to the skills (Step 4) he developed with his first mentor, Peter Nicholson at Nova Scotia Bank, and his bachelor's degree in economics from UPenn, he refined his abilities in finance, economics, negotiations, and public relations to strive in the new game level. Those skills helped Zip2 raise $3 million from the venture capital firm Mohr Davidow Ventures.

Elon's cold-calling skills also secured a mind-blowing deal with the digital maps and directions company Navteq: namely, Zip2 could use all their technology for free. He also developed his visionary leadership and stoic management skills – something that he would rely on greatly in his future ventures.

This was extremely important for Musk's life game progress, as he explains, "I had never really run a team of any sort before. I'd never been a sports captain or a captain of anything or managed a single person. I had to think, "Okay, what are the things that affect how a team functions? The first obvious assumption would be that other people will behave like you. But that's not true."

While his stoic management skills were empowered by his re-lentless problem-solving, goal obsession, and emotional resilience attributes (Step 2), it also fed on his possible attribute weaknesses (often the other side of the coin for his strengths) such as being extremely demanding, lacking empathy, and having a blunt com-munication style.[32]

Luckily, and true to the 10K HP ethos, Musk had allies (Step 5) to make up for his weaknesses. His brother Kimbal Musk was

---

[32] In 2021, during his appearance as a host on the renowned US television show, *Saturday Night Live*, Musk candidly disclosed that he has Asperger's syndrome, a condition that is part of the autism spectrum disorder, often characterized by difficulties in social interaction and nonverbal communication. He would often speak so harshly to his team that he would make them feel humiliated and demoralized – something not very productive when being a manager.

an extremely upbeat sales leader at the company and helped with improving the mood and culture of Zip2. According to one of their sales staff, Jeff Heilman, "Kimbal was the eternal optimist, and he was very, very uplifting. I had never met anyone quite like him."[11]

On top of that, Musk also had an ally in the form of cofounder and mentor named Greg Kouri, who became an ally through Musk's alliance building (Step 5) efforts while still in Canada. Kouri invested $6,000 and moved to California to join Zip2 as a cofounder in early 1996.

Most importantly, being in his 30s and a higher-level businessman, Kouri moderated Musk's more impulsive behaviors and helped reduce the "toxicity" in his work culture. Eventually, this helped Musk become more patient and empathetic alongside his stoic management skills. Later he reflected back, "You have to put yourself in a position where you say, 'Well, how would this sound to them, knowing what they know?' "

Eventually, all these skills, hard work, and sleepless quests led Zip2 to sell to Compaq for $307 million dollars in 1999, with Musk personally making $22 million ($16 million after paying his taxes) at the age of twenty-eight.

This marked the Musk brothers' first significant triumph while infusing Musk with the capital to dream bigger. As the new millennium dawned, Musk plunged headlong into his next venture, a new quest (Step 6) called X.com, which began as an internet bank but later became known as PayPal.

Continuing his game of "realizing the transformative potential of the internet to change the world," Musk remembered from his previous internship quest at Bank of Nova Scotia that banks are slow-moving and often herd-like. He also believed that the future of finance would be in the realm of the internet. With some knowledge (Step 4) of how banks work and a few allies (Step 5) he met while interning at the Bank of Nova Scotia, he started X.com (Step 6) to create a comprehensive online financial institution offering services like checking and savings accounts, brokerage services, and insurance.

So how would Musk achieve such an audacious undertaking within the institutionalized banking industry equipped with only an intern's level of experience and knowledge?

In the 2012 movie *Marvel Studios' The Avengers*, when S.H.I.E.L.D Agent Maria Hill questioned Tony Stark's know-it-all comments with, "When did you become an expert in thermonuclear astrophysics?" Stark, known as Iron Man, promptly replied, "Last night," indicating he had absorbed all the necessary knowledge in this new environment through reading.

True to Iron Man's style, the way Musk sought to disrupt and replace all the banks and insurance companies was this: he read a book about the banking industry.

As tongue-and-cheek as that sounds, this theme of Musk taking on learning quests through reading books would become a recurring theme in his SpaceX and Tesla days. The takeaway? The activity you are doing right now seems to truly be an effective way to exercise Step 4: Enhance Your Skills, in your 10K HP journey.

After X.com was founded, Musk quickly discovered there was a barrage of regulations and compliance issues that felt impossible to overcome, and he even experienced betrayal when all his cofounders deserted him and left him with a shell of a company and a handful of employees.

This was when Musk's powerful attributes (Step 2) of relentless problem-solving, adaptability, and emotional resilience allowed him to persist in the game. Eventually, X.com overcame most of the regulatory issues, merged with another company called Confinity, and was soon rebranded as PayPal.

Here Musk would build some "frenemy" allies (Step 5) with the Confinity cofounders Peter Thiel and Max Levchin, who later pulled a coup to replace Musk as the CEO but also invested in his future companies.

In 2002, PayPal was finally sold to eBay for an astounding $1.5 billion. Given his ownership stake in the company, Musk reportedly walked away with $176 million after paying $74 million in taxes.

A happy ending for a bullied boy with big dreams and determination.

Except that, for an OP Hero like Musk, this was just the beginning of his 10K HP journey.

To the Stars: SpaceX

After a brief attempt to live out a normal family life in Los Angeles, California, Musk was ready to evolve his game again, this time shifting upwards – out of the Earth Server and toward the stars.

The transformative catalyst that set this shift into motion can be traced back to a book that captivated Musk during his formative teenage years – *The Hitchhiker's Guide to the Galaxy*. Within the pages of this ingenious blend of science fiction and comedy, Musk discovered a profound truth: the power of asking the right questions over possessing all the answers.

He came to the realization that humanity's current level of consciousness was insufficient to comprehend the true meaning of life. However, Musk envisioned a future where generations of humans, tens of thousands of years ahead even, would possess heightened consciousness and possess the ability to unravel life's ultimate purpose.

He then saw his own purpose as maximizing the probability that humans would survive for that long.

So, with his newfound centimillionaire status, Musk transitioned his role (Step 3) uniquely into *existential innovator* and upgraded his life game (Step 1) to safeguarding the existence of humanity and to extend consciousness beyond Earth.

Why beyond Earth? Well, according to Musk, if we as a species are stuck on a single planet, our ultimate fate is doom. If we don't destroy ourselves or run out of resources, the grim fact that the sun is slowly expanding means humans will inevitably go extinct if we can't leave this planet.

Because of this, Musk strategically selected Los Angeles to be the place of his residence (Musk applies zone shift quests regularly), particularly because it was the hub of aeronautics and space engineering.

There he joined a new guild (Step 5) called the *Mars Society*, a nonprofit with prestigious members such as the legendary movie producer James Cameron and NASA planetary scientist Carol Stoker, dedicated to exploring and eventually settling on Mars. Musk built a great deal of alliances there before starting his own guild, the *Life to Mars Foundation*, where he would invite all sorts of experts to understand the viability of exploring space.

This was also where he connected with some of the highest-level players in the field of rocket science and space engineering, such as Tom Mueller, Chris Thompson, and Michael Griffin. Griffin helped Musk understand various implications of physics and rockets, allowing him to level up these key skills (Step 4) before Griffin went on to become head of NASA a few years later. This ally would become instrumental to Musk's future quests.

After some unrealized quests of trying to send a plant to Mars as well as failed visits to Russia to buy intercontinental ballistic missiles, Musk applied his attributes (Step 2) and skills (Step 4) to come up with a game plan so audacious and so ingenious that even the highest-level players in any role considered it ludicrous.

Using his attributes such as learning agility, comprehensive recall, and, importantly, proactive optimism, Musk leveled-up his knowledge in engineering and acquired the skill of *rocket science* by delving into textbooks such as *Rocket Propulsion Elements* by George P. Sutton, *Structures, Or Why Things Don't Fall Down*, and

Introduction to Rocket Science and Engineering, among others.

Through his research and his school of thought of first principles, Musk realized that he could make his own rockets for a fraction of the cost that the Russians or NASA were making them for. In 2002, Musk decided that he would start his own rocket company, the Space Exploration Technologies Corporation, better known as SpaceX, to make space travel accessible and affordable, with the ultimate objective of colonizing Mars.

This was a difficult task: of the 400 rockets blasted into space between 1957 to 1966 by the US government, with its unparalleled deep pockets and "an army of people," 100 of them crashed and burned. For a mere man and tech startup to do the same thing more effectively would be considered blasphemous.

Beyond just understanding rocket science, Musk needed to acquire additional skills in scientific problem-solving, resource utilization, quality assurance, and supply chain management.

Equipped with the stoic management abilities he had leveled-up earlier, Musk faced a series of setbacks with SpaceX, including multiple failed rocket launches. Each failed attempt cost tens of millions of dollars and countless person-hours.

However, despite the escalating challenges and the dismissive voices of critics, his stoic management and visionary leadership remained unyielding.

Finally, in 2008 Musk was able to launch SpaceX's first successful rocket out of orbit. This was truly astonishing, because normally only governments of top-tier world powers get to play in space. But Musk applied his physics, economics, engineering, and management skills to make it happen on his own terms.

Now with international recognition and credibility, SpaceX was awarded a significant contract by NASA for $1.6 billion, which took the company out of financial distress and imminent bankruptcy. Oh... remember that Michael Griffin guy who became an ally to

Musk back in the days of Musk's Life to Mars Foundation guild? Griffin visited Russia with Musk and almost became a cofounder of SpaceX but turned it down because he didn't want to do the zone shift quest and move to Los Angeles.

This same Michael Griffin later leveled-up and was the head of NASA when SpaceX received $1.6 billion in contracts after their successful launch. Though Griffin and Musk's relationship was reportedly bumpy at times, it is compelling that many milestones of SpaceX became possible because Musk had taken the initiative to start a guild and establish various allies (Step 5) who shared his vision (Step 1) and who joined him on numerous quests (Step 6). Aren't you excited that we're almost at the chapter on Step 5: Build Your Alliance?

Later on, Musk's skills (Step 4) in scientific problem-solving, resource utilization, visionary leadership, and rocket science allowed SpaceX to become the first entity in the world to have reusable rockets that land back on earth. SpaceX has since launched hundreds of rockets into orbit and released thousands of internet-providing satellites through its Starlink services.

Innovation on the Ground: Tesla

Of course, when most people think about Musk, they don't immediately think about SpaceX. They think about Tesla. As if one crazy company weren't enough at one time, while Musk was building SpaceX, he concurrently embarked on the monumentally difficult quest of building the first significant electric car company in the world.

As Musk's game set his mind to tackling the world's sustainable energy challenges, his ultracapacitor battery technology skills (Step 4) from places like Pinnacle Research Institute naturally led to the Tesla Saga and the following quest lines.

At the time electric cars were not seen as viable because of the immense amount of battery energy needed to move heavy machinery and people over long distances. They were mostly seen as golf carts for very light and small-distance usages. But with the skills Musk acquired over physics, battery technology, and visionary leadership, alongside some allies (Step 5) such as JB Straubel, Martin Eberhard, and Marc Tarpening, Tesla was able to create the first compelling electric car company, which eventually pushed most of the other automobile companies to invest in electric vehicles.[33]

Creating any car company in 2004 was pretty insane if you didn't compare it to creating a space exploration company. In fact, no car company since Ford's founding in 1903 has ever been successful in the United States. To accomplish these overwhelmingly hardcore quests, Musk had to again refine his engineering skills and delve into manufacturing optimization to realize his vision.

As the company scaled, he faced new sets of challenges that required brand new skills such as supply chain management, resource utilization, manufacturing optimization, and he also had to further develop his skills in visionary leadership and stoic management.

All this led to breathtaking results as a company CEO for any industry. In 2024, Tesla sold close to 1.8 million vehicles and made $98 billion in revenues, up from 936K vehicles and $53.8 billion in revenues in 2021. Out of the total 7.25 million total vehicles that Tesla has sold since 2008, 25% were sold in 2024 alone. Because of that, in March of 2025 Tesla has a market cap of $804 billion and is the world's eleventh most valuable company in terms of market cap. This made Musk the richest man in the world based on his Tesla shares alone.

---

[33] Martin Eberhard and Marc Tarpening originally registered the company and invited Musk to become the leading investor. At the same time, Musk was supporting JB Straubel in his own electric car startup. Musk suggested they join forces under the Tesla entity, with him becoming the Chairman of the Board. Later, there was a falling out where Musk claimed Eberhard was dishonest with funds and nearly drove the company to the ground, forcing Musk to take over and save it. As a result, there is debate about whether Musk should be considered a "founder" of Tesla or just an early investor, similar to Tony Hsieh of Zappos. Regardless, it would be accurate to say that Musk was the most critical individual leading to Tesla's success today.

Yes, with all the other awe-inspiring quest lines Musk tackled, such as integrating the human brain with computers via Neuralink, co-founding OpenAI (which birthed ChatGPT), excavating massive tunnels with The Boring Company, or addressing the profitability issues of the social media platform formerly known as Twitter, he had to continuously master new skill sets and abilities that exceed many professionals in those respective fields.

Without turning this book into a full-fledged biography of Musk, I want to emphasize how, at each stage of his early life, he was focused on acquiring the right knowledge and skills for advancing forward in his game. These were not isolated instances of learning but pivotal acquisitions that he later integrated and applied synergistically to conquer new major quests, many of which were of legendary difficulty.

Some have argued that Musk doesn't have actual skills of his own, but he just gets a lot of money to hire the best people to do the amazing work for which he takes credit. However, when asked, the "best people" he hires such as Kevin Watson – a SpaceX Engineer who built a $10 million avionics systems onto the SpaceX Dragon Rocket for $10,000 – had this to say about Musk:

"Elon is brilliant. He's involved in just about everything. He understands everything. If he asks you a question, you learn very quickly not to go give him a gut reaction. He wants answers that get down to the fundamental laws of physics. One thing he understands really well is the physics of the rockets. He understands that like nobody else. The stuff I have seen him do in his head is crazy. He can get in discussions about flying a satellite and whether we can make the right orbit and deliver Dragon at the same time and solve all these equations in real time. It's amazing to watch the amount of knowledge he has accumulated over the years. I don't want to be the person who ever has to compete with Elon. You might as well leave the business and find something else fun to do. He will outmaneuver you, outthink you, and out-execute you."[12]

Out of all the skills Musk possesses, one that is extremely applicable to everyone reading this book is the real-life game skill *siphoning*. Siphoning is a Warlock skill that absorbs the power of its targets and uses it for the caster's own purposes.

You've likely heard Picasso's saying, "Good artists copy, great artists steal," which Steve Jobs repeated as one of the keys to his success. This refers to the ability to quickly learn everything there is about others and effectively apply it to your own creations.

I like the term siphoning because it adds an element of power and scaling to the concept of "learning as much as you can from another person." It elevates a potentially mundane process to something that feels dynamic and captivating. Eric Siu, in his book *Leveling Up*, notes that, "Kobe Bryant, five-time NBA champion, was said to imitate basketball legend Michael Jordan so extensively that when Jordan was asked who could have beaten him in his prime, he said Kobe Bryant – because Kobe stole all his moves."[13]

Elon Musk has that same skill generally maxed out. To understand how high-leveled Musk's siphoning is, consider what biographer Ashley Vance wrote about Musk's special ability in his 2015 biography:

Musk initially relied on textbooks to form the bulk of his rocketry knowledge. But as SpaceX hired one brilliant person after another, Musk realized he could tap into their stores of knowledge. He would trap an engineer in the SpaceX factory and set to work grilling him about a type of valve or specialized material. "I thought at first that he was challenging me to see if I knew my stuff," said Kevin Brogan, one of the early engineers. "Then I realized he was trying to learn things. He would quiz you until he learned ninety percent of what you know." People who have spent significant time with Musk will attest to his abilities to absorb incredible quantities of information with near-flawless recall. It's one of his most impressive and intimidating skills and seems to work just as well in the present day as it did when he was a child vacuuming books into his brain.

After a couple of years running SpaceX, Musk had turned into an aerospace expert on a level that few technology CEOs ever approach in their respective fields.

If you think about the implications of learning ninety percent of another person's knowledge on a regular basis, you'll realize this is actually mind-boggling and a key reason why Musk is able to dominate in so many different high-skill industries.

Jim Cantrell, a co-founding member of SpaceX, said this about Elon's intelligence: "He is by far the single smartest person that I have ever worked with ... period. I can't estimate his IQ but he is very, very intelligent. And not the typical egghead kind of smart. He has a real applied mind. *He literally sucks the knowledge and experience out of people that he is around.*"

OP Hero Elon Musk: Takeaways

OP Hero Elon Musk was relentless in enhancing his skills, reading all the books in his local library, and learning how to code in his youth. In college, he cold-called successful people to learn from them and took on multiple impactful internships, alongside double majoring in economics and physics in order to understand the world better.

After hiring the best talents, Musk applied the real-life game skill *siphoning* to absorb as much knowledge from his teammates as possible, which led him to become the most knowledgeable and skilled individual in his entire company. All this skill enhancement allowed him to dominate in multiple established industries.

Although Musk has mastered the siphoning skill to the ultimate degree, you too possess the capacity to apply this skill by learning from the most formidable players globally. That's precisely why I've dedicated numerous pages to dissecting the playthrough of the Earth Server's most accomplished OP Heroes – their paths to acquire and apply skills, their techniques for building alliances, and their strategies for embarking on quests.

With these skills acquired, you are ready to become a historical OP Hero yourself.

Chapter 5 Highlights

- Focus on mastering synergistic skills (skills that power up each other) to achieve success in your chosen role.
- Skills are developed in months through practice, education, and diligent effort, unlike innate attributes, which can take many years or decades.
- Prioritize essential skills for your mission to enhance your progress.
- Balance between specializing in a few synergistic skills and diversifying to other skills – so you are not only a specialist, nor a dabbler, but something in between.
- Map and rank your current skills to identify areas for improvement by creating a Skill Triangle.
- Develop a Target Skill Triangle by studying top masters in your desired role.
- Enhance your skills through deliberate practice, learning quests, and targeted development.
- Utilize real-life game skills categorized under different classes (Warrior, Ranger, Mage, Rogue, Druid, Paladin, Warlock) to improve specific areas of your life.
- Build and leverage alliances to support your skill development and achieve significant breakthroughs.

Chapter 6: Build Your Alliances (Network)

STEP 1	STEP 2	STEP 3
Choose Your Game MISSION	*Know Your Attributes* TALENTS	*Select Your Role* SPECIALTY

STEP 4	STEP 5	STEP 6
Enhance Your Skills CRAFT	***Build Your Alliance*** **NETWORK**	*Achieve Your Quests* MILESTONES

"Alone, we can do so little; together, we can do so much."

—— Helen Keller

Now that you have determined the game you are playing, identified your attributes and roles, and assessed the skills you have and should acquire, it's time to look for allies.

Allies are generally people who are playing the same life game as you (with similar passions or goals) but who have complementary roles and skills. They could also be individuals who share the same quests (Step 6) as you at any given time.

In most co-op dungeon games like *World of Warcraft*, the dungeons and raids are designed to be tackled by five to forty players. If you decide to take on any raid containing relevant rewards by yourself, no matter how strong you are, you will fail miserably. In team competition games like *Counter-Strike* or *League of Legends*, five players are pitted against five other players. Even if one of those five players becomes AFK ("away from keyboard" – basically inactive), it almost certainly leads to a team loss. If you decide to fight the other team of five by yourself, your skills won't be able to turn any meaningful game around.

Similarly, in our life games, each achievement or milestone reached is typically the product of combined efforts, the culmination of multiple minds working in unison. The value of building alliances, finding allies, and networking cannot be underestimated. As we embark on our life game, the relationships we cultivate often play a pivotal role in achieving important milestones (Step 6).

If we break down the foundations of life success, it usually boils down to two key factors: *ability* and *opportunity*. Ability comes from applying your attributes (Step 2) to learn powerful and synergistic skills (Step 4). On the other hand, one main source of opportunity – besides degrees, credentials, and reputation – is your connections.

As you can see, building alliances, often referred to as networking, is just as important, if not more important, than securing an advanced degree or possessing high skill. From seeking professional advice, building a team, and creating career opportunities, to developing friendships, networking has not only enriched my own life but also enhanced the lives of many people on their 10K HP journeys.

The Importance of Building Alliances

Here are some concrete benefits of having a strong alliance:

- **Power of Collaboration**: No matter how talented you are, you can't achieve much alone. Society thrives on teamwork, and the most remarkable achievements result from people working together. Architects need builders, business leaders need teams, and even individual athletes rely on coaches and support staff. Teamwork is essential to create the most value in the world.
- **Being Resourceful**: Connections make you resourceful. Knowing people and being known opens up opportunities. Networking and building alliances ensure that the right skills and rewards find their way to you.
- **Life Sharing**: Meaningful companionship is crucial. Achieving success is hollow if you are alone. What truly matters are the people who struggle with you, whom you trust and love as you reach the top. Sharing your journey makes life fulfilling and your game worth playing. Support, time, and care spent with others make life truly worth living. In Dr. Jane McGonigal's book *SuperBetter*, she explains that playing competitive games alone can harm mental health, while playing with friends enhances emotional well-being.[1] Amidst striving for success, many forget the importance of human connection. Make life complete by sharing fellowship with others.

So how does this play out in your 10K HP journey? If you are a businessperson trying to start a tech company, you would likely want to find an engineer partner who shares your passion for solving the same problems. If you are an extroverted, well-spoken person, perhaps you can find allies who may not be as loquacious but are more organized and detail-oriented. By partnering up, one of you might take on a marketing or sales-oriented role, while the other focuses on finance or operations.

Sometimes your allies will be working on the same project, in the same company, or even in the same household with you. Other times, they might be in different companies. Either way, you know that when there is a need, they are there to support your game, and you are there to support theirs.

Below are various types of allies and ally entities relevant to your 10K HP life game:

Factions

A faction is a large group of people tied together by a high-level belief or identity. Religions, movements, alma maters, and cultural groups can all be considered factions. They are driven by belief, heritage, or history, rather than organizational structures.

A notable characteristic of a faction is the lack of an organized hierarchy with authority over the entire group. There might be a *guild* within a faction that has an organized hierarchy directing members toward a common goal, but the faction itself consists of individuals who share a common belief without being organized by any authority.

This also means it is often impossible to know everyone within the faction, as there isn't an organized member list for communication. Even as a faction leader, knowing every member is not feasible, nor is having direct control over them. However, when two people of the same faction meet, they immediately feel connected and are much more likely to help each other and support the faction's purpose.

As an example, when I transitioned from a skeptical and argumentative atheist to a Christian in 2003 (the same year I discovered gamification!), I joined a large worldwide faction of Christians who support me spiritually, mentally, physically, and sometimes financially. Similarly, I volunteer more of my time to help people and organizations when they reveal to me that they share the same faith and, hence, are from the same faction.

On the other hand, when I meet someone who graduated from UCLA, I feel intrinsically motivated to help them more than usual. The same applies to members of the international business fraternity of Delta Sigma Pi, which I joined while at UCLA (yes, you can have two factions overlapping in the same environment). Even if someone attended a different university and pledged for Delta Sigma Pi ten years after I did, if I encounter this "DSP brother," I feel an immediate connection and a desire to help them, similar to how I would help a distant nephew.

You could also categorize people who believe in gamification, the Octalysis Framework, or the 10K HP lifestyle as a faction. There are over a million people around the world who have learned the Octalysis Framework, most of whom I do not know nor manage. They find my book, my videos, or my literature from somewhere, and they become fans or practitioners. Of course, they also don't all know each other. But when one Octalysis fan meets another, they immediately feel connected and want to spend more time with each other. And as you might guess, there are way more people who are believers of gamification in general, which would be an even bigger faction.

Tesla or Elon Musk fans is another example of a faction bonded by beliefs. Most of these fans don't know each other, aren't part of the same organization, and aren't controlled by Musk, but when they bump into each other they can go on for hours about the merits of Musk while feeling very connected. Similarly, there are factions organized around a hatred or distrust toward Musk, which share similar characteristics as his fans in the opposite direction.

If the faction is too broad, such as "nine-to-five workers," it might not have the cohesive and relatedness power that more specific factions have. Nevertheless, people still relate to each other more than to those outside the faction. Some factions can be smaller and more specific, such as "women who work in mining." It may not be populous, but it is a group that shares a common background and, likely, similar challenges. They tend to be able to build a strong supportive circle with each other compared to the generic nine-to-five workers group.

However, since they are united by background but may not know each other personally or be part of an organized group, this would still be considered a faction and not yet a guild. A guild forms within a faction when there is an organized group that coordinates people toward specific objectives. Other examples of factions include yoga practitioners, anime fans, Asian Americans, NBA fanatics, hippies, freelancers, movie buffs, and more.

Depending on the game you are playing, it is often a good idea to become part of a big and powerful faction. However, not all factions are equally supportive in terms of members helping each other.

As much as I hate to admit it, the USC (University of Southern California, which is UCLA's main rival) alumni network is a much more supportive faction than UCLA's. USC alumni are known for being extremely proactive in helping each other and current students. Many USC alumni make it part of their life's mission (a game in itself!) to help other USC students and alumni become successful. Based on my own observations and discussions with others in my faction, UCLA alumni, on the other hand, are mostly just friendly and supportive toward each other but not as proactive as the average USC alumni.

Some factions have faction-wide communication channels that allow you to connect with other members, whether it be via a Facebook group, a LinkedIn group, Telegram, or a Discord channel. These are not centrally organized by a hierarchy; they are simply communication spaces for people who want to connect under the same banner.

If you consistently communicate via faction channels and help others there, you might become a known individual within the faction, creating a variety of new opportunities and possibly taking on leadership roles. Generally, the strength of a faction lies in the inherent "relatedness" that exists when members reach out to each other. This shared sense of belonging significantly increases the likelihood of mutual assistance.

Guilds

Guilds are small to large organizations where members share the same mission under an organized hierarchy. This hierarchy can be extremely flat or even decentralized, but it is structured to facilitate decision-making and ensure that everyone works toward a common goal.

A guild could be your company, the school you are currently attending, a chapter of an organization focused on a certain cause or craft, or a membership club you join. For example, as part of the Christianity faction, my guild would be my local church or the Christian leadership organizations I belong to.

Similarly, to be part of the UCLA faction, I first needed to join the UCLA guild as a student. During this time, I was under the authority, management, and curriculum of the university (guild) to accomplish the mission of graduating as an educated individual.

After graduating, I am no longer in the UCLA guild but remain in the UCLA faction, where the university no longer has any authority over me. Of course, some people decide to join the UCLA Alumni Association, which is another guild but includes a smaller percentage of actual UCLA faction members.

A guild could also be my local chapter of Delta Sigma Pi while attending UCLA. During my three to four years there, more than a hundred "brothers" bonded together, helping each other grow professionally under an elected hierarchy. I treat each of these guild members like direct family members. However, if I encounter DSP brothers from other chapters or those who joined after I graduated, I treat them like distant relatives – part of the faction but not the same guild.

Depending on the size of the guild, it is often realistic for someone to know everyone in it. In fact, some leadership teams know every single guild member and how they are performing toward the common goal.

My education platform, Octalysis Prime, serves as a guild for believers in the Octalysis Framework and in gamification. Members don't necessarily know everyone, but they communicate and help each other, coordinating on missions and quests.

In Octalysis Prime, my leadership and community team generally know the most active participants in the Octalysis Prime guild and keep track of how everyone is learning and growing. As the guild leader, I have even provided no-interest loans to OP members to help them pay off their credit card debts, referred them to jobs, or guided them to transformative experiences – anything that helps the guild become more successful and high-level in the world.

Another common example of a guild is the company you work for. Google, for instance, stands as one of the most influential guilds, characterized by its highly vetted talent and meticulous evaluation of cultural fit among members. Employees at Google can effortlessly connect and assist each other with endeavors within the company, as well as with favors outside the corporate sphere.

Similarly, my own company, The Octalysis Group, is a much smaller guild, yet each member feels they have joined a respected and close-knit family. Members of The Octalysis Group often spontaneously organize tours of Europe, form book clubs, and create highly creative birthday greetings for each other. They also collectively choose their teammates for various client projects, sometimes even opting for reduced compensation to ensure other team members receive more.

Almost all guilds have communication channels that allow members to connect and, more importantly, enable guild leaders to coordinate activities. Most guilds use publicly available social media platforms or internal intranet solutions to communicate and organize tasks.

When a guild becomes big enough, it can evolve into a faction (many religions or movements started off as guilds). The faction-leading guild then becomes the organizing unit that might trigger a global movement.

Parties

Parties are generally the small groups you work with to accomplish an immediate mission or quest. Unlike factions or guilds, everyone in the party knows each other intimately and understands how to collaborate effectively. This could be your company unit, your startup, your local basketball team, or your dance club.

Much like in *World of Warcraft*, where a guild leader deploys different guild members to take on dungeons and raids, a party is the group that works together to tackle those challenges and achieve immediate results.

Similar to a game where you have various roles like tank, damage dealer, and healer, your party should consist of complementary skills (Step 4) to help support each other toward the goal. Maybe someone excels in communication and persuasion, while another is strong in analytical skills. Perhaps one party member has a background in marketing, while another specializes in engineering. One might have experience in childhood development, while another knows how to make custom candy. The key is that these skills come together to complete the shared team quest.

When you form parties, it's important to know whether they are long-term or short-term. Long-term parties could be your company team that stays with you for years. Short-term parties might be like flash mobs, where you practice for one performance and then disband.

Long-term parties need careful planning and vetting. If someone isn't contributing meaningfully, you should consider changing teammates or finding ways to improve their performance. Constructive communication and chemistry are crucial for continuous success.

For short-term parties, there are still significant differences between high-impact and low-impact performances. However, after the project, the team disbands until another project brings you together. The current project's end result or outcome (while maintaining your reputation) is a high priority for these parties.

In my company, The Octalysis Group (the leading guild within the Octalysis Kingdom/faction), we differentiate between core team members and the Octalysis contractor network, also known as the bigger Octalysis family. Octalysis core team members continuously work together to improve the guild overall, investing time in team building, gaming, research, innovation, and more. This constitutes our long-term party.

Conversely, the Octalysis contractor network consists of talented individuals who are brought together for revenue-generating projects. They collaborate with core team members to deliver the highest value based on the Octalysis Framework. These teams, assembled for specific client projects, are short-term parties, and teammates likely won't work with the exact same people again within the year.

Partnerships

A partnership involves one or two other people with whom you are bonded to accomplish a long-term mission. These could be significant others, co-founders, business partners, sparring/research partners, or the colloquial "wingman." Duos like Steve Jobs and Steve Wozniak, Larry Page and Sergei Brin, Helen Keller and Anne Sullivan, Warren Buffett and Charlie Munger, or even Batman and Robin come to mind.

A partnership is like a team, but generally smaller and longer-term. Often, partnerships stay intact over decades, whereas parties are formed or changed as new needs arise or situations demand. As you can imagine, a good partnership is extremely important due to the intimate interactions, mutual reliance, and long periods of time spent together over many major quests. Trust and chemistry are imperative for a partnership.

It is also important to differentiate between the two types of trust within a partnership: *character trust* and *ability trust.* Character trust refers to the belief in a person's intentions to treat you with good faith, whereas ability trust relates to confidence in their skill set to achieve a desired outcome. For example, I have complete trust in my mother's intention to save my life if I was in danger. However, I wouldn't trust her to pilot a fighter jet to rescue me, simply because she lacks the necessary flying skills. In this scenario, I possess character trust in her but not ability trust.

I have witnessed numerous unnecessary emotional arguments between individuals who are shocked that their friends or family do not "trust" them enough to lend money to start a company. Indeed, while they may love and trust you as a good person, they may not have confidence in your skills to successfully run a business based on the actions you have demonstrated thus far.

No one inherently deserves ability trust – it is earned through prolonged hard work, self-improvement, and demonstrated results.

Therefore, don't feel hurt if someone close to you doubts your capability in a certain area. In fact, their closeness and concern for your well-being may make them more accurate evaluators of your abilities than mere acquaintances. It's up to you to prove to them that you have grown and are no longer the same person they knew years ago.

Ideally, only form partnerships with people in whom you have both character trust and ability trust. You know you can rely on them because they have the integrity to do the right thing, as well as the skills to deliver good outcomes. If either of these trusts is missing, it is difficult to form a strong partnership.

Additionally, chemistry is very important in a partnership. Strong trust enables good chemistry, which helps coordinate seamlessly while enjoying the process together. Let's look at an example of how great chemistry can result in world-class results.

Can Being Funny Help You Win a Nobel Prize?

The iconic father of behavioral economics, Daniel Kahneman, is the first psychologist to win a Nobel Prize in Economics. In his book, *Thinking, Fast and Slow*, he talks about how he was only able to accomplish his OP feats because of his late research partner, Amos Tversky.[2]

Amos Tversky, according to Kahneman, was an absolute genius. In their research community, there was a tongue-in-cheek way of gauging the intelligence of any particular person: how quickly they could realize that Tversky was smarter than them. If someone immediately recognized that Tversky was much smarter, they were considered highly intelligent. But if someone believed they were smarter than Tversky, it was seen as proof of their low intelligence. This alone highlights Tversky's legendary status in his 10K HP journey.

What struck me as most interesting about Kahneman's partner was that in his book, Kahneman repeatedly mentioned that Tversky was extremely funny. He would regularly make statements such as, "He was also blessed with a perfect memory for jokes and an exceptional ability to use them to make a point. There was never a dull moment when Amos was around." When they were discussing whether they should work together on their eventual breakthrough research, Kahneman also wrote, "It would be fun to explore the topic further together."

At first, I didn't think much of it. But it was mentioned so often that it caught my attention and curiosity, as if Kahneman was afraid the reader would miss this important quality about Tversky.

Finally, Kahneman revealed why this was so relevant and important before introducing his life's work to the reader: "Amos and I discovered that we enjoyed working together. Amos was always very funny, and in his presence, I became funny as well, so we spent hours of solid work in continuous amusement. The pleasure we found in working together made us exceptionally patient; it is much easier to strive for perfection when you are never bored."

Essentially, Kahneman is stating that the reason they could achieve more than anyone else in the industry was that he and Tversky had fun working together as allies and partners. With good chemistry, a partnership can thrive above teams that are supposedly smarter or more competent but lack similar synergy. This is akin to many multiplayer games, where coordination and team combos often prove to be the winning formula.

Other Alliance Relationships

While you normally would have a main role in your own 10K HP journey, you would also have relationship roles with others in their own 10K HP journeys. You already explored the foundations for some relationship roles such as partner, teammate, guildmate, and faction allies. But there are a few more that are worth mentioning.

Mentors and Coaches

One of the most transformative categories of allies in your 10K HP journey is the *mentor*. Just like in games, where a higher-level player can help you navigate challenging stages and level up faster, a high-level mentor in your life game can elevate your endeavors to a whole new trajectory. In fact, having a good mentor (or mentors) can assist with all six steps (!) in your 10K HP journey. Here's how a mentor can help any 10K HP Player, as long as they are proactive in seeking guidance:

- Help you identify the life game you should focus on (Step 1). A good mentor can listen to your dreams and aspirations and help you identify the true game you should pursue. Often, our judgment is clouded by fears and social friction, and wise guidance from someone who has already traveled that path can clear the air.
- Recognize your unique attributes (Step 2). Sometimes, we fail to recognize our own strengths. A mentor, with their external perspective, can help identify attributes that make you unique and guide you in leveraging them effectively. This insight is invaluable, as it helps you sharpen your strengths and address your weaknesses, setting you on a path of self-awareness and optimal choices in your life game.
- Help you define the role and specialty (Step 3) that makes the most sense for your game. A mentor, with their seasoned perspective from similar paths, can guide you in carving out a role that aligns perfectly with your unique attributes. They help you understand where your talents and attributes can be most effectively utilized, ensuring that you don't just play the game, but that you play it in a role that is relevant in the current "meta" (most effective tactical approach) and is something at which you could excel.

- Help you focus on the skills and abilities you should learn to achieve the best success (Step 4). Your mentor can help pinpoint the skills vital for your role's growth. They can provide a roadmap, much like a Skill Tree in a game, highlighting the skills that will maximize your potential and propel you toward victory. Their guidance ensures you invest your time and energy into learning what matters most, turning each new skill into an effective powerup against future obstacles.
- Introduce you to other high-level allies who can help you along your journey (Step 5). A mentor can introduce you to a network of people who can be instrumental in your journey. Imagine being introduced to a guild of experienced players, each bringing their own expertise and support. These connections can open doors to new opportunities and collaborations, much like forming a party with seasoned adventurers in a game, enhancing your journey with their wisdom and experience.
- Guide you toward the right quests and introduce previously unavailable ones (Step 6). A mentor can provide insightful advice on selecting quests that align with your game and role. Should you take this high-paying job, or join that startup you're passionate about? A mentor can ensure your quests align well with your game. Additionally, mentors can often introduce you to new quests that you wouldn't otherwise have access to, acting almost as a "cheat code" for your journey.

Depending on your industry, *coaches* can be very similar to mentors. They often assist when you already have a defined game, role, and quest, helping you leverage your attributes to improve your skills and synergize better with your allies. A good coach can help a mediocre team achieve astonishing results.

My alma mater, UCLA, is renowned for its tradition of excellence in basketball. UCLA ranks first in the number of NCAA championships won, boasting a total of eleven. In comparison, the University of Kentucky holds second place with eight championships, and the University of North Carolina is third with six. Most universities haven't won any championships at all, as by definition, only one out of the 358 NCAA Division I basketball teams can become the champion in any given year.

So UCLA is undeniably impressive. As a result, if a basketball player decided to take on the major quest of playing for UCLA, he would have the best odds of becoming a champion, right? Not necessarily. What might be less known to those outside the basketball community is that most of UCLA's championships, ten out of eleven to be precise, were won under the leadership of a single coach: John Wooden.

John Wooden was the UCLA basketball coach who led the team to ten NCAA championships between 1964 and 1975. This means that, during those years, his team won ten out of twelve possible championships, including an astounding seven-year streak. Remarkably, Wooden achieved this feat without relying on the same players throughout, as college basketball players typically leave every few years to graduate or join the professional NBA. John Wooden consistently transformed new students into champions. In fact, his last championship team wasn't composed of star players; instead, it was described as a group of "rugged opportunists" by sports analysts.[3]

Consequently, when John Wooden retired after the 1975 season, the championships stopped pouring in. It would only be in 1995, twenty years later, that UCLA won its last championship. Since then, UCLA has joined the ranks of the other hundreds of NCAA teams, not having won another championship to this day.

So, no: if you joined UCLA today as a basketball player, you would not have the highest odds of winning an NCAA championship. You would, however, have had the highest odds of winning a championship if you had played under John Wooden as your *coach*.

A good coach with a solid framework can literally turn mediocre players into consecutive champions. John Wooden's "pyramid of success" framework not only helped his players perform better on the basketball court, but it also helped many of them achieve career success afterward.

Andy Hill, who played under John Wooden and achieved three NCAA championships, later became president of two major media companies: CBS and Channel One News. Twenty-five years after graduating from UCLA, he reconnected with John Wooden and decided to co-write the bestselling book *Be Quick – But Don't Hurry! Finding Success in the Teachings of a Lifetime With Wooden* to showcase how John Wooden's framework and principles had helped him become successful in business and life.

While John Wooden's 10K HP journey can already qualify him as a legendary OP Hero, the lesson here for your own 10K HP journey is that you should actively seek out, even chase after, the best coach you can find.

Agents and Patrons

For creative and freelancing professionals who don't have a stable paycheck, *agents* and *patrons* are important allies who help you obtain opportunities so you can continue to create value in the world with freedom and flexibility.

Agents act as intermediaries, representing your interests and helping you navigate complex landscapes. They are crucial in fields like entertainment, sports, and literature, but their utility extends to any area where specialized knowledge and networks provide an advantage. Talent agents connect artists and performers with opportunities, business agents open doors to new markets and partnerships, and real estate agents guide significant property transactions.

Patrons provide crucial financial and institutional support, allowing creators to focus on their craft without financial stress. Universities, foundations, and investors act as financial patrons through grants, scholarships, and funding, while also enhancing credibility and visibility. For many roles (Step 3), cultivating these relationships is key to becoming a 10K HP Player.

Mentees, Sidekicks, and Staff

Mentees, sidekicks, and *staff* are essential allies who support your journey and can grow into powerful players themselves.

Mentees – those for whom you act as a mentor – bring fresh perspectives and energy to your organization. They often possess unique insights and innovative ideas that can invigorate your approach to various challenges. By investing time in mentoring, you help them develop their skills and build a loyal, capable team. This relationship creates a robust support system where mentees feel valued and motivated to contribute their best efforts.

A well-mentored individual can evolve into a key player who significantly contributes to shared goals and may even become a mentor themselves, perpetuating a cycle of growth and excellence. This continuous development ensures your organization remains dynamic and forward-thinking. Mentees who grow under your guidance are likely to become strong allies, championing your vision and advancing mutual objectives, leading to long-lasting professional relationships and sustained success.

Sidekicks are trusted companions who share your vision and complement your strengths and weaknesses. Think about famous sidekicks such as Robin for Batman, Samwise Gamgee for Frodo Baggins (from *The Lord of the Rings*), Dr. Watson for Sherlock Holmes, and Luigi for Mario.

A reliable sidekick offers honest feedback, emotional support, and shares the burden of leadership, bringing out the best in you and helping navigate complex situations. With a good sidekick, you can focus more on the tasks you excel at or enjoy most, reducing your worries. Over time, sidekicks can grow into leaders, taking on more responsibility and becoming pivotal in achieving your objectives. Their close working relationship with you allows them to internalize your values and goals, making them ideal candidates for future leadership roles. As they develop their own leadership skills, they drive projects independently, mentor other team members, and uphold the organization's vision, creating a legacy of competent and committed leaders.

Staff members form the backbone of your operations. Well-selected staff are crucial for maintaining a strong foundation. These individuals handle day-to-day tasks, ensuring your organization runs smoothly. Investing in their growth ensures your team remains capable and aligned with your vision. Providing opportunities for professional development and career advancement leads to higher job satisfaction, increased loyalty, and improved performance.

Empowered staff members create a supportive network, driving success and helping achieve long-term goals. When staff feel valued and empowered, they are more likely to take initiative, offer innovative solutions, and work collaboratively to overcome challenges. This fosters a positive work environment where everyone feels part of the mission, contributing to a cohesive and motivated team. Recognizing and nurturing talent within your staff builds a pipeline of future leaders, ensuring the continuity and growth of your organization.

Networking Starts With the Self

Now that we have established the structure of alliances, let's explore the strategy guide to expand on building alliances. In 10K HP, we call top-tier alliance-building *OP networking*, in the same spirit of being "overpowered" as the highest level of play within our life games.

So how do you actually apply OP networking and build your alliances within your 10K HP journey? The first thing to remember is this: OP networking starts with the *self*.

If you are a regular reader of self-growth books, I'm sure you have seen quite a bit of content out there that explains the steps to go out and network with others. However, in 10K HP, we believe that true OP networking begins with self-improvement. To network effectively, *you must be worth networking with*. Networking is reciprocal; you're not only seeking to enrich your life through your friends and allies, but you are also aiming to enrich *their* lives. Knowing a million people is counterproductive if they all think poorly of you.

Some might think, "Good networking is an attribute people are born with! I know I lack these skills, but I can't do anything about it!" The truth is, we have more control over our growth and development than many people realize. While attributes can't be learned quickly like skills, they can be developed over time through life experiences, attitude, and effort.

All it takes is a positive attitude and a constant will to improve. With a good attitude toward trying and growing, your brain activates a special superpower called neuroplasticity,[4] which is the ability of your nervous system to reorganize its structure, functions, or connections in response to intrinsic or extrinsic stimuli. Of course, you likely can't change yourself immediately, just like you can't become a great musician overnight. But continuous investment into growth and improvement can yield transformative results.

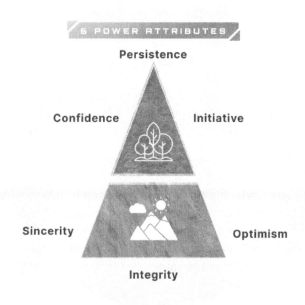

Figure 27. Six Power Attributes

Six Power Attributes for OP Networking

Within OP networking, there are six power attributes that help you start with the self: *integrity, sincerity, optimism, confidence, initiative,* and *persistence.* (See Figure 27.) Each power attribute builds on top of the previous one, with the first three being foundational, while the latter three are expansive.

Power attributes are the keystones of exceptional individuals, often seen in historical OP Heroes who have wielded these qualities to achieve great success. In the realm of building alliances, these attributes are indispensable. Without them, networking becomes a series of hollow actions, akin to playing notes in music without regard for rhythm, dynamics, tone, or emotion.

Integrity

Integrity transcends cultivating a reputation as a good person. It's about *being* a great person, especially when no one is watching. Integrity enables you to have pride in who you are and the life you lead.

Back in my high school English class days, I learned about archetypes in mythology: heroes, villains, sidekicks, and more. What was uniquely memorable to me was the teacher's explanation that heroes might vary in strength, wealth, or wisdom, but they all shared a defining trait: moral character. Without moral character, strength is meaningless. You cannot be the hero or main character in your own story without it.

From a young age, I taught my twin daughters, Symphony and Harmony, that constant self-improvement is vital. However, without integrity, all efforts are futile. You risk becoming a powerful villain, a far worse fate than being a weak hero or even a weak villain, as the latter causes less harm to society.

Integrity begins as personal accountability, but over time, others will recognize you as a person of principle. Earning this reputation is a hallmark of success in OP networking. Even if your actions go unnoticed, you can move through the world with confidence, knowing you stand for what is right. This inner strength naturally attracts the right allies to your life game.

Sincerity

After establishing strong integrity, the next crucial step is sincerity. It's possible to have high Integrity and always do the "right thing" without genuinely caring about others. In OP networking, it's equally important to care about your fellow human players. Shift your focus from self-benefit to empathy. Aim to help others as much as possible. Authenticity is key – find joy in others' successes, especially when you've contributed to them.

Sincerity is about deriving immense joy from others' achievements and feeling genuine sadness when things don't go their way. This mentality transcends seeking returns; it prioritizes genuine friendship. When you are truly sincere, people sense it, fostering trust beyond mere acquaintances.

Throughout my life, I've been consistently surprised by how quickly acquaintances trust me after just meeting, often sharing very personal insecurities or seeking advice. I didn't fully understand why, and it still surprises me to this day, but it seems my natural empathy and sincerity are immediately detected by people, who open up to me the moment we meet.

When people perceive you as sincere, trust builds swiftly, enabling you to build your alliance more effectively and undertake greater quests with a strong, supportive network.

Optimism

Optimism is essential in any journey. No one likes to be around people who are sad and grumpy all the time. Being optimistic means you can be a source of motivation that others draw hope from.

Some may worry they have little to offer, especially if they are young or low-level in their 10K HP journey. However, positive energy and happiness are invaluable. Bringing joy and optimism to interactions significantly enhances the daily lives of others. Don't be the "game over, man!" guy you see in movies. Be the person who is always thinking positively and encouraging others. Always inspire hope and creativity toward new solutions.

Optimism is also necessary when you face potential rejections while practicing your OP networking and honing your skills to build new alliances. An optimistic mindset helps you brush off rejections and prevents past failures from paralyzing your future efforts.

Winston Churchill aptly said, "Success consists of going from failure to failure without loss of enthusiasm." This captures the essence of optimism. It's a driving force that keeps you productive. How can you accomplish much if you're constantly coping with your own sadness? Feeling good and happy most of the time allows you to focus on growth and leveling up, rather than being bogged down by repeated moping timeouts.

At the end of the day, if you live life with optimism, not only will you bring value to those around you, you'll also have more fun while playing your life game.

Confidence

When you are optimistic and maintain a high level of integrity, it is easy to be confident.

Confidence is not about thinking of yourself as superior to others – that's arrogance. *Confidence is simply being optimistic about yourself.* It's knowing you are valuable because of who you are, not just what you can do. Therefore, your performance should not determine your confidence and self-worth.

A confident person recognizes their own strengths and appreciates the strengths in others. They understand that everyone excels at something they struggle with themselves, and they genuinely admire and celebrate these abilities. Confidence is crucial because when people don't know you, they rely solely on the image you present.

How you view yourself is often projected onto others. If you see yourself as insignificant, you will behave that way, and others will treat you accordingly.[34]

You must be the first person to believe in yourself for others to follow suit. Essentially, you teach people how to treat you, and you lead others to believe in themselves.

Initiative

Nothing will happen if nothing starts. Unless you are already an extremely high-level player, people won't automatically come to you. You have to take the initiative to grow your alliance. This attribute transitions from "who you are" to "what you must do" to have effective OP networking.

Taking initiative means overcoming the allure of your comfort zone. Be adventurous and willing to explore beyond your personal circle. Engaging and talking to strangers can be intimidating for many, but the fear of reaching out is often based on illusions.

In reality, there's nothing to lose. If you express respect and admiration for someone, even if they don't reply or they respond negatively, at worst you've made a snobby person feel good about themselves that day. While your networking attempt may be unsuccessful, you might never see this person again, which is the default scenario if you never reached out at all.

I often use the analogy of the "harmless dragon": outside your comfort zone lives a scary dragon with sharp claws and teeth, breathing fire that seems like it could consume your soul. However, you are completely invulnerable to this dragon. The dragon does zero damage to you because of your "invincibility" trait. Knowing

---

[34] Robert K. Merton first described this phenomenon in 1948 and labeled it the Self-Fulfilling Prophecy and Labeling Theory. In sociology, labeling theory also discusses how people's perception of themselves can be influenced by the labels others apply to them, which can then influence their behavior. "Self-Fulfilling Prophecies." *The Oxford Handbook of Analytical Sociology.* Peter Bearman, Peter Hedström, eds. Oxford University Press, 2009: pp. 294-314. https://users.ox.ac.uk/~sfos0060/prophecies.shtml

that the dragon cannot hurt you, you must ignore its intimidating appearance and confront it. Even if you don't have enough strength to slay the dragon, knowing that it cannot harm you should encourage you to try often.

Rewards will be given to those who bravely confront the harmless dragon.

Persistence

To many, persistence is the most challenging out of all the power attributes. It means never giving up, and it goes hand-in-hand with taking Initiative. People need to see that you are genuinely determined to connect with them. If someone ignores your email, send another one.

However, to avoid appearing desperate or pushy, give time between follow-ups so people can process the information. Provide value in your communication so that those you are reaching out to begin to see how you might help them. In life, good things that seem out of reach will open up for those who go the extra mile and persist even after facing rejection.

The hard part is finding the balance between being persistent and being annoyingly tone-deaf. If people say no and you keep pushing until they feel compelled to say yes, that is clearly a terrible approach. It will backfire, as people will start avoiding you. However, if someone doesn't reply to your email, it's likely because, despite feeling positive about it, they didn't have time to respond and then forgot. Think about how long it takes you to reply to some of your friends.

It doesn't matter if you're not a CEO of a large firm or a Nobel Prize winner. If you are willing to help when needed, bring pleasantness into people's lives, and believe that you have something to offer, either now or later, you give people a reason to know you. Even if you are just a student, if you demonstrate potential and ambition toward a great future and project an uplifting attitude, professionals will usually be interested in helping you.

Finally, having an existing strong alliance is another great reason for people to want to be your ally. The key is to start building it now!

Remember: To build alliances, you must become a worthy ally yourself.

It's Your Turn to Play: Establish Your Alliance

It's time for you to explore your allies and make sure you are part of the right group to help you become successful in your game.

Pick from One of the Three Game Modes

Easy: Identify the Factions, Guilds, Parties, and Partners you are already part of in your life game. Write down one thing each alliance has contributed to your game so far.

Medium: Take action to join a new Faction, Guild, or Team that aligns with your current game. Research and select a group that would strengthen your abilities, such as a professional association, mastermind group, or recreational club. Attend your first meeting, introduce yourself, and actively participate. Remember, showing initiative is key to being a valuable ally in return.

Hard: Step outside your comfort zone and build new alliances by reaching out to strangers. Identify individuals who inspire you or could be instrumental in your growth — these could be potential mentors, industry leaders, or role models. Craft a genuine, personalized message that highlights your admiration and clearly states how you'd like to connect or collaborate. Send out three of these messages this week. Even if you don't hear back, you've taken initiative and started building momentum.

To bring structure and focus to your journey, visit 10KHP.com/worksheets to unlock practice worksheets and discover the 10K HP Workbook.

OP Hero Profile: From Failed Freelancer to Timeless Genius – the Inventive Polymath

It's time to examine another historical OP Hero from the 15th century - someone who was considered a loser for decades until his mid-40s. Initially recognized as one of the most promising youths of his time, he became a struggling man facing rejection after rejection throughout his adult years. While he embarked on various commissions, his insatiably curious mind often led to a string of unfinished projects. Consequently, he frequently encountered instances where he did not receive payment for his diligent efforts.

At age twenty-five, he opened his own crafting workshop for freelance work, but it quickly failed. Over the next five years, he received only three known commissions; two were left unfinished, and one was never started. At one point, he wrote in his journal, "Two years of my salary still not received." Zero out of three in a five-year timespan – he indeed seemed like a loser.

After closing his workshop, he was so desperate to find work that he applied for a variety of jobs, from being a writer to a musician, an artist, and even a weapons inventor. Despite his diverse capabilities, his reputation for unfinished work persisted.

By the age of thirty, he was struggling with deep sadness and sorrow. Occasionally, he would finally receive the good news of being hired, but his emotional struggles and distracted mind would get him fired again, reinforcing the belief that he was a loser. Many times, he would pour months of effort into projects, only to have them abruptly canceled because he was distracted and couldn't stay on schedule, leaving his invested time wasted.

In his personal journal, our OP Hero expressed deep feelings of emotional pain, melancholy, and desperation. Seeking answers within himself, he wrote, "Tell me if anything was ever done... tell me... tell me..." These heartfelt words reveal his inner turmoil and longing for actual progress and success. He further captured his anguish, reflecting, "While I thought that I was learning how to live, I have been learning how to die."

Distressed by his lack of employment, our OP Hero once desperately submitted a proposal in pursuit of any available job with the Duke of Milan. In his application, he offered his skills as:

- An engineer capable of constructing the most exceptional bridges.
- A military engineer who could enhance fortifications, develop advanced weaponry, and invent innovative war machines for both offensive and defensive purposes.
- An architect capable of designing captivating public and private structures to enhance the beauty of the city.
- A sculptor skilled in working with marble, bronze, and clay.

This job application reveals his desperation for any available opportunity. Despite facing years of rejection, our emotionally perseverant (Step 2: Know Your Attributes) OP Hero finally received a chance to join the Court of Milan, where he was responsible for staging plays within the theater. This quest (Step 6) allowed him to apply his diverse interests and skills (Step 4) such as playwriting, music, art, and engineering to create stunning effects on the stage.

This demonstration of synthesized talent made him well-known among the royalty of Milan, Italy, and gained more favor with the

Duke of Milan. So that's when his life should take off and he should become a respected OP Hero, right?

Unfortunately, no. After years of sparse projects from the Duke of Milan, our determined *stage artist* (Step 3: Select Your Role) finally received a big-break opportunity. He was commissioned to create an epic monumental bronze horse sculpture known as the Sforza Horse. Our resolute hero, now aged forty years, embraced this chance to make his mark in history.

He eagerly delved into the project, devoting his time to studying horses, their anatomy, and meticulously planning the sculpture. With his characteristic attention to detail (Step 2), he diligently measured quantities and devised innovative techniques to conserve bronze while bringing his vision to life. After many jaded experiences, this quest (Step 6) ignited a renewed sense of purpose and excitement in our OP Hero, as he channeled his artistic prowess into capturing the grace and majesty of the horse in his work.

But at the same time, our OP Hero still grappled with his own personal weakness attributes (Step 2). He often found himself consumed by his inclination to daydream, leading to bouts of disorganization, a lack of focus, and a tendency to procrastinate. Even at this point in his life journey, these weaknesses hindered his progress and caused significant delays in his work.

This delay in delivery cost our OP Hero greatly. After months of hard work, a *plot twist event* occurred: the King of France waged war against Italy. Due to the outbreak of war, the Duke abruptly canceled the project in order to redirect the bronze for the production of cannons. This plot twist event left our OP Hero devastated, deepening his sense of disappointment and frustration. Not only was he unable to collect any payment, but this cancellation meant that his months of hard work were reduced to nothing. He was, once again, a failure in life.

This incident was such an embarrassing failure that it was later met with mockery from one of history's greatest artists: Michelangelo di Lodovico Buonarroti Simoni. In a confrontational encounter many years later, a much younger (twenty-three years to be exact) Michelangelo disdainfully remarked to our OP Hero, "So those idiots from Milan actually believed in you?"

Seeing countless projects slip through his fingers and falling behind contemporaries he considered less talented, our OP Hero lamented in his notebooks, "We do not lack devices for measuring these miserable days of ours..." He was pondering giving up his life, but fortunately, our OP Hero found the strength to persevere and continue the arduous journey.

Finally, at the age of forty-five, he stumbled upon and completed the pivotal quest that would solidify his place among the great masters of art. This pivotal quest was to paint one of the most iconic and revered masterpieces in history – *The Last Supper*. (See Figure 28).

Figure 28. The Last Supper

Yes, you might have guessed it: our OP Hero who was a distracted "loser" until his mid-40s is none other than the illustrious *Inventive Polymath* – Leonardo da Vinci.[5]

Leonardo da Vinci's remarkable contributions spanned a diverse range of disciplines, making him a truly interdisciplinary genius. Not only was he an extraordinary artist, his staggering impact on the world encompassed an extraordinary array of fields, from art and science to engineering and architecture.

To genuinely encapsulate the expansive breadth of Leonardo da Vinci's skillset and the visionary nature of his intellect, here is a catalog of the diverse fields to which he made substantial contributions. Regrettably, his practice of keeping his notes private (and in mirrored script, making them incredibly challenging to decipher) meant that many innovators in the fields listed below were unable to leverage his work before independently arriving at the same discoveries or inventions centuries later.

da Vinci's Achievements

While you read through the following list of da Vinci's achievements, keep in mind that unlike other OP Heroes who were photographed during their lives, he was born almost 600 years ago, before most things we enjoy today were invented.

- **Art**: Da Vinci's work in art needs little introduction. He painted some of the most recognized pieces in the world, including the *Mona Lisa* and *The Last Supper*. His work in art *alone* gave him equal standing to other historical OP Heroes like Michelangelo, Monet, and Picasso. His techniques, such as *sfumato* for soft transitions between colors, influenced many future artists. More on that later.
- **Anatomy**: Da Vinci conducted detailed studies of the human body. He created over 240 detailed drawings and wrote about 13,000 words on the topic. His findings included understanding the functions of the skeletal muscles and the principle of "antagonism," the structure of the human heart with its chambers and vessels, and how the aortic valve works.
- **Neuroscience**: Leonardo made some of the first wax castings of the human brain and cranium, providing a new way to study its structure. He theorized about the function of various parts of the brain, linking certain mental functions to specific areas of the brain, a precursor to modern neurobiology.
- **Engineering**: Da Vinci designed a variety of machines in his notebooks, some of which were precursors to modern inventions. These include early versions of a helicopter, an airplane, an armored tank, a machine gun, a parachute, a mechanical calculator, a self-propelled vehicle that could move straight or at "pre-programmed" angles, and even a robotic knight that could make theatrical movements without any human intervention. Many of these mechanics and

inventions were independently invented 100 to 400 years after his death by other individuals or teams.[35]

- **Architecture:**   Leonardo designed various architectural structures, from simple residences to complex fortifications. His architectural designs were innovative, with concepts such as revolving stages and portable bridges.   He was commissioned to design a dome for Milan's cathedral and an *Ideal City* for the Duke of Milan that improved communications, sanitation, and featured an innovative sewage system to deal with the plague killing a third of Milan's population.
- **Optics:** Da Vinci was one of the first to consider the possibility of using lenses and mirrors – 100 years before the first telescope was ever invented. He also conducted several investigations on the nature of light, reflections, and shadows. He also wrote about the *camera obscura,* a precursor to the modern camera.
- **Hydraulics:** He made extensive studies of water, documenting its movement, the action of waves, erosion, and sedimentation. These studies were practically applied in his designs for canal systems and river diversion plans.
- **Geology:** Da Vinci has been called a "Pioneering Geologist" for prefiguring the principle of stratigraphy and tectonic plate shifts, correctly interpreting fossils as ancient life forms, and anticipating processes of erosion and sedimentation. This also wasn't understood by the human race until 300 years later.[36]

- **Physics:** Leonardo da Vinci's private notes revealed that he understood many advanced concepts in physics, including

---

[35]While skepticism initially surrounded da Vinci's inventions due to their untestability before the Industrial Revolution (which occurred 300 years after his birth) and the advent of the steam engine, the 21st century has witnessed many engineers bringing his creations to life. Many researchers have successfully re-created and validated the practicality of many of da Vinci's designs, from the helicopter and vehicle to the parachute and beyond.

[36]Daniel J. Jones. "Leonardo da Vinci –Pioneering Geologist." *Brigham Young University Studies.* Winter 1962; Vol. 4, No. 2: p. 119.

detailed studies about friction, its properties, and its implications. He also demonstrated an understanding of the fundamental principles of force, motion, and waves. Two-hundred years later, Isaac Newton would get hit by a falling apple, and Guillaume Amontons would publish his Three Laws of Friction.

- **Mathematics**: Declaring in his notebook, "Let no one read me who is not a mathematician," Leonardo's mathematical work largely supported his interests in art and engineering. He used geometry extensively, including his exploration of the *Golden Ratio*, reflected in his other legendary work, the *Vitruvian Man.*[37]

- **Botany**: Leonardo was one of the first to describe the process of tree growth, noting that the rings in a cross section of the trunk represented the tree's age and environmental conditions over time. He also examined how water is taken up through the roots of a plant and transported to its leaves, marking an early investigation into plant physiology.

- **Theater**: In the realm of court pageants and theatrical spectacles, Leonardo curated spectacular visual effects, designed intricate stage settings, and significantly influenced the narrative flow and presentation of the performances. His deep insights into storytelling, along with his intricate understanding of human gestures and expressions, greatly contributed to the expressive character portrayal of that time.

- **Music**: Leonardo was known for his beautiful singing voice and skill as a musician. He improvised and composed music, played many musical instruments, and even invented several, such as the *viola organista.*

- Additionally, Leonardo da Vinci reportedly created a sort of home gym with ropes and pulleys to perform resistance

[37] The Mona Lisa Foundation. "Leonardo and Mathematics." https://monalisa.org/2012/09/12/leonardo-and-mathematics-in-his-paintings/ and Klaus Schröer, 2018. http://www.klaus-schroeer.com/leonardo/

exercises, which could be considered a forerunner to modern gym equipment. So, you could also say he was a pioneer in the fitness industry.

Imagine if, 300 years ago — long before the United States existed — someone secretly sketched detailed plans for computers, the internet, blockchain, AI, gamification, augmented reality, social media, lithium-ion batteries, and even reusable rocket landings. Sounds impossibly ahead of their time, right? That's exactly how OP Leonardo da Vinci was.

Had Leonardo da Vinci's revolutionary theories and discoveries been disseminated on a broader scale during his lifetime, our collective comprehension across various domains could have leaped forward by centuries, instigating incalculable transformations for humanity.

Regrettably, during his lifetime, Leonardo did not receive recognition or rewards commensurate with his extraordinary breadth of skills. Despite Leonardo's prodigious attributes (Step 2) and the unparalleled skills (Step 4) mentioned earlier, even regular recognition and success eluded him for many years. True to the ethos of this chapter, his fortunes turned only when he sharpened his capacity for building alliances (Step 5). In fact, you will see that whenever he was surrounded by suitable allies, he excelled in his quests (Step 6). But when he focused on solo endeavors, our OP Hero struggled to make significant strides in his life game.

After mastering the art of building alliances, Leonardo spent his final years in France, wealthy and comfortable, basking in the companionship of royalty and enjoying a close friendship with King Francis I. So, how did the strategic building of alliances catalyze the transformation in Leonardo da Vinci's circumstances? Let's take a closer look at his OP Player journey.

Leonardo da Vinci grew up with an immense amount of intellectual curiosity matched with the astute observation attribute (Step 2) within him. He was fascinated by nature and studied every little detail he could so he could reproduce it through another creative medium. Even though he always had unique attributes that empowered his skills, his big break came from his first important ally in his life: his father, Ser Piero Fruosino di Antonio da Vinci.

Ser Piero held a substantial role in Florentine society as a Notary. Though not of noble lineage, he nonetheless garnered respect and possessed a certain status emblematic of the middle-class strata of the time. And even though Leonardo was an illegitimate son with a peasant woman, Ser Piero and his family still helped Leonardo occasionally. The early help wasn't significant, as poor Leonardo didn't even have the opportunity to learn how to read or write until he was twenty-one years of age. But when he was fourteen, Ser Piero recognized his immense talent and skills in drawing, and he decided to utilize his own alliance to put Leonardo onto a new trajectory.

In Chapter 3 I discuss how middle-to-upper-class families adopt a "concerted cultivation" parenting style over a "natural growth" parenting style. True to this pattern, once Piero da Vinci discovered Leonardo's strength attributes, he secured for him an apprenticeship with one of his clients, Andrea del Verrocchio, an artist and engineer who ran one of the best workshops in Florence.

From this point on, Leonardo da Vinci joined one of the top guilds in the world to train multidisciplinary artists, and the guild leader Verrocchio became Leonardo's first mentor ally. In Verrocchio's workshop, young Leonardo learned a variety of skills (Step 4) alongside other students, such as drawing and painting, anatomy, mechanical physics, and techniques such as *chiaroscuro*, which applies effects of light and shadow on materials like draperies.

Through this apprenticeship quest, Leonardo developed a strong foundation for his polymath tendencies and laid the groundwork for his ultimate technique, *sfumato*, the craft of subtly blending and softening the edges between colors and tones to create a magical effect. This was the main technique he applied to the *Mona Lisa* (Figure 29), making it an amazing, timeless masterpiece.[38]

Figure 29. Painting of La Gioconda – The Mona Lisa, Louvre, Paris

Many years into this apprentice quest, Leonardo da Vinci slowly started to surpass his master. According to Vasari, an early biographer of Leonardo, when the teacher-student duo together painted *The Baptism of the Christ*, Verrocchio was so impressed that he "resolved never again to touch a brush."[39]

When Leonardo was twenty, Verrocchio, who later became more of a partner to Leonardo, advocated for him, helping him become a highly respected painter. Despite many believing that Leonardo

---

[38]One intriguing effect of the *Mona Lisa* is the elusive nature of her expression. Upon direct inspection, her lips hardly seem to curl into a smile. However, when your gaze shifts, the power of the *sfumato* technique imbues her with a coy grin, as if she's quietly mocking you from your peripheral vision. But the moment you redirect your attention to confront her mockery, she of course quickly reverts to her original, bland expression so that you won't get offended by her.

[39]Isaacson, Walter. *Leonardo da Vinci.* Simon & Schuster, 2017: p. 52.

da Vinci could leave the guild and succeed independently, he valued this alliance and chose to continue living and working in the workshop for the next nine years.

During his years in Verrocchio's workshop, Leonardo benefitted from another guild: the guild of Saint Luke in Florence. Although Leonardo was never a member, Verrocchio's membership allowed Leonardo to be exposed to many high-level allies, enabling him to learn and grow his cultural and artistic skills (Step 4). These experiences significantly impacted his later work.

At twenty-nine, Leonardo da Vinci finally decided to step out on his own and create his own guild. He wanted to prove his ability to succeed independently but, more importantly, he sought the freedom to pursue his artistic vision without the constraints of Verrocchio's workshop operations and client requirements.[40]

However, without a well-operated guild and teammates to compensate for his weaknesses, Leonardo da Vinci soon found himself struggling again. Leonardo couldn't meet deadlines when given too much freedom. He was frequently distracted by exploratory or "learning side quests" (Step 6) that were not mission-critical.

For instance, when he needed to draw people, he undertook many stealth quests to dissect human bodies, aiming to understand and accurately depict the human form. At the time, dissecting human cadavers was restricted to medical professionals, and those outside the profession faced condemnation by the church. Yet, Leonardo's intellectual curiosity (Step 2) drove him to perform many dissections in secret, enhancing his abilities (Step 4) to portray the human body with precision.

This led to famous examples of unfinished work, such as the *Adoration of the Magi* for the monastery of San Donato. After initially conceiving the image, his interest waned, leaving it tragically unfinished.

---

[40]The actual reasoning of his departure is undocumented, but you will soon see why I believe this reason seems the most logical based on Leonardo's psychographic profile.

Due to the lack of the right teammates and partners (aside from agreeable sidekicks within his workshop) to offset his weaknesses of being unfocused and disorganized, Leonardo da Vinci's reputation for failing to complete projects severely impacted his business. As a result, he faced financial hardship for over a decade.

Fortunately, during these years, he became part of the *faction* of Renaissance Humanists, a cultural movement emphasizing human potential, the study of classical literature and art, and empirical observation. This cultural context shaped his approach to art and science, providing the intellectual framework for his diverse studies. Even though Leonardo was not a promoter of books and considered himself a *discepolo dell'esperienza* – disciple of experience – he encountered many books that helped him study and deepen his understanding of the world.

It was within this faction that his reputation grew. Despite his weaknesses and the associated reputation still haunting him, he continued to receive commissioned projects due to his charismatic persuasion skills (Step 4), in addition to his diverse artistic skills, which included painting, drawing, and sculpting, among others.

However, it still wasn't enough. Eventually, Leonardo da Vinci shut down his own workshop in Florence and, like Gandhi, pressed the reset button by moving to Milan in hopes of finding better opportunities. (This was when he sent the job application to the Duke of Milan, Ludovico Sforza, mentioned earlier in this section.)

Unfortunately, despite enlisting himself for all sorts of occupations, Leonardo's initial applications to Sforza were all rejected.[41] Luckily, one of Leonardo da Vinci's strength attributes (Step 2) was *emotional perseverance*. Despite often feeling depressed and emotional, he had the resilience to carry on and keep trying. After *five years* of persistent networking (more on these principles in Chapter 8), he was finally accepted as a stage engineer for the

---

[41] He was without a job from 1482 to 1487. "Letter from Leonardo da Vinci to Ludovico Sforza." https://nicofranz.art/en/leonardo-da-vinci/letter-from-leonardo-da-vinci-to-ludovico-sforza

theaters in the Court of Ludovico Sforza. Thus, Leonardo da Vinci was able to join another powerful guild in Milan.

It was during these years in this new guild that Leonardo started forming strong alliances (Step 5) with key people. As part of his quests to develop his charismatic persuasion skills (Step 4), he began observing how people interacted with each other. In his notes, he wrote to himself, "As you go about town, constantly observe, note, and consider the circumstances and behavior of men as they talk and quarrel, or laugh, or come to blows." This quest (Step 6) to study human interactions significantly contributed to his later reputation for having a charismatic and delightful personality.

Key among his newfound allies was Ludovico Sforza, the Duke of Milan himself. Sforza was not only a patron of Leonardo's art but also provided him with a vineyard, ensuring a stable source of income. Another supporter during Leonardo's time in Milan was Beatrice d'Este, Sforza's wife. Additionally, Francesco Melzi, who wasn't directly associated with Sforza's court, became Leonardo's pupil during this period in Milan. Melzi remained a close companion and assistant to Leonardo for the rest of his life.

While serving in Sforza's court, Leonardo also joined a distinguished cadre of mathematicians and engineers. Among this illustrious group was Fra' Luca Pacioli, a mathematician who shared Leonardo's passion for math and science, who quickly became a close friend. Their mutual interests led to a collaboration on a book titled *De Divina Proportione* (*On the Divine Proportion*), which delved into the mathematical nuances of proportions and harmony.

Finally, after all the trials and tribulations, Leonardo da Vinci's fortunes began to improve. He embarked on a series of successful projects that secured his finances and cemented his reputation as the renowned Inventive Polymath (Step 3). Leonardo's success exemplifies the alignment of his unique attributes (Step 2) such as imaginative vision, intellectual curiosity, and keen observation; his relentless pursuit of knowledge and skills (Step 4) in art, scientific inquiry, and charismatic persuasion; and his strategic formation of alliances (Step 5) with key figures.

It's important to highlight that, despite Leonardo's monumental talents and skills, he thrived best within the camaraderie of others. His periods of prosperity coincided with his tenure under his mentor Verrocchio and his association with the Duke of Milan's court. Conversely, when left to his own devices, his fortunes faltered. This correlation underscores the crucial role of supportive alliances that complement one's attributes and skills.

As the years passed, Milan succumbed to a French invasion, prompting Leonardo to explore new opportunities. With his well-honed skill of forging alliances, he quickly secured a position with Cesare Borgia, the Duke of Valentinois and commander of the Pope's forces. In this role, Leonardo spent two years applying his extraordinary talents and skills as a military engineer and advisor. He masterfully crafted fortifications and devised military campaigns and strategies. After this productive period, he ended up establishing the ultimate alliance with the King of France, the very ruler whose forces had once invaded Milan.

OP Hero Leonardo da Vinci: Takeaways

In 10K HP, we understand that one significant advantage of forming robust alliances is the accrual of one's reputation score. Through his active engagement with numerous luminaries, Leonardo's fame spread far and wide, reaching the ears of King Francis I of France. Intrigued by the reports of this charismatic polymath behind seminal works like *The Last Supper* and other inventions, King Francis I extended an invitation to Leonardo, welcoming him to join the French court.

Thus, Leonardo found himself ensconced in the Château du Clos Lucé, a majestic castle nestled in Amboise, France. Here, he was afforded the freedom to delve into his artistic pursuits, scientific explorations, and inventive endeavors. Graced with the title of "Premier Painter, Engineer, and Architect to the King," Leonardo secured a distinguished position in the French court. At long last, our Renaissance man finally attained the apex accolade he aptly deserved.

Chapter 6 Highlights

- Success in life often comes from collaboration and teamwork. Achievements and milestones are typically the result of combined efforts.
- It's key to find allies who share your passions but who have different talents and skills.
- The right connections can open doors, provide opportunities, and offer support.
- Mentors and coaches can help you develop skills and complete quests, elevating your journey to higher levels.
- For effective networking, focus on self-improvement by leveling up your integrity, sincerity, optimism, confidence, initiative, and persistence.
- Collaborative efforts and strong networks are essential for achieving long-term success. Surrounding yourself with supportive and capable allies can propel you toward your goals.
- OP Hero Leonardo da Vinci was a financially struggling genius who faced repeated rejection until he formed the right alliances, which brought him fortune, reputation, and success, writing his name in history.

Chapter 7: The Alliance-Building Playbook

STEP 1	STEP 2	STEP 3
Choose Your Game MISSION	*Know Your Attributes* TALENTS	*Select Your Role* SPECIALTY

STEP 4	STEP 5	STEP 6
Enhance Your Skills CRAFT	***Build Your Alliance*** **NETWORK**	*Achieve Your Quests* MILESTONES

"The most important single ingredient in the formula of success is knowing how to get along with people."

—— Theodore Roosevelt

As a 10K HP ally, I want to share a secret lifehack from my low-level days — something even the majority of my most avid fans don't know about. One of my first ventures ever was an online networking service designed to facilitate connections among professionals. This entrepreneurial endeavor took shape during my freshman year at UCLA after I read an educational article in the campus newspaper, *The Daily Bruin.*

The article emphasized the importance of networking, urging students to proactively engage with professionals who spoke at campus events and to stay in touch with professors even after courses ended. This was something I had not considered at all!

Around the same time, I was captivated by movies like *Mission Impossible*, where characters could immediately recruit specialized experts from their network to tackle challenging missions. Whether it was a skilled hacker or an explosives expert, the seamless utilization of their alliances intrigued me and inspired me to explore the transformative potential of building my own network in my life game.

One final straw that made me realize the profound power of having a vast network was when I watched another iconic movie, *The Godfather.* At the beginning of the movie, an undertaker or funeral director named Bonasera pleaded with the head of a major mafia family named Don Vito Corelone to avenge his daughter. In exchange, he willingly submitted himself and honored Corleone to become his Godfather. "Someday, and that day may never come, I will call upon you to do a service for me. But until that day, consider this justice a gift on my daughter's wedding day."

At the time, I thought, "What would Corleone get out of this? I can see having a movie star being very valuable to the Godfather in exchange for his influence, but how does this guy who works with coffins deliver any value in return to this all-powerful mafia boss?"

It then became a revelation to me when much later in the movie (spoiler alert for this 1972 classic) when Don Vito Corleone's son Sonny was brutally murdered by a rival gang, Corleone went to Bonasera with Sonny's dead body and requested in deep sorrow, "I want you to use all your powers, and all your skills. I don't want his mother to see him this way."

That's when I fully realized that everyone's attributes (Step 2), skills (Step 4), and allies (Step 5), no matter how niche, can become essential in the right situation. Having an alliance with anyone could potentially help you complete important quests (Step 6) sooner or later. As a freshman at UCLA, I decided to go out and build my alliances and network my heart out. Recognizing how crucial it was to my game, it was a quest I couldn't refuse.

But I also stumbled upon a challenge: "Why would anyone want to network with me? I'm just a freshman in college with nothing to offer." This led to another insight: "If a person can connect someone to thousands of other experts and professionals, their value would be the accumulated value of all those thousands of professionals combined!"

My First 10K HP Guild: The FD Network

Realizing that as a young student I could still be valuable by leveraging the capabilities of other professionals, I started my first public guild in 2004 – the FD Network (FD stood for "Future Delivery," a screen name I used in my earlier gaming days). The FD Network was designed to be an online service where professionals in all walks of life sign-up and offer up their expertise, specialties, and hobbies to help other FD members.

FD Members had two requirements when they joined:

1. Update their profile once a year (this was before LinkedIn became mainstream)
2. If someone reaches out to them via the FD Network, treat the FD member like a friend.

FD members aren't necessarily required to offer help, but if they are unable to help, they should at least reply and say something like,

"Sorry I can't help you. But I know this other person who might be able to help. Maybe check out these other resources too."

Different from open professional platforms like LinkedIn, the FD Network was service-oriented and highly personalized. Whenever a member in the FD Network needed help, they would reach out to the "FD link" (me) via a form, and I would personally connect them with the right information (website, book, course) as well as people who could help.

How some members described the FD Network was like this, "Everyone wants to be friends with that person who knows everything and everyone. However, someone like that is obviously very successful and may not have time to help you out. That's why you join the FD Network, where the FD Link is connected with all sorts of people and resources but dedicated to helping you as an FD Member."

While still in my freshman year of college, I successfully attracted a diverse array of professionals to join the FD Network, including a nuclear propulsion engineer, a VP at a bank, a florist, a Hollywood actor, a rabbi, and many more.

That was my way of forging my first alliance through creating a guild as a teenager.

One particularly memorable moment was when I had the opportunity to meet an FD member who was not only a prominent game designer but also twice my age. His work was highly influential, and he was someone whom I greatly admired. But to my surprise, after engaging in an hour-long conversation, he unexpectedly exclaimed, "I still can't believe I'm meeting with the FD Link!" Somehow it looked like my effort to build my alliance (Step 5) as a young 10K HP Player worked!

Although I eventually ceased operating the FD Network to pursue my next startup venture – a gameful platform aimed at assisting students and young professionals in building their real-life careers – the connections forged through the FD Network continue to impact my life game to this day. Moreover, I still believe in the model and regularly think of restarting a similar service again, maybe as part of my current Octalysis Prime guild or through some sort of 10K HP academy.

Because of my experience running the FD Network, I spent an extensive amount of time studying and learning how to build alliances through OP networking. I share some of these principles and strategies in this chapter as a strategy guide to help those who need a power-up.

OP Networking Principles

Many people associate networking solely with events and view it as primarily transactional, focusing on the benefits it can bring. However, OP networking takes a different approach, inspired by the spirit of playing games with friends and cultivating alliances. In gaming, interacting with allies is not only about utility and progress but also about finding intrinsic joy and a sense of warmth. It embraces the idea that building meaningful connections can be both personally fulfilling and instrumental in achieving success within the game.

Following are some important OP networking principles that you can use on your 10K HP journey.

The First and Second Rule: Always Ask for Contact Information

Have you ever encountered someone who was doing something interesting at an event, and after a very good conversation, you depart with, "It was nice meeting you. See you later!" That statement would be a lie. Because the odds are, you will never see this person again. Even if you did meet them for a second time a year later at another event, you still wouldn't know if you will ever talk again after that. That's because you didn't obtain their contact information.

Someone is not an ally if you have no means to get in touch with them. They would just be a zone NPC who was there to entertain you and irrelevant to your life game afterwards. In the iconic movie *Fight Club*, the main character (played by Edward Norton) describes these zone NPCs as "single-serving friends." You can use their companionship once, and then you throw them away. Fortunately, when Edward Norton's main character meets Tyler Durden (played by Brad Pitt), Durden gives Norton's unnamed character his business card. This allowed – as far as we are concerned – Norton's character to get back in touch with Tyle Durden when he was in desperate need of some help.

In today's questing landscape, whether it's exchanging business cards and phone details, or connecting on professional networking platforms, these seemingly small gestures are essential and lay the groundwork for inviting them into your life game and becoming true allies.

Before you say goodbye, do your life game a favor and say, "Hey, I would like to stay in touch with you. Can we exchange contact information?" You have now transitioned them from a zone NPC to an ally in your game.

The Art of Following Up

In the grand adventure of relationship-building, regular check-ins are like secret power-ups often missed by players. Think of these not as mundane tasks, but as opportunities to strengthen the fabric of your alliances. Imagine each connection as a unique superhero in your game, each requiring a different strategy for engagement. Some should be nurtured quarterly, while others can be reinforced yearly. This personalizes your approach and sets a natural rhythm for each relationship in your journey.

When you reach out, you can give an update of your 10K HP journey thus far, reminding them of the game you are playing and your recent quests, milestones, and accomplishments. You should then ask them to share about their journey and explore how you can help them as their ally. Show genuine curiosity in their quests, be it their latest business achievements, hobbies, or personal milestones. Let them be the protagonist of this interaction and that you view them as comrades rather than mere contacts.

Later in this chapter, I describe how OP Hero Sun Yat-sen, master of building alliances, stays in touch with everyone he meets at each life phase and utilizes them in all his future quests, even decades later.

Overkill to Outshine: Build a Remarkable Reputation by Exceeding Expectations

In games, the term *overkill* means applying far more damage than is necessary to defeat an enemy. If a monster has 100 health points, and your attack dealt 2,000 damage, then you have achieved an overkill of 1,900. While there aren't any in-game benefits to overkilling – hence the word "over" – it feels great and often impresses other people.

Same in the real world: regardless of your position or experience, there's a principle that can significantly boost your professional reputation – doing more than what's expected. In many workplaces, I've noticed individuals who quickly complete their assignments only to indulge in nongrowth activities like browsing the internet or going on social media. If an individual is capable of finishing their work swiftly, it implies they possess capabilities beyond their assigned tasks. Wouldn't it be advantageous for others to recognize this?

Consider two employees: One completes their work quickly and then diverts their attention to online games, while the other finishes their tasks at a slower pace but then seeks out additional responsibilities. Who do you think is more likely to receive a promotion or a referral to new opportunities and quests? Despite the obvious answer, I've witnessed numerous individuals wonder why their careers aren't going anywhere, even though they all "did their jobs."

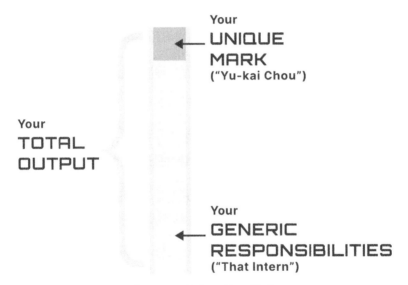

Figure 30. Making Your Mark

The key insight here is that fulfilling your assigned tasks, your "responsibilities," is merely meeting the baseline expectation. Anyone in your position should be achieving this, which means that there's nothing special about the individual who does it. Your true merit begins where your mandatory responsibilities end, and where your voluntary efforts begin. When you willingly undertake extra tasks, you transcend from "That Intern/Teller/Analyst/Associate/Accountant/VP" to "Yu-kai Chou" (of course, insert your own name here). (See Figure 30.)

This is an amazing realization because we know that the moment we finish our required responsibilities, *every minute* of additional effort in creating value will gain us unique credit and reputation points.

When I was still a high school student in Southern California, I did an internship at a local bank. They gave me menial activities like organizing papers within big binders. It would take many hours of busy work each day to get these tasks done. Some other interns took their time and made sure a whole day was spent on doing these activities, while others finished them quickly and began to surf the web. I wanted to learn as much as possible so I could level up my game, so I finished my activities as quickly as I could, and I went to each executive at the bank and asked them if there was anything I could help with (remember the harmless dragon?). If nothing else, people at the bank would recognize that I was competent and could finish my activities very quickly.

One executive told me that there was a problem with the bank's software vendors and asked if I could represent the bank and call their support team to resolve the problems. I did and ended up saving the bank tens of thousands of dollars per month. During this time, I made a unique impression with the institution's FVP (First Vice President) to the point that he invited me to help him with a startup that he was incubating. I learned a tremendous amount from this mentor and improved my skills (Step 4) in banking, financing, startup operations, and more.

Additionally, a few years later, when I was running my own boot-strapped startup as a twenty-year-old, this FVP mentor invested his own money into my startup – twice – just so that we wouldn't run out of money and die. (I did eventually raise over $1 million for this startup.) And all of this profound learning, quests, and being carried by a high-level mentor was because during my high-school internship, I did "more than my responsibilities."

I *overkilled*, and I received some epic loot.

Horizontal vs Vertical Networking

When it comes to enhancing your professional network, the most prevalent strategy for those who are not 10K HP Players is to broaden their circle by meeting more people – a process I like to call "horizontal networking." However, an often-overlooked, yet equally potent, approach lies in the second dimension – *vertical networking*.

The common definition for horizontal vs vertical networking is that the former involves connecting with individuals who are at a similar level or position as you, whereas the latter refers to establishing connections with individuals who are at a higher level than you are. But in the 10K HP playbook, it almost follows the opposite spirit.

In our world, vertical networking isn't about climbing up by connecting with higher-ups. It's about powering up the people already in your circle, helping them level up, sometimes even faster than yourself. It's being the supportive teammate who boosts their allies' journey to success. This in turn amplifies the collective strength and reach of your own network and alliance.

The beauty of this approach is that it doesn't necessitate a direct return of favors. The very fact that you've contributed to someone's success story means you have a strengthened bond with someone who is high level. And of course, sincerity is paramount. If everyone in your network became successful because of you, there's almost no game in the world where you would still be stuck at the bottom and struggling.

Vertical Networking: The Pit Analogy

In the famed manga and anime series *Hunter x Hunter*, one of the protagonists, Killua, after saving and then being saved by a converted enemy, said, "Let's just get one thing straight. The next time something like this [saving my life] happens, I won't bother taking time to thank you. So next time, if I'm the one who saves you, you don't need to thank me either. Friends are supposed to help each other out. I'm sure that you and I will be helping each other all the time from now on. But helping your friends isn't anything special. It's expected. Don't you think it's not cool to thank someone for doing something mundane like this?"

Helping your allies is not a transaction, but a natural extension of the six power attributes mentioned in Chapter 6. Let go of the expectation of getting something in return. Instead, view the act of helping as a reward in itself. You may subtly acknowledge that your assistance might endear you to others, but the minute your actions become driven by what you might gain in return, your sincerity attribute fades, and the effectiveness of your networking diminishes.

Even if your assistance propels someone else to a level of success you have coveted for yourself, that's still a victory. You've played an important part in their achievement, and they are likely to remember that. The resources and opportunities you may access through their success could very well catapult you to new, even more exciting heights in your own journey.

Consider this analogy: imagine that you are stuck in a deep pit alongside a crowd of many others. Everyone is trying to climb out, with some clambering over others or employing tactics of manipulation and betrayal for their survival. They have an outlook that life is a dog-eat-dog game.

Now imagine that amidst this chaos, you extend your arms to help push people around you up and out of the pit. After pushing five or more people out of the pit, they can now easily help grab you out of the pit. Even if some of them were selfish and just ignored you, as long as you have helped enough people up, there will surely be enough grateful hands to pull you up.

Not only have you facilitated their success, but you've also earned their appreciation. You've simultaneously positioned yourself amidst successful individuals and strengthened your bonds with them.

What's even more interesting is that life turns out to be a multi-layered pit, where climbing out of one pit puts you in a wider, higher one. Now imagine those who stepped on other peoples' shoulders to climb to this second-level pit. No one trusts them anymore and they find themselves without allies. Not you. Since you have helped so many people get to this level, you have built an alliance that you can continue to help push to higher levels, and in return they can lift you up to levels far beyond what was possible by yourself.

In the Biblical scriptures, Jesus Christ imparted a timeless piece of wisdom: "It is more blessed to give than to receive."[1] This principle rings true in the realm of building alliances, proving its universal applicability and transformative power in fostering relationships rooted in empathy, mutual respect, and success.

Cold-Emailing: One-Two Punch and the Uppercut

Have you ever felt like you're on a not-so-epic quest of cold-emailing, reaching out to elusive contacts, only to be met with deafening silence? This can leave you second-guessing your tactics or whether you should be playing this game in the first place. Cold emailing, admittedly not the most thrilling part of the OP network-ing game, becomes crucial when you're chasing opportunities that don't just fall into your lap. Whether it's for potential clients, mentors, advisors, or investors, it's like venturing into unknown territories for hidden treasure that wasn't revealed to you by the game.

But what happens when there's no reply? Do you send another carrier pigeon into the void? Should you email them again? Haven't they already implicitly rejected you by not responding? Aren't you annoying them? The entire experience can be very demoralizing, as their silence can feel like a subtle "game over" screen.

Well, let me tell you a story. In 2007, I decided to take on a networking quest (Step 6) by attending a vibrant entrepreneurship event called StartupLA, hosted at the UCLA Anderson School. After the event, my workload piled up, and I only managed to follow up with a few key individuals. Unfortunately, not so OP.

Fortunately, a struggling entrepreneur I met at the event was doing a much better job in their OP networking quest and emailed me instead. He expressed his appreciation for meeting me and suggested getting together for food or coffee. Being in my stressful catch-up mode, I felt warm about the email but ultimately ignored it. I didn't want to "feel" like a jerk by replying and rejecting such a polite and sincere offer.

A couple of weeks later, I received another email from him, saying that he knew I was busy but it would be great if we could catch coffee sometime. When I read the email, I actually wanted to respond, but it sat in my inbox for almost a week, and it felt too awkward to respond with, "Sorry I didn't get back to you earlier..." so I unimpressively let it go.

Luckily for me, this individual had the tenacity to do an *uppercut* (which I'll discuss further) by sending me another email. At that point, I had no excuse, and I felt compelled to respond immediately. We arranged a dim sum outing, and I'm grateful that he reached out a third time.

Our friendship blossomed from there, and we became mutually supportive allies, assisting each other in a variety of ways. Likely due to his embodiment of the six power attributes of OP networking, his startup soared to new heights and gained over 300,000 users.

In 2011, he sold his company for tens of millions of dollars.

As you can see from this story, if he had become discouraged and given up after the first or second "rejection," our friendship/alliance would never have formed. It serves as a powerful reminder that persistence can lead to incredible opportunities and meaningful connections.

So don't be shy – slay that harmless dragon!

Love Letters and Uppercuts

A lot of people say that cold-emailing is a numbers game. You email 100 people, and X% of them will respond. Once you finish trying that 100, you move on to another 100.

Since I, alongside many of my high-level allies, have a lot of experience on the receiving end of cold emails, I slowly derived a conclusion that could be insightful: the odds of your cold-email getting a response from someone you already cold-emailed before is often higher than the odds of cold-emailing someone new.

This idea is similar, but the reverse of the fundraising concept of how people who have donated before have a much higher chance of donating again. This says that the people who have *ignored* you in the past have a higher chance of responding to you this time.

Now obviously this assumes everyone you targeted at the beginning is relevant to you. If they ignored you because you were trying to sell things that are completely irrelevant or you reached out in an inappropriate way, then of course the frequency of follow-ups wouldn't really matter. It's like writing dozens of romantic love letters to someone who isn't looking for a partner.

As a result of this insight, I started calling this mentality the "one-two punch and uppercut." To draw a parallel with boxing, imagine the first email as a weak jab, the second as a stronger right cross punch, and the third as the powerful uppercut that can defeat most opponents.

It is important to note that this doesn't involve any special skills or abilities (Step 4). The key lies in a shift in *mentality*. Typically, when you send out your first cold email, receiving no response might already make you feel like a failure. You may gather the courage to send a second email, but once that goes unanswered as well, you deem yourself a failure in this quest. You start feeling insignificant and that nobody wants to engage with you, despite your heartfelt and carefully crafted email. It can become a disheartening experience, as if the world has turned quiet and gloomy.

But with the one-two punch and uppercut mentality, your aim is to defeat as many opponents as possible. Some opponents are easily taken down with just a jab – they respond to your initial email (and I genuinely encourage you to be those amazing people who respond right away). Others require a jab and a strong cross punch before they yield and finally reply.

And then, for those opponents who withstand the first two punches, you deliver the knockout blow with the uppercut.

By adopting this mentality, you no longer perceive being ignored as a rejection. Instead, you view the person as a stronger opponent who requires the full combo one-two punch and uppercut. In doing so, you maximize your chances of receiving a response from them.

Jabbing 100 People Once Does Not Give You the Most Wins in Cold-Emailing

With this concept, you can easily see why cold-emailing a lot of people once and moving on to more is not ideal. Imagine if you quickly jabbed each of the 100 opponents you encountered. No doubt, you'd achieve many victories. Only a few novices would be defeated, and you might start doubting your abilities, feeling downcast and discouraged.

Instead, consider a different approach. Focus on finding thirty opponents with whom you can execute the complete one-two punch and uppercut technique. Choosing those thirty will be a good task in and of itself to help you discover why you want to connect with each of them and what value you might be able to provide to them. By investing more time and effort into each interaction, you're likely to defeat a significantly larger number of opponents. This not only improves your success rate but also boosts your confidence and overall outlook.

Quality over quantity becomes the key to effective cold-emailing, allowing you to build more meaningful connections and achieve greater results. This is why I also call this "writing love letters" over "sending cold emails," which awkwardly describes the same activity as punching them in a boxing match. Both activities leave the other person reeling, as if stars are dancing before their eyes, breathless with a flurry of butterflies in their stomach, and utterly swept off their feet in a head-over-heels fashion.

What If the Uppercut Fails?

If you have completed your three-hit combo but have yet to get a response, it's completely up to you if you want to continue fighting or just give up for now. I would say that in most cases the odds of the fourth email getting a response is actually lower. If your opponent took your three-hit combo and still stands firm, then they just might be too high level for you. For instance, for most people, their three-hit combo would not work on the President of the United States, as the president's level is too high. You can't really damage the president no matter how many emails you send.

In that case you'll just have to first level-up before you try again. If you become one of the legendary OP Heroes like Elon Musk,

Oprah, or Gwynne Shotwell, then you actually might have a decent chance of succeeding with the one-two punch and uppercut on the president.

Just remember, there is really no harm in trying. The worst that can happen is that you never talk to this person, which is by default the result if you never tried at all. Well, the actual worst that can happen is that you make a jerk feel very good about how important they are, brag about it to their friends, and reply to you that they think your email is ridiculous. Don't worry if you just made a jerk's day by cold-emailing them. Keep leveling-up, and one day you'll knock them out.

Building Your Alliances Everywhere

Each individual we encounter in our game of life – be it a barista at our favorite coffee shop, the mailman who delivers our packages, or the mechanic who fine-tunes our car – has a unique life story, a different set of experiences, and, potentially, vast untapped knowledge. Treating each person we meet as a potential networking connection isn't just an excellent career strategy; it's a way of embracing the diversity of human experience and fostering a culture of mutual respect and shared growth.

Depending on your dedication to OP networking, you could try to build amazing relationships with everyone you encounter (some very successful people do that), or you could be more targeted and focus on higher-level players. Some people also dedicate a lot of time to helping mentees grow and level up in their life games. Who knows – seven years later, they might even become higher level than you!

I have many experiences where a high school or college student reached out to me and asked for mentorship. At the time, I understood that they didn't have any impressive skills or a high profile that could push my own life game forward, but because I genuinely enjoyed helping people when I could, I spent some time guiding and encouraging them.

A few years went by as I focused on pursuing my own quests. Suddenly, I realized some of these mentees had become startup CEOs of unicorn companies that raised over $50 million!

A compelling example of this dynamic is the relationship between Elon Musk and Greg Kouri, as witnessed from Kouri's perspective. At the time, Kouri was an accomplished and prosperous entrepreneur, while Musk was still a student with almost no notable achievements. Despite this, Kouri chose to invest his time, support Musk's endeavors, and provide both financial and mentoring resources.

Years later, the impact of Kouri's mentorship became abundantly clear as Musk rose to great heights of wealth, influence, and innovation. Musk's ventures, such as SpaceX and Tesla, revolutionized their respective industries and propelled him to become an iconic figure. Kouri's decision to guide and assist Musk paid off handsomely, showcasing the immense power and potential within mentorship relationships.[42]

Beyond Blood and Bond: Family and Friends

Your existing connections, which predominantly consist of friends and family, typically form the core of your network. These are the people who have journeyed with you over the years, sharing your personal milestones and experiences. They tend to be your most loyal advocates, often genuinely invested in your well-being and success.

[42]Regrettably, despite Kouri's iconic success as an investor and businessman, his life was tragically cut short by a heart attack in his early 50s. This serves as a poignant reminder that no matter how adept you are at playing your life game and achieving remarkable feats, your health must also be safeguarded. Just like in a game, if you deplete your health points (HP), it doesn't matter how high your "stats" are or how much gold you've accumulated – you end up arriving at the "game over" screen prematurely! We all need to constantly remember the importance of nurturing both our ambitions and our well-being within our game.

The essence of networking isn't simply about extending your contact list; it's fundamentally about nurturing and sustaining relationships that already exist in your sphere. Engaging with your existing contacts, therefore, is as critical as establishing new ones.

The good news? You're already an expert at maintaining these relationships – after all, these individuals are already part of your life. Now, it's just about integrating the six power attributes of networking into these existing relationships.

The fundamental rule to remember here is to *always keep up-to-date contact information.* Think about all the acquaintances from your past – elementary school buddies, middle school companions, high school friends. Even if not all of them have accomplished great feats, each one of them possesses unique knowledge, experiences, and networks that you don't have. The wealth of potential connections lost by not keeping in touch is quite staggering.

Even in my 30s, one of my elementary school classmates helped me design some logos for my companies. I also have been helping him with my behavioral design and empathetic persuasion skills to improve his communications with others.

My middle school friend who became a musician generously gave me usage rights of all his 100-plus songs to use on my Octalysis Prime Island, and all I have done was to provide lifetime guidance when he needs it. I have another middle school friend who was scammed and ran into financial troubles. Since I was doing quite well, I decided to hire him to ease his living. It turned out he had immense animation and 3D design skills, which helped make the Octalysis Prime Island vibrant, as well as saving a $180,000 client project when the 3D design firm we relied on fell through and even the backup agency couldn't step up.

None of these win-win scenarios would have been possible if I didn't stay in touch with my childhood classmates.

Clearly, one of the most essential steps to 10K HP success is to consistently reach out and touch base with your contacts. Depending on the relationship, sending a friendly email or making a catch-up call once a year or so could suffice. This doesn't have to involve deep, lengthy conversations; the goal is simply to let them know you're still around and still care about them. Over time, you'll also gain a better understanding of how you might assist each other should the need arise.

During this process, it's crucial to uphold the six power attributes: integrity, sincerity, optimism, confidence, initiative, and persistence. These values should become second nature, forming the backbone of your interaction style. Always strive to create an atmosphere that reassures your contacts that they can count on you for support.

As for your own family members, they form an enduring part of your life game network. They are your lifelong support system, typically willing to extend substantial care and help. Even if they don't agree with your life game and even interact with you rudely, when you are in the most need of help, they are usually the ones who step out and save you from disaster.

Now, you don't really need a strategy guide to explain how to make your family members your allies. Therefore, the only reminder I'll give here is that it's easy to take this unconditional support for granted and only foster these relationships when you need assistance. However, *it's essential* to continually invest in family ties intrinsically without any ulterior motives. After all, the goal is not to be the family member who only shows up when in need but to be an integral part of the family network who values and respects others' individuality and contributions.

Workplace Warriors: From Superiors to Supporters

Your workplace is a dynamic landscape teeming with diverse individuals, each playing their own life games (or being NPCs).

However, your perception of these individuals often extends only to their designated roles instead of encompassing and valuing their worth as individuals. In fact, when you think, "Yeah, these people are definitely NPCs," that's exactly the scenario that prevents you from seeing their own unique 10K HP journeys toward the games they are passionate about.

In the vast game of corporate life, where numerous players fill the arena, it's common to form closer alliances with a select few. Yet, just because your quest naturally aligns you with certain teammates, don't overlook the rest of the guild. This doesn't need to be extremely time-consuming. A genuine smile can work wonders in a stress-laden environment, offering a much-needed breath of fresh air and brightening someone's day.

This approach extends to both your superiors and subordinates. When interacting with higher-ups, exhibit confidence and approachability, and apologize respectfully for any mistakes. When dealing with subordinates, avoid arrogance and display the same confidence and sincerity. A leader who can admit faults will likely earn more respect and inspire greater effort from their team.

Prove your mettle through your work. Instead of resenting your current role or responsibilities, strive to overachieve and demonstrate your capabilities. Maintaining relationships with peers requires a bit more finesse, as some may view you as their competitor, especially when you are reliably leveling up your skills and completing quests better than they are. They might even view your hard work as a strategic move to win over superiors. However, consistently exhibiting integrity and offering assistance can mitigate such suspicions. Through patience and dedication, most will recognize your sincere passion and accept your work ethic as part of your character.

If you support your coworkers in their upward trajectory (even if they surpass you), you earn a supportive superior who values your contribution. They may recommend you for opportunities or provide glowing references to prospective employers. Over time, you will find yourself achieving your career goals, surrounded by a network of positive relationships.

It's also rewarding to not overlook the often-undervalued roles, such as the janitors. People in such positions also possess a wealth of hidden experiences, networks, and potential opportunities that you may not be aware of. A simple smile, greeting, or inquiry about their day can brighten their spirits. This connection can yield unexpected opportunities, once again showcasing the value of being genuinely nice in all interactions.

Imagine being Thomas A. Scott, an executive in the Pennsylvania Railroad Company. One day, Scott noticed a humble telegraph messenger boy who exhibited strong attributes (Step 2) in diligence and determination. Intrigued by the boy's work ethic, Scott decided to impart some valuable business lessons and eventually hired the boy as his personal assistant. This relationship became the foundation for a profound journey of personal and professional growth.

Little did anyone know at the time that this humble messenger boy would go on to become one of the greatest tycoons in history – Andrew Carnegie. Can you imagine being the mentor of one of the richest and most successful men in human history? That is literally an ally money cannot buy (how much money do you think you can offer Carnegie for him to treat you like a mentor?) and only possible because of the relationship investment made before Carnegie leveled-up.

Remember: Greatness can emerge from unexpected places within an organization, showcasing the incredible value of investing in the development of all individuals, no matter their starting point. In your pursuit of growth, focus on uplifting others as well. Competing yields short-term victories, whereas collaborative success paves the way for long-term accomplishments.

Unplanned Conquests: The Power of Spontaneous Networking

Harnessing the power of spontaneous networking requires a certain flair, as it involves creating connections in the most ordinary places – the library, the elevator, or even while waiting for a bus. These spontaneous interactions can be the catalyst for remarkable opportunities. Rather than passively awaiting chances, proactive networking enables you to create a myriad of possibilities for yourself.

Initiating these interactions need not involve a profound conversation; indeed, the beauty lies in its simplicity. Recognizing that there's no risk involved, as described by the harmless dragon principle, a simple comment on your surroundings, the weather, or any shared experience can break the ice. Once this initial contact is made, introduce yourself, always accompanied by a warm smile and a confident handshake if appropriate.

Though spontaneous networking may seem unconventional, many successful business partnerships and employment opportunities have sprouted from these unexpected interactions. Projecting confidence and competence can make others perceive you as a valuable addition to their own guild or alliance.

In 1980, Jay Elliot walked into a restaurant in the small town of Los Gatos, California. Having spent some time taking on major career quests (Step 6) as a high-level executive of Intel (Step 3), he was starting to feel bored. At the reception desk of the restaurant, he bumped into a young man in his 20s who was passionately bragging about his startup company. Elliot decided to exchange a few sentences but was surprised when the young entrepreneur audaciously said, "Maybe I'll hire you into my company."

Elliot smirked and said, "You can't afford me."

"Oh yeah? Tell me your price." Turns out, this kid founded a computer company that Elliot had never heard about but had already made $150 million! It also had a really peculiar name for an electronics company – Apple Computers.

Four weeks later, Jay Elliot joined the young Steve Jobs' guild and became the SVP of Operations. He helped Apple launch the first Macintosh and brought the company's revenue from $150 million to $3 billion.[2] This unplanned conquest in spontaneous networking enabled Elliot to embark on one of the most historically epic quests in technology and made his 10K HP journey more legendary. I believe your next spontaneous encounter could also have life-transforming effects. You just have to take that first step in building you're alliance.

It's Your Turn to Play: Slay The Scary Dragon

Now that you have absorbed the Alliance-Building Playbook, it's time for you to put it in action.

Pick from One of the Three Game Modes

Easy: Find a person in your contacts that you haven't spoken to in a while. Reach out to them and share that you're on your 10K HP journey. Let them know they've been an important Ally in your life and ask how you might be able to support them. This is a simple yet powerful way to rekindle valuable connections.

Medium: Identify higher-level players online who could be pivotal to your game. Use the "Jab, Cross Punch, and Uppercut" Technique and follow-up with them at least three times over the next four weeks. You can use this exercise to persistently reach out to the same individuals as in Chapter 6's Hard Mode, ensuring this time your efforts are persistent and consistent.

Hard: Step into the real world and sign up for a local event where you can meet new people. Conquer the Harmless Dragon by following these steps:

1. Making eye contact and greeting people energetically.
2. Engaging in a short, meaningful conversation.
3. Say that you would love to keep in touch and collect their contact details
4. Do Steps 1-3 with as many people as possible.
5. After the event, follow up with everyone within 24 hours to express your interest in staying connected. Request a follow-up coffee or online meeting to deepen the relationship.
6. Two months later, reach out again to nurture the connection and explore ways to help each other.

To bring structure and focus to your journey, visit 10KHP.com/worksheets to unlock practice worksheets and discover the 10K HP Workbook.

OP Hero Profile: From Exiled Loser to Founding Father – The Revolutionary Architect

The previous chapter examined the life playthrough of the Inventive Polymath, Leonardo da Vinci. His story involved a remarkable display of innate talents (Step 2) and developed skills (Step 4), yet it took decades for his genius to be fully recognized, partly due to his initial struggles in forging alliances (Step 5). Now, I'd like you to consider another OP Hero – a master of alliance-building, and a strategist whose adeptness in this art played a pivotal role in achieving what seemed like an insurmountable goal: the overthrow of a millennium-old empire.

While Sun Yat-sen might not be a familiar name in Western circles, he is revered as a legendary figure in the Chinese-speaking world, which is nearly twenty percent of the global population. A visionary idealist in the late 1800s, he masterminded the dismantling of imperial rule in China and laid the legal groundwork for a modern, democratic nation. His story is not just about political acumen but is also a testament to the power of strategic alliances in realizing world-changing missions (Step 1).

Of all the OP Heroes covered in this book, I consider Sun Yat-sen's mission to be the most monumental. Coming from a poor peasant background without status or money, he needed to rally people willing to die for his cause of overthrowing the corrupt Manchus who ruled China as the Qing Dynasty. In a seventeen-year saga, he had the largest questing zones of all OP Heroes: places like China, Japan, England, France, the United States, Hawaii (which wasn't yet officially part of the United States), Singapore, Malaysia, the Philippines, Indonesia, Thailand, Russia, and more. He tirelessly traveled across the world to establish allies and secure money and weapons for his cause, all in an era before airplanes and emails were options.

Needless to say, he didn't travel luxuriously or leisurely. He was often on the run, in exile by his host nation due to pressure from the Chinese Qing Dynasty government, avoiding assassination, or being kidnapped. Sun Yat-sen once wrote to his audience, "I have often for weeks together lived on a little rice and water, and I have journeyed many hundreds of miles on foot." His British Medical School dean and professor James Cantlie also wrote this about him, "For safety Sun frequently lived on board junks on the river as he traveled in the interior of China."

Due to Sun Yat-sen's multiple attempts at overthrowing the foreign-invaded Qing Dynasty, his 10K HP journey was dangerous for himself and for those who allied with him. At one point, the Chinese Qing Dynasty government set a $500,000 bounty on his head – in 120-years-ago dollars![43]

Our OP Hero wrote that if he was caught, "I well knew the fate that would befall me – first having my ankles crushed in a vice and broken by a hammer, my eyelids cut off, and, finally, be chopped to small fragments, so that none could claim my mortal remains."

But the greatest devastation is the fact that after he abandoned his medical clinic as a doctor to become a revolutionist, Sun Yat-sen failed a total of ten armed revolutions within his seventeen-year saga. Failing ten businesses in a row would already be soul-crushing for almost anyone, but these failed revolutions aren't even at comparable levels. Each time he failed, his friends and colleagues died, their families tortured, he lost his patrons substantial amounts of money enough to fund militias, and his life was put in even greater danger.

In fact, not only did his older brother, a self-made business tycoon in Hawaii, end up in bankruptcy after supporting Sun Yat-sen for many years, Sun's childhood best friend Lu Hao Dong was also captured in the first failed revolution when he voluntarily abandoned his escape and rushed back to his office to destroy the secret member list of their guild. Lu was tortured to death before ratting out any information about any member. For the following few decades, Sun had to live with the fact that his best friend was tortured to death because of his ideals as he orchestrated the next nine failed revolutions.

After Sun's former allies succeeded in the eleventh revolution independent of him and overthrew the Qing Dynasty government (yes, Sun never succeeded in his own revolutions), they respected his character, his struggles, and his writings on democracy enough to give him the presidency of the new republic.

His legacy was carried even further by his successors, with the most prominent ones being Mao Zedong and Chiang Kai Shek, supreme

---

[43]This would be approximately $20 million in 2024.

leaders of the Chinese Communist Party in China and the Republic of China in Taiwan.[44]

As someone who spent five childhood years in the Republic of China in Taiwan, I was required to sing the national anthem to Sun Yat-sen's portrait and the flag of his guild every day. I didn't know much about him other than that he was like a George Washington figure to my homeland. When I finally read his life story thirty years later to write this book, I surprisingly felt disappointed in this revered legend.

I saw failure after failure, rejection after rejection, and dismissal followed by exile from previously supportive nations. Huh? I thought he was supposed to be amazing at persuading people and making allies! Why did so many people reject him and disassociate themselves from him? The only strong attribute (Step 2) I gave him credit for was perseverance. After all, who would keep trying after the seventh, eighth, or ninth devastating failure?

It wasn't until the second time I read through his biography that I realized why he didn't appear impressive the first time: it was simply because of the hardcore difficulty level of his game mode. Being from a poor peasant class meant the Chinese elite class looked down on him. As a Chinese man during the period when China was labeled the "Sick Man of East Asia," the Japanese, British, Americans, and other Western nations dismissed him. His role as a revolutionary positioned him as a threat against those who benefited from a stable Qing Dynasty – current government workers, reformists, foreign governments with exploitative treaties, and wealthy Chinese living overseas who had bought prestigious titles from their motherland. Furthermore, advocating democracy over monarchy made him a threat to nations still under monarchic rule, which was still most of the Western world, as well as potential

---

[44]Chiang Kai Shek was Sun's direct lieutenant, student, and protégé, who implemented Sun's "Three Principles of the People" democracy system rigorously in Taiwan. Mao Zedong grew up admiring Sun and often stated that he had been "our great revolutionary forerunner" and that "the cause of national revolution started by Dr. Sun Yat-sen has not yet been completed, and we must carry it through to the end."

Asian allies such as Japan and Thailand. Finally, as a man who expected his faction to be willing to die for their mission, he alienated those who valued their own lives or their family members, making association with him unthinkable.

But despite all that difficulty, he was able to forge allies willing to support him in all those places and demographics. How did he do that? It was because of his wide range of attributes (Step 2), including the six power attributes for OP networking mentioned in Chapter 6: integrity, sincerity, optimism, confidence, initiative, and persistence.

He was also an eloquent speaker (Step 4: Enhance Your Skills) who could adjust his speeches to the audience listening to him. He was able to persuade many guilds throughout the world – weaponized gangs, governments, Japanese ronin, American adventurers, British intellectuals, Christian pastors, and Qing Dynasty renegades – to become part of his faction by convincing them that fulfilling his mission would be aligned with their own individual agendas. Many of the guilds he united had ideological differences and would otherwise never have worked toward the same cause.

Paul M.A. Linebarger, often known by his pen name Cordwainer Smith, was a successful science fiction writer, a scholar on East Asia at Duke University and Johns Hopkins University, and US military colonel who advised the British Forces, the CIA, and John F. Kennedy himself on psychological warfare and war information. Linebarger once wrote that Sun was, "in all probability a more assiduous and widely read student of political science than any other world leader of his day except [Woodrow] Wilson; he studied innumerable treatises on government, and was surprisingly familiar with the general background of Western politics and theory."[3]

But I find the highest form of flattery toward Sun not from the Chinese who revere him as a founding father, but from his medical school professor and dean, James Cantlie. In his book, Cantlie wrote numerous enthusiastic compliments about Sun, which made

Cantlie look like a fanboy.

When explaining why he took a trip away from his Hong Kong duties to Macau in order to support Sun execute a high-risk surgery on a patient, Cantlie wrote: "His is a nature that draws men's regard towards him and makes them ready to serve him at the operating-table or on the battlefield; an unexplainable influence, a magnetism which prevails and finds its expression in attracting men to his side."

Keep in mind that Sir James Cantlie was an extremely well-respected figure in British society and even medical history. He had published many medical books and was a pioneer of first aid methodologies in 1875 that we still use today. He was also a pioneer in degeneration theory (unrelated to the modern-day Web3 fanatic). In today's field of human anatomy, the term *Cantlie line* refers to an imaginary division of the liver that is useful for performing hepatectomies. He is the founder of Royal Society of Tropical Medicine and Hygiene, a founding member of the London School of Tropical Medicine as well as *Journal of Tropical Medicine*, a Fellow of the Royal College of Surgeons, and cofounder of Hong Kong College of Medicine for Chinese, which later grew into the University of Hong Kong. In other words, James Cantlie would qualify as an OP Hero himself!

Cantlie was a medical school professor and dean at the Hong Kong College of Medicine when he met Sun Yat-sen as a twenty-year-old student. Perhaps predicting that some "gamification author" 100 years later would scoff at him for being a fanboy to his own student, Cantlie wrote:

"My respect and regard for [Sun] may appear to have warped my judgment and directed my pen in too narrow a channel. Let there be no mistake in this matter, however; I have restrained, not exaggerated, my feelings towards him. I have never known anyone like Sun Yat Sen; if I were asked to name the most perfect character I ever knew, I would unhesitatingly say Sun Yat Sen."

Knowing how much Western nations, especially the British, looked down upon Chinese people at the time (they were the ones who brought the Opium War to China in the first place), I found myself tearing up as I read this. I wondered if I could ever become as respected by unlikely audiences as Sun Yat-sen was, purely based on my character, mission, and endeavors (attributes, game, and quests). It inspired me to strive to become a better person, which is why I share the stories of these OP Heroes with my readers. I hope that you, too, can be inspired to become a better person and take on your life missions with the passion of a gamer.

So how exactly *did* Sun Yat-sen built his alliances and caused the overthrowing of a dynasty?

How Sun Yat-sen Built His Alliance

Since Sun's life story was the most complicated among all of our OP Heros to digest and explain (it also took me the longest to research), I'll focus on his early life and how the allies he built during that time made a difference to his quests years or even decades later. Pay close attention to how Sun made new allies (Step 5) on every step of his 10K HP journey by wearing his game like a badge (Step 1), applying his persuasion and perseverance attributes (Step 2), building his role into a faction leader (Step 3), and applying organizational and press skills (Step 4) in order to power his multiple uprising quests (Step 6).

(Also, since you may not be well acquainted with the hundreds of Chinese names in Sun's journey, I will keep the mentioning of actual names to a minimum, favoring readability over historical documentation. If you are interested in the full details of all Sun's allies, visit 10KHP.com, where I map it out for readers to explore.)

Born in the small village of Cuiheng, Guangdong Province, Sun Yat-sen's early years in the late 1860s were quite humble. His father, a farmer and tailor, provided a simple life for the family. This modest beginning laid the groundwork for Sun's empathetic understanding of the common people, a trait that would become crucial in his later quests for change. His family village was so poor that his father's three brothers couldn't support themselves as farmers and decided to venture overseas, resulting in two of them dying on their journeys. Luckily, a third brother landed in Hawaii and was able to start a small business there. Sun's father, knowing that his two brothers had died on journeys to secure livelihoods, still sent Sun's older brother, then just seventeen, to Hawaii because of how difficult conditions were at home. This older brother, Sun Mei, later became extremely successful in Hawaii, but from this story, we get an understanding about how difficult Sun Yat-sen's small starting zone was.

In this starting zone, Sun forged a critical alliance with Lu Haodong, a friendship that would later become instrumental in starting his revolutionary game. When Sun Yat-sen turned five, he was sent to Honolulu in Hawaii by his father to join his older brother. During this time, Sun observed his brother's success as a sugar planter and farm equipment dealer, and after jumping islands eventually became known as "the King of Maui." Sun's brother, Sun Mei, became Sun's first major powerful ally who supported him during the school years and many parts of his revolutionary activities.

At the same time, Sun's exposure to a different world of British and American systems, where success was linked to governance and justice, began to shape his thoughts on leadership and reform. Sun's exposure to Western governance contrasted heavily with the Qing Dynasty's corrupted monarchy rule back home. There, the seeds of revolutionary thought were quietly sowed.

In 1882, Sun Yat-sen attended Oahu School (which was also the high school of former US President Barack Obama, but at that point had been renamed Punahou School) and formed a meaningful alliance with his Chinese tutor from British Malaya (modern day Malaysia), Too Nam. Nam was impressed by Sun's integrity, sincerity, optimism, and confidence as a teenager (remember those six power attributes of OP networking?) and decades later became a supporter of Sun's cause, joining Sun's revolutionary faction and expanding his guild in Southeast Asia.

It was also during this time that Sun Yat-sen converted to Christianity, joining his first and dominant faction that supported many of his future quests. There he met another important ally, Deng, who later became a leader in Sun's future guild as well as a top official in the newly established republic. Unfortunately, Sun's conversion to Christianity met heavy resistance from his sponsoring brother, and as a result, Sun Mei sent him back to China to avoid further exposure to his new Christian faction.

To everyone's surprise, once Sun was back in his old village, alongside his childhood ally Lu Haodong, he went into his local village's temple and destroyed the worshiped idol, believing they were harmful superstitions that held the village back. This, of course, angered the other villagers, so Sun's father arranged for Sun to escape to Hong Kong in case his life was in danger.

In Hong Kong, Sun attended the Diocesan School and later the Central Government School. Here he took initiative in building relationships with fellow members of the Christian faction, such as Chinese Christian pastors, and notably the American Congregationalist missionary, Dr. Charles Hager. Dr. Charles Hager baptized Sun Yat-sen and Sun's childhood buddy Lu Haodong, as well as gave Sun his new Christian name that we regularly use to refer to him today, *Yat-sen*.

Unfortunately, toward the end of 1884, Sun's brother Sun Mei was so infuriated by Sun's baptism that he "summoned" Sun back to Hawaii. Sun Mei threatened to cut off all Sun's financial support and forced him to return a property that Sun Mei had registered in his name. Sun Yat-sen had to oblige and was therefore returned to Hawaii for over a year without getting his high school diploma.

During this time a major world event occurred. In 1885, the French military struck a dominating victory against China over the control of Vietnam, which in turn spurred England to seize Burma and

Japan to claim Korea. The Qing Dynasty government behaved very passively, believing that it did not have the forces to resist foreign aggressors, and also because many Chinese monarchy leaders took personal benefits from various arrangements of corruption.

At the time, the local Governor-General of Guangzhou city called the people to resist the French. Many peasants in Guangzhou banded together to boycott France, including refusals to repair French warships. Sun was impressed by how the peasants' fighting spirit surpassed the cowardly inaction of the Qing Dynasty government and felt deeply that those leaders did not represent the strength of the Chinese people. This highlighted the need for strong, grassroots leadership – a role (Step 3) Sun was gradually preparing to embrace. He needed a way to get back to China.

Sun's resourcefulness in leveraging his allies became instrumental in 1886. Despite his brother controlling all his finances, Sun reached out to senior faction member Reverend Francis Damon, superintendent of the Hawaiian Board of Mission, and pleaded for funds from the Christian community to return to China so he could study there. He successfully raised $300 (about $11,000 today), which allowed him to go back to Hong Kong. This ability to mobilize support was an early testament to his emerging leadership and persuasive skills (Step 4).

Returning to China for higher education posed its challenges. As a peasant in China's class-based system, Sun's options were limited. He could not pursue higher learning, nor attend military or naval academies. He considered becoming a pastor, but there were no seminaries in Hong Kong at that time. Law was also not an option in the British colony.

Yet, Sun managed to persuade his former faction ally, Dr. Charles Hager, to write a letter of introduction to the medical school of Boji Hospital, which admitted Sun and his childhood buddy Lu Haodong. Here, not only did Sun strengthen his bond with Lu Haodong, he also met Zheng Shilang, a rich Shanghai merchant's son who had connections to secret gang societies. Many of these societies, such as the Triads, were created to overthrow the "foreign-ruled" Manchu government so they could abolish the Qing Dynasty and reinstall the previous Han-led Ming Dynasty.[45] But after more than 300 years, these secret societies did not have the organizational force or momentum to succeed in their missions.

Sun's Alliance with Zheng and his secret society guilds served as the main muscle for Sun's early revolutionary quests.

During this period Sun's older brother, Sun Mei, finally realized that he could not sway Sun Yat-sen's chosen path. Sun Mei therefore relented and resumed financial support for his brother's education, acknowledging the stubbornness of Sun's convictions. Having Sun Mei as a financial ally was not only important for Sun Yat-sen's schooling, but it was also a main source of funding for Sun Yat-sen's early revolution attempts, until Sun Mei himself became bankrupt.

In October 1887, Sun's transfer to the new College of Medicine for Chinese in Hong Kong marked another significant arc in his 10K HP journey. There he proactively established alliances with another Christian faction member, Sir Ho Kai, who became Sun's *mentor*. Ho Kai was one of Hong Kong's most distinguished civic leaders and one of the Chinese community's principal representatives with the British colonial authorities. Ho Kai served on the Legislative Council for three terms and sat on almost every major public board.

Sir Ho Kai, with his extensive connections and deep understanding of both Eastern and Western political landscapes, became more than just a mentor to Sun; he was a gateway to a world of potential allies and resources. Through Ho Kai, Sun was introduced to influential figures in both the Chinese community and the British colonial administration. This was a strategic networking master-

---

[45]Han is the ethnic group that is the far-majority population of the Chinese people. When people talk about their Chinese heritage, they mostly are referring to Han Chinese. There are many other ethnic groups, such as the Mongols, Manchus, Tibetans, and Uyghurs. As you might guess, ethnic tensions and discrimination issues persist to this day.

class (Step 4), as Sun navigated these interactions with the finesse of a seasoned diplomat, gaining insights and forging connections that would later prove invaluable.

It was also at this college that Sun met his dean and professor, Dr. James Cantlie, whom I described earlier as having a prestigious background in the medical world while being extremely fond of Sun Yat-sen. During this time, Cantlie would have Sun follow him around as a translator when Cantlie studied diseases across China. Cantlie would later become critically important in saving Sun from certain and torturous death.

Sun also connected with many peers during this time. Sun became part of a team with three other friends and met regularly to discuss ideas about governance, societal reform, and revolutionary strategies. These four individuals were so consistent and infamous to the neighborhood locals that they garnered the nickname the "Four Bandits." These friends, once considered naive dreamers, would later emerge as crucial players in Sun's revolutionary narrative, underscoring the long-term value of these early alliances.

Of course, during this time, Sun's life game (Step 1) wasn't truly to become a revolutionist and risk his existence to overthrow the governing empire. Initially, it was just to save people and improve the country. He couldn't do that as a pastor, so he chose to do that as a doctor (Step 3: Select Your Role). But, like many people we might know, he loved talking about politics and what was deeply wrong with his country. During this period, he wrote some of his political views describing what China should focus on: "The adoption of Western practices, the diffusion of institutions to promote talent, and improvements to advance China's agriculture and sericulture." Sun believed that the spread of literacy was essential. "If human talent is not in abundance and if customs are not good, then the nation cannot be strong."

By 1892, Sun Yat-sen's medical journey reached a pivotal milestone. Despite topping his class, a bureaucratic tangle over accreditation meant that Sun could only practice in the Portuguese colony of Macau. In Macau, entire villages would gather around the house where he operated on patients, peeking through the windows, as they didn't have access to TikTok yet. Some recoiled at the gory sight of surgery, yet all were in awe of this doctor who fused Western medical techniques with an empathetic understanding of the people's needs.

In 1893, Sun relocated to Guangzhou, setting up the East-West Apothecary with a physician partner who had the proper medical license to practice (Step 5: Build Your Alliance). With Sun at its heart, the apothecary quickly garnered an excellent reputation and made Sun a respectable living. If Sun's game were merely being a successful doctor who could live comfortably, similar to Gandhi's initial game of being a successful barrister, then he could have continued to cruise in life and become an NPC.

But Sun was too passionate about healing the woes of his country and not just those of his patients. So, a year later, at the age of twenty-eight, he abandoned the apothecary and started his Hero's Journey into his main life game.

At this point, instead of starting his own guild in the revolutionary faction, he still hoped to join an existing reformation faction aimed at improving the current Qing Dynasty, as opposed to overthrowing it. In a bold move, Sun and his childhood buddy Lu Haodong traveled toward the capital city of Tianjin, around 1,300 miles away, seeking an audience with the influential government leader Li Hongzhang, in hopes of being hired and having at least a minor role to help reform China.

Sun didn't just blindly travel without a plan. He still utilized his alliance abilities to maximize his chances. They first took a stop at Shanghai so they could meet the famous reformist comprador, Zheng Guanying, who once incorporated one of Sun's articles in his influential book *Words of Warning to an Apparently Prosperous Age*. The comprador connected Sun to a reformist journalist who had friends in high places and gave Sun a letter of recommendation into Li's entourage.

Unfortunately, the journey ended up being a *Plot Fail Quest* (a quest that was meant to fail so the story could carry on), so Sun's petition fell on deaf ears. Furthermore, Sun saw firsthand how wealthy and corrupt the people were in the capital city and began to feel that China needed more than just reform.

The same year, Sun, alongside other reformers, openly protested against the government, hoping to see change. But instead of changing, the government arrested most of the protesters, with Sun being one of the few who escaped.

Sun's Real-Life Game: Revolution

At this point, Sun realized that reform was hopeless, and the only reasonable way to save the country was the path of revolution. This time, he finally started his real-life game: lift up China by overthrowing the Qing Dynasty government and establish a democratic republic.

To start, he needed to recruit the allies he made in his youth. He returned to Hawaii to recruit people into his new guild. He tried to convince many of the Chinese who had settled in Hawaii to join him, but most people only admired his audacity but refused to join, in fear that their families and relatives in China would be tortured to death. At the end, only twenty people who were either Sun's relatives, including his brother Sun Mei, or Christian idealists similar to Sun committed to the new guild.

On November 24, 1894, Sun Yat-sen established the Revive China Society, which became a pioneering guild in the revolutionary faction. With a membership fee set at $5 (close to $200 in 2024), the society later grew to 100 members and represented the first seeds of revolution.

It was during this time that another world event happened: the Sino-Japanese War in 1895, resulting in Japan's victory and significant territorial losses for China. Before that, most of the Chinese population had accepted the fact that China would always lose to a Western nation, but they had been expecting an easy victory over the small island nation of Japan.

This loss shocked everyone, and the following Treaty of Shimonoseki was so outrageously humiliating against China that Russia, Germany, and France all decided to intervene and restrict what was agreed upon in fear of losing their own spoils from the defeated nation. This, historically known as the Triple Intervention, sparked the later Russo-Japanese War. For the entire time, China was simply at the mercy of how foreign nations were scrambling against each other to divide up what had been plundered.

These events sparked a new quest line for Sun Yat-sen. After forming the Revive China Society, he had planned to travel to America to raise more funds from the Chinese diaspora overseas, but he saw this uproar of discontentment in China as an opportunity. So he abandoned his plans and traveled back to Hong Kong.

When his ship briefly stopped in Yokohama, Japan, Sun met a Chinese bookseller inspired by Sun's faction, and Sun recruited him into the Revive China Society. This encounter not only expanded Sun's influence beyond Hawaii into Japan, but also laid the foundation for future support. The bookseller's son later also joined Sun's guild at the age of fourteen and became an important historian for the movement.

Once back in Hong Kong, Sun by chance met with a Japanese photography studio owner, Umeya Shokichi. Inspired by Sun's revolutionary aspirations, Shokichi decided to join Sun's guild and facilitated the procurement of armed shipments for the uprising. Through a member of his previous group of allies, the Four Bandits, Sun also connected with another guild called the Furen Literary Society, which shared similar revolutionary goals. The Furen

Literary Society consisted of westernized Chinese individuals who were influenced by Confucian ideals. Sun convinced their leader that, since they were part of the same revolutionary faction, they should join forces into a single guild. However, the Furen Literary Society's leader, Yang Quyun, also aspired to lead the joint guild. Consequently, the leadership position became temporarily vacant, with Sun coordinating revolutionary operations while Yang managed the finances.

On February 18, 1895, Sun was able to gather his previous allies and officially establish the Hong Kong Branch of the Revive China Society. This branch was a remarkable amalgamation of diverse elements: the passionate Four Bandits, Hawaiian daredevils who had traveled with Sun and were ready to risk their lives for the cause, and the Furen Literary Society of westernized Chinese individuals who valued Confucian principles.

Illustrating the depth of their dedication, one of the wealthier guild members sold his apartment and contributed all the proceeds to fund the inaugural revolution. Sun also donated his entire savings from his medical career to the cause. Meanwhile, Sun's earlier mentor from his medical school days, Ho Kai, though not officially joining, played a critical role by influencing the British press in Hong Kong. He portrayed the uprising favorably, framing them as righteous revolutionaries fighting against corruption and deserving support from European nations.

Sun then demonstrated his strategic organizational skills (Step 4) by establishing the Agricultural Study Society, housed within a bookstore run by a pastor. This "front" for the Revive China Society, alongside Sun's previous excellent reputation as a medical practitioner in Guangzhou, was well received in gentry and bureaucratic circles with its educational and reforming focus. Many influential locals began to help Sun's guild, directly or indirectly. The guild also attracted Liu Xuexun, a man of high esteem who had one of the most prestigious degrees in China. Liu's involvement was a significant boost, lending an air of respectability and intellectual weight to the movement, which until then was largely seen as a collaboration between peasant Chinese Christians and gang members.

During this period, the global questing landscape changed for Sun in the form of a faction war. Opposing Sun was a rival Reformists faction that advocated for a moderate approach to reform within the existing imperial framework, rather than the outright over-throw of the Qing Dynasty. Led by two esteemed figures, this faction gained significant traction due to their intellectual acumen and high societal standing, which far exceeded Sun's.

The Reformist faction's less radical approach made it much harder for Sun's revolutionary faction to garner support and resources from the overseas Chinese population overseas, as their moderate path was more appealing to a much wider following, including foreign governments, intellectuals, and even progressives within the imperial court.

The faction war intensified over the following decades as the rival faction leaders consolidated power and influence. In a surprising twist, one of the two reformist leaders began befriending Sun Yat-sen, bonding over their mutual disdain for the weak Qing Dynasty. However, in an unexpected act of betrayal, Sun discovered that this reformist leader had used his recommendation letter to lure away the Hawaiian revolutionary faction members to join the Reformist faction instead. Even Sun's older brother, Sun Mei, was persuaded to join the rival faction and started donating to their cause instead.

On a more important front, Sun's first uprising was scheduled for October 26, 1895. His Revive China Society had 153 offi-cial members, including wealthy merchants, small business own-ers, physicians, English teachers, clerks, and technicians in for-eign enterprises. This group would coordinate a strike force of 3,000 Triad members within the same revolutionary faction, armed with weapons supplied by the Japanese photography studio owner Umeya Shokichi. Of course, a mere force of thousands could not overthrow the Qing Dynasty, but Sun's calculation was that, once the revolution ignited, it would inspire widespread uprisings across the nation, creating a domino effect of fed-up Chinese that would ultimately lead to the dynasty's downfall. This eventually became true – almost twenty years later.

The first revolution was just the first of many failures. There were logistical problems with weapons arriving a day late, secretive postponement telegraphs not arriving in time, and the brother of a guild member tipping off the government due to fear of torturous repercussions to his own family. This allowed the government to anticipate the uprising, giving them time to request many more troops to reinforce the garrison as well as intercept the unarmed Triad members while they were still on ships.

Many guild and faction members were arrested. Sun and his childhood best friend, Lu Haodong, narrowly escaped. However, Lu suddenly remembered that the member list of the Revive China Society was still in the office. He turned back, ran to the office, and burned the list. As mentioned earlier, he was then arrested and tortured to death without revealing the details of any ally.

With the help of a Chinese Christian minister in Guangzhou, a lawyer referred by Sun's medical school professor, Dr. Cantlie, and Japanese photography studio owner Umeya Shikichi, Sun and two allies took the first available ship out of Hong Kong, which happened to be heading to Kobe, Japan. Surprisingly, their arrival was covered with respect by the Japanese press, which called Sun "the leader of the Chinese revolutionary party." From that day on, Sun was a public fugitive on the run and exiled from China as well as Hong Kong.

Without time to mope, Sun quickly changed his appearance and set up a new Revive China Society branch in Yokohama. They realized that Zheng Shilang, the rich Shanghai merchant's son with connections to secret gang societies, was not on the Qing Dynasty's wanted list, so he was sent back to lay the groundwork for a future uprising. Meanwhile, Chan Siu-bak, one of the Four Bandits, would first go to Tokyo and later to Taiwan to setup the Taiwan branch of the guild, along with many other guilds within the revolutionary faction in the years to come.

For the next year, Sun worked on creating new chapters and raising more funds across Hawaii and North America, with very little success. He then received an invitation to London from his former Professor, Dr. James Cantlie. This trip was intended to be an opportunity for study and networking, a chance to engage with Western ideas that could further develop Sun's design for the future democratic republic's government. However, his stay in London soon took a dramatic turn.

On October 11, 1896, Sun Yat-sen was kidnapped by agents of the Qing Dynasty and was scheduled to be sent back to China for his execution. As fate would have it, the Chinese legation (diplomatic office) where he was held was just a block away from Dr. Cantlie's residence. After twelve days of continuous begging, the emaciated Sun finally convinced the legation's English porter to deliver a message to Dr. Cantlie down the street.

Upon receiving the message at midnight, Dr. Cantlie immediately sprung into action. Unfortunately, the midnight police force felt it was none of their business, so Dr. Cantlie persisted and hired a detective agency to keep an eye on the building (ironically, it was the same agency the Chinese legation hired to follow Sun in the first place), while pushing for higher officials such as Lord Salisbury and the foreign office to intervene.[46] Finally, this story was picked up by the *London Globe* and was newsworthy enough that most of the British press surrounded the Chinese legation, challenging the legitimacy of the Chinese government to kidnap someone in British

---

[46] To add even more irony to reality, before Dr. Cantlie went to the police, he first knocked on the door of a friend whom he knew was very influential with the Chinese government to see if that friend could help. However, this friend wasn't home because he was actually the mastermind behind Sun's kidnapping and was at the location where Sun was being interrogated. Had this man been home to answer the door, he would have received a heads-up about Dr. Cantlie's efforts, likely resulting in Sun being quickly shipped away, which could have led to Sun's death.

society. This forced the Chinese legation to release Sun. This story, in effect, turned him into an international hero.

Following his release, Sun Yat-sen leveraged this traumatic incident to gain public sympathy and support in London and worldwide. He published the book *Kidnapped in London*, which made many parts of the world see him as a romantic and valiant revolutionary, fighting against an oppressive regime. His new reputation of being caught but released with dignity by the Qing Dynasty enabled him to establish many future alliances, as well as cement himself as a figurehead for the revolutionary faction.

During this time, he also immersed himself in study at the British Museum Library, improving his knowledge and skills (Step 4) in politics, law, diplomacy, and military affairs, while building more alliances in London. He connected with new contacts such as Felix Volkhovsky, the Russian editor of *Free Russia*, who had recently gained his freedom after seven years of imprisonment and eleven years of exile.

Volkhovsky helped Sun publish the Russian version of *Kidnapped in London*, which later aided Sun's alliance with the Soviet Union. Another significant outcome of Sun's time in London was the alliance he formed with Rowland Mulkern, an Irish soldier. Mulkern became not only Sun's bodyguard in London but also a lifelong Western ally, supporting him through various phases of the revolution.

The next stop for Sun was Japan, which had successfully undergone the Meiji Restoration and was a beacon of modernization and reform in Asia, starkly contrasting the stagnation of the Qing Dynasty. However, the Meiji Restoration left many Japanese from the Samurai class in search of a new purpose. Observing how Westerners invaded Asia, many began adopting the principles of *Pan-Asianism*, the philosophy that all Asian nations should unite and become strong against Westerners as a whole.

During this time, these Japanese "ronins," who held high positions, also saw a weak China as suboptimal. They believed that once the Western nations finished splitting China into their respective colonies, Japan would likely be next. Sun and his allies managed to convince these Japanese ronin and pan-Asianists that they, too, should be part of the revolutionary faction to help overthrow the weak Qing Dynasty.

Sun Yat-sen leveraged his network of former classmates and key figures in Singapore – including a prominent legislative councilor and a former reformist turned revolutionary – to bolster his support base. Singapore became a crucial headquarters after his exile from Japan. In Hong Kong, one of Sun's Four Bandits allies also founded the Chinese Harmony Society to spread revolutionary ideas.

Expanding to Vietnam, Sun established a branch in Saigon, forging alliances within the Chinese-Vietnamese community and even persuading the French colonial governor to become an ally. In the Philippines, he mediated an arms deal between Japanese pan-Asianists and the Filipino independence movement, gaining substantial financial support and an offer of military assistance from their leader.

Recognizing the power of the press after his London abduction, Sun used funds from his Philippine ally to establish the *China Daily* in Hong Kong, supported by his Four Bandits teammate as well as his mentor, Sir Ho Kai.

Through Japanese connections, he united the Society of Elder Brothers and the Triads with his Revive China Society, forming the *Revive Han Society*. Elected as leader, Sun consolidated his position at the forefront of the revolution.

His strategy was multifaceted: overseas allies provided financial support, secret societies supplied manpower for uprisings, and the educated elite trained for political leadership in the new republic. Unlike many revolutionaries who focus solely on toppling a regime — only to become tyrants themselves — Sun emphasized long-term governance. To ensure a stable future for China, he even sent his allies abroad to study various subjects, preparing them for leadership roles.

Unfortunately, efforts to ally with the French and use Vietnam as a base saw little success due to France's policy of keeping a weak Qing Dynasty for ongoing exploitation. However, Japan, seeking discreet expansion, promised resources for a second uprising and agreed to allow Sun to use Taipei as his headquarters.

Japan, which occupied Taiwan, wanted a way to gain control of Xiamen, a treaty port in Fujian province close to Taiwan. However, they didn't want to alarm other powers with this aggression, so they met with Sun in Taiwan and agreed to support him with military aid. By allowing Sun to use Taipei as his guild headquarters, they could take over Fujian, giving Japan access to Xiamen.

Sun meticulously planned a coordinated attack from eastern Guangdong and Guangzhou, aiming to unite in Xiamen and leverage Japanese supplies. However, restless forces launched a premature assault in Guangdong. Despite this, as Sun envisioned, young men from neighboring towns eagerly joined the cause. In just ten days, their numbers grew from 600 to 10,000, crushing any resistance the local governments could throw at them.

Victory seemed within reach — all that remained was to unite in Xiamen and secure Japan's promised aid to start their regional momentum towards the capital. But then came a devastating blow — Japan reneged on its pledge. Deprived of crucial supplies, Sun had no choice but to disband the uprising, ending the revolt after two and a half weeks.

The consequences of this failure were dire. Many guild leaders fled to Singapore, but two key allies — Sun's college friend Zheng Shilang and his former leadership rival from the Furen Literary Society, Yang Quyun — were killed. The Revive Han Society was effectively dismantled, and Sun was again alone and powerless.

This devastating failure would have crushed the soul and spirit of most 10K HP Players.

But not Sun. He continued to push forward in his game, forging new alliances and plotting new major quests. After the second failed uprising, he pressed the reset button and pushed for the next uprising, this time with more developed attributes (Step 2), more skills (Step 4), and stronger allies (Step 5).

Prepare, Fail, Repeat

To prepare for the next revolution, Sun attracted young Chinese students in Japan, establishing a military academy. He then did one of his most important quests within his 10K HP journey: merging his Revive China Society with their faction guilds to form the main faction-leading guild, the *Revolutionary Alliance.* As the most experienced, persuasive, and internationally respected member, Sun naturally assumed leadership, again being recognized as the guild, and hence, faction leader.

Furthermore, his Four Bandits expanded the Chinese Harmony Society globally, consolidating into the Revolutionary Alliance. A wealthy Chinese antiques dealer he met on a boat trip pledged significant financial support whenever Sun would send a secret code. In the United States, Sun recruited a Yale-educated scholar who would draft the republic's constitution and an American military strategist who became a mission-driven general under Sun's leadership.

After persistent efforts, France finally agreed to support Sun, establishing the *Intelligence Service on China from France,* providing financial and military aid, and granting international legitimacy. Sun effectively utilized media, founding publications and establishing reading clubs worldwide to expand recruitment and propagate revolutionary ideas. He absorbed various guilds—including societies in Saigon, Bangkok, and Malacca—and secured pledges from disillusioned Qing officials for them to defect during uprisings.

But despite all these impressive feats of allying with stronger entities and absorbing weaker ones, Sun still faced failure after failure. His third Chaozhao uprising failed because some of his rebel soldiers became restless and attacked too early again, while accidentally killing a Qing general who had agreed to deflect and join them. They were able to successfully occupy the local government for three days, but reinforcements couldn't get there on time. In that era, it took days to even receive the message that the rebel forces attacked prematurely, let alone coordinate any real-time improvisations. They were then quickly taken down by the national Qing forces.

The fourth uprising involved working with a feminist ally, who was the passionate founder of a modern girls school. That, too, failed, and she was beheaded. The fifth uprising failed after a bomb assassination attempt failed.

After the sixth failed uprising, the French cut all ties with Sun and exiled him from modern-day Vietnam. The seventh uprising failed after a general who had agreed to defect betrayed Sun and decided to take a better deal somewhere else.

The eighth uprising failed when Sun's second-in-command, Huang Xing, was prematurely arrested in Vietnam. The ninth uprising also failed due to a premature conflict between a shopkeeper, the police, and the military, resulting in the death of Sun's partner.

In the tenth uprising, an independent assassination event occurred days before the planned attack, prompting the government to tighten control. This forced Sun's troops to again attack early, leading to the capture of the governor's home. However, the chaos and communication difficulties caused the defecting government reserve forces, who had intended to join Sun, to be misunderstood and slaughtered. Consequently, this uprising also ended in failure.

Unshakeable Perseverance

If it feels exhausting just reading through all of these failures, imagine what it was like to actually experience them. This alone demonstrates that Sun had one of the strongest unshakeable perseverance attributes (Step 2) on the Earth Server. Even though the attempts all failed, the last few uprisings struck fear into the Qing Dynasty government and gave hope to the Chinese citizens. The British intelligence at the time even reported that they believed the next uprising would cause a national shift in China.

Unfettered by the failure, Sun continued traveling the world to raise funds and organize troops for his next uprising. However, it became increasingly difficult as he had lost credibility in the communities that once respected him but had suffered significant financial losses and casualties due to his failures.

In a twist of fate, while Sun was preparing for another uprising in the United States, some of his faction's offshoot guilds and former members, including his previous second-in-command Huang Xing, successfully overthrew their local governments. This led to uprisings across China, with key members of Sun's faction overpowering the Qing Dynasty government's national forces. A mutiny then erupted in the capital city, and military leader Yuan Shikai seized control from the imperial family on March 10, 1912. For the first time in over two thousand years, China was without an emperor.

From Revolutionary to President

Initially, the debate over who would be the first president of China was between Huang Xing and a respected Qing general who had been reluctantly forced to lead the revolutionaries at gunpoint. Ultimately, because the revolutionaries respected Sun Yat-sen as the faction leader who had toiled for the cause for many years, and because he had the most comprehensive structure for a new democratic government, they elected him as the first president of the new Republic of China. His faction guild, the Revolutionary Alliance, then transformed into a political party, the Kuomintang (KMT), marking the transition from a guild for revolution to a guild for political governance.

If Sun Yat-sen's 10K HP journey were a TV series, this would have been the perfect ending: a man who pursued his dreams and, after seventeen years of turmoil, finally achieved his goal.

Unfortunately, that was just a perfect ending for "Season One."

After that, there was a-whole-nother "Season Two" where Sun's struggles resumed again. In order to unite the nation and avoid another civil war with warlords, Sun surrendered his presidential position just forty-five days later to the Qing military head Yuan Shikai, who still had many loyal commanders. Sun did this to prevent civil war, recognizing that Yuan was still viewed by Western powers as the more legitimate leader to take over.

This decision led Sun into a new series of political setbacks, including Yuan's betrayal and attempt to establish a monarchy with himself as emperor. Shockingly, Yuan assassinated Sun's KMT guild members, who were winning majority votes, to retain all the power.

Devastated by this new tyrant, Sun's unyielding spirit led him to again seek support in Japan and the United States for overthrowing Yuan. Even after Yuan's death from uremia in 1916, commanders loyal to him emerged, plunging China into the infamous *Warlord Period.* During this tumultuous time, Sun became the President of Southern China, tirelessly working to unify the chaotic North. This period was fraught with danger, including assassination attempts and internal conflicts within Sun's government.

Despite these challenges, Sun's charisma and vision continued to inspire people to his cause.

Sun's strategic foresight led to the establishment of the *Whampoa*

Military Academy with the help of his protégé, Chiang Kai-shek, who later became a key leader in defeating the northern warlords and formally unifying China under a common Republic. Unfortunately, before Sun could see his vision fully realized, his health deteriorated rapidly. In 1925, Sun passed away from gallbladder cancer[47].

Sun continuously struggled through his meaningful life game right up to the last year of his playthrough. Japan, England, and the United States ceased supporting his regime for their own political reasons, forcing him to turn to the Soviet Union for aid. He faced many enemies and political adversaries who painted him in a negative light. One of his most remembered nicknames, even to this day, "Sun Big Cannon," was propagated by his tyrant opponent Yuan Shikai to discredit him as a big talker, not a doer. Many in China looked at Sun's numerous failures and wondered if he was losing relevance, getting too close to the Soviet Union, or merely a big talker without accomplishments.

Ironically, after his death, Sun Yat-sen rapidly became the most revered figure among Chinese intellectuals by a landslide, as reflected in polls. This widespread respect was due to several reasons. First, his modest will, which left only a humble house and many books to his wife, set him apart as the only high-ranking official known to control vast funds – enough to operate armies and governments – yet he kept nothing for personal gain.

Second, recognition grew that he was the original and most steadfast patriot, tirelessly working to save his country. His writings on the *Three Principles of the People*,[48] his visions for China's improvement, and his thoughts on democratic governance were widely read and esteemed.

Last, his gentle yet charismatic nature earned him posthumous

---

[47]Sun was originally thought to have died of liver cancer. But 91 years later, in 2016, an American pathologist toured and examined his historical autopsy report and corrected the record.

[48]This is an extension of Abraham Lincoln's "Government of the People, for the People, by the People" in his 1863 Gettysburg Address.

praise even from his rivals and adversaries, now that he posed no threat. Throughout his life, Sun emphasized "nonretribution" against the Manchus, echoing the ancient Chinese adage, "He who delights not in killing a man can unify all men." In reflection, Chinese intellectuals acknowledged that Sun "was a patriot of unique simplicity."

Because of this newfound popularity, his political rivals, including future generations, began to appropriate the writings of the respected Sun Yat-sen for their own endeavors. He is the only modern Chinese figure revered and respected by both China and Taiwan. Chinese leader Xi Jinping often invokes Sun Yat-sen's name as a persuasive tactic to convince Taiwan to fulfill Sun's dream of creating a unified China.[49]

Figure 31. A US postage stamp featuring Sun Yat-sen

One of Sun's biographers, the Indonesian scholar and investment banker Tjio Kayloe, marveled that in both China and Taiwan, "in

---

[49]This gesture unfortunately motivated many Taiwanese people to disassociate themselves from Sun Yat-sen, despite living in a government system that Sun designed.

virtually every city there is at least a public park, a thoroughfare, a square, or another public landmark named in his honor." He noted that adding up public facilities and landmarks in other nations, such as "a Chinese garden in Vancouver, a museum in Chicago, a memorial park in Honolulu, a street in Port Louis, Mauritius, a road in Kolkata, India, a memorial hall in Kobe, and a relief at the Hakusan Shrine in Tokyo," there might be more public landmarks dedicated to Sun Yat-sen, often called "Zhongshan," than there are to any other historical figure worldwide. Given China's vastness alone, this might not be far from the truth.

OP Hero Sun Yat-sen: Takeaways

Sun Yat-sen was able to secure such a legacy and orchestrate the dismantling of a whole dynasty because he built alliances every step of the way. Despite being born into virtually no social circle, he seized every opportunity to approach anyone who could benefit his cause and immediately sought to make them his allies. In every moment, he embodied the six power attributes: integrity, sincerity, optimism, confidence, initiative, and persistence. Because of these qualities, he helped achieve what his countrymen thought was impossible and toppled an empire.

What about you? Have you ever felt that your goals seem insurmountable and you lacked the proper connections to make them a reality? If so, you should take a page out of Sun Yat-sen's playbook and bravely approach anyone you feel could even remotely help you toward your quests.

At school, you should find one-on-one time with your professors like Sun did with his Hong Kong mentors like Ho Kai and Sir James Cantlie. You should talk about your goals often and wear your game like a badge, so people in your social circles can be enlisted into helping you. You should reach out to or approach anyone who could be a great connection to set you off on the next step. Even if many people don't reply or even reject you – it's the ones who see greatness in you who will move your story forward.

Chapter 7 Highlights

- Networking is key to your game strategy. It should be strategic and intentional, focusing on meaningful connections rather than transactional benefits.
- Always obtain contact information with consent to turn acquaintances into allies. This simple step ensures that you can maintain and grow your network.
- Follow up regularly with your allies. Personalize your approach, showing genuine interest in their journey and how you can support them.
- Exceed expectations in all your interactions. This builds a remarkable reputation and encourages others to view you as a valuable ally.
- Treat every interaction as a potential alliance-building moment because spontaneous networking can create unexpected opportunities.
- The one-two punch and uppercut strategy in cold-emailing involves three respectful, persistent follow-ups to increase response rates. Quality over quantity is key.
- OP Hero Sun Yat-sen orchestrated the eventual overthrowing of the Qing Dynasty by recognizing and leveraging the unique attributes and skills of each ally. Since his childhood, he built alliances that mattered to his game everywhere he went.

Chapter 8: Achieve Your Quests (Milestones)

> *"Dream big dreams, but start small. A journey of a thousand miles begins with a single step."*
>
> —— Lao Tzu

Now that you have determined your game, attributes, roles, abilities, and alliance, it's time for the final step: achieve your quests. Quests are activities that help you get closer to your game objective, acquire necessary skills to become stronger, and grow with your allies.

A quest could be reading a book (like you are doing now), taking a class, doing an internship, volunteering in an underprivileged country, starting a family, writing a book, or climbing to the next position within your organization.

This is where the previous five steps culminate in actions that help you succeed in the game you set out to play. In essence, Steps 2 to 5 are about helping you choose the right quests, and completing quests allows you to grow in those areas too.

Your attributes and role help identify the skills you need to acquire and the allies with whom you need to connect. The quests are the actions required to make that happen. And once you have completed those quests, you will have grown in skills and allies too. Occasionally, it leads to a role transition, such as Gandhi transitioning from a barrister to an activist lawyer when he moved to South Africa.

Beyond skill acquisition and leveling-up, quests also furnish you with higher *scores* and *resources*. These not only elevate your status and provide enhanced "gear" but also enable you to do more activities of self-expression. Moreover, some quests provide the keys to unlock new zones or subsequent steps in a quest line. For instance, securing an undergraduate degree paves the way for potential master's programs or specific entry-level corporate roles. Similarly, successfully navigating a nation's immigration procedures (a minor "gatekeeping quest"), or achieving financial freedom through strategic career quests, can initiate a zone shift quest, granting access to new countries and a variety of new activities and quest lines.

Indeed, examining the journeys of our previous OP Heroes reveals that many embraced pivotal zone shift quests, propelling them toward their ultimate game. Elon Musk's path took him from South Africa to Canada, Pennsylvania, Silicon Valley, and finally to Los Angeles' aerospace realm. Gandhi transitioned from India to England, South Africa, and then back to India. Disney migrated from

Missouri to Los Angeles, Oprah from Mississippi to Tennessee, and Leonardo da Vinci ventured from Florence to Milan. Oftentimes, when your questing landscape isn't optimal, the best quest is to work toward moving to a new environment. You will see more of this from this chapter's OP Hero – someone who worked with an ally toward a multi-year plan just to complete a zone shift quest.

Dimensions of a Quest

To understand the anatomy of a quest, we can examine the variables that give each one its unique nature. There are generally three dimensions for each quest: the *scope* of completion, the *significance* to the game, and the quest *type*.

Quest Dimension 1: Scope

Quests can be broken down into various hierarchies based on the scope needed to complete them, including sagas, arcs, major quests, minor quests, and tasks. First, consider the more fundamental blocks like major quests and minor quests.

Major quests are long-term and significant commitments that usually take many months to multiple years to complete. These might include taking up a new job, moving to a new country, starting a new company, joining an important club, or enrolling in a new school. When someone declares, "I'm starting a new chapter in my life!", it usually means they have embarked on a new major quest (which could also mark the beginning of a new arc or even a saga, which I will discuss later).

Minor quests are shorter and smaller commitments that still enhance your skills, build alliances, and hopefully advance you toward your game objectives but are easier to pick up and complete. For instance, taking a class or reading a book are minor learning quests, whereas getting a college degree would be considered a major learning quest. Generally, a person would be on one or a few major quests, while constantly tackling a variety of minor quests that are often built into the major quests. Minor quests can be required or optional for beating the game, and they often still give some source of stats boost, whether it's for skills, reputation, resources (money, etc.), network, or other tangible benefits in the game.

Minor quests could be part of a major quest or independent of it. For instance, let's say my major quest is to launch a product into the market. Within this major quest, there are a variety of minor quests, such as recruiting people, planning marketing, quality assurance, etc. However, a minor quest could be completely independent of a major quest, such as doing a philanthropy trip to a third world country over a weekend. This would be known as a "minor side quest."

Within minor quests there are certain *tasks*, which are activities that can be done fairly quickly and do not qualify for being quests on their own. These tasks are often the line items you put into your to-do list (if you aren't overly vague or ambitious), such as, "Write this email," "Come up with a bullet point list," "Create a presentation," or "Spend thirty minutes with kids."

On a daily basis, you may accomplish dozens or even hundreds of these tasks, which become part of a minor quest. Then, a string of minor quest lines often become a major quest.

When many major and minor quests string together toward a single objective, especially when one directly leads to another, it becomes a major quest line we call an *arc*.

At the most macro level, when many major quest lines or arcs come together to define a new "act" or "era" in a person's life, they form a *saga*. While a person might have hundreds of major quests and thousands of minor quests throughout their life, they would only experience a few to two dozen sagas. For instance, my first saga was in South Africa (from ages two to eight), comprising only two major quests and one minor quest. There weren't many arcs during that period, as I was primarily focused on growing up and learning foundational skills.

At the time of this writing, I am only on my seventh saga, with six major quests and one minor quest. It's often difficult to detect our true progress in life, even between major quests, but when we look at the different sagas, we can see notable advancements in our life game.

For instance, after Elon Musk concluded his PayPal saga, he officially started his SpaceX Tesla saga. If we examine his Starting SpaceX Arc, we can identify various major quests. His first major quest was to inspire space travel. This led to numerous minor quests, such as moving to Los Angeles, joining the Mars Society, exploring how to fly mice into space, interviewing various experts, starting the Life on Mars Foundation (this would have been a major quest if he had done more with it), recruiting experts to his cause, and a trip to Russia to buy rockets.

That trip was unsuccessful, but it led to his next major quest: founding SpaceX. In this major quest, there were again various minor quests, including recruiting founding employees, researching various space components, and securing office space in Hawthorne, California. And, of course, each of these minor quests was filled with tasks.

The reason why I think it is important to differentiate between the scope of quests is because when you look at the available published literature related to turning life into a game, the word "quest" is often used to represent any type of activity. Visiting a country, writing an email, launching a software product, and becoming a billionaire are all called "quests," even though we intuitively understand the major differences in scope among these activities. I think it's useful in this literature to have a more precise term than just "a fun way to call stuff you have to do."

Quest Dimension 2: Type

Besides scope, quests can also be categorized by the nature of their activities. There are a variety of quest types, such as learning quests, health quests, spiritual quests, relationship quests, career quests, alliance quests, and more. Starting a new job that would take years of commitment is considered a major career quest, whereas doing a small gig on the side is considered a minor resource quest.

Following are some descriptions of a variety of common (but not exhaustive) quest types.

- **Career Quests**: These shape your professional journey. They can involve climbing the corporate ladder, transitioning careers, or pursuing side hustles that align with your life game.
- **Learning Quests**: These focus on acquiring knowledge and skills. Whether you're studying a new subject, learning a language, or attending a workshop, these quests enhance your intellectual growth.
- **Resource Quests**: These aim to accumulate valuable resources essential for sustaining and improving quality of life. If your job doesn't align with your life game but your side hustle does, then the job is a major resource quest and the side hustle a minor career quest. For instance, Peter Parker's reporter job at *The Daily Bugle* is a resource quest compared to his real career quest of fighting crime as Spider-Man.
- **Health Quests**: These focus on physical well-being, such as starting a fitness regimen, following a new diet, or addressing specific health issues. It's about staying in top shape to handle other quests.
- **Spiritual Quests**: These involve one's inner journey through meditation, religious practices, or philosophical studies, aiming to find meaning, purpose, and inner peace. For some, spiritual quests can be the most important of all.

- **Relationship Quests**: These focus on building, maintaining, or ending relationships, including friendships, family ties, and romantic connections. Keep in mind these relationship quests are not necessarily for work partners who can push your game to new heights, since we reserved that for...
- **Alliance Quests**: These involve building networks, forming partnerships, or joining communities aligned with your game objectives. Strong alliances can make a significant impact, as seen with Sun Yat-sen, who leveraged them to help overthrow an entire dynasty.
- **Discovery Quests**: These personal journeys uncover your true self. They involve introspection and self-discovery, fostering awareness and growth. Perhaps you decided to take a whole new job thinking that it would start a new saga in your life. But two weeks in, you realized it was not for you, and you quit the job. This major career quest ended up transforming into a minor discovery quest of what you don't want to do in your life.
- **Service Quests**: These involve altruistic pursuits like volunteering, community projects, philanthropy, or serving your country. Gandhi's life was filled with service quests, where he excelled as a Strategy Sage.
- **Adventure Quests**: These focus on exploration and novelty. Whether traveling to a new country, trying a new activity, or breaking routine, these quests add excitement and unpredictability to the life game.

These are just examples of the most common quest activities, but they are by no means exhaustive. Quest activities can be as varied and diverse as the endeavors we pursue in our lives and should not be limited by a dropdown of selections. If you go on vacation, feel free to call it a "resting quest." If you are fighting in court for custody of your children, labeling it as a "court quest" is just as valid as calling it a "relationship quest."

Some quests might also overlap across categories. For example, an international work assignment could be both a career quest (professional growth) and an adventure quest (new experiences). In such cases, we may simply reference the one that aligns most closely with the game objectives.

While the naming of the quest type is not as important, what's vital is to recognize where each quest lies in your journey and how it advances (or sometimes hinders) your overall game objectives – and that brings us to the next quest dimension.

Quest Dimension 3: Significance

Besides scope and activity, the third dimension for quests are their significance toward the game objectives. Quests can be divided into main quests and side quests, with some quests ascending to the "pivotal" level.

Main quests are quests that advance you significantly toward your game objectives. Often, they are seen as requirements for progressing further in the game and usually unlock new quests and opportunities that are higher leveled. As mentioned, enrolling in a good university is often a "major learning main quest" that unlocks other major main quests such as joining a professional fraternity or finding your first job. Without these major main quests, it would be very difficult to advance to higher level "dungeons," which is important for leveling up and beating your game.

What is considered a main quest depends on the game (Step 1) you chose to play, as the same tasks could be seen as either instrumental or a complete waste of time depending on what your goals are. Occasionally, one might change their game after realizing all their past quests would align better with a different game, or at least a different role (Step 3) in that game.

For instance, a mediocre engineer might discover that they are happiest when mentoring engineering interns or helping aspiring students find their passions. Although these activities might be seen as distractions (or side quests) from becoming a top engineer, they realize that switching their game and role to that of a career coach or counselor allows them to help as many young people as possible. The seemingly unimportant activities from the past then become crucial main quest experiences for their new game objective.

Side quests, on the other hand, are activities that do not directly contribute to the actual game objectives but are done because of some hobby, interest, or distraction. For instance, if my game and role isn't about becoming a great chess player but I am preparing to compete in a local chess tournament, that would be considered a side quest.

If I decided to write music or a novel, play games, or travel the world, but these activities do not directly contribute to beating my game by learning the right skills or building the right alliances, they would be considered side quests. These are not inherently bad, as they can be quite meaningful, such as spending time with family or picking up a sport. However, they tend to slow down progress toward beating your actual game, which is why hardcore players tend to avoid too many side quests.

In the game *The Legend of Zelda*, the main protagonist, Link, is tasked with fighting quests to improve his combat skills in order to stop the ultimate evil from taking over the world. However, he can also engage in side quests such as fishing and catching chickens for local villagers. While these activities are entertaining and can sometimes provide benefits for future quest lines, they are generally not efficient ways to save the world.

More often than not, side quests exist to provide a break from the main game, offering a chance to focus on something more relaxing to enhance quality of life or improve mental states. Many people also end up doing side quests because of what their friends are doing, leading to significant distractions from their own major quests. This is why it's important to apply good immersion design, or the real-life game skill (Rogue skill class) *batcave crafting*, much like Batman designed his perfect environment for gearing up to fight crime.

When an activity is so important that it sets the player on a new trajectory in their game, it is called a *pivotal quest.* Many major main quests are inherently life-altering to some degree (unless you didn't do your 10K HP exercises and didn't align your major quests to your life game), but pivotal quests can also be special minor quests that change everything. Consider Steve Jobs attending the Homebrew Computer Club, where he met his future co-founder, Steve Wozniak, or Gandhi's relocation to South Africa, where a discriminatory train experience galvanized his mission. Sometimes, a single book can offer such profound insights that a person dedicates their life to a newfound cause.

For me, a few of my pivotal quests included starting my first business at seventeen, conceptualizing the Octalysis Framework, and publishing *Actionable Gamification: Beyond Points, Badges, and Leaderboards.* If I hadn't taken on any one of these quests, my life today would be distinctly different, likely at a significantly weaker level.

As I'm sure you know by now, a big part of being successful at your 10K HP game is to have full clarity of what your game is, what role you should play, and to ensure you spend more time on main quests rather than side quests.

Of course, main quests don't need to be solely related to work. I noted in Chapter 2: Choose Your Game, that my game also involves optimizing my spiritual life and being there for my family. In that way, volunteering at my church or taking my kids to a chess tournament would still be counted as main quests instead of distracting side quests.

If you don't know what game you are playing yet, and therefore cannot determine your main quests and side quests, it's still beneficial to engage in various minor quests. Explore courses, volunteer opportunities, books, clubs, documentaries, or new hobbies. As you do more minor quests, you might stumble upon something or someone that transforms a discovery side quest into a pivotal quest, which would then help you determine your life game.

Major side quests are also fine as you explore what your game is, but, given the fact that major side quests can last multiple months or years, committing to something for a long period without knowing how it aligns with your overall mission can be costly. I know many individuals who pursued advanced degrees, such as Ph.D.s, primarily because they didn't know what they wanted to do with their lives.

Opting for a Ph.D. as a default might be considered high-level and prestigious, but it's a considerable commitment. Not only does it demand years of dedication, but it can also inadvertently narrow one's career options due to the specialization involved. It is not recommended to spend five years specializing in something that does not align with what you truly want to do in your life game.

By now, you might recognize the great tragedy of having a major career side quest – holding a long-term job that has nothing to do with what you truly want to do in life. Unfortunately, many people are stuck in such quests.

If you plan to improve your health over the next year with an actionable plan, that could be considered a major health main quest, as you won't be able to complete your game if your health deteriorates. Joining my online community, Octalysis Prime, could be seen as both a "major learning and alliance main quest." Getting married is likely a "major relationship main quest," whereas a two-week trip with a significant other might be considered a "minor relationship side quest," depending on the game you set out to play.

So, What Is Not Considered a Quest?

If activities that align with your game objectives are main quests and those that don't are side quests, does that mean everything we do is a quest? It's important to understand what doesn't qualify. Here are criteria that prevent an activity from becoming a quest:

- **Daily Chores and Indulgences**: Tasks like grocery shopping, doing laundry, or paying bills are essential but aren't quests. They are maintenance tasks for daily functioning but don't advance your life game. Occasional indulgences like eating out or shopping are also not quests unless they serve a larger purpose. All quests have tasks, but tasks themselves are not quests.
- **Passive Consumption**: Activities like binge-watching TV, mindlessly scrolling through social media, or surfing the internet might be relaxing but don't qualify as quests unless they serve a larger purpose. For instance, watching a documentary to learn could be part of a learning quest, but watching TV to pass time doesn't advance your game objectives. Quests require intentional effort, not passive consumption.
- **Trivial Activities Within a Quest**: Minor actions like walking to the office or opening your laptop are not quests. In a game, killing one monster or opening a door isn't a quest – those are tasks that contribute to completing a quest.

If activities are done out of habit or social expectation rather than intent, they don't count as quests. You might spend countless hours on certain activities but still live like a passive NPC, not engaging in true quests that advance you toward your goals.

Auditing your daily activities can reveal how you spend your time and highlight areas for adjustment. Reorganizing or reducing certain activities may create time for more fulfilling minor or major quests you've been postponing. It's important to prioritize tasks that truly matter, advance your objectives, and resonate with your purpose in the grand game of life.

How to Decide on Your Quests

Embarking on quests is a significant commitment, entailing the investment of time, energy, and often, resources. Therefore, the process of selecting the right quests to pursue should be carefully considered. In this juncture of your 10K HP journey, let's examine the avenues you can explore to make informed and effective decisions on what quests to undertake.

Simple Method 1: Ask a Role Model or Mentor

An integral part of Step 5: Build Your Alliance (Network), is identifying a role model who aligns with the role (Step 3) you envision for yourself in your game (Step 1). This should be someone who has successfully navigated similar paths and has valuable experience and insights.

Approach them with your defined game, communicate your objectives, and seek their guidance on which quests to undertake to level up effectively. Once the role model agrees to help you, they become your mentor and can offer valuable advice on your next steps for growth.

Simple Method 2: Model After a Role Model

In addition to seeking guidance from mentors, you can also model your journey after a role model by emulating their actions. That's what role models are for, right? In the context of this book, historical OP Heroes serve as good examples for this method.

Start by choosing a role model whose journey resonates with you. Ideally, this should be someone who not only shares a similar role in the game but also has carved out an inspiring trajectory. Study their history, accomplishments, and the choices they made at crucial points in their life.

Break down their journey into tangible quests they undertook. Analyze the skills they honed, the alliances they formed, and the personal attributes that played key roles in their success. Then, map out how you can replicate these quests in your own journey, tailoring them to fit your personal circumstances and objectives.

Simple Method 3: Progressing Your Skill Triangle

To transform yourself into a high-level player, you need to constantly evolve and sharpen your skills (Step 4). If you haven't yet, start by analyzing your Current Skill Triangle and comparing it to your Target Skill Triangle. What gaps do you observe? What skills are you lacking that are crucial for becoming a top player in your role?

Create an action plan detailing how you intend to acquire and enhance these missing skills. This might involve enrolling in relevant courses, becoming an apprentice, or undertaking quests focused on honing these skills. If it isn't clear which skill to pursue first, it's okay to choose one and treat it as a Discovery Learning Quest.

Simple Method 4: Join Your Allies' Quests

As incorporated in Step 5, you want to align yourself with allies who are engaged in the same game as you. Engage in discussions, brainstorm ideas, and explore opportunities to undertake quests together. This collaborative approach not only enhances learning but also makes the journey more enjoyable and fulfilling.

If you've chosen your allies well, consider joining the quests they are already pursuing. Whether as a co-founder, sidekick, study buddy, or gym partner, surrounding yourself with the right people will naturally involve you in their quests. Many early classmates of revolutionary patriot Sun Yat-sen joined his revolutionary activities against the Qing Dynasty because they didn't have a clear game and quest strategy but were passionate about a better and respected China. By joining Sun Yat-sen's quests, no matter how small their roles, they contributed to the legendary achievement of ending thousands of years of the imperial system and impacting billions of people.

If you don't have allies doing quests that resonate with you, consider joining a guild where you can engage in activities that enhance your skills, expand your network, and boost your accomplishments. This could be a professional fraternity, local Toastmasters club, Brazilian Jiu-Jitsu academy, church gathering, or cooking club. It doesn't matter what it is. As long as you're interested in the activities and can meet others with the same interests, it can inspire you to discover your next important quest in your life game.

"But I Can't Do It!"

Don't have a mentor yet so you can't do Method 1? Perfect! Now your first quest can be to find a role model and turn them into a mentor! Don't know your Current and Final Skill Triangles yet? No problem – make today the day you delve into understanding and mapping out your Skill Triangles. Finding yourself isolated without allies playing the same game as you? It's time to venture out and align with a guild, a place where like-minded individuals converge.

The point is that, in the 10K HP journey, there should never be a moment where you don't know what quest you should take on. If you don't know, that means you have a variety of discovery quests waiting for you to tackle and find out. Just like most games, the only way to lose is by not playing. If you don't proactively think about what quests you are doing in relation to your game, you are not "playing" and, therefore, just being a passive NPC.

Crafting Quests: Make Them SMART

Quests are the milestones of your 10K HP journey, and to ensure they lead you to success, they should be SMART – Specific, Measurable, Achievable, Relevant, and Time-bound. Originally outlined by George T. Doran in a 1981 *Management Review* article and often linked to Peter Drucker's management principles,[1] the SMART framework is an invaluable guide for goal setting, or in our context, quest design.[2] So let's see how the SMART framework could be applied to the 10K HP context.

Specific: Define the What and Who

To carve a clear path to victory, your quests must be specific. They should clearly outline the quest activity type – be it a relationship, career, or philanthropy quest – and the desired actions within these quests. A specific quest dispels ambiguity, focusing your efforts on well-defined objectives and necessary resources.

Measurable: Set Clear Win Definitions

Measurability is crucial for gauging progress and keeping motivation high. Your quests should have distinct milestones, making it evident what you've achieved and what lies ahead. This answers the crucial question: How will I know when I've succeeded?

Achievable: Ensure Urgent Optimism

Your quests should challenge you but remain within the realm of possibility. Setting unattainable goals only leads to frustration and potential abandonment of your quest. By ensuring that your quests are achievable, you align them with your current skills, resources, and time constraints, fostering a sense of attainable challenge and achievement.

Relevant: Align With the Why

The relevance of your quest ensures it's in harmony with your broader life goals, ensuring that every step you take is a stride in the right direction. A relevant quest resonates with your core values and long-term objectives, making the journey not just a series of tasks, but a meaningful pursuit toward your ultimate game.

Time-Bound: Set a Clear Fail-State

Finally, your quests need a deadline. Time-bound quests create a sense of urgency and focus, preventing endless procrastination. They help you organize your efforts and stay on track toward timely completion.

Designing your quests using the SMART framework turns them into powerful, purposeful steps in your 10K HP journey. This approach allows you to craft a journey that is not only ambitious but also structured, meaningful, and, ultimately, achievable within your game.

Gamify Your Quests

Besides making your quests SMART, here are a few ways to add gamified structure to your quests. These simple mechanics primarily rely on extrinsic motivators such as progress, achievement, and reward, and can be easily incorporated into your endeavors. While there are many ways to add intrinsic motivators to your quests, they typically require a bit more learning to design and implement. For creating holistically gamified quests that are fun, enjoyable, and meaningful, consider joining the Octalysis Prime Community or reading my book, *Actionable Gamification: Beyond Points, Badges, and Leaderboards.*

Adopt a Three-Star Achievement System Into Your Quests and Tasks

For each quest you set for yourself, it can be helpful to establish tiers of completion based on how well you achieve it. This approach prevents setting a quest that is either too difficult or too easy due to fear of failure. A good method is to implement a three-star achievement system, as seen in the iconic game *Angry Birds* and many other mobile games. For performance-driven tasks, the system can easily reflect the level of achievement. For example, if you are aiming for a high score on an exam, you could grant three stars for a score of 90 percent or higher, two stars for at least 80 percent, and one star for above 70 percent.

In my learning community, Octalysis Prime, I could set reward tiers based on the number of members who sign up by the end of this month (remember, it ideally should be time-bound). If 1,000 members join by the month's end, I would earn a three-star achievement for this quest. If 500 sign-ups are reached, that would be a two-star achievement. If only 100 sign-ups occur, it would be a one-star achievement.

There are also many quests based on labor-driven tasks, typically items on your to-do list awaiting completion. Generally, as long as you spend time on these tasks, you will complete them. However, there isn't a clear criterion for performance metrics besides the perceived quality. In this case, the three-star system can be based on the speed of completion. For example, if my goal is to finish proofreading this manuscript, I could set a three-star achievement for completing it within three days, a two-star achievement for finishing it within a week, and a one-star achievement for taking more than two weeks.

They can apply to smaller activities too. Remember the quest hierarchy of Sagas $\Rightarrow$ Arcs $\Rightarrow$ Major quests $\Rightarrow$ Minor quests $\Rightarrow$ Tasks? Writing a book could be an arc, while completing the first draft might be a major quest. Smaller activities, such as "finish writing Chapter 3," "proofread Chapter 2," or "study Gandhi's biography," would be minor quests. Tasks within minor quests should also be SMART and have their own three-star achievements, provided the task isn't so mundane that specifying the requirements takes more time than completing the task itself. For instance, it would be a mistake to create a SMART plan with a three-star achievement for reading and responding to each email.

Consider the example of sending out an important project proposal to a potential client. A three-star achievement could be sending the proposal today, a two-star achievement could be sending it within three days, and a one-star achievement could be sending it within five days. If the proposal isn't sent within five days, the task is considered failed.

It's crucial to ensure that each achievement is attainable. A one-star achievement should feel easy to reach with effort. A two-star achievement should be challenging but manageable under optimal conditions. A three-star achievement should be a stretch goal, where hitting it would be cause for celebration with your allies. Incorporating urgent optimism into your quest designs helps you feel like you can actually reach the goal, but you must act urgently to avoid running out of time and failing.

Counting Your Stars

Once you've integrated the three-star achievement system into your quests and tasks, the next step is to monitor and evaluate your performance. Instead of simply tallying your achievements, focus on understanding the nature and difficulty of the tasks you've accomplished and use this insight to motivate further progress. By tracking the number of quests you've completed with one, two, or three stars, you gain valuable insight into your performance, effort levels, and areas for improvement.

At the end of each week, month, or any other time-bound period you set, take some time to review the quests you've completed. Categorize them based on the number of stars achieved: count how many quests were completed with a one-star rating, how many with two stars, and how many reached the exhilarating three-star status. This breakdown provides a clear picture of your performance across varying levels of difficulty and effort.

Create a Reward Schedule

Once you've tallied your stars, it's time to reward yourself. This not only reinforces positive behavior but also keeps you motivated for future quests. Rewarding yourself based on the difficulty and impact of the tasks completed makes the system even more meaningful.

A Star Is a Star

Count your total stars and reward yourself equally. For example, every ten stars could earn you a movie night or a nice dinner out, regardless of how the stars were earned. This approach encourages consistent effort across all tasks. To add more fun, use each star as a raffle ticket for your reward pool. At the end of each month, draw tickets for different prizes based on your total stars. This element of excitement and anticipation will keep you motivated to earn more stars.

Rewarding Impactful Tasks

Three-star achievements represent your highest efforts and deserve special recognition. For every three-star quest completed, treat yourself to something significant, like a day off or a special purchase. For an even bigger boost, offer a grand reward for every ten three-star quests completed. This creates anticipation and excitement for reaching high achievements.

Acknowledging Consistent Efforts

One and two-star tasks, while less challenging, showcase your consistent effort and commitment. Regular, smaller rewards for these tasks keep your motivation high. For example, treat yourself to your favorite coffee for every five one-star tasks completed. Adjust the rewards based on the scope of these quests.

Personalized Reward System

Use the star count system as a tool for reflective learning. If you find you're racking up one-star achievements but struggling to hit those two- and three-star marks, it might be time to reassess your quest-setting strategies. Are you setting achievable stretch goals? Are you allocating enough time and resources to your higher-tier quests? This reflection can help you adjust your approach, ensuring that your future quests are not only SMART but also aligned with your ultimate objectives in your 10K HP journey.

By implementing a fun and structured reward system, you reinforce positive behaviors and maintain high motivation, making your journey through your quests both enjoyable and productive.

What If I Failed My Quest?

What if you failed to accomplish the task in general and didn't even get one star? We all face moments when, despite our best efforts, we fail to complete a task. It's a part of the learning and growing process. However, how we respond to these failures can significantly impact our motivation and progress in our life game. Following are some ways to process quest failure in a psychologically productive way.

Implementing the Two-Week Break Rule

If you fail to accomplish a task and don't earn even a single star, I recommend enforcing a two-week break from that specific task or quest. This break serves two purposes: it acts as a consequence for not meeting your goal, and it offers a mental reset.

- *Reflect and Recharge*: Use this break period not only as a consequence but also as an opportunity for reflection and rejuvenation. Stepping back from a task can provide new perspectives and renewed energy.
- *Remove the Weight*: A lingering, incomplete task can become a mental burden, constantly reminding you of an unmet goal. I've seen many people have the same tasks on their to-do lists for months, which can feel demoralizing. By temporarily removing it from your list, you free yourself from this weight, allowing space to focus on other productive tasks.
- *Re-evaluate*: When you reintroduce the task after two weeks, reassess its importance. Is it still relevant and necessary? If so, approach it with fresh eyes and a rejuvenated spirit. This break can help you tackle the task more effectively.

Handling Mission-Critical Tasks

If a task is urgent and cannot be postponed, it's imperative to push through and complete it, even if it means earning zero stars. Failing to complete a mission-critical task on time should be a learning experience. Analyze what went wrong and how you can prevent similar situations in the future.

Consistently failing to complete tasks can lead to a negative spiral of demotivation. Remember that even late completions help maintain a positive mindset and forward momentum. Ensure your one-star thresholds are low enough that your brain feels it's a piece of cake as long as you engage and play the game.

This approach balances accountability with compassion for your own limits and challenges. The goal is not to punish failure but to encourage growth, learning, and continuous improvement. Remember, the 10K HP journey is about progress, not perfection.

Should I Adapt the Three-Star System to Tasks or Major Quests?

Given your 10K HP quest hierarchy of sagas, arcs, major quests, minor quests, and tasks, the question is whether you should assign a three-star system to all of them, despite their differing scopes. The key is to focus on areas where rapid feedback and a sense of accomplishment are achievable – primarily tasks and minor quests.

Tasks, the smallest units in our quest hierarchy, are ideal for the three-star system. They are short-term, clearly defined, and their completion brings immediate results. Whether it's finishing a chapter of a book, working out for a day, or completing a small project at work, applying the three-star system here allows for quick feedback and a sense of progress. It's like scoring points in a game – the instant gratification keeps you engaged and motivated.

Minor quests, slightly larger endeavors than tasks, are also well-suited for this system. They offer enough immediacy to make the three-star rating meaningful and motivational. For example, organizing a small event, completing a short course, or achieving a monthly sales target can all be structured as minor quests with a three-star rating system.

By focusing the three-star system on tasks and minor quests, you create a framework that provides rapid feedback and fosters a sense of achievement, keeping you motivated and engaged in your journey.

Why Not Major Quests?

While it might be tempting to apply the three-star system to major quests like starting a new career or launching a significant project, the feedback loop for these endeavors is much longer. Major quests often span months or even years, and the slow pace of feedback can diminish the system's effectiveness. Imagine waiting a year to find out how well you did in a game; the lack of immediate feedback can lead to a loss of engagement and motivation, which is contrary to the goals of the three-star system.

Applying the three-star system to tasks and minor quests aligns with the principles of cognitive ease and urgent optimism - a term coined by Dr. Jane McGonigal. Cognitive ease refers to our preference for things that are easy for the brain to process. By focusing on smaller, more manageable components, we make the process of achievement less daunting and more digestible.

Urgent optimism, the desire to act immediately to tackle an obstacle combined with the belief that success is attainable, is more realistically achieved by applying the three-star system to tasks and minor quests. This creates a sense of urgency and a belief in attainability, setting short-term goals that keep us motivated and moving forward.

Focusing the three-star system on tasks and minor quests creates a gaming-like environment with constant rapid feedback and a sense of accomplishment. This approach keeps us engaged, motivated, and steadily progressing toward our larger goals within our sagas and arcs. Remember, the journey of 10,000 hours is not just about the destination but also about enjoying and making the most of every step along the way.

Questing With OKRs

Every quest serves a larger purpose — advancing the ultimate game objective. To understand this, consider how game objectives, quests, and tasks connect. In any video game, the objective is the primary goal. Reaching it requires completing quests, each made up of tasks, which are the concrete steps needed to progress.

Take the role-playing game *Witcher 3: Wild Hunt* as an example. The game clearly outlines main quests and the associated tasks required for completion. In the game, the protagonist Geralt is on a critical mission to find his adopted daughter, Ciri, who is being pursued by nefarious forces known as the "Wild Hunt." To find Ciri, Geralt first needs to locate Yennefer, who possesses crucial information.

In *Witcher 3*, the game objective is to "find and protect Ciri from the Wild Hunt." Before tackling this, you must complete the main quest "locate Yennefer." This main quest includes several minor quests:

Kaer Morhen (a tutorial quest): Learn the game controls. Lilac and Gooseberries: Track down clues to find Yennefer. The Incident at White Orchard: Discover Yennefer is in Vizima. Imperial Audience: Reunite with Yennefer.

For example, the "Lilac and Gooseberries" quest includes several tasks:

Ask the Nilfgaardians about Yennefer. Kill the ghouls. Follow Vesemir. Go to the tavern in White Orchard. Ask travelers about Yennefer.

The power and allure of RPG games come from these core elements: game objectives, quests, and tasks. They create an immersive journey with a constant sense of progression, keeping players engaged.

A similar structure is used by companies like Intel and Google with the management methodology of OKRs (Objectives and Key Results). First introduced by Andy Grove of Intel in the 1970s, it was popularized by Google's investor John Doerr. In Google's early years, Doerr introduced OKRs, which played a key role in the company's explosive success.[3]

If you pay close attention, you'll see that OKRs echo the quest mechanics of video games. In games, there's a clear game objective, similar to OKRs' objectives. To accomplish these objectives, players complete a set of predefined quests, similar to key results. Every quest then has its own specific tasks, which mirror the initiatives in OKRs. In most video games, the paths to achieve the game objectives are limited; players simply navigate through them. In the game of life, however, the challenge lies in charting your own course from thousands of possible choices to advance toward the game objectives (or side quests that distract you). If you've been diligently applying the first five steps of the 10K HP journey (or working on the 10K HP Workbook), outlining the correct main quest lines becomes a creative endeavor rather than a daunting task.

Mark Diaz Quest List Example

Take Mark Diaz from my mentorship guild of Octalysis Prime, who later became a co-author of this book. One of his game objectives is to "Live a long, healthy life." To support this goal, his main health quest was to lose weight. To make his quests SMART, instead of vaguely wanting to lose weight, the minor quest becomes: "Shed twenty pounds of (ideally) body fat in two months."

- **Specific**: Setting a clear target of twenty pounds.
- **Measurable**: The goal is quantified in pounds, making progress tracking straightforward.
- **Achievable**: With a plan, shedding around two to three pounds per week is realistic.
- **Relevant**: This weight loss directly ties into better health, aligning with the game objective of a longer, more fulfilling life.
- **Time-Bound**: There's a clear deadline of two months. This SMART goal gives Mark a crystal-clear vision of victory. Starting at 190 pounds, he'll know he's succeeded when the scale displays 170 pounds. When that moment arrives, it'll be time to celebrate. This minor main quest consists of two task lists, each broken down into specific tasks.

Task List 1: Adopt a Balanced Diet

- Consult with a nutritionist to understand his specific dietary needs.
- Plan and prepare weekly meals ahead of time, ensuring they are balanced and aligned with his calorie goals.
- Avoid "empty calories" like processed foods with low nutritional value.
- Create a list of healthy foods he enjoys and incorporate them into his meals regularly.
- Track daily caloric intake using the Fitbit app.
- Drink at least eight glasses of water daily.

Task List 2: Incorporate Regular Exercise

- Get a Fitbit smartwatch to count steps.
- Join a local gym or get home gym equipment.
- Schedule workouts at least three times a week.
- Walk at least 8,000 steps a day, or at least 56,000 steps a week using the Fitbit watch.
- Set incremental weekly goals for strength (increasing dumbbell weights or reps).
- Track workouts, noting duration, intensity, and how he felt afterward.
- Get an accountability buddy to report to weekly and ensure that he is doing the workouts.

Many of these tasks require consistent effort to reach the goal, indicating the need to form new habits. If he consistently carries out these tasks week after week, he should be able to shed two to three pounds weekly and be on the path to victory. Mark followed this plan and achieved great results.[50]

---

[50] Being a TEDx Speaker with over 340K views, Mark regularly attributes his success to being in the Octalysis Prime Guild, where he tapped into a variety of gamification techniques to boost his motivation, incorporating rewards and incentives throughout his journey. Octalysis Prime also connected him to a community of like-minded, goal-driven individuals. Within this supportive network, he found a dedicated accountability partner who was also on a fitness journey. Together, they seamlessly integrated gamification into their routine, transforming their goals into a fun and engaging adventure.

Figure 32. Mark Diaz Before and After

Question: Did Mark Achieve His Game Objective in Just Two Months?

The Answer: Not quite! While Mark initially set a two-month time-line, believing it was attainable, it actually took him six months. Old habits die hard, and Mark had several to overcome. However, because his progress was measurable, he stayed motivated, setting a new deadline every two months until he achieved his goal. If Mark doesn't perform as well as he wants, he can use a three-star system for his weight-loss results (performance-driven activities): One star for ten pounds, two stars for fifteen pounds, and three stars for twenty pounds. Stars can be collected and used in a larger lifestyle gamification reward system. If he doesn't earn even one star, he should set a new SMART quest with a fresh three-star system. If Mark doesn't complete his labor-driven activities over two months, he should set a two-week cooldown period before tackling the quest again. This approach encourages seriousness and discourages procrastination. Consistently failing deadlines creates self-esteem and stress problems, which hinder a fulfilling life. Enforcing a rule such as, "If I don't finish this today, I can't touch it for a week," creates a sense of urgency (what I call "black hat motivation" within the Octalysis Framework), making people more likely to complete tasks. In the upcoming OP Hero story, I'll describe how game objectives, quests, and tasks propelled someone to an exceptional life far exceeding their goals.

It's Your Turn to Play: SMART Quests

Now that you have acquired the knowledge of 10K HP quests, it's time for you to reflect on your own quests and determine future ones to level up in your journey.

Pick from One of the Three Game Modes

Easy: Reflect on the Major Quests in your life that have made a significant impact on shaping who you are today. Write down three to five meaningful milestones or achievements that stand out. Consider what made them important and how they contributed to your growth journey.

Medium: Identify a goal you want to accomplish in the next month and turn it into a SMART Minor Quest: Specific, Measurable, Achievable, Relevant, and Time-bound. Use the Star Reward System to track your goal and define meaningful rewards along the way. Share your Minor Quest with two trusted allies and ask them to help keep you accountable.

Hard: Think big by planning your Five-Year Goals and breaking them down into Major and Minor Quests. Explore the variety of Quests you need to tackle to achieve your goals: Learning Quests to gain new skills, Alliance Quests to build connections, Career Quests to enhance your profile, and Health Quests to maintain your best condition. Break each goal into smaller, actionable steps and assign timelines to each Quest. Create a Visual Roadmap to outline your game plan and track your progress.

For a bit of structure, visit 10KHP.com/worksheets to download practice materials or find the 10K HP Workbook to guide your progress.

OP Hero Profile: From Oppressed Girl to Double Nobel Laureate – the Scientific Trailblazer

Here's the 10K HP journey of another OP Hero whose life was entangled with failed relationships and emotional depression. As a young girl, this OP Hero was joyful and carefree, loving to "dance the night away." Unfortunately, she grew up in a poor family in Russia-occupied Poland during the 1870s, where pro-Polish sentiments were suppressed. Additionally, her life's opportunities were limited since many quest lines, such as obtaining an advanced degree, were available only to boys.

At eighteen, our OP Hero worked for an esteemed family as a governess, a nanny-like tutor. She fell in love with the oldest brother in her employer's household. As her feelings intensified, she wrote to a friend, "Some people pretend that in spite of everything I am obliged to pass through the kind of fever called love."

Unfortunately, her employer disapproved of the relationship, claiming it would bring shame and stain the family's honor. Heartbroken, the son complied and ended their bond. Emotionally depressed, our OP Hero confided in a letter to her sister:

"I have been stupid, I am stupid and I shall remain stupid all the days of my life [...] I shall never be lucky. [...] I don't know what to do... I am exceptionally unhappy in this world."

Despite the heartache, humiliations, and constant whispers from the household, she continued to work there for many years. She needed the money and still hoped that her lover would eventually have a change of heart and ask her to marry him.

When it became clear that he never intended to marry her, she wrote, "I feel everything very violently with physical violence and then I give myself a shaking, the vigor of my nature conquers and it seems to me that I am coming out of a nightmare..."

After this heartbreak, she decided to continue pursuing an advanced education. However, due to the restrictions on women in her country, she was not allowed to study her field of interest at any university. This forced her to use all her savings and move to Paris, where women were allowed to pursue advanced degrees.

While studying at the Sorbonne University in Paris, our OP Hero was reportedly so poor that she wore all the clothes she owned during winters because she could not afford a coat. During this time, she fell in love with a French physicist, whom she eventually married. She was hesitant about marrying a Frenchman because she wanted to return to Poland, and such a decision "meant abandoning my country and my family." Their shared passion, however, led her to commit.

For a few years, she enjoyed the life of a working wife and mother of two daughters. Then, a tragic plot twist event occurred when her husband was killed in a "wagon accident," leaving her a devastated single mother. Unsure of how to carry on, she found strength in her late husband's words of encouragement and continued working hard to carry on his legacy.

Five years after her husband's death, she fell in love again, this time with a former pupil of her deceased husband. Unfortunately, this man, who was also a reputable physicist, was married with four children. Our OP Hero was immediately shunned by the French press and branded with the Scarlet Letter: "This foreign home-wrecker had tarnished the good name of her deceased husband!" read one newspaper report. Some reporters even hinted that her affair had begun five years prior while her ex-husband was still alive, suggesting he committed suicide in despair.

On top of the public humiliation and accusations, she returned home one day to find an angry mob terrorizing her fourteen-year-old and seven-year-old daughters. This ordeal led to severe depression and acute illness, resulting in a kidney operation. Feeling unworthy of her deceased husband's name, she used only her maiden name and forbade her daughters from addressing letters to her legal name. To escape the press, the shame, and the mobs, she fled to England and spent a summer there, hiding under her maiden name, sick, dishonored, and lonely.

So, you might wonder, "Yu-kai, I thought we were talking about historically amazing OP Heroes who have conquered many quests in their lives. Why are we discussing this drama-filled individual who seems to belong in a soap opera?"

That's because I've only been sharing the relationship main and side quests of this OP Hero, and have not yet touched on her other main quests and achievements.

Despite all the drama and setbacks she experienced in her life, our OP Hero found her true life game (Step 1) in helping humanity through science, with her role (Step 3) as a scientific researcher. She possessed the right attributes (Step 2) to uncover the secrets of our physical world and *proactively* took on many quests (Step 6) that helped her gain the necessary skills (Step 4) to achieve feats no human had ever accomplished.

Our OP Hero is the *Scientific Trailblazer*: Marie Skłodowska-Curie.

Legacy of a Trailblazer

So why do I call Marie Curie a trailblazer? Even though this phrase is commonly used in many scenarios as hyperbole, I never use it figuratively. Marie Curie stands as a true beacon of the trailblazing spirit, pioneering paths in numerous uncharted fields.

She was the first woman to win a Nobel Prize, one of the highest honors on the Earth Server. Not only that, she was the first person to win two Nobel Prizes. If that isn't impressive enough, she is the first and one of only two human beings in history to have won two Nobel Prizes in two different categories (physics and chemistry), out of only a handful of possible categories.[51]

It might impress you further to learn that Marie Curie is also the first Nobel Laureate whose child – her daughter, Irène Curie – won a separate Nobel Prize.[52] By now, it might seem like Nobel Prizes fly around like hotcakes in their family, but it's important to remember that having a child win a Nobel Prize is already a legendary parenting achievement in itself. Just consider the number of books about parents who guided their children into prestigious universities like Harvard. While getting into a prestigious university is no doubt impressive, it pales in comparison to winning a Nobel Prize.

Besides her Nobel Prize achievements in physics and chemistry, Marie Curie pioneered and coined the field of radioactivity, discovered two elements on the periodic table (polonium and radium), and founded the Radium Institute in Paris (now the Curie Institute). She was also a member of the League of Nations' Committee on Intellectual Cooperation alongside Albert Einstein, and when she toured the US, President Harding personally presented her with a gift of radium for her research. In honor of her work, a unit of

---

[51]The other person being Linus Pauling, who was awarded the Nobel Prize in Chemistry in 1954 and the Nobel Peace Prize in 1962.

[52]William Bragg and his son Lawrence Bragg also won Nobel Prizes after Marie Curie but before Irène Curie. However, the father-son pair won the same Nobel Prize together in 1915, which is why I emphasize Irène Curie's separate Nobel Prize from her mother's.

radioactivity was initially named a "Curie."

In addition to being a scientific (and parenting) legend, Marie Curie was also a war hero. She engineered vehicles with gas-powered X-ray machines and personally drove these "Little Curies" into World War I battle zones, saving countless lives by performing X-ray examinations on wounded soldiers in field hospitals. Not only did she learn how to drive and fix cars, but she also fundraised for the campaign, eventually training over 150 women volunteers to operate twenty Little Curies and treat over one million soldiers during the war.

Marie Curie is truly a legendary Scientific Trailblazer on our precious Earth Server.

How Did She Do It?

So how did this drama-filled woman proactively tackle important quests in her life to accomplish such legendary "World's First" feats and achievements?

As young as four years old, Marie Skłodowska-Curie embarked on her first minor exploration quest, aligning with her future life game. She observed and imagined the possibilities of the items in her father's glass cabinets, examining scientific tools like glass tubes, small scales, and mineral specimens. Her father, a math and physics professor, lost his job during the Polish uprising against Russian authorities in 1863, four years before her birth. Despite their poverty, he was well-educated, had a scientific mind, and believed in women's rights to higher education.

While most level 1 players on the Earth Server didn't know their game, due to Russian oppression and her father's teachings, Marie committed early to her first game: obtaining higher education at all costs. With this clarity, she embarked on her first major main learning quest: enrolling at the Flying University in Warsaw. Conventional advanced degrees were unattainable, so Marie and her sister, Bronya, attended this illegal underground institution that admitted women.

The university was called "Flying" because classes had no fixed locations but were held in various private homes to avoid Russian detection. It accepted both men and women, and classes were taught in Polish. This major main learning quest included "stealth conditions," with high consequences if failed!

Because of her impoverished background and compassionate, patriotic personality, Marie took on the minor resource side quest of tutoring younger students at the Flying University while studying there. However, as an underground guild, the university had limited resources, lacking professional faculty, infrastructure, and lab equipment. Marie realized her gameplay was too limited in this questing landscape.

During this time, Marie and Bronya learned of Sorbonne University in Paris, celebrated for its inclusive policy of offering higher education degrees to women. This dream-like place was destined to be where Marie could beat her game.

Armed with this knowledge, Marie and Bronya charted a bold zone shift quest: relocating to Paris and enrolling at the esteemed institution. Like any zone shift quest, there were difficult prerequisites, such as obtaining the right legal status and enough money to make the move. Since they didn't have the funds, they devised a strategy to pursue a major resource main quest: to earn enough money for one of them to first go to Paris and enroll at Sorbonne University. Once that sister established herself professionally and earned a steady income, she would then sponsor the other's journey and education to fulfill the same quest.

As imagined, this type of group quest requires a great deal of trust and is usually only feasible between family members or perhaps childhood friends. Since it would take years to fulfill, if the partnership were based solely on mutual self-interest, the one who first goes to Paris might later back out from the commitment and not financially sponsor the other due to "changing circumstances" such as having a child or lacking money themselves. But when you have trust like the Skłodowska sisters did, this becomes an extremely powerful quest that can elevate both individuals to new realms. Take a moment to think about how many people in your life you could trust to undertake a quest like this. Unfortunately, if you don't have any potential partners like that, it is extraordinarily difficult to meet new ones who have those criteria.

In the case of the Skłodowska sisters, because Marie was the younger, Bronya was chosen to first realize her ambition by moving to Paris to become a physician. The plan was that upon graduation, she would send money back to Poland, paving the way for Marie to journey to Paris and pursue her life game.

To make more money than she received from tutoring students, Marie Curie took on a higher-level major main resource quest: becoming a governess for the Zorawski family, a wealthy household in northeastern Poland. Because Warsaw was very far away, Marie lived with the family.

During this time, Marie's living expenses were covered, allowing her to send most of her income to Bronya in Paris while saving the remaining amount for her own trip to meet her there.

As mentioned earlier, this was when Marie Curie fell in love with Kazimierz, the oldest son of the Zorawski family. However, this major relationship side quest was rejected by both the Zorawski family and Kazimierz himself. This is termed a major relationship side quest because it was a long-term relationship taking many years (major, not minor) and served as a distraction from her primary goals (side quest, not main quest). If Kazimierz had agreed to marry Marie, she likely would have given up on her higher education goals.

This hypothesis is not unfounded. When Bronya completed her medical studies and invited Marie to join her in Paris to pursue her dreams, Marie initially declined. She confided in a letter: "I dreamed of Paris as a redemption, but the hope of going there left me a long time ago and now that the possibility is offered to me, I don't know what to do." She was still waiting for Kazimierz's family to accept her.

During her lonely and shameful hours working in the Zorawski villa, Marie decided to take on additional minor learning main quests to explore her academic interests. She read sociological studies, literature, physics, and chemistry textbooks and studied advanced math through correspondence with her father by traditional mail.

As a result of this failed major relationship side quest, Marie Curie discovered she had strength attributes (Step 2) in mathematics and the physical sciences. She wrote, "During these years of isolated work, trying little by little to find my real preferences, I finally turned towards mathematics and physics, and resolutely undertook a serious preparation for future work."

Understanding that her role (Step 3) should be a *science researcher*, she needed to acquire relevant skills (Step 4), so she took on the additional minor learning main quest by taking chemistry lessons from a chemist at the local beet-sugar factory.

Even with her hands full with work and study, Marie still found time for minor service side quests, such as teaching the illiterate children of the Zorawski family's peasant laborers. They were fond of her, and she began to feel that her game might also involve helping others. Since teaching illiterate children did not directly support her goal of becoming a woman of higher education, it was classified as a side quest. However, if her game were centered around helping others, this activity would become a main quest. This realization helped her figure out the next game she wanted to play after achieving her initial goal.

It's important to note that not all relationship quests are considered side quests for career-oriented players. Later, you will see how Marie's relationship and marriage with Pierre Curie were instrumental in her career and game achievements, classifying them as major relationship main quests.

Finally, after years of struggling emotionally at her relationship side quest, Marie shook off the weight of her despair and decided to join her sister in Paris to continue her main quests. Of course, in all side quests we still learn valuable lessons and skills. Marie Curie left with an impactful one: "First principle: never let one-self be beaten down by persons or by events."

With her major resource main quest completed, she was now ready to officially start her zone shift quest and move to Paris.

Marie was twenty-three when she began attending Sorbonne University in Paris. However, she quickly realized that her less formal educational background left her struggling to keep up with her classmates, who had accumulated more experience and skills from their previous major learning quests. Determined to succeed, Marie took on a major learning main quest to immerse herself completely in math and science, understanding that she needed to invest more game time than others to catch up.

Initially, Marie stayed at her sister's apartment with her brother-in-law. However, she found the lively atmosphere distracting from her hardcore main learning quests. Frequent visits and conversations with her family became a relationship side quest she could not afford.

To focus better on her main quests, Marie committed to a minor zone shift quest. She used her limited funds to rent an unheated garret room on the sixth floor of a building closer to the university. Although the room was cold, small, and claustrophobic, it provided the ideal questing environment for her to deeply concentrate on her studies.

This zone shift quest significantly boosted her questing journey. She wrote to her father, stating she was getting a thousand times more work done than when she lived with her sister. Of course, this move added new challenges, as she now had to pay rent, which strained her financial resources. Marie often became malnourished and exhausted, so much so that she fainted in the library one day. When she woke up at her sister's home, she quickly returned to her tiny garret room to resume her learning quest.

Within a year, her dedication to her questing paid off in a literal way when she earned the Alexandrovitch scholarship. Managed frugally, this quest reward provided enough finances to complete her degree.

Later, her questing abilities attracted the attention of Gabriel Lippmann, her professor at Sorbonne, who became one of her major mentor allies (Step 5). This new ally arranged for the Society of the Encouragement of National Industry to pay Marie an even greater sum to study and chart the magnetic properties of various steels.

This endeavor started as a minor resource main quest because she needed money for her studies (her actual game), but it eventually transitioned into a major career main quest as she shifted her focus. The lab work she performed for the Society of the Encouragement of National Industry later evolved into Marie's ultimate legendary quest that led to her two Nobel Prizes in physics and chemistry. However, before achieving this, there were many minor quests and smaller achievements she needed to tackle.

At the age of twenty-five, due to her diligence and hard work, she completed her major learning main quest, finishing as the top student in her physics degree within two years of enrolling. At this point, she had beaten her life game "to obtain a higher education by any means necessary!"

Like many people who have beaten a game worth playing, Marie Curie immediately sought a new challenge and enrolled in another program in mathematics. This time, as a much higher-level player, she finished the program and earned her second degree in math, graduating as the second-place student just a year later. This mirrors common gaming experiences where initially insurmountable goals, like beating a tough dungeon, become manageable and even easy with dedication and leveling up. While the challenges in our life game remain constant, our enhanced skills and experiences prepare us for more difficult quests.

Finding a New Game to Play

Having completed her degree game twice, Marie Curie needed a new game to play. She found it in her laboratory work on magnetic properties and steel. Her growing curiosity about her research led her to take on a game similar to those played by young Elon Musk and Leonardo da Vinci: to uncover the truths of the universe.

With her new game (Step 1) and full-time role as a scientific researcher (Step 3), Marie recognized the need to upgrade her lab environment to perform the highest quality work possible. Much like her initial move away from her sister's house, she understood the importance of designing an environment conducive to immersion and equipped for success.

Marie Curie's quest to find a new lab led her to her most important ally (Step 5): Pierre Curie, a French physicist and expert on magnetism. Marie and Pierre connected deeply, ironically because neither was initially interested in romance. Marie, still scarred by her heartbreak in Poland, had vowed never to let passion distract her from her life game. Pierre, too, believed women distracted him from his research but was intrigued by Marie, whom he considered "a woman of genius."

In their shared laboratory, each focused on their own research endeavors. Marie quickly recognized Pierre's scientific prowess, and they discovered a mutual passion for scientific exploration. Their discussions covered their personal research interests as well as broader scientific concepts and philosophies. As their professional relationship blossomed, so did a deep personal bond. What began as a minor resource main quest for a larger laboratory space turned into a major relationship main quest that would change her life and human history forever.

Despite their closeness, when Pierre first proposed marriage, Marie hesitated, torn between her devotion to her homeland and her love for Pierre. She was apprehensive about leaving her country and family behind. Pierre, demonstrating his deep affection, was ready to give up his established career in France and start afresh in Poland, just to be with her. Touched by this gesture and realizing their unparalleled companionship, Marie remarked, "Our work drew us closer and closer, until we were both convinced that neither of us could find a better life companion." They married in 1895, marking the beginning of an iconic scientific partnership (Step 5).

By 1897, their family expanded with the birth of their daughter, Irène. Seven years later, their second daughter, Ève, was born. Despite the demands of parenthood, their dedication to science remained unwavering. They poured their energy into various relationship, resource, and career quests.

While Marie Curie was still short on funds for her new family, after completing the well-compensated study of metals in 1897 (the same year her daughter Irène was born), she used a portion of her earnings to repay the Alexandrovitch scholarship she had received four years prior. She took on this minor service side quest to ensure that another Polish student could benefit from the same financial support that had paid for her own education.

During this period, Marie began tackling research quests related to the then-overlooked uranium rays discovered by Henri Becquerel. This major research main quest, alongside partners like her husband Pierre and Henri Becquerel, eventually led to the groundbreaking discovery of radium and polonium. This discovery earned her the first Scientific Trailblazer achievement in the form of a Nobel Prize in Physics, a prize she shared with her two partners.

However, a plot twist event occurred when she lost her beloved husband to a tragic accident. Devastated, she found strength in Pierre's previous words. Reflecting on her grief, she said, "Crushed by the blow, I did not feel able to face the future. I could not forget, however, what my husband used to say: that even deprived of him, I ought to continue my work."

After Pierre's death, Marie Curie entered the Brave Widow Saga in her life game, focusing on continuing the mission they shared and carrying on Pierre's legacy. She took on Pierre's former position as a professor of physics at Sorbonne University, becoming the first woman in France to hold such a position (as a Polish woman too!). She continued her major research quests, which eventually led to her second Nobel Prize in Chemistry after determining radium's atomic weight.

Achieving More Career Quests

Following another major career quest of publishing the textbook *A Treatise on Radioactivity*, the international scientific community named the unit of radioactivity a "Curie." Marie was not interested in personal accolades but wanted to ensure that her husband's legacy lived on.

During this saga, Marie Curie evolved her game into its final form, helping humanity through science, focusing on using her research to improve the lives of others.

She tackled a major career main quest by founding her own guild: the Radium Institute (later the Curie Institute). With her new life game, she saw the Radium Institute as both a contribution to human society and a tribute to Pierre's memory. In this quest, Marie had to orchestrate support from patrons, scholars, and politicians, enlisting the help of the government-funded University of Paris to work alongside the private Pasteur Foundation to create a research institute for radium. She even renamed the street of the building *Rue Pierre-Curie* (Rue is French for "street").

At this point, Marie had already become a legendary OP Hero, achieving feats unmatched on the Earth Server. Unfortunately, toward the end of the brave widow saga, Marie fell in love with another married physicist, creating much drama that led her to flee France for a while. However, after a resilient recovery and returning to France, she was ready to embrace a new life without further drama.

It was just at this time that another world event occurred. In fact, it was one of the biggest world events of them all on the Earth Server: World War I.

In Marie Curie's World War I saga, she embarked on many service quests to aid wounded soldiers during the war, leading to the famous *Little Curies Arc* – a chain of major quests, each composed of multiple minor quests.

The arc began with the major resource quest line of fundraising for a special vehicle to carry X-ray machines to the battlefield. This quest line included the following major and minor resource quests:

- Securing funds and vehicles from affluent families.
- Persuading automobile workshops to convert cars into specialized vans.
- Rallying manufacturers to support the nation by donating essential equipment.
- Equipping these vans with state-of-the-art X-ray machines, including installing petroleum-powered generators.

After completing the major resource quest line, Marie moved on to a new major quest line to learn the skills needed to operate the vehicles. This involved minor learning quests, such as:

- Mastering the operation of X-ray machines.
- Learning how to drive a car.
- Deepening her understanding of anatomy to treat wounded soldiers better.

- Understanding automobile mechanics to fix cars in war zones.

Finally, after completing these quest lines, she tackled further major service quests, including:

- Driving the vehicles, now known as Little Curies, into war zones to help soldiers.
- Training over 150 volunteer women to embark on the same mission.
- Raising funds to construct 20 Little Curies.
- Treating over one million soldiers during the World War I saga.

After the World War I saga, Marie Curie continued with two more sagas in her life: the legend-building saga and the succession saga. During these sagas, she took on many courageous and inspiring quests, such as:

- Visiting America twice and meeting Presidents Harding and Hoover, facilitated by her new journalist ally, William Brown Meloney.
- Founding the Curie Institute to provide the Radium Institute with resources.
- Establishing the Warsaw Radium Institute (now the Maria Skłodowska-Curie National Research Institute of Oncology).
- Raising the next generation of scientists, including her daughter Irène Curie and her husband Jean-Frédéric Joliot.

Sixty years after her death, Marie Curie achieved her final Scientific Trailblazer achievement badge. She became the first woman whose remains were placed in France's national mausoleum, the Panthéon in Paris, alongside the country's most eminent men.

OP Hero Marie Curie: Takeaways

Beyond admiring Marie Curie's trailblazing accomplishments, the main focus of this book is to highlight how she *proactively* undertook a variety of major and minor quests to advance toward her life game. In fact, very few of her quests were given to her by others or brought to her by her environment. She pursued them independently because she understood her game (Step 1), her attributes (Step 2), her role (Step 3), the skills she needed to learn (Step 4), and the allies she needed to partner with (Step 5).

Naturally, there were moments when she stumbled upon side quests that distracted her, but she quickly adjusted and returned to her main quests. Curie also skillfully handled the intricate dance between major and minor quests, too. She didn't just aim for grand goals but meticulously mapped out and accomplished numerous main quests that collectively propelled her toward her ultimate game objectives.

Reflecting on Curie's monumental legacy, it becomes clear that her extraordinary life was a product not just of her genius but also of her understanding of her questing landscape and the interplay between various types of quests.

Chapter 8 Highlights

- Quests are actions aligned with your game objective, they range from reading a book to starting a family or climbing career ladders, integrating all previous steps.
- Attributes and roles guide which skills to acquire and allies to connect with, defining the actions needed to win.
- Quests unlock resources, growth, and new opportunities.
- Major quests are long-term commitments like working at a new job or relocating to a new country, whereas minor

quests are shorter, endeavors that could be completed in a few months, weeks, or even days.

- A quest hierarchy includes sagas (life eras), arcs (objective-based periods), major quests (significant goals), and minor quests (short-term objectives).
- Quests vary by type: career, learning, resource, health, spiritual, relationship, alliance, discovery, service, and adventure quests.
- Main quests directly advance game objectives, whereas side quests may not but can be meaningful distractions.
- Pivotal quests significantly alter your trajectory toward beating the game.
- Use role models and mentors to guide quest choices, model after successful individuals, progress your Skill Triangle, or join allies' quests.
- Marie Curie was not allowed to play her game and study in Russia-occupied Poland. As a result, she had to proactively pursue many Quests to relocate, learn, and discover, ultimately becoming the highest achieving academic Player on the Earth Server.

Chapter 9: Achieving 10K HP Alignment

At this point, I have explored a variety of OP Heroes who, through their 10K HP alignment, achieved extraordinary results that have secured their place in human history.

It is important to note that none of these luminaries began their journeys from a place of great advantage. Instead, most of their paths were marked by hardships that likely surpass those of my readers. However, a common thread unites them: an unwavering determination to keep playing the game, despite overwhelming setbacks.

While it's easy to attribute the success of accomplished OP Players to mere luck or fate, these individuals took extraordinary actions that others don't commonly take, resulting in achievements most others never accomplish. No matter your age or circumstances, if you haven't taken steps similar to those our OP Heroes took before becoming legendary, it means there is likely more you could be doing to improve your conditions and success within your game.

If you're feeling lost as a student, consider building relationships with your professors like Sun Yat-sen did, cold-calling successful professionals you see on the news like Elon Musk did, or moving to different countries to find better environments for personal growth like Marie Curie did.

For young professionals in their 20s feeling stuck, hopeless, and poor, look to develop new essential skills for the future and potentially start selling new services like Disney and Musk did. You could also consider relocating to a new quest zone to restart your career, like Gandhi moving to South Africa after failing as a lawyer in London.

If you're in your 30s and have suffered great losses, try to put enthusiastic effort into your compromised position, like Oprah did after being demoted to hosting a morning talk show. Alternatively, bounce back from repeated setbacks, as Sun Yat-sen did after ten failed revolutions. Push harder to overcome personal grief and public humiliation, like Marie Curie did following her husband Pierre's death, when the mainstream media and angry mobs accused her of being a murderous whore.

For those middle-aged or older who feel stable but not thriving or passionately engaged, consider changing your questing zone entirely. Think about Gandhi moving back to India later in his life, Elon Musk betting all his money and moving to Los Angeles, or Leonardo da Vinci relocating to France after Milan fell. If anything, start meeting new allies who can take your life on exciting new journeys, or mentor younger 10K HP Players so their growth within their own quests brings you excitement and fulfillment.

Remember, none of the OP Heroes knew they would become historical legends while they were in the trenches of their struggles. Many were ordinary individuals navigating society's challenges or experiencing moderate career successes well into middle age. It was their persistent effort and attainment of 10K HP alignment, coupled with fortunate circumstances, that catapulted them to legendary status.

If at this point you still doubt that any person, no matter their circumstances, can necessarily achieve remarkable success, the next section will explore the life of an individual who likely faced more obstacles and setbacks than any reader of this book. Yet, this person achieved extraordinary accomplishments, setting an inspirational benchmark for anyone aspiring to reach extraordinary heights.

10K HP OP Hero Story: Suzy Batiz

Now that you have explored all six steps of 10K HP, it's time to see how the steps collectively apply to you playing your game in today's society. While we've examined various OP Heroes – figures so legendary that most people today are familiar with them – their stories might be difficult to relate to. Additionally, I have focused on only one of the six steps for each OP Hero, without exploring how all six steps synergize to unlock the OP Mode in which they operate.

This chapter will show how these six steps can holistically apply to someone whose story might hit closer to home, yet is an extraordinary journey we can all aspire to and learn from. This amazing OP Hero, with whom I happen to have the privilege of working closely with, is Suzy Batiz: the *Scential Alchemist.*

Suzy's life game began amid poverty, family molestation, two bankruptcies, multiple divorces, depression, and a suicide attempt. Yet, she triumphed over these challenges and built a $500 million company, earning a spot on Forbes' Top 100 Self-Made Women of 2020. She is the creative force behind Poo~Pourri, an innovative, eco-friendly before-you-go toilet spray known for its natural essential oil-based odor neutralization. Rebranded as ~Pourri, the brand gained international recognition with its viral video "Girls Don't Poop," which amassed over 44 million views, secured a Webby Award, and was named AdAge's "Funniest Viral Video of the Year" in 2014.

After her success with Poo~Pourri, Suzy Batiz founded another successful venture, Supernatural. This brand offers a line of natural cleaning products made from essential oils, known as "conscious concentrates," which are beneficial for the environment, your home, and your well-being. Additionally, she is a dedicated teacher and mentor with AliveOS, where she guides budding individuals to harness their inner power and achieve the lives they truly desire.

Suzy Batiz's journey has been one of the most heartbreaking I've ever seen, which makes her ultimate triumph even more glorious. Her path was marred by harrowing struggles that deeply challenged her spirit and resilience. Despite enduring the devasting trauma of her early life, she demonstrated an inspiring amount of perseverance through seemingly insurmountable challenges.

This chapter will examine her journey and achievements through the lens of the six steps journey within 10K HP. To effectively illustrate her path, I have structured her story around her game (Step 1) and her quests (Step 6), breaking down her life's journey into sagas, arcs, major quests, and minor quests. As her narrative unfolds, it will interlace the other steps, revealing her attributes (Step 2) as they emerge, her role (Step 3) as it evolves through various sagas, the skills (Step 4) she acquired and utilized to advance to the next level, and the allies (Step 5) she formed relationships with along her journey. Note that many names in Suzy Batiz's story are aliases to protect the identities of those involved.

I. Growing Up Saga: Stepfather Arc

Everyone's Hero Journey starts with their origin story. As you will see, in the early years of Suzy's life, her phases were heavily influenced by the relationships she was in. Despite her proactive efforts to improve her living conditions, she was often an NPC when it came to relationships, meaning whoever she was with largely defined that period of her life. Consequently, most of her early sagas are named after the men she was involved with.

Due to her high dependency on her circumstances and the men in her life, the first game (Step 1) she pursued – like many people – was to "Escape Life's Tribulations and Become Financially Secure." It took her five challenging sagas to finally beat this game and find a new mission in life. It all started in 1965 when Suzy was born into a poor household in Arkansas, marked by a chaotic childhood and a bipolar, alcoholic father.

Her father's erratic behavior and addiction issues made her early life full of instability and unpredictability. Instead of a haven of safety and comfort, her home was a place of uncertainty. Suzy recalls constant fights between her parents, often triggered by her father's sudden outbursts of rage.

Her mother struggled with depression and became reliant on pain pills, further destabilizing their home environment. Her mother's mental health and addiction issues left her emotionally and physically unavailable.

Eventually, Suzy's life took a significant turn when her parents divorced, a major event in her life. As a child, Suzy saw this as a chance for the turmoil to end. With her mother still psychologically affected by her father's issues, Suzy took on the responsibility of caring for her. Despite her young age, she demonstrated a unique attribute: selfless nurturing.

During this time, another major event occurred: her mother met a new partner who would become Suzy's stepfather. This prospect of her mother's newfound happiness filled Suzy with joy, feeling she had finally reached a *win-state* amid her family's trials and tribulations.

Unfortunately, a devastating plot twist occurred when she was twelve. During what should have been a joyful period, her new stepfather began molesting her. Despite her fear and confusion, Suzy chose to keep this a secret from her mother. Surprisingly, this wasn't because she feared her stepfather. Instead, Suzy saw her mother finally happy with her new husband, and she didn't want to ruin it for her. As a result, Suzy embarked on the challenging quest of staying silent about her molestation, bearing the burden of her trauma alone.[53] This continued for four long years.

Regardless of whether her decision to take on such a heart-wrenching quest was correct or not, it was a testament to her

---

[53]Many years later, that same stepfather also walked her down the aisle when she got married, which she described as "gross."

empathy and resilience attributes. This choice profoundly shaped her life, influencing her future relationships and her journey toward healing and self-discovery.

I. Growing Up Saga: First Hustles Arc

As Suzy entered young adulthood, she began her first official resource main quest by landing her first Burger King job at fifteen. Excitement coursed through her veins, as this job symbolized her newfound freedom. Her mother and stepfather had always tightly controlled her finances, providing little money and making her beg for even the smallest amounts.

During this resource quest, Suzy showcased her exceptional *energized communications* and *diligent work ethic* attributes. These skills allowed her to transform the Burger King resource quest (just doing it for the money) into her next career main quest. By the time she was eighteen, she was managing a prominent clothing store, becoming one of the youngest managers in Tampa, Florida.

Driven by her mission to reduce her reliance on her mother and stepfather, Suzy applied her self-reinvention attribute to embrace the role of a *hustler*. She used her optimistic creativity and empathetic inspiration to craft paintings and sell clothes, generating additional income.

One notable career main quest was designing denim pumps for women. Fortunately, her college boyfriend, Christopher, had a mother who worked at a shoe factory, and that factory brought her designs to life. Suzy's shoes ended up being so impressive that clothing retailer Guess invited her to New York to discuss a potential partnership. Unfortunately, she did not continue this quest because of an *NPC limiter* in her environment: her mother told her to forget about it, saying she was just a girl from Arkansas and would never succeed in the big city.

Without the real-life game skill of *aegis* (Paladin skill), the ability to ignore criticisms and naysayers while pushing toward a quest, Suzy was defeated by the NPC limiter and unable to continue. When you recognize the NPC limiters in your life and understand that you can acquire skills like *aegis* or *heroic strike* (a bold and confident gesture that is socially surprising and audacious) to overcome them, you can instantly become a higher-level player with access to more zones and quests.

However, Suzy did develop other real-life game skills, such as *charge* and *execute* (Warrior skills). These skills enabled her to approach strangers (charge) and close deals with them (execute). Later in life, by completing the appropriate quests, she unlocked *divine shield* (Paladin skill), the ability to say "no" regardless of persuasion.

Beyond these special real-life game skills, Suzy continued to develop her attributes and acquired various *traditional world skills* (Step 4) such as caregiving, sales, management, entrepreneurship, painting, and fashion design.

It is important to note that her skills were more effective when they harnessed her unique attributes, which evolved over time to better suit her quests. For instance, she transformed her empathy attribute, developed while caring for her mother, into *empathetic inspiration*. This advanced attribute allowed her to generate creative ideas and conceptualize things that resonated emotionally with people.

Suzy's attributes and skills continued to evolve throughout the next few sagas, as she faced quests that were beyond her initial level.

II. Christopher Saga: First Marriage Arc

After Suzy declined the New York visit with Guess, an unexpected plot twist event occurred. During a family reunion, Christopher surprised everyone by proposing to her in front of everyone. The atmosphere was filled with joy, and Suzy became the center of attention, with eager smiles and expectant faces all around her, awaiting her response.

Despite appearing joyfully surprised to comply with social expectations, Suzy was panicking inside. In truth, she didn't want to marry Christopher, but the social pressure and overwhelming enthusiasm from her family made her feel that she had no choice but to say yes. In that moment, Suzy found herself in a situation where she lacked the necessary skills (Step 4) to deal with the unexpected pressure. In the context of the 10K HP real-life game skills, Christopher had executed a heroic strike.

Christopher's heroic strike in front of Suzy's entire family was difficult for anyone to counter. Like many others, Suzy had not yet acquired divine shield (Paladin skill), which would have allowed her to calmly and confidently say *no* in such a pressurized situation. Consequently, she was defeated by a more skilled opponent.

This turn of events drastically altered Suzy's questing landscape, leaving her trapped in a marriage she didn't want in the first place. To amplify the crushing desolation, her stepfather, who had molested her in her youth, walked her down the aisle to a man she didn't want to marry. For Suzy, the game was not going so well.

II. Christopher Saga: Bridal Shop/Salon Arc

Around the same time Suzy married Christopher, she embarked on a major entrepreneurial quest: she bought a bridal salon with her soon-to-be husband and started running the business at the age of nineteen. Unfortunately, things didn't go according to plan, and after managing it for a year and a half, she failed the quest and filed for bankruptcy.

This failure compounded her frustration with marrying Christopher out of social pressure. Even though she lacked the divine shield skill earlier, this time she decided to execute a heroic strike of her own. She took a deep breath and tackled a challenging and stressful relationship quest: divorcing Christopher at the age of 21.

The quest was particularly difficult because her family loved Christopher and still wanted them to be together. This is why the heroic strike skill was so crucial. Despite the difficulty, she succeeded with a bold and audacious move, allowing her to carry on with her life. That was when she moved into the third saga of her 10K HP journey: the Barbossa Saga.

III. Barbossa Saga: New Relationship Arc

By this time, Suzy was still playing the same game (Step 1) of "escaping life's tribulations and becoming financially secure." She was developing important attributes (Step 2) such as empathetic inspiration and emotional perseverance, while also upgrading her traditional world skills like sales, entrepreneurship, and management.

In this saga, Suzy set out to find a new ally (Step 5), but instead, she ended up bringing a top villain into her home.

Following her divorce from Christopher, Suzy married a man named Barbossa. This major relationship quest led to a marriage filled with both love and abuse.

From the start, she faced a tough zone event where her parents and family strongly disapproved of Barbossa, making her feel that her divorce from Christopher was a huge mistake. Despite their disapproval, Suzy's love for Barbossa, the archetypal bad boy with immense confidence, compelled her to pursue this major relationship quest and marry him.

The first signs of Barbossa being a villain in her 10K HP journey became evident when they settled down in Kentucky and his abusive tendencies surfaced. During her first pregnancy, he severely kicked her, leaving her with a broken tailbone. To make matters worse, he was regularly unfaithful, seeing many other women throughout their marriage.

III. Barbossa Saga: Life and Death Arc

Caught between her abusive husband, whom she loved, and her family, who were eager to say, "I told you so," Suzy became depressed. The emotional exhaustion drove her to a breaking point, resulting in her first suicide attempt. Fortunately, she overcame this survival pivotal quest and successfully prevented her own "rage quit."

Then, a ray of sunshine broke into Suzy's life with the birth of her first son, Dustin. However, her moments of happiness were over-shadowed by Barbossa's recurring violence. The pattern of abuse followed a troubling cycle. After each violent episode, Barbossa would apologize profusely, making Suzy question whether she was somehow at fault for provoking his anger. In reality, Barbossa was using the real-life game skill *feign death* (Rogue skill), pretending to be weak or pathetic to avoid punishment for his wrongdoings. Suzy, unequipped to handle such cheap-shot tactics from someone she loved, knew she had to find strength from somewhere to defeat this villain or escape the environment.

III. Barbossa Saga: First Resistance Arc

During one abusive exchange, Suzy finally undertook the minor quest of calling the police. As the officers were on their way, she felt empowered by her actions and had a glimpse of hope that things would improve. But then, another plot twist event occurred. When the police arrived, they treated Barbossa as a friendly buddy, completely dismissing Suzy and her cry for help. This dismissal left Suzy feeling even more isolated and confused, leading her to believe that she was the problem.

Barbossa's manipulation intensified as he used another real-life game skill *mind shift* (Warlock skill) to convince Suzy that she was losing her sanity. Desperate to save her marriage, she found herself pregnant with their second child. Confusion, ongoing abuse, and self-doubt led Suzy to seek help from a psychiatrist. In therapy, she repeatedly claimed to be crazy, attributing the turmoil in her marriage to her own actions.

However, the psychiatrist, digging deeper, uncovered the truth: Barbossa was an abusive husband who relentlessly subjected her to physical abuse for the smallest transgressions. The session lasted far longer than anticipated as the psychiatrist became a critical ally (Step 5), realizing that Suzy was a victim in need of escaping her abusive marriage.

III. Barbossa Saga: Escaping Barbossa Arc

The interactions with her new psychiatrist ally helped Suzy embark on the journey toward the real-life game skill *self-mastery* (Rogue skill), which allowed her to gain a higher sense of self-awareness. She now saw the reality of the situation: she was not crazy, but rather, she was being abused and needed to escape Barbossa. Despite her love for him, Barbossa's infidelity and escalating violence convinced Suzy that she had to tackle the new relationship main quest of leaving him. This proved to be a high-difficulty major quest that took over a year to complete.

Thinking about leaving an abusive husband is one thing, but actually executing on such a high-difficulty quest is another. For this, she first needed to complete a minor quest of seeking legal advice. Shockingly, one attorney she approached warned her that Barbossa's involvement in an influential criminal guild, involving shady syndicates and corrupted cops, could cost her custody of her children if she pursued a divorce.

Suzy recalled the rumors surrounding Barbossa's alleged criminal activities. At the time, she had regarded them as nothing more than a joke, even engaging in playful banter by mockingly claiming, "Yeah, we're drug dealers." Now, the gravity of those rumors struck her with unsettling reality. To secure her children's safety, the attorney suggested a game plan: move to another state and file for divorce there. This would legally protect her from Barbossa's corrupted influences and enable her to keep her kids.

But escaping Barbossa was fraught with danger, as he frequently threatened to kill her and dispose of her body. The fear felt real and palpable, but Suzy was determined to break free in order to have a shot at her game of obtaining freedom from her harsh reality and becoming independent.

III. Barbossa Saga: Barbossa Jailed Arc

However, a zone event occurred in Suzy's favor when Barbossa was arrested in Memphis, found with $10,000 cash, a pound of cocaine, and a gun. This shocking revelation confirmed her suspicions about his criminal activities. Despite the opportunity to leave him behind, Suzy couldn't bear to abandon the man she loved. She flew to Memphis, hired top-notch attorneys, and secured his release from jail.

Suzy succeeded in getting Barbossa out of jail, but his trial still loomed. Amidst this turmoil, she found herself back in Kentucky, torn between her desire to break free and her love for Barbossa. Nevertheless, Suzy held strong and exercised another real-life game skill, *ninja focus* (Rogue skill), staying disciplined in executing her relationship quest of escaping. She convinced Barbossa to move to Memphis, where the trial would take place. Barbossa thought it was a great idea, fulfilling the first step of her plan to move away from the corrupt officials who could help him.

As they settled in Memphis, Suzy was ready to execute the next part of her plan. She promptly secured an attorney who advised her to wait six months before filing for divorce. The plan was to endure another six months with Barbossa, believing that his lack of ownership of corrupt officials or influence in the new town would provide her with the opportunity to divorce him while retaining custody of her children.

III. Barbossa Saga: Memphis Hustling Arc

During the six-month waiting period, Suzy pursued several minor resource quests to earn some income. One of these quests led her to a job at a Merry-Go-Round store, where she met another important ally (Step 5), Andrew, with whom she developed a flirtatious connection. Alongside her job, Suzy also had a side hustle selling overstock goods from her car trunk. Despite making some money, she handed it all over to Barbossa, who controlled their finances.

The abusive pattern persisted during those six months, with Barbossa repeatedly subjecting Suzy to violence and isolation. On several occasions, he beat her, took all the phones in the house, and drove away in their only car, leaving her and their kids stranded at home. One dark night, Barbossa discovered Suzy was seeing an attorney and planning to file for divorce. While Suzy was still in the shower, Barbossa ripped the curtains open and unleashed a torrent of abuse.

Afterward, Barbossa again employed his feign death (Rogue skill), apologizing profusely and asking for forgiveness, saying, "Do you love me?" In that pivotal moment, Suzy found the strength to activate her divine shield (Paladin skill) for the first time. She courageously responded, "How can I love someone like you?" This display of strength and confidence unsettled Barbossa, who remained silent and walked away.

This minor relationship quest of standing up to the arch-villain Barbossa became a crucial step for Suzy as she entered the next arc of her journey.

III. Barbossa Saga: Breaking Free Arc

The following day, while Suzy was working at the Merry-Go-Round store, Barbossa called and informed her that he would drop off their kids in front of the store. However, when Suzy retrieved her children, she was met with another shocking and life-changing plot twist event. Barbossa had not only departed for good, but he had also taken the only vehicle they owned, emptied their bank account, and had neglected to pay rent for several months. As a result, she was evicted from their home.

Suzy's questing landscape suffered a detrimental hit. She was now a homeless single mother with two kids. The only silver lining was that she still had her job. She had taken the first steps toward breaking free from a life filled with abuse and torment. In the face of adversity, she embarked on a journey of survival, determined to build a new life for herself and her children. In order to survive, she couch-surfed for a while until she saved enough to rent a place to stay. With Barbossa gone from her life, she now bravely stepped into her next saga.

IV. Andrew Saga: Andrew Rescues Arc

During a particularly challenging Christmas season, Suzy found herself in a difficult situation. With no money for presents and her life in a state of chaos, she was given a lifeline when her mother offered her $200 to buy gifts for her two boys. Grateful for the support, Suzy took her children to the mall, all the while wrestling with the overwhelming turmoil in her life. She was juggling the responsibilities of being a single mother with no stable place to call home, and the weight of these challenges pressing down heavily on her mind.

Amid her contemplations, another plot twist event struck. Her purse was stolen in the bustling mall, becoming a devastating blow as the $200 was the only hope of happiness she could provide to her children. Despite being emotionally strong, the plot twist event acted like the final straw on the camel's back. Suzy broke down and cried.

Fortunately, amid hopelessness, an ally came to the rescue. Her workplace friend Andrew, recognizing her struggles, rallied his colleagues at work, and together they collected money to buy Christmas presents for Suzy's children. This unexpected support provided a glimmer of hope during a trying time. Suzy saw Andrew as an angel who saved her from her miserable circumstances.

However, Suzy's challenges were not limited to financial difficulties. She confided in Andrew about her lack of a stable home and need for long-term assistance. In response, Andrew offered a solution, suggesting she move in with him. Suzy found him cute, and even though she liked him, she was struggling with her emotional life and was initially hesitant to accept such an offer. Ultimately, Suzy found herself without other viable alternatives, and she decided to take Andrew up on his offer.

This significant moment marked the start of a new chapter in Suzy Batiz's life. Thanks to her new ally (Step 5), she managed to secure Christmas presents for her children and a place to live. This milestone addressed her basic needs, leading to a pivotal shift in her questing landscape. Now, she was better positioned to pursue additional main quests aimed at achieving her life game of becoming financially secure.

IV. Andrew Saga: Broken Leg Arc

Despite the initial support from Andrew, their relationship went through many ups and downs. One particularly devastating event added to Suzy's difficult life. During an argument, Suzy became so angry that she impulsively punched Andrew in the stomach. As a former kickboxer, Andrew's reflexes activated, and he counter-kicked her leg, resulting in a painful break.[54]

When Suzy went to check on her injuries at a hospital after she saw her toes turn blue, she realized that she had a decompressed fracture. The doctor recommended major surgery to address the issue. Suzy faced a lengthy and challenging road to recovery as she was placed in a full cast for the next ten weeks. It was a period marked by pain, physical limitations, and uncertainty about the future. Of course, Suzy had to continue to work throughout that process because she had yet to complete her game of reaching financial security.

Another plot twist event happened upon Suzy's return from her surgery, Andrew presented Suzy with an engagement ring, asking her to marry him. Conflicted and feeling trapped between her desire for independence and her reliance on his support, Suzy found herself in a difficult dilemma. Fortunately, this time she was higher-leveled against social pressure, so she decided to give it some time, especially after the injuries Andrew gave her. She continued living with Andrew without marrying him.

IV Andrew Saga: Postpartum Depression Arc

When Suzy was twenty-nine years old, a significant zone event happened that would change her questing landscape again. Andrew expressed a strong desire to have a child with her, despite Suzy's reluctance to expand their family. Andrew reassured her that he would shoulder the full responsibility, both emotionally and financially.

Suzy didn't want to do it initially because she felt she was not in the circumstances to have a third child, but she felt she owed Andrew for all the help that he gave her when she was in the most

---

[54]Unlike Barbossa, who continuously abused Suzy, this was the first and last time Andrew hit her. Suzy describes Andrew as a very kind and protective man, who tried his hardest to take care of Suzy and her kids throughout their relationship.

desperate times of need. As a result, their daughter Cassidy was born, a radiant addition to Suzy's family.

But then another plot twist event happened. Andrew, despite his promise to provide financial support, was facing his own financial challenges. Suzy's questing landscape was changed once more. Now a mother of three, Suzy found herself in a situation where she had to work tirelessly to support her family. This unforeseen twist added even more weight to her shoulders as she juggled the demands of two significant roles (Step 3) – that of a mother and a provider. Striving to fulfill these roles, she worked tirelessly to ensure both her family's well-being and financial stability.

To make matters worse, Suzy had to return to work sooner than anticipated after giving birth. Contrary to her expectations, her job did not provide her with the four to six weeks of leave she had hoped for after pregnancy.

This situation led to an unfortunate personal event for Suzy. She experienced postpartum depression, a debilitating condition that cast a dark cloud over her life. In her desperation to find relief from the overwhelming emotional burden, she turned to an *item buff* by taking Zoloft, a medication that offered her a brief respite from the depths of her despair. This helped her better manage some of the depression and allowed her to focus more on her quests ahead.

V. First Success Saga: Casino Arc

With a strong determination to succeed in her role as a provider, Suzy fully focused on tackling as many resource main quests as possible to increase her income. When someone suggested she could do well working in a casino, she applied for the job and successfully secured a position as a cocktail waitress.

Had Suzy been living the life of an NPC, without a true game to engage in or quests to undertake, she might have simply learned about the casino job, felt a spark of interest, and, like many

NPCs in society, taken no further action. However, powered by her attribute of *optimistic creativity*, she exhibited signs of *track treasure* (Ranger skill) – the ability to identify hidden opportunities not apparent to others – and jumped on this quest.

At her casino job, using her optimistic creativity coupled with her other attributes like empathetic communication, personal charm, and diligent work ethic, Suzy consistently garnered substantial tips each night, frequently making $600 to $800 in cash. This marked a notable advancement in her ongoing resource main quest, helping fulfill her role as a provider.

V. First Success Saga: Settling Down Arc

Suzy's job at the casino was taking off, and since Andrew was no longer providing for her and her children, she finally accomplished the achievement of buying her own house and moved out of his residence. This was another huge step toward completing her game of becoming financially secure.

However, despite her newfound stability, Suzy realized that she couldn't manage everything on her own. She decided to use the real-life game skill *summon* (Druid skill) by reaching out to Andrew again for assistance. Andrew therefore moved in with her and started to help her with household tasks.

V. First Success Saga: Recruiting Agency Arc

In a twist of fate, someone Suzy met at the casino noticed her great talents and selling skills and connected her to a job opportunity at a recruiting agency. At the age of thirty-four, she embarked on a new major career quest.

Reapplying her attributes of optimistic creativity, personal charm, and diligent work ethic, as well as her real-life game skills charge and execute (both Warrior skills), Suzy quickly leveled-up as a headhunter. The charge skill allowed her to approach candidates with confidence and determination, while the execute skill enabled her to close deals and secure signed contracts. This helped her become the top recruiter in her agency. Her efforts were rewarded handsomely, with her income surpassing $200,000 a year – in 1998! This financial success marked a significant achievement and a turning point in her quest to achieve financial security.

V. First Success Saga: Spontaneous Move Arc

Amid her recent success, Suzy's attribute of profound intuition kicked in as she suddenly had a random yet strong feeling to take on a zone shift quest and move from Saint Louis to Dallas, Texas. This would be a very difficult commitment as she had just bought a new house in Saint Louis with her upgraded finances. Despite Andrew's logical opposition of moving out of their newly settled home, Suzy was adamant about moving, even though she couldn't pinpoint the exact reasons behind her intuition.

Andrew eventually agreed to the move, and they embarked on a new chapter in Dallas, settling into a spacious house in the suburb of Plano. Suzy's profound intuition turned out to be correct, but she wouldn't know until a decade later, when her son, then seventeen, disclosed that during their time in Saint Louis he was being molested by a neighbor. Suzy's decision to follow her gut feeling and relocate had unknowingly shielded her family from terrible hardships. This is a demonstration of the high-tier Ranger skill *instinctual pathfinding* – the ability to use your instincts to find the right path forward.

V. First Success Saga: Turning Point Arc

In Dallas, Suzy continued her work with the recruiting agency, and their enhanced financial situation enabled them to enjoy a more luxurious lifestyle, which included the addition of a Range Rover and a Mercedes Benz to their possessions. This phase represented a significant period in Suzy's life; having undertaken and conquered numerous main quests, she finally secured a home, landed a very well-paid job with a six-figure income, and elevated her lifestyle.

At this point in her 10K HP journey, Suzy managed to achieve a monumental milestone – she beat her first life game: "Escape life's tribulations and become financially secure!" It was a triumphant moment in her life, a testament to her unwavering dedication and resilience over three decades. Suzy had not only overcome adversity but also positioned herself as a self-reliant and financially independent individual. Her attribute of optimistic creativity allowed her to always pursue new opportunities, expecting the best and finding solutions to problems she encountered. The journey that had begun with uncertainty and challenges had led her to a place of accomplishment and empowerment.

At this point, she transitioned to a brand new game in her life: *to build impactful companies that make the world better.*

Ironically, in a turn of events, Suzy took on a new major relationship quest with Andrew because of an all-expenses-paid vacation offered by her recruiting agency. For the package, if you had a married partner, they would be fully covered by this benefit. This unexpected offer served as the catalyst that pushed Suzy to make a pivotal decision: to marry Andrew.

Her choice wasn't solely about their relationship; it was also driven by her caregiving attribute, as she deeply considered the decision for the sake of her family, particularly Cassidy, who was also Andrew's daughter. The ally who had helped her when she was a single mother without a home was now her husband, forming the foundation of a new family.

VI. Second Bankruptcy Saga: Culture Startup Arc

In 1999, Suzy transformed her game into building impactful companies that make the world better. Leveraging her attribute of adventurous risk-taking, Suzy made a bold move by investing all her personal savings into her startup, Greener Grass, which aimed to match individuals' cultures to company cultures. She hired many employees, including psychologists, to help refine their value offering. Utilizing her attribute of persuasive communication, Suzy secured $5 million in funding commitments for her venture. Unfortunately, before the deal could go through, she was hit by the detrimental *world event* known as the dot-com crash of 2001. Without any financial liquidity in the investor market, her company ran out of cash and had to shut down. This plot twist led to Suzy's second bankruptcy and severe financial consequences. Creditors seized her hard-earned house and cars. They came with such force that Suzy had to scramble to grab everything in her car's glove compartment before it was taken away. During this time without a home, Suzy and her family moved from one place to another. Her kids didn't understand why they were moving so much, and she would tell them it was because of her work. In reality, she was struggling to make ends meet. However, Suzy didn't let this experience crush her. She used the real-life game skill *phoenix rebirth* (Paladin skill) to rebuild her life bit by bit. Relying again on her attribute of optimistic creativity, she turned to creative pursuits and enrolled in faux painting classes, eventually becoming a teacher in this field. These decisions were not only a response to financial necessity but also marked a determined effort to regain her footing and move forward after the challenging times she had endured.

VI. Second Bankruptcy Saga: Bootstrapped Entrepreneur Arc

Driven by her resourcefulness attribute (Step 2), Suzy launched her own interior design company — a new resource main quest. Alongside this, she maintained her hustle by selling products, including merchandise directly from the trunk of her car. Suzy's ability to adapt, pivot, and persevere in the face of adversity continued to shape her extraordinary journey.

Between 2000 and 2004, although it seemed like Suzy had reverted to her old role as a hustler (Step 3), this time it was completely different because her game had changed (Step 1). Earlier in her life, her game was to obtain financial security, and she took on the role of a hustler, trying everything to escape her tough circumstances. But after she succeeded in that game, her new game became building impactful companies that make the world better. Within this new game, her role was not a hustler but a *bootstrap entrepreneur*, staying afloat with small projects while building toward her next world-changing idea.

VI. Second Bankruptcy Saga: "The Work" Arc

Despite playing a new role in a different game, Suzy's failure and lowered self-esteem still hindered her ability to face new challenges. In 2004, she contemplated suicide again, but a strong sense of responsibility toward her children helped her pass another survival quest and avoid a "rage quit" attempt. Had she succumbed to her despair, the future success and happiness in her 10K HP journey would have never materialized. This serves as a reminder that even in our darkest times, the next chapter of our story, filled with potential joy and achievements, is always waiting to be written.

The following day, as Suzy took her daughter Cassidy to play, she stumbled upon a book titled *Loving What Is* by Byron Katie. Her instinctual pathfinding (Ranger skill) compelled her to purchase it. This book fascinated her, as it allowed her to answer questions to find her truth and regain responsibility for her life. Suzy was developing new breakthroughs from this minor learning pivotal quest.

This transformation was so pivotal that Suzy immediately decided to continue on that quest line, tackling Byron Katie's wellness quest just two weeks later. This ten-day retreat, led by Katie herself, allowed Suzy to obtain an additional ally (Step 5) in the form of a mentor.

Through Byron Katie's transformative methodology, known as *The Work*, Suzy started to embrace the philosophy of assuming 100 percent responsibility for her own life and choices. She realized that she had been unwittingly victimizing herself and, in doing so, had relinquished her personal power. This newfound awareness enabled her to reclaim control over her life and reshape her destiny.

After that retreat, for six months Suzy dedicated herself to pursuing a self-discovery quest using *The Work*, specifically focusing on unraveling and reshaping her beliefs surrounding money. She started detaching her self-worth from money and saw money as merely a tool to get things done. This intensive self-examination allowed her to confront and dismantle the barriers that had been holding her back, giving her new attributes (Step 2) toward a brighter and more empowered future.

VI. Second Bankruptcy Saga: Failed Course Arc

After her mental power-up, Suzy Batiz embarked on a new teaching quest by creating a course titled "Inside Out: How to Create a Life You Desire by Going Within," aiming to guide individuals through a journey of self-discovery and inner transformation.

Unfortunately, because of her own lack of career success at that point in time, she only managed to enroll five women. What's worse, none of the five women completed the course. Suzy realized that to effectively teach success she needed to achieve greater success herself. Though still passionate about teaching and uplifting others, she knew she had to find her own big success to inspire others.

She decided to shelve her course and pursue another venture first, called Poo~Pourri. Years later, after achieving her 10K HP alignment, Suzy would come back to this quest and help aspiring women and men alike find themselves and achieve success.

VII. Poo~Pourri Saga: New Idea Arc

In 2006, a pivotal zone event occurred during a casual dinner party conversation. As Suzy and her relatives chatted, the topic unexpectedly shifted to the awkwardness of using a shared bathroom for "number two." In a light-hearted moment, Suzy's brother-in-law jokingly suggested the idea of trapping unpleasant odors. This seemingly innocuous remark ignited "God-given" inspiration in Suzy. While clearly seeing the solution visually in her head, she seized the moment and confidently declared, "I can do that!"

This marked the beginning of a new quest line for Suzy, setting off a series of subsequent quests. Harnessing her unique traditional world skill of imaginative forecasting, Suzy envisioned a toilet with a magical oil floating atop the water, acting as a barrier to prevent bad odors from emerging while releasing a pleasant aroma throughout the bathroom. During my talks with Suzy, she continued to emphasize to me that this vision was crystal clear to her, as if it was divinely downloaded from a higher place.

Suzy had been passionate and knowledgeable about essential oils (Step 4: Enhance Your Skills) for many years because she preferred natural solutions over harsh chemicals. With a clear goal in mind, she embarked on a major invention quest to use essential oils to solve the embarrassing problem of bathroom odors in shared spaces. She tapped into her traditional world skill of essential oil blending and her real-life game skills of *adaptive foraging* and *mastermind* (both Ranger skills) to create innovative solutions. For nine months, Suzy delved into the world of essential oils, conducting countless experiments in her kitchen. These activities (Step 6) were powered by her attributes (Step 2) of keen observation, resourcefulness, and passionate perseverance.

Fueled by passionate perseverance and optimistic creativity, Suzy endured repeated failures. Where others might have given up after the second, fourth, or even eighth setback, Suzy pressed on. Her newly developed attribute of self-belief convinced her that her goal was not only achievable but also destined to be lucrative. She was confident she possessed the skills and attributes needed to bring her vision to life. This time, she refused to let NPC Limiters tell her she was in over her head.

Suzy's 10K HP Alignment

As Suzy created and scaled Poo~Pourri, she transitioned her role (Step 3) from a bootstrap entrepreneur to an *eco-product entrepreneur*, focusing on products that are environmentally friendly and nontoxic to our bodies. This pivotal change propelled her into finally achieving her 10K HP alignment, which involved pursuing the right game, harnessing the right attributes, choosing the right role, honing the right skills, aligning with the right allies, and embarking on the right quests, as shown in her Talent and OP Skill Triangles, depicted in Figures 33 and 34.

- At the heart of her 10K HP journey, Suzy started to engage in the **right game (Step 1)**, dedicated to building impactful companies aimed at making the world better. Importantly, this angle of being eco-friendly and environmentally sustainable was aligned to her actual passions. Her first game of just making enough money was necessary but not aligned with her passions, making it difficult to achieve 10K HP alignment.

- Suzy leveraged the **right attributes (Step 2)**, beginning with her edge attribute of optimistic creativity, supplemented by her ring attributes, which included authenticity, profound intuition, empathetic inspiration, and resourcefulness, all underpinned by foundational base attributes like relentless problem-solving, passionate perseverance, and diligent work ethic, among others.

Figure 33. Suzy's Talent Triangle

- Embracing the **right role (Step 3)** as an eco-product entrepreneur, Suzy eventually evolved into her Hero role: the

Scential Alchemist. But before that full transformation happened, Suzy was excited and motivated to play her game as an eco-friendly entrepreneur.

- Suzy honed the **right skills (Step 4)** powered by the right attributes, including traditional world skills like imaginative forecasting, fueled by her profound intuition and optimistic creativity attributes. This skill helped her envision potential futures that were less obvious to others. Other essential skills she developed were branding and marketing, driven by her energized communications and authenticity attributes; leadership and team building, inspired by empathetic inspiration; and product development and innovation, rooted in keen observation and relentless problem-solving. Her expertise in entrepreneurship, sales, management, and persuasive communication further enriched her abilities. Additionally, her real-life game skills played a significant role in her success. These included charge and execute (Warrior skills), as well as instinctual pathfinder, mastermind, and adaptive foraging (Ranger skills), which greatly empowered her in her gameful skill class as a Ranger.

Figure 34. Suzy's OP Skill Triangle

- The journey also involved gathering the **right allies (Step 5)**. Her mentor Byron Katie, who helped her overcome her depression and aligned her to tackle the right quests, as well as other mentors she found along the way like Gay Hendricks, a psychologist and best-selling author known for his knowledge in the fields of personal growth, relationships, and body intelligence. Suzy also attracted a great passionate and talented team to become her Poo Crew guild. Later on, she evolved her guild to become an overarching Suzy Batiz faction.
- Tackling the **right quests (Step 6)**, with each quest developing her existing attributes, enhancing her role skills, attracting new allies, and continues to develop the success of Poo~Pourri. From getting the first sales of Poo~Pourri, to expanding into more retail stores, and selling it online,

every quest allows Suzy to get closer to beating her game of building impactful companies that make the world better. It also allows her to transition to her eventual next game: Lift up the human condition and make everyone more *Alive* (which will become the name of a future entrepreneurial venture).

Once Suzy achieved her 10K HP alignment, she was poised to play her life game with unparalleled prowess, embodying the true essence of an OP Hero and ready to tackle all the challenges of the world – all while enjoying it every step of the way.

With her 10K HP alignment, Suzy was able to grow her sales and expand her team over the following years. In 2013, she expanded her lineup of allies (Step 5) by working with comedic and viral video experts, the Harmon Brothers. Together, they embarked on a Career Pivotal Quest (Step 6) to create a marketing video titled "Girls Don't Poop." The video quickly went viral, amassing an astonishing ten million views in just two weeks. Its popularity continued to soar, ultimately reaching over forty-four million views. In 2014, it won a Webby Award and was named *AdAge's* "Funniest Viral Video of the Year" – major achievements unlocked! This viral sensation not only boosted Poo~Pourri's sales but also catapulted the brand to newfound levels of recognition and acclaim.

Despite this success, a devastating challenge quietly crept up on their doorstep – a threat that could bring Suzy back to her old fate of bankruptcy.

VII. Poo~Pourri Saga: Starting Poo~Pourri Arc

In 2007, despite a history of past failures, Suzy Batiz drew on her adventurous risk-taking attribute to secure $25,000 from her brother-in-law and embark on a new entrepreneurial endeavor: Poo~Pourri. With unwavering determination and a crystal-clear vision, she boldly launched her first batch of bottles containing the new "spray-before-you-go" toilet fragrance, ingeniously designed to trap bathroom odors.

At the beginning, Suzy encountered significant challenges as retailers struggled to categorize her innovative product, leading to numerous rejections. But relying on her now-developed attributes, she remained undeterred and forged ahead, determined to prove the value of her creation. Eventually, she was able to apply the execute skill (Warrior skill class) and convince the first few shops to put her product on their shelves.

To everyone's delight, customers who tried Poo~Pourri were so satisfied with the experience that they kept going back for more and told their friends about it. People who owned their own stores started to order Poo~Pourri for their retail shelves. The product seemed to be catching on!

Buoyed by new momentum, Suzy assembled a team of allies (Step 5) who proudly called themselves the Poo Crew. Together, Suzy used her optimistic creativity attribute (Step 2) to empower her branding and marketing skills (Step 4) and transform a traditional cleaning product into something fun, funky, and delightfully unexpected. Additionally, Suzy applied her resourcefulness attribute to establish a website for direct consumer sales, skillfully bypassing traditional retail channels.

In 2008, within a year of launch, Suzy unlocked a major new achievement in her 10K HP journey: Poo~Pourri had reached $1 million in sales, driven primarily by her website and word of mouth. By 2010, the Poo Crew had grown into a family of ten employees. Suzy's alliance guild (Step 5) was officially established and growing steadily.

VII. Poo~Pourri Saga: Avoiding Bankruptcy Arc

In 2013, following the viral success of "Girls Don't Poop," Suzy Batiz's Poo~Pourri business exploded beyond expectations, catapulting her into a whirlwind of success and imminent chaos. Orders poured in, overwhelming the young company with more demand than they could handle. The website collapsed under the heavy traffic, and the team was stretched thin, resorting to sleeping on bubble wrap in the office to manage shipments.

This overwhelming success, however, teetered on the edge of disaster. Poo~Pourri found itself drowning in a sea of back orders, running critically low on its unique sprayers, and facing severe understaffing. The company's lifeline – the sprayers essential for their product – was at risk as suppliers were sold out and couldn't provide anything for months. When Suzy called the CEO of one of the sprayer suppliers, he explained that he couldn't help her due to his own supply chain issues and commitments to bigger clients.

The inability to fulfill orders threatened to create an avalanche of problems. First, the surge of new customers would become enraged, accusing Poo~Pourri of being a scam for taking their money without delivering the product, turning every customer into a negative press agent.

Second, the supply chain disruption could alienate smaller suppliers, who could no longer work with them, while larger suppliers wouldn't take them seriously due to the one-time surge in orders.

Finally, and most critically, angry customers would demand millions of dollars in refunds, which could drive the company into bankruptcy. Poo~Pourri would have invested heavily in operations, and the initial processing and return fees alone could make the company insolvent.

If Suzy had been in her previous form – before achieving 10K HP alignment – these challenges might have crippled her and led to bankruptcy. But not for this new Suzy. With the new skills learned from *The Work* by Byron Katie, Suzy understood the importance of taking full responsibility for her company. She needed to proactively take action to achieve positive results. Powered by her base attributes of passionate perseverance and hopeful proactivity,

Suzy used a high-tier Warrior skill: *power leap* – traveling directly to someone to meet them without an invitation.

Remembering that the CEO of the sprayer supplier had declined to help, Suzy made the bold decision to fly directly to meet him. That morning, she sent a message to the CEO, informing him that she had purchased a ticket to meet him in person. She explained that if he could say "no" to her face, she would accept it and leave, but she was confident he wouldn't.

Despite receiving no response, Suzy proceeded with her power leap and traveled to the airport. While waiting to board, she received a phone call from the VP of North America of the sprayer company. He informed her that the CEO was on vacation and not at the office.

However, the sprayer company CEO had been so impressed by her powerful Warrior skill that he wanted to work out a creative way to assist her. In fact, the VP took a stand in their board meeting to advocate for Poo~Pourri and explored a solution based on their manufacturing overflow.[55] He devised a strategy to manually spin off the excess sprayers from their large client production runs, one by one, and allocate them to Poo~Pourri.

Although this strategy was still limited in how much they could supply Poo~pourri, it provided just enough resources to keep Poo~Pourri operational. Through Suzy's proactive skills to save Poo~Pourri and her ability to turn the sprayer company executives into her allies (Step 5), Suzy was able to prevent her company from going into bankruptcy. Now she was at the pivotal point of her iconic rise to become the Scential Alchemist.

VII. Poo~Pourri Saga: Suzy Rising Arc

In the aftermath of Poo~Pourri's early triumph, having overcome the challenge with sprayers and now capable of fulfilling much

---

[55] Manufacturing overflow refers to a situation where a factory produces more goods than planned or required, leading to excess inventory that exceeds current demand or storage capacity.

larger orders, Suzy recognized an opportunity to expand her product range. Her ambitions extended beyond her home country. Pursuing another entrepreneurial main quest, she aimed to increase her brand's global presence by branching into retail locations in various countries. By 2014, her efforts bore fruit as Poo~Pourri's international distribution network expanded to over ninety countries, marking a significant milestone in the brand's journey.

That same year, Suzy embarked on a distinctive and ambitious major lifestyle quest. She purchased a century-old, vacant church in Dallas with the vision of transforming it into her new home. This ambitious renovation project reflected Suzy's passionate perseverance, a key attribute in tackling challenges with vigor and creativity. The task required meticulous attention to detail and a deep understanding of the real-life game skill batcave crafting (Ranger skill). Transforming a church into a home required careful consideration to create a space that catered to Suzy's spiritual, productive, and social needs. Suzy's project showcased her ability to adapt and reimagine spaces, aligning them with her personal style, and transforming them into a unique sanctuary that reflected her identity and vision.

Suzy's journey of innovation and entrepreneurship was further recognized when she received an Edison Award in 2014, honoring her as the creator of one of the world's most innovative products. In 2017, Suzy Batiz celebrated a significant milestone: the ten-year anniversary of Poo~Pourri. By then, Poo~Pourri had achieved remarkable success, selling over 25 million bottles.

Suzy was named Ernst & Young's "Entrepreneur of the Year" and gained recognition from prominent media platforms such as *Forbes, The New Yorker, TODAY, People,* and *CNBC*. To share her journey and lessons learned, the Poo Crew guild published *The Woo of Poo* in 2018, a friendly yet provocative book chronicling the founding of Poo~Pourri.

At this point, Suzy, who had endured sexual, physical, emotional, and financial abuse throughout her life, finally unlocked her OP Mode, a state of empowerment and readiness to expand her influence globally, driven by her 10K HP alignment.

VIII. Scential Alchemist Saga: Supernatural Arc

In 2018, Suzy Batiz, steadfast in her life game (Step 1) to create impactful companies that better the world, delivered a compelling speech at the Conscious Capitalism Annual Conference in Dallas, Texas. During her speech, she offered a profound insight, declaring, "money is energy." This message, steeped in her attributes of empathetic inspiration and authenticity (Step 2), resonated deeply with her audience. She emphasized the symbiotic relationship between wealth and the energy we invest in the world. Additionally, drawing on her profound intuition, she underscored the significance of listening to one's intuition and heeding the body's signals when making conscious, ethical financial decisions.

Guided by her profound intuition and relentless problem-solving, Suzy aimed to create more products and companies that help the planet and enhance the atmosphere of households. With the success of Poo~Pourri, Suzy was ready to evolve her role (Step 3) from eco-friendly entrepreneur to her current form: the Scential Alchemist.

In this new role, she embarked on a major entrepreneurial quest (Step 6) focused on the environmental impact of cleaning products. Recognizing that many conventional cleaning products contain harmful chemicals detrimental to both home and planet health, Suzy was driven to make a positive change in the industry.

In 2018, Suzy Batiz launched Supernatural, an innovative venture providing eco-friendly, sustainable, and nontoxic cleaning solutions. These products prioritize household well-being and environmental preservation, revolutionizing the cleaning industry with a more conscious and sustainable approach.

Utilizing her essential oil blending skills (Step 4) and relentless problem-solving attributes (Step 2), Suzy crafted the first batch of Supernatural products. The foundation of Supernatural's offerings lies in organic essential oil blends, reducing potential irritation and allergic reactions associated with synthetic substances.

Supernatural's commitment to eco-friendliness is evident in its sustainable packaging strategy. Products are sold in glass containers with refill vials designed to be mixed with water, minimizing plastic waste and reducing the environmental impact of transportation and disposal. These glass bottles are also aesthetically pleasing, encouraging reuse and adding decorative value to homes.

As the Scential Alchemist, Suzy transformed cleaning into an elevated extrasensory experience, described as "a calming aromatherapeutic ritual." Supernatural's branding emphasizes nature, inspiration, and simplicity, turning cleaning into an enjoyable and mindful activity. This innovation aligns with a vision of conscious living and sets a new standard in the industry.

To underscore Supernatural's commitment to transparency, quality, and environmental responsibility, Suzy established an alliance (Step 5) with Bureau Veritas, a globally recognized leader in testing, inspection, and certification services. This partnership ensured that Supernatural's products, operations, and logistics adhered to stringent sustainability standards and certifications.

Further enhancing the brand's digital journey, Suzy enlisted The Octalysis Group, my consulting and design agency, to refine the online shopping experience of Supernatural and Poo~Pourri, making them more delightful and human-focused. This is how I first met Suzy, and we have been close allies since, with my company supporting her on a variety of ongoing endeavors.

In 2019, Suzy Batiz received several prestigious accolades in recognition of her exceptional contributions to conscious business practices and environmental sustainability. She was celebrated as "Conscious Company's World-Changing Woman" and honored as

"EarthX's Community Leader of the Year." These awards reflect her impactful work and ongoing commitment to positive change.

Perhaps most impressively, Suzy Batiz was listed among *Forbes'* Richest Self-Made Women in America in both 2019 and 2020, ranking between Oprah Winfrey and Rihanna.[1] She was one of the few women on the list with a perfect "self-made score" of 10 out of 10, indicating that she not only emerged from an impoverished family but also endured various levels of physical or sexual abuse.[2] Interestingly, our other OP Hero, Oprah Winfrey, was also among the handful who had a 10 out of 10 self-made score.

VIII. Scential Alchemist Saga: Alive OS Arc

After undergoing the transformative process of *The Work* with Byron Katie, Suzy Batiz experienced a profound shift in her game (Step 1).   After succeeding in her quest of building impactful companies with ~Pourri (the newly expanded name of Poo~Pourri) and Supernatural, she felt it was time to revisit a previous quest that she was passionate about.

Remember Suzy's initial attempt at launching the course "Inside Out: How to Create a Life You Desire by Going Within"? Despite enrolling five participants, the course saw no completions, largely due to Suzy's lack of personal achievements at the time.   Fast forward to 2019, Suzy was now poised for a comeback, with her 10K HP steps fully aligned.

Suzy introduced ALIVE OS, an eight-week program aimed at guiding individuals on their journey to self-discovery and empowerment.   ALIVE OS became a platform for Suzy to utilize her empathetic inspiration and authenticity attributes (Step 2) to help others unlock their potential and create meaningful lives.

This revitalized approach involved redefining her game (Step 1) from building impactful companies to "elevating the human spirit and helping people and organizations become more alive." With her newfound wisdom and developed self-belief attribute, Suzy embarked on a remarkable journey. She transformed her concepts into a thriving nine-figure business empire with Poo~Pourri. Now, it was time to teach what she learned from conquering her self-discovery quests.

Drawing from her own experiences, Suzy taught her students how to access their inner profound intuition (Step 2: Know Your Attributes) and develop their instinctive pathfinding (Ranger skill – my terminology, not Suzy's). Her philosophy suggests that intuitive wisdom is an inherent gift that fades as we immerse ourselves in external distractions. Her approach seeks to reforge this lost connection, guiding others to use intuition for similar success.

As of this book's publication, ALIVE OS is still growing, inspiring people to find their own 10K HP alignment and live with passion and meaning. Even members of my own guild have signed up for the ALIVE OS program, inspired to operate at a higher level.

VIII. Scential Alchemist Saga: The Ninth Arc

Now in her late 50s, Suzy shows no signs of slowing down. Like all 10K HP Players, she's not content with complacency. Achieving 10K HP alignment has transformed the world into an expansive questing zone for her, making it unimaginable to rest on past glories. Recognizing that her unique Druid-Ranger skills are ideally suited for devising creative strategies to elevate companies, Suzy understands that her perfect occupational role isn't as a CEO dealing with logistical intricacies. Instead, she's drawn to work where her passion lies, where she excels, and where she can generate the most distinctive value.

To this end, Suzy has launched another venture within her Suzy faction: The Ninth. This creative agency is her platform to replicate the ingenious successes of ~Pourri and Supernatural with other brands. Shortly after its launch, The Ninth has already driven innovative holiday campaigns and remarkable conference alternate reality games (ARGs).

Regardless of the trajectories of The Ninth and AliveOS, Suzy is committed to living her life in pursuit of her game, fueled by passion and her 10K HP alignment. Her upcoming sagas promise fulfilling successes, paving the way for grander quests and world-changing impact. Even in the face of potential failure, Suzy's clarity about who she is and the game she's destined to play serves as her steadfast anchor. Having seen and overcome various failures, she is ready for whatever comes next.

10K HP Alignment and Unlocking OP Mode

As I've stated throughout, the aim of this book is to equip you with strategies to beat the game of life. Think of it as a comprehensive strategy guide to fully leverage the insights discussed herein. The strategy involves following each of the six steps for mastering your game and achieving 10K HP alignment throughout your journey.

Reaching this milestone significantly increases your life's momentum toward success. This triggers a compound effect, where success creates tools, resources, and boosters that enable even more success. You'll also attract more formidable allies along the way while constantly enhancing your questing landscape. These improvements make it possible to embark on more advanced quests that were previously unavailable.

As you achieve 10K HP alignment and find success in quests that make a significant difference, you unlock OP Mode. In OP Mode, you transition from a 10K HP Player to an OP Player, becoming considerably successful and powerful in your game. At that point, if you push your game even further and make a legendary difference for humanity, you ascend to become an OP Hero, much like Steve Jobs, Oprah, Gandhi, and all the other OP Heroes highlighted throughout this book.

Suzy's journey, from poverty and despair to founding a company valued at $500 million and attaining happiness, underscores the transformative power of 10K HP alignment. This enables not only financial success but also profound personal fulfillment.

In the previous chapters, we have examined each OP Hero through the lens of a specific step within 10K HP. In the following sections, I will review the moments when each OP Hero achieved 10K HP alignment with all six steps and began playing their game in OP Mode. Pay close attention to how all our OP Heroes unlocked massive success after achieving 10K HP alignment: playing the right game (Step 1), relying on the right attributes (Step 2), choosing the right role (Step 3), honing the right skills (Step 4), aligning with the right allies (Step 5), and embarking on the right quests (Step 6).

10K HP Alignment: Mahatma Gandhi

Gandhi's 10K HP alignment is illustrated by the following analysis of his six steps.

Gandhi's Game Alignment (Step 1)

Gandhi's initial life game was modest – aiming for a stable career and a good life in England. However, a pivotal incident where he was thrown off a train in South Africa due to racial discrimination triggered him to change his mission. He shifted his life game's focus from personal comfort to the grand purpose of liberating India from British rule.

Gandhi's Attributes Alignment (Step 2)

Initially, Gandhi might not have fully understood his attributes, as evidenced by his struggles in court due to his shyness. However, his resilience, logical reasoning, and compassionate charisma became evident as he engaged in civil law and activism. These attributes were more aligned with helping people and leading civil rights movements rather than pursuing criminal cases.

Gandhi's Role Alignment (Step 3)

Gandhi transitioned from a barrister role, which was not well-suited to his attributes, to an activist lawyer in South Africa. This role allowed him to unify the Indian people against discrimination and build significant political alliances. His ultimate role evolved into a Strategy Sage upon his return to India, where he led the nation toward independence through the philosophy of *satyagraha*, or "truth force."

Gandhi's Skills Alignment (Step 4)

Gandhi honed skills such as diligent research, logical persuasion, and empathetic listening, which were crucial in his activism and legal work. His strategic application of satyagraha and leadership during the Salt March demonstrated his adeptness at nonviolent resistance and mass mobilization.

Gandhi's Alliance Alignment (Step 5)

In South Africa, Gandhi built influence and networked with key political figures, uniting the Indian community through the Natal Indian Congress. These alliances were crucial in fighting discrimination and later rallying support for India's independence. After unlocking OP Mode, he expanded his allies to include influential figures like the last Governor-General of India, the first Prime Minister of independent India, and a Nobel laureate poet.

Gandhi's Quest Alignment (Step 6)

Gandhi undertook significant quests such as leading the Salt March, a 390-kilometer journey that defied British salt laws and inspired thousands to join him. This act of civil disobedience and others like it were crucial steps toward achieving his game objectives and ultimately led to India's independence.

Gandhi's 6-Steps Alignment

Once Gandhi aligned his 10K HP six steps and unlocked OP Mode in South Africa, everything started to flow momentously. When he went back to India (a zone shift quest), it seemed like he was starting from scratch at a place where he didn't build his career, on a game that he didn't have much experience in.

In reality, since he had already unlocked OP Mode, Gandhi was able to build momentum immediately upon his arrival in India. People quickly became inspired by him, preferring him over other more established leaders in the community. He swiftly began to develop his strategy in press, politics, and alliance-building, all while nurturing the next generation. Even when he was imprisoned, the momentum he had generated through his OP Mode caused such a significant stir from his alliance and press quests that his release became imperative. With OP Mode unlocked, Gandhi leveled through being an NPC, a 10K HP Player, an OP Player, all the way to becoming an OP Hero.

10K HP Alignment: Walt Disney

Disney's 10K HP alignment was achieved by the following analysis of his six steps.

Disney's Game Alignment (Step 1)

From a young age, Disney was driven by a powerful mission: to bring joy and happiness to children and alleviate life's hardships through enchantment and laughter. This mission, rooted in his own difficult childhood experiences, shaped his life's work to create magical worlds where children could find solace and happiness.

Disney's Attributes Alignment (Step 2)

Disney's journey was fueled by optimistic creativity, passionate perseverance, and persistent perfectionism. These attributes allowed him to envision wondrous worlds beyond grim realities. By leveraging his primary attributes, he continuously innovated in the animation industry. As an Industrious Storyteller, he cultivated imaginative vision, ambitious confidence, and harmonious team building. This strategic approach not only enhanced his craft but also revolutionized the field, highlighting the importance of aligning attributes with goals to foster growth and change.

Disney's Role Alignment (Step 3)

Inspired by Charlie Chaplin, Disney began as a comedic entertainer. His true calling emerged in animation, transforming him into an enchantment storyteller who captivated both children and adults. But after the heartbreaking experience of having his IP taken away, Disney learned that to fulfill his game of making every child smile, it doesn't matter who creates the IP — it only matters who owns it. That's when he transitioned his role to become an Industrious Storyteller. With this more industrious role, he assembled a team under his vision and built an empire that with all sorts of magical experiences. This strategic alignment amplified his creativity and established a legacy that reshaped the entertainment industry for over a century.

Disney's Skills Alignment (Step 4)

Disney honed his art skills through relentless practice, study, and experimentation. He immersed himself in animation, storytelling, and character development, pushing the boundaries of what was technically and artistically possible to bring his enchanting stories to life. As he grew his company, he developed business skills such as leadership, resource allocation, quality management, marketing, public speaking, and negotiation.

Disney's Alliance Alignment (Step 5)

Recognizing the importance of collaboration, Disney found a crucial ally in Ub Iwerks, a talented artist who played a significant role in creating Disney's first studio. Later, his brother Roy Disney became indispensable, managing the financial and business aspects of their ventures, allowing Walt to focus on creative innovation and scaling their meteoric guild.

Disney's Quest Alignment (Step 6)

Disney's journey was marked by a series of bold quests that challenged the status quo and expanded the horizons of animation and entertainment. He achieved 10K HP alignment when he created Mickey Mouse, supported by the right intellectual property and organizational strategy. From that point, Disney's quests revolutionized storytelling and entertainment, leaving an indelible mark on the cultural landscape.

Disney's 6-Steps Alignment

Walt Disney's journey to becoming an international media icon began with major setbacks. One of the most pivotal was losing the rights to Oswald the Lucky Rabbit to distributor Charles Mintz — an event that, while not causing bankruptcy, was a deeply disheartening blow after earlier struggles like the failure of Disney's first studio, Laugh-O-Gram Films.

The path to becoming an OP Hero often includes a "plot fail quest" — a significant setback that sparks greater growth. For Disney, losing Oswald was a turning point. It taught him the importance of owning intellectual property and ultimately led to the creation of Mickey Mouse. That lesson transformed him into the visionary Industrious Storyteller who would reshape global entertainment.

Fueled by optimistic creativity, passionate perseverance, and persistent perfectionism (Step 2), Disney didn't succumb to defeat. Instead, this setback catalyzed a shift in his perspective and strategy. Where others might have given up, Disney's unique attributes spurred him to re-enter the game with renewed vigor.

With OP Mode unlocked, Disney won his first Oscar in 1932 for *Flowers and Trees*, pioneered full-length animated features such as *Snow White*, and developed magical worlds like Disneyland and Disney World. Despite obstacles, achieving 10K HP alignment propelled his life forward with momentum, passion, and impact, transforming him from a creative animator into the visionary entrepreneur necessary to fulfill his ultimate destiny.

10K HP Alignment: Oprah Winfrey

From the six-step perspective, Oprah Winfrey's 10K HP alignment looked like this:

Oprah's Game Alignment (Step 1)

Oprah set a life game to become a renowned media personality, inspired by figures like Diana Ross and Barbara Walters. Her mission was to break through the barriers of a male-established industry and use media to significantly impact the world.

Oprah's Attributes Alignment (Step 2)

Oprah's journey was distinguished by her inspirational charisma and empathetic intelligence. These attributes set her apart early on and were instrumental in her numerous achievements, enabling her to connect deeply with people and excel in her roles and endeavors.

Oprah's Role Alignment (Step 3)

Oprah initially pursued the role of an actress, inspired by her idol Diana Ross. Her career took a pivotal turn when she became a news reporter, following in the footsteps of Barbara Walters. However, her most transformative role was as an empathetic interviewer, fully utilizing her innate attributes and resonating with a wide audience. After she started playing her game in OP Mode, she eventually became the Inspirational Mogul of our generation.

Oprah's Skills Alignment (Step 4)

Throughout her career, Oprah developed and honed skills such as empathetic interviewing, charismatic presentation, and inspirational storytelling. These skills were crucial in her ability to connect with audiences and inspire millions through her television presence. If Oprah had focused on developing her other skills, such as acting or reporting, she might never have achieved true 10K HP alignment and become the OP Hero we know today.

Oprah's Alliance Alignment (Step 5):

Oprah's Step 5 alignment activated when she sought guidance and wisdom from influential figures like Maya Angelou, who served as a mentor and helped her refine her interviewing and storytelling skills. This alliance was vital for her growth and success in the media industry. Once she unlocked OP Mode, she began to attract more allies who helped her scale her inspiration and expand her business as a mogul.

Oprah's Quest Alignment (Step 6)

Oprah's Step 6 alignment happened when she started interviewing people as a morning talk show host. Upon achieving OP Mode, she embarked on various quests that expanded her influence beyond television, including creating her own production company, Harpo, and launching the Oprah Winfrey Network (OWN). Her philanthropic quests through The Angel Network, The Oprah Winfrey Foundation, and The Oprah Winfrey Operating Foundation further exemplify her commitment to making a meaningful impact.

Oprah's 6-Steps Alignment

Oprah Winfrey's path to 10K HP alignment and unlocking OP Mode began by chance when she was demoted from news reporter to morning talk show host. This unexpected shift aligned her role with her game, attributes, skills, and quests. With OP Mode unlocked, she was on the trajectory to become one of the world's most influential women.

Her transformation into the Inspirational Mogul OP Hero role represented the culmination of her journey, where she not only entertained but also educated, uplifted, inspired, and empowered millions globally. Through her company, Harpo, and various other ventures, Oprah guided multiple organizations toward her goals of inspiration and philanthropy, evolving from an OP Player to an OP Hero.

10K HP Alignment: Elon Musk

Elon Musk's six steps to 10K HP alignment played out like this:

Musk's Game Alignment (Step 1)

Elon Musk's insatiable curiosity about the universe and his desire to extend human existence and consciousness set the foundation for his life game. His mission evolved from uncovering the truths of the universe to safeguarding humanity and extending consciousness beyond Earth, particularly through the colonization of Mars.

Musk's Attributes Alignment (Step 2)

Musk's journey is driven by attributes like logical intelligence, learning agility, relentless problem-solving, risk-seeking, and goal obsession. These traits enabled rapid learning and practical application, essential for founding SpaceX, expanding Tesla, and tackling high-risk challenges. Beyond intellectual prowess, Musk uniquely embodies a relentless entrepreneurial drive, embracing risks with uncommon vigor. Many 10K HP Players who have the same attributes as Musk, which include intellectual curiosity, logical intelligence, and learning agility, would likely not be comfortable with regularly negotiating for rockets in Russia, running up and down factory floors, and firing employees in large batches. In that sense, Musk is like a blend of both Leonardo da Vinci and Walt Disney, having strong mental capability yet focused on relentless industry domination.

Musk's Role Alignment (Step 3)

Beginning with a passion for software engineering, Musk's initial success came from transitioning his role from entrepreneurial engineer to internet entrepreneur by co-founding Zip2 and what became PayPal. Its sale made him a centi-millionaire, providing the resources to become an existential innovator. In this capacity, he founded SpaceX and scaled Tesla into a world-dominating brand. Musk's major quests, including founding The Boring Company and acquiring Twitter, align with his goal of extending human existence.

Musk's Skills Alignment (Step 4)

Musk cultivated a diverse skill set critical to his ventures' success. Starting with programming and scientific problem-solving, he expanded into engineering, strategic thinking, and economics, complemented by finance, stoic management, and public relations. These skills, essential for his roles, were foundational to his achievements. Without these tailored skill sets powered by his unique attributes, notable triumphs like SpaceX and Tesla might have been deemed impossible. His refinement in visionary leadership and resource utilization was key to his evolution as an Existential Innovator.

Musk's Alliance Alignment (Step 5)

Musk proactively built his alliance by cold-calling successful individuals featured in newspapers, engaging in and initiating guilds focused on Mars and space travel, and consistently replacing underperforming team members. Key allies, including his brother Kimbal Musk, early mentor Peter Nicholson, Tesla co-founder JB Straubel, SpaceX President Gwynne Shotwell, and investor Peter Thiel have significantly contributed to his expanding faction aimed at transporting humanity to Mars.

Musk's Quests Alignment (Step 6)

Musk's early quests consistently aligned with his attribute of intellectual curiosity, evident in his voracious reading and fascination with space. Recognizing that his starting zone, South Africa, was not ideal for his game, he embarked on a zone change quest, relocating to Canada. There, he attended Queen's University to acquire skills in business and physics and connect with potential mentors. He then strategically changed zones again, first to the University of Pennsylvania and then to Stanford University, positioning himself in the heart of Silicon Valley.

In Silicon Valley, Musk made the bold decision to quit his Ph.D. program at Stanford – a major education quest that most would not forsake – to embark on his major entrepreneurial quest with Zip2. This venture's success led to his subsequent entrepreneurial quest with PayPal, netting him close to $200 million. With these resources, his true game commenced, leading to major entrepreneurial quests such as the founding of SpaceX and the expansion of Tesla.

Musk's 6-Steps Alignment

Elon Musk's 10K HP alignment was arguably realized once he exited PayPal and shifted his game to safeguarding humanity and extending consciousness beyond Earth. With this true game and his role as an Existential Innovator in sync, he leveraged his attributes to enhance his skills in engineering, manufacturing optimization, and supply chain management.

Musk also strategically assembled allies with the necessary skills, resources, and connections to advance his game. He then undertook significant major quests, such as founding SpaceX and expanding Tesla. Once Musk achieved alignment across all six steps within the 10K HP framework, he began playing his game at the highest levels. Despite immense challenges and daily agony, his exceptional performance enabled him to accomplish tasks deemed impossible by experts, ultimately leading him to top the wealth leaderboard on the Earth Server.

10K HP Alignment: Leonardo da Vinci

Here's how Leonardo da Vinci's 10K HP alignment was achieved through his six steps:

Da Vinci's Game Alignment (Step 1)

Leonardo da Vinci's life game was driven by insatiable curiosity and a desire to explore and understand the world. His goal since childhood was to "uncover the secrets of the universe and convey them through timeless works of imagination." Despite early failures and struggles, his game was not about conventional success but about pushing the boundaries of art, science, and invention. Various employment opportunities that he pursued later were merely means to secure resources to continue playing this game.

Da Vinci's Attributes Alignment (Step 2)

Da Vinci's journey was marked by powerful attributes that uniquely qualified him to become a polymath, such as imaginative vision, intellectual curiosity, astute observation, and logical intelligence. These attributes aligned with his skills, allowing him to produce incredible works. However, due to a misalignment with Step 5: Build Your Alliance, he faced limited success during most of his life. Fortunately, his emotional perseverance helped him endure financial instability and mockery until he reached true 10K HP alignment.

Da Vinci's Role Alignment (Step 3)

Initially, Leonardo pursued his game through the role of craftsman, either under his mentor or on his own. He then advanced to being a stage artist for the royal courts, leveraging connections and allies to further advance his role into an artistic inventor. This progression led to his 10K HP alignment, ultimately establishing him as the best-known Inventive Polymath in human history.

Da Vinci's Skills Alignment (Step 4)

Powered by his immense attributes, Leonardo's skills were vast and varied, perfectly aligning with his OP Hero role of Inventive Polymath. Utilizing his extraordinary attributes, he acquired skills in art, anatomy, engineering, physics, geology, and more, centuries before others even recognized these skill trees. However, it was only when he mastered the craft of charismatic persuasion that he achieved his full 10K HP alignment.

Da Vinci's Alliance Alignment (Step 5)

Despite the common perception of Leonardo da Vinci as a solitary genius, his journey to 10K HP alignment was achieved only once he learned to build alliances. Key figures such as mentor Andrea del Verrocchio and patron Ludovico Sforza were instrumental. The support of these allies, especially the King of France, enabled him to transition into the role of an Inventive Polymath by providing opportunities to showcase his talents and gain recognition. Additionally, connections with individuals like Francesco Melzi and Fra' Luca Pacioli deepened his intellectual skills (Step 4) and enhanced his collaborative quests (Step 6).

Da Vinci's Quest Alignment (Step 6)

Da Vinci's quests were as diverse as his interests, ranging from painting masterpieces like the *Mona Lisa* and *The Last Supper* to designing innovative machines and studying the human body. While not all his quests were completed, each helped him level-up his skills and grow toward the role of Inventive Polymath.

The major career quest that set Leonardo on the path to 10K HP alignment was being a stage artist for the royal courts, which allowed him to evolve into an artistic inventor. Once he learned to utilize his allies at the royal courts, he started playing his game in OP Mode, becoming an OP Player. However, it took a few more years in OP Mode before he painted *The Last Supper* and became an OP Hero. This masterpiece symbolizes the zenith of his artistic prowess and marks the point where his life became legendary for centuries to come.

Da Vinci's 6-Steps Alignment

As we can observe, Leonardo da Vinci had many elements of the 10K HP steps aligned, but his initial failure to address the critical step of building alliances meant he was perceived as a loser until his 40s. Many readers on their own 10K HP journey may also be just one step away from achieving 10K HP alignment. This shortfall could have led to years of frustration and depression, similar to da Vinci's experience. However, this implies that, regardless of whether you're still facing challenges in your 40s or even later, as long as you embark on your 10K HP journey with the correct approach, success is achievable. By playing the game correctly, you too can become an OP Hero for future generations.

10K HP Alignment: Sun Yat-sen

Sun Yat-sen's six steps to 10K HP alignment played out in the following manner:

Sun's Game Alignment (Step 1)

Sun Yat-sen's initial game was driven by a profound desire to save lives, initially aspiring to do so as a pastor. This ambition was fueled by deep compassion and a desire to make a tangible difference. Unable to find qualifying ways to become a pastor, Sun Yat-sen transitioned to saving lives as a doctor, addressing the physical well-being of individuals. As he recognized that China's issues were deeply entrenched in its political, economic, and social systems, his game evolved to encompass lifting China by reforming the Qing Dynasty government. While this was a step in the right direction for his 10K HP alignment, he eventually realized that mere reform was insufficient. He then pursued the ultimate solution: overthrowing the Qing Dynasty government and establishing a democratic republic.

Sun's Attributes Alignment (Step 2)

Sun Yat-sen's journey to transforming China was driven by key attributes essential for achieving his ambitious game. His visionary leadership allowed him to dream of a democratic China when most governments of the Western world were not democracies. His unwavering persistence empowered him to relentlessly pursue the revolutionary cause despite setbacks and failures. This was complemented by his charismatic gentleness, which enabled him to inspire and rally diverse groups with a persuasive yet gentle leadership style. His adaptability allowed him to navigate shifting political landscapes and adjust strategies to maintain revolutionary momentum. Together, these attributes were crucial for Sun Yat-sen's success in leading China toward a new era and overthrowing the Qing Dynasty.

Sun's Role Alignment (Step 3)

Sun Yat-sen's journey from a medical physician to a global visionary for China exemplifies a remarkable evolution of roles. Initially, as a medical physician, he expanded his role into that of a reformist, advocating gradual changes. Realizing the need for more radical actions, he transformed into a revolutionary. This transition was crucial for his 10K HP alignment, culminating in his advancement to the role of Revolutionary Architect, where he founded guilds and united others. This role, emerging naturally from his attributes and skills, positioned him as a pivotal figure in overthrowing the Qing Dynasty. As the founder of the Revolutionary Alliance and later the Kuomintang, Sun unified various factions under a shared cause.

After achieving his initial goal of overthrowing the Qing Dynasty, Sun briefly served as the country's President before ultimately embodying his final role as a Revolutionary Architect. This role went beyond political leadership, symbolizing his status as a visionary capable of inspiring change and steering the nation toward a brighter future. When China descended into chaos after President Yuan Shikai's betrayal and the rise of warlords, Sun Yat-sen, revered as the Revolutionary Architect, adapted his game to "Unite China under a thriving democratic republic," a vision ultimately realized by his protégé, Chiang Kai-shek.

Sun's Skills Alignment (Step 4)

Sun Yat-sen's revolutionary endeavors required a multifaceted skill set, prominently featuring the ability to forge alliances, strategic planning, and persuasive communication. His diplomatic skills were evident in securing both domestic support and international recognition for his revolutionary cause. He adeptly navigated international politics, seeking allies and resources crucial for his mission. Strategically, Sun was a master planner, orchestrating uprisings and coordinating efforts across various revolutionary groups with precision. His ability to communicate his vision compellingly through persuasive communication skills allowed him to mobilize diverse groups toward a common goal, powered by his exceptional attributes of unwavering persistence, charismatic gentleness, and adaptability.

Sun's Alliance Alignment (Step 5)

One of Sun Yat-sen's most remarkable qualities was his ability to forge alliances wherever he went. From his childhood village to his school days in Hawaii, from his medical training in Hong Kong to his travels between countries, he consistently formed alliances that would significantly contribute to his game, often years or even decades later. Recognizing the vast scope of his mission, Sun Yat-sen established his own guilds, namely the Revive China Society and subsequently the Revolutionary Alliance. The Revolutionary Alliance, serving as the faction-leading guild, propelled Sun Yat-sen's 10K HP alignment, elevating him to OP Player status. The successful overthrow of the Qing Dynasty by the Revolutionary Alliance and its allies marked Sun Yat-sen's ascent from an OP Player to an OP Hero, cementing his legacy in numerous history books.

Sun's Quest Alignment (Step 6)

As a Revolutionary Architect, Sun Yat-sen embarked on numerous challenging quests, from early uprisings to the pivotal revolution that led to the fall of the Qing Dynasty. Despite frequent failures, each endeavor served as a critical milestone toward establishing a republic. Forming the Revolutionary Alliance and amalgamating various guilds into this faction-leading entity was one of Sun Yat-sen's most crucial quests, playing a key role in his achievement of 10K HP alignment.

Sun's 6-Steps Alignment

The Wuchang Uprising of 1911 eventually led to the Qing Dynasty's downfall and the proclamation of the Republic of China. Although Sun Yat-sen was not the direct organizer of this uprising, his foundational revolutionary efforts, alliances, and political writings played a pivotal role. His contributions were so significant that the Wuchang revolutionists, including his former second-in-charge, proposed that Sun become the first President of the Republic as the previous faction leader.

As a 10K HP Player, are you constantly building alliances and establishing connections to propel your game forward? Consider how Sun Yat-sen's strategic networking became pivotal in his revolutionary journey, reminding us that each relationship we cultivate could play a critical role in our own 10K HP journey. Or perhaps you need to learn from Sun's tenacity, marked by unfazed resilience in the face of multiple failures.

Remember, each setback is a stepping stone, much like Sun's numerous failed uprisings before his monumental success. By embracing these principles – recognizing the value of both alliances and persistence – you can equip yourself to navigate your path with determination and insight, steadily evolving into an OP Hero in your own life game.

10K HP Alignment: Marie Curie

Marie Curie's 10K HP alignment was achieved through these six steps:

Marie Curie's Game Alignment (Step 1)

Marie Curie's initial life game focused on securing higher education despite societal constraints on women. This pursuit led her to France, where her game evolved into "Uncovering the Secrets of the Universe," starting her 10K HP alignment. Her dedication resulted in two Nobel Prizes: Physics in 1903 for radiation research and Chemistry in 1911 for discovering radium and polonium. Curie's ultimate game became "helping humanity through science." She exemplified this by driving mobile radiography units, Little Curies, into WWI war zones and nurturing her daughter Irène Joliot-Curie's scientific career. Irène and her husband won the Nobel Prize in Chemistry in 1935 for synthesizing new radioactive elements.

Marie Curie's Attributes Alignment (Step 2)

Marie Curie's 10K HP journey was propelled by key attributes essential to her groundbreaking achievements. Her relentless problem-solving and logical intelligence enabled her to navigate complex scientific and personal challenges methodically. These attributes sustained her through failures and heartbreaks, providing resilience even during emotional lows, allowing her to recover through logic and problem-solving. Combined with her comprehensive recall and imaginative vision, Curie could retain and integrate vast amounts of information. This unique blend of memory and creativity fueled her capacity to formulate innovative hypotheses, ultimately leading to her legendary achievements.

Marie Curie's Role Alignment (Step 3)

Marie Curie's career was a journey of evolving roles, each marked by significant milestones. Her initial role as a student in Poland was constrained by financial hurdles and political barriers that precluded higher education. She then became a governess, strategically saving funds for her move to France. In Paris, her enrollment at the University of Paris and receipt of the Alexandrovitch scholarship marked her transition to a scientific researcher. This period led to her 10K HP alignment, paving the way for her extraordinary scientific achievements. Curie's career culminated in her recognition as the Scientific Trailblazer. Her pioneering work in radioactivity distinguished her as the first female Nobel Prize laureate and the only person to win Nobel Prizes in two separate science categories. During World War I, she took on a new role as a medical war hero, developing Little Curies to advance medical care for injured soldiers, adding a new dimension to her role sphere.

Marie Curie's Role Alignment (Step 4)

Marie Curie's journey to becoming a scientific researcher was fortified by a solid foundation of skills, honed through her academic pursuits. At the University of Paris, she achieved two high-level academic degrees, excelling as the top student in her physics class and ranking second in mathematics.

This exceptional academic record established the necessary skills in physics, chemistry, and research methodologies critical for her 10K HP alignment. Curie's mastery in isolating radioactive isotopes directly resulted from this rigorous academic training. Her proficiency in these areas was instrumental in her pioneering research and in being honored with Nobel Prizes. These skills extended beyond research, profoundly impacting medicine, particularly in cancer diagnosis and treatment, revolutionizing medical practices and establishing new benchmarks in healthcare.

Marie Curie's Alliance Alignment (Step 5)

Marie Curie's ascent in the scientific world was significantly influenced by key allies. Her sister, Bronya, provided crucial emotional and financial support, enabling Marie to study at the Sorbonne in Paris. This support led to her meeting Pierre Curie, her most significant ally, marking a key moment in her 10K HP alignment. Their collaboration on radioactivity research was a convergence of personal and professional harmony, catalyzing Marie's major scientific breakthroughs.

This meeting was impactful because Marie had already developed the necessary skills and attributes and was in the right role. Their complementary attributes – Pierre's romantic idealism and Marie's pragmatic problem-solving – formed a robust partnership. Both shared a dedication to scientific research, aligning them in the same life game. Marie Curie's legacy continued through her daughters, Irène and Ève. Irène, particularly, followed in her mother's footsteps, achieving a Nobel Prize in Chemistry and continuing the family's remarkable scientific lineage.

Marie Curie's Quest Alignment (Step 6)

Marie Curie's path to 10K HP alignment was a remarkable saga of intellectual discovery, personal resilience, and societal impact.

From her student days, she pursued zone shift quests — overcoming societal barriers by moving to France for higher education. At the University of Paris, she excelled in a male-dominated environment, becoming a top student in physics and mathematics.

Her studies evolved into groundbreaking research quests, including the discovery of radioactivity and the isolation of radioactive isotopes. Through relentless dedication and methodical problem-solving, she pushed the boundaries of science despite immense challenges.

Curie later proved her devotion to her game by launching a major quest of raising funds to deploy fleets of women driving "Little Curies" into WWI battlefields, treating over a million soldiers, and becoming a war hero in the process.

Marie Curie's 6-Steps Alignment

Marie Curie's life epitomizes the alignment of the right game, attributes, role, skills, allies, and quests, all unified toward the noble vision of advancing science for humanity's benefit. Despite facing numerous setbacks, rejections, and even humiliation, Curie's relentless problem-solving and dedication to her craft led to her pivotal 10K HP alignment when she met Pierre Curie. Together, they embarked on profound scientific quests, undeterred, harnessing their combined strengths and shared vision to unravel the mysteries of the universe and leave an indelible mark on the world.

It's Your Turn to Play: Your 10K HP Alignment

You've seen how achieving 10K HP alignment became life-changing for our OP Heroes. Now it's time for you to find your own 10K HP alignment.

Pick from One of the Three Game Modes

Easy: Reflect on your current progress through the six steps of the 10K HP journey: Are you playing the Right Game? Do you understand and use your Attributes effectively? Have you identified your Role? Are you building and honing the Skills you need? Are you surrounded by the Right Allies? Are you pursuing meaningful and SMART Quests? Write down what feels aligned and what might be out of sync. Identifying these gaps is the first step to achieving full 10K HP alignment.

Medium: Build an Action Plan to align your life game fully and move toward OP Mode: Choose the top 2 areas where you are most out of alignment. Define concrete, actionable steps to bring those areas into alignment. For example: If you lack Allies, commit to networking events or outreach strategies. If your Skills are falling short, design a 3-month plan to master a critical skill. Set clear milestones and timelines for your action plan.

Hard: Work with others to enhance your alignment and amplify results: Partner with a trusted Ally to tackle your alignment challenges together. Share your Action Plan and hold each other accountable. Join a Guild or community where others are also on their 10K HP journey. Collaborate, share ideas, and seek support from players with similar goals. Consider working with a 10K HP Coach — someone who can offer personalized guidance and strategies to accelerate your alignment and help you operate at OP Mode.

Take the exercises you have done in the previous chapters and organize them in your 10K HP Canvas to see what you are lacking and missing to achieve 10K HP alignment. For steps on how to do this, go to 10KHP.com/alignment.

Chapter 9 Highlights

- Achieving 10K HP alignment means unifying the right game, attributes, role, skills, allies, and quests to reach peak performance.
- Every OP Hero faced significant hardships before their alignment, which often became catalysts for profound personal growth and mission clarity.
- The success of OP Heroes results from persistent effort and strategic 10K HP alignment, not pure luck.
- Building relationships and seeking new environments can propel you forward. Examples include Sun Yat-sen's connections with professors, Elon Musk's cold-calling successful professionals, and Marie Curie's move to France.
- Each life stage offers opportunities for alignment and growth. Young professionals should focus on skill development and potential career shifts, while those in middle age can seek new quests or mentor younger players for renewed excitement.
- Embrace setbacks as learning opportunities. OP Heroes often turn their failures into pivotal moments that propel them toward their goals.
- Cultivate your unique talents and seek strategic alignment. By following the examples of these OP Heroes, you can unlock great achievements that significantly impact your chosen game.

Chapter 10: The Playing Never Stops

Wow. You have finally made it. You have reached the concluding chapter of this book! If you are feeling a sense of relief and accomplishment, imagine how I must feel reaching this chapter after four long years of writing it (in contrast, my first book, *Actionable Gamification* only took two years to write). I have completed another major main quest in my life and am excited to connect with a whole new realm of reader allies, ready to tackle this exciting yet complex life journey together.

If you have read all the way to this point, I believe I can safely assume that something about the 10K HP journey resonates with you, and that I can see you as an ally on my own journey. Welcome to officially becoming my ally.

In the previous chapters, we've embarked on a grand journey through the landscape of gameful living. We've dissected the elements that make life a captivating game worth playing: choosing your game, knowing your attributes, selecting your role, enhancing your abilities, building your alliances, and achieving your quests.

Now, as we approach our final narrative milestone, it's crucial to remember that this is not the end of your 10K HP journey, but the beginning. Just as the conclusion of the original Star Wars trilogy in the 1980s marked the start of a vibrant pop culture franchise, this book opens the door to endless exciting possibilities. The Star Wars universe has thrived with fan art, novels, and community engagement for decades. Similarly, the 10K HP journey is about opening doors to new adventures and opportunities, not closing chapters.

Through 10,000 Hours of Play, you have learned to strategize your life's quests and master the intricacies of a gameful mindset. But remember: true mastery requires more than reading — it demands constant practice and a willingness to keep pushing your boundaries.

From Book to Life Game

Of course, it is impossible to cover all aspects of the 10K HP six steps within the confines of these pages, as each step could warrant dozens of books on its own. There are many great books out there that aim to help you find your passion in life and understand your talents and identity. There are even more textbooks focusing on acquiring a single skill or body of knowledge, as well as books that teach readers how to win allies and network with others.

The aim of this book is to string all these important aspects of life together in a holistic yet gameful manner and showcase how the alignment of all these disciplines is what creates a truly playful and purposeful life. To achieve true transformational change, it's not enough to simply read a book and move on with your life. You need to integrate the knowledge and methodologies into your lifestyles through multiple mediums and contexts. This is why throughout the book I have included a list of exercises, additional workbook materials, and a library of other books, videos, and courses on 10KHP.com to help 10K HP Players level up in their games.

When you read the biographies of other successful people, pay attention to how their lives reflect the six steps and how they achieve 10K HP alignment. When you read nonfiction books to improve your skills or knowledge, be aware of how those skills align with your game, attributes, and roles. When you read fictional novels or comics, observe how the main character fulfills their Hero's Journey (and most likely, also achieves 10K HP alignment).

When making important decisions in your life, consider whether they will become a main quest in your life game or just a side quest that might distract you from your main quest. Think about proactively joining guilds that could connect you to like-minded allies, such as my Octalysis Prime community, a professional fraternity, or a local church. Use 10K HP terminologies on a daily basis with each other. You will find that sharing this vernacular with each other becomes a fun and effective way of bonding, separating the NPCs from the true 10K HP Players.

This type of daily integration is why my first book, *Actionable Gamification: Beyond Points, Badges, and Leaderboards*, became so impactful. People who learned the Octalysis Framework have told me it's like being unplugged from the *Matrix*, where they see "green code" everywhere. Every conversation, email, marketing campaign, and political speech can be driven by the 8 Core Drives within the Octalysis Framework. By seeing and applying them daily, those who have learned the Octalysis Framework have effectively changed their lives and transformed everything they do. That is the power of just one real-life game skill: *enchant.* Imagine if you acquired dozens more and applied them effectively to your life game and main quests. You would become an unstoppable OP Player.

This type of integration into your daily life will help you go from an NPC to a 10K HP "Reader," to a 10K HP Player, to an OP Player, and who knows, maybe even an OP Hero.

Spreading 10K HP

My primary goal in writing this book is not simply to become a published author or to have a bestseller, but to transform as many lives as possible into joyful, meaningful existences filled with fun and achievement. I want to make sure the knowledge and impact can reach a **wide** audience and impact them in a **deep** way.

For **width**, I believe this book would make an excellent gift for those you care about. For someone in their 50s who isn't fully satisfied with their life, this book can help them find passion and meaning in their ongoing endeavors. If you have friends worried about their high school children's lack of direction, gifting them this book can help turn their lives into a game worth playing.

Of course, if you truly found this book helpful and you want others to give it a fair chance, consider taking the step to leave a review from where you found it. Based on my experience with my previous book, critics would likely say I'm extremely conceited, make up a bunch of new terminology, all while pretending to be authoritative. I won't argue against these claims, but I believe it's important to passionately share one's journey and quest achievements with confidence. I encourage all my 10K HP allies to do the same. True allies will celebrate alongside you, so don't hide your shine, as long as you aren't belittling others. The night sky is vast enough for every bright star to radiate its brilliance.

I also believe, and have seen repeatedly, that giving playful names to existing patterns can breathe new life into well-established literature, making it more enjoyable to study, memorize, and apply. That's why I don't plan on changing my writing style for the critics. However, it would be unfortunate if people miss the value this book offers due to these reasons. This is why I rely on my reader allies to encourage others to look past superficial critiques of the writing style and experience the deeper, life-changing insights this book provides.

For **depth**, besides adding workbooks, library resources, a World Leaderboard, and more, if there are enough 10K HP Players who really want to take their lives to the next level, it makes sense for me to start another guild, a "10K HP Academy" of sorts, and guide aspiring 10K HP Players to find their 10K HP alignment. Currently, Octalysis Prime is the platform where my reader allies acquire a variety of useful skills (Step 4) and connect with me and a whole community of other reader allies (Step 5).

As of 2024, I have already made over 1,600 videos on Octalysis Prime (also "OP") to help upgrade its members' skills and abilities. However, to achieve 10K HP alignment requires more one-to-one or one-to-few hand holding, so the 10K HP Academy might be the most sensible next step to deliver more value to my reader allies.

The envisioned 10K HP Academy is founded on three pillars:

1. Every successful person we studied in history has aligned with the six steps of 10K HP.
2. By applying this methodology, we aim to bring about the rise of 100 new Steve Jobses, Walt Disneys, Marie Curies, and Leonardo da Vincis into the world.
3. As a 10K HP reader, you could become one of these 100 OP Heroes — or at the very least, an OP Player who is both successful and fulfilled. Ultimately, as the tagline of this book suggests, our goal is to help you obtain your Legendary Achievement in life.

When I envision the boundless possibilities that 10K HP could unlock for myself and the world in my upcoming saga, I am both exhilarated and terrified. But I know I won't be alone. With all you "Chapter 10 Readers" supporting me, we will embark on the most epic 10K HP journey I could ever ask for. Your support transforms this journey into an incredible adventure, filled with limitless potential and extraordinary achievements. Together, we will create a legacy that transcends boundaries and inspires countless others to join us in our quest.

10,000 Hours and Beyond

So, what happens after you've integrated 10K HP principles into your daily life and invested those proverbial 10,000 hours into your life game? The journey doesn't end. Like any great game, the landscape evolves, new challenges arise, and so do opportunities. The skills and networks you've developed open new paths that were once hidden. Now, equipped with a hero's arsenal, you are ready to redefine your goals, expand your horizons, and play the next epic game. This is why many successful entrepreneurs can't seem to retire despite having tens of millions of dollars: they love the game too much.

As you stand at this juncture, look back at how far you've come, and then forward to the endless possibilities that await. It's time to set new quests, perhaps more daring than before. Whether it's tackling a new industry, learning a new skill, or starting a new venture, you are never out of moves as long as you have the will to play.

This is an invitation to keep playing the game of life with gusto, strategy, and insatiable curiosity. Your 10,000 Hours of Play have prepared you for whatever comes next. The only way to lose in this game is by choosing to stop playing, as many adults do before experiencing a midlife crisis. Never give up!

Remember, in your own life game, you're not just a player - you're the most qualified designer of your world. So, design wisely, play passionately, and transform your life into an epic journey celebrated by generations to come.

It's Again Your Turn to Play

Beyond The Book

If you want to transition 10K HP from just an engaging reading experience into a life-changing transformation, here are ways you can get involved:

1. Dive Deeper into 10K HP – As mentioned throughout the book, if you want more in-depth content, visit 10KHP.com to access Worksheets, Workbooks, Stories of OP Players and Heroes, Global Leaderboards, and a library of recommended books, experts, and courses to help you level up.
2. Get Personalized Coaching – If you're interested in 1-on-1 10K HP Coaching with me or a certified coach, or if you'd like to become a Certified 10K HP Coach yourself, you can apply at 10KHP.com.
3. Join the Community – If you're looking for a casual yet supportive 10K HP community, hop into our Discord at 10KHP.com/Discord.
4. Join an Elite Guild – If you're serious about leveling up and want to be part of an intense, dedicated Guild, consider joining Octalysis Prime at OctalysisPrime.com.
5. Connect with Me Directly – You can reach out to me via my website at yukaichou.com/contact or on X.com (@yukaichou). If you message me and say you're one of my "Chapter 10 Allies," I promise to reply if I see it.
6. Explore More on YouTube – Check out our YouTube channel at youtube.com/@10KHP-Academy to see if we've cooked up new videos, insights, and stories about our 10K HP Journeys and OP Heroes.

Notes

1 Introduction Notes. Malcolm Gladwell. *Outliers*. Little Brown and Company, 2011.

2 K. Anders Ericsson, Ralf Th. Krampe, and Clemens Tesch-Römer. "The Role of Deliberate Practice in the Acquisition of Expert Performance." *Psychological Review 100*, No. 3 (1993): 363-406.

3 Daniel J. Levitin. *This is Your Brain on Music: The Science of a Human Obsession*. Dutton, 2006, p197.

4 https://www.salon.com/2016/04/10/malcolm_gladwell_got_us_wrong_our_re-search_was_key_to_the_10000_hour_rule_but_heres_what_got_oversimpli-fied/

1 Chapter 1 Notes. Campbell, Joseph. The Hero with a Thousand Faces. Princeton University Press, 1949.

2 Vogler, Christopher. The Writer's Journey: Mythic Structure for Writers

1 Chapter 2 Notes. Simon Sinek. *Start With Why: How Great Leaders Inspire Everyone to Take Action*. Portfolio, 2009.

2 Bronnie Ware. *The Top Five Regrets of the Dying: A Life Transformed by the Dearly Departing*. Hay House, Inc., 2012.

3 Stuart Brown, Christopher Vaughan. *Play: How It Shapes the Brain, Opens the Imagination, and Invigorates the Soul*. Penguin, 2009.

4 Champy, James, and Nitin Nohria. The Arc of Ambition: Defining the Leadership Journey. Perseus Books, 2000.

5 Ferrazzi, Keith. *Never Eat Alone: And Other Secrets to Success, One Relationship at a Time*. Crown Currency, 2014

6 James Cameron. *Terminator 2*. TriStar Pictures, 1991.

7 Mohandas Karamchand Gandhi. *M.K.Gandhi: An Autobiography – The Story of My Experiments With Truth*. Prabhat Prakashan, 2018.

1 Chapter 3 Notes. Annette Lareau. *Unequal Childhoods: Class, Race, and Family Life. University of California Press, 2003.*

2 Ryan, Richard M., and Edward L. Deci. Intrinsic Motivation and Self-Determination in Human Behavior. Plenum Press, 1985

3 Neal Gabler. *Walt Disney: The Triumph of the American Imagination.* Vintage, 2007.

1 Chapter 4 Notes. Bryan CJ, Walton GM, Rogers T, Dweck CS. Motivating voter turnout by invoking the self. *Proceedings of the National Academy of Sciences of the United States of America.* 2011; 108 (31): 12653-12656.

2 Nir Eyal. *Indistractable: How to Control Your Attention and Choose Your Life.* BenBella Books, 2019.

3 *Forbes* profile, Gwynne Shotwell. https://www.forbes.com/profile/gwynne-shotwell/?sh=2128552f2b96

4 Joris Beerda. *How Rebel Soldier Guns Started Joris Beerda's Octalysis Journey.* The Octalysis Group blog. https://octalysisgroup.com/2024/03/how-rebel-soldiers-created-my-octalysis-journey/

1 Chapter 5 Notes. Klaff, Oren. *Pitch Anything.* Chapter 3: Status. McGraw-Hill, 2011, p87-90.

2 Isaacson, Walter. Steve Jobs. Simon & Schuster, 2011, p. 16.

3 Isaacson, Walter. Steve Jobs. Simon & Schuster, 2011, p. 45.

4 Robbins, Tony. Awaken the Giant Within. Simon & Schuster, 1991.

5 David A. Vise. *The Google Story.* Chapter 19: Space Race. 2018 Anniversary Edition. Delacorte Press, 2018: 225-230.

6 Hugh McIntyre. Taiwanese Music Star Jay Chou Scores The Bestselling Album Of 2022 Globally. March 27, 2023, Forbes.com. https://www.forbes.com/sites/hughmcintyre/2023/03/27/taiwanese-musical-star-jay-chou-scores-the-bestselling-album-of-2022-globally

7 Jon Christian. "Why Elon Musk Got Bullied in High School." Futurism.com, May 6, 2022. https://futurism.com/elon-musk-bullied-high-school

8 Isaacson, Walter. *Elon Musk.* Simon & Schuster, September 12, 2023: p. 3.

9 Zameena Mejia. "Elon Musk's mom worked 5 jobs at once as she struggled to raise 3 kids after her divorce." CNBC.com, June 1, 2018. https://www.cnbc.com/2018/06/01/elon-musks-mom-worked-5-jobs-to-raise-3-kids-after-her-divorce.html

10 Vance, Ashley. *Elon Musk: Tesla, SpaceX, and the Quest for a Fantastic Future.* Ecco, 2015: p 33.

11 Vance, Ashlee. Elon Musk: Tesla, SpaceX, and the Quest for a Fantastic Future. Ecco, 2015, p.39.

12 Vance, Ashley. *Elon Musk: Tesla, SpaceX, and the Quest for a Fantastic Future.* Ecco, 2015: p. 207

13 Siu, Eric. *Leveling Up: How to Master the Game of Life.* Page Two, 2021: chapter 13.

1 Chapter 6 Notes. McGonigal, Jane. SuperBetter: A Revolutionary Approach to Getting Stronger, Happier, Braver and More Resilient. Penguin Books, 2015.

2 Kahneman, Daniel. *Thinking: Fast & Slow.* Farrar, Straus and Giroux, 2013.

3 "A Rough, Wild, Wonderful Land." Chicago Tribune, 17 June 1990, www.chicagotribune.com/1990/06/17/a-rough-wild-wonderful-land.

4 Doidge, Norman. *The Brain That Changes Itself: Stories of Personal Triumph From the Frontiers of Brain Science.* James H. Silberman Books, Penguin Publishing Group, 2007.

5 Isaacson, Walter. *Leonardo da Vinci.* Simon & Schuster, 2017: p. 367.

1 Chapter 7 Notes. *The Bible*, Acts 20:33

2 Elliot, Jay. *The Steve Jobs Way: iLeadership for a New Generation.* Vanguard, 2011.

3 Source: Linebarger, Paul M.A. Sun Yat-Sen and the Chinese Republic. The Century Co., 1925.

1 Chapter 8 Notes. Dorian, George T. "There's a S.M.A.R.T. Way to Write: Management's Goals and Objectives." *Management Review.* November 1981.

2 This is the "SMART Goal Setting." You can check the ProductPlan website here: https://www.productplan.com/glossary/smart-goal-setting/

3 Doerr, John. *Measure What Matters: How Google, Bono, and the Gates Foundation Rock the World with OKRs.* Portfolio, 2018.

1 Chapter 9 Notes."America's Self-Made Women." *Forbes.* October 13, 2020. https://www.forbes.com/profile/suzy-batiz/?list=self-made-women&sh=6e5b1a253d40

2 Jonathan Ponciano. "The *Forbes 400* Self-Made Score: From Silver Spooners to Bootstrappers." *Forbes.* September 8, 2020. https://www.forbes.com/sites/jonathanponciano/2020/09/08/self-made-score/?sh=28ad152041e4